# Musical Encounters at the 1889 Paris World's Fair

# Eastman Studies in Music

Ralph P. Locke, Senior Editor
Eastman School of Music

(ISSN 1071–9989)

## Additional Titles of Related Interest

A complete list of titles in the Eastman Studies in Music Series, in order of publication, may be found at the end of this book.

# Musical Encounters at the 1889 Paris World's Fair

Annegret Fauser

University of Rochester Press

First published 2005

University of Rochester Press
668 Mt. Hope Avenue, Rochester, NY 14620, USA
www.urpress.com
and of Boydell & Brewer Limited
PO Box 9, Woodbridge, Suffolk IP12 3DF, UK
www.boydellandbrewer.com

ISBN: 1–58046–185–9

**Library of Congress Cataloging-in-Publication Data**

Fauser, Annegret.
  Musical encounters at the 1889 Paris World's Fair / Annegret Fauser.
     p. cm. – (Eastman studies in music, ISSN 1071-9989 ; v. 32)
  Includes bibliographical references (p.353) and index.
  ISBN 1-58046-185-9 (hardcover : alk. paper)
  1. Music–France–19th century–History and criticism. 2. Exposition
universelle de 1889 (Paris, France) 3. Music–Social aspects–France. I.
Title. II. Series.
  ML270.4.F38 2005
  780′.78′44361–dc22
                                    2005014454


A catalogue record for this title is available from the British Library.


This publication is printed on acid-free paper.
Printed in the United States of America.

For Tim

# Contents

# Figures

# Tables

# Music Examples

# Acknowledgments

My project on music at the Exposition Universelle in Paris in 1889 turned out to be a fascinating undertaking revealing a rich universe of sound from all parts of the world, whether Java, Paris, or even the future. My scholarly journey took me around the globe, both figuratively in terms of the immense wealth of materials I uncovered, and literally: from Paris to Melbourne, and from London to Chapel Hill. Many a travel companion accompanied me on my voyage; they have contributed to the adventure and opened up new horizons. I cannot express how grateful I am to you all.

Work on this book began during a period of sabbatical leave from City University London that I spent as an honorary fellow at the University of Melbourne, from January to April 2001. The fellowship offered the space and time to outline the book and to try out ideas with colleagues in Melbourne. Various libraries in Paris and London made the detective work of research a pleasure. I am grateful to the staff of the Bibliothèque Nationale de France, the Bibliothèque Historique de la Ville de Paris, the British Library, and the Edison National Historic Site, in particular its archivist Leonard DeGraaf. The book was finished during my time as a Pardue Fellow at the Institute for the Arts and Humanities of the University of North Carolina. The weekly discussions at the Institute provided inspiration and companionship which were invaluable. Meanwhile, Tim Carter, Katharine Ellis, and Steven Huebner read the manuscript and offered elegant suggestions, astute criticism, and much-needed encouragement. M. Elizabeth C. Bartlet, Edward Berenson, Barbara Kelly, and Ralph P. Locke commented on sections of the manuscript and contributed precious information and critique. Thank you so much for the cherished gift of your time and intellectual engagement.

Over the past years, 1889 has become a constant reference point in conversations with friends and colleagues. Your interest, patience, suggestions, and encouragement contributed so much to this enterprise. Many thanks to Kevin Bartig, David Charlton, Michael Christoforidis, Martin Elste, Catherine Falk, Gerry Farrell †, Joël-Marie Fauquet, Jon Finson, Jane Fulcher, Patrick Gillis †, Diana Hallman, Roy Howat, Mi Gyung Kim, Hervé Lacombe, Peter Lamothe, Ethan Lechner, Arthur Lawrence, Kerry Murphy, Jann Pasler, Cassidy Pratt, Clair Rowden, Debora Silverman, Ingrid Sykes, Helena Tyrvänien, Philip Vandermeer, Sarah Weiss, Lesley Wright, and the members of the Research Triangle French Study Group. The production of this book went smoothly thanks to the great support of the team at the University of Rochester Press, and in particular due to the elegant and patient copyediting of Louise Goldberg. Rachel Porcaro typeset the music examples efficiently and professionally. One companion, however, shared all the adventures of this trip around the musical world. It would have been only half the fun without my strongest supporter and fiercest critic, Tim Carter.

Two recently published texts contain material of the book. An earlier version of a section of chapter 1 was published as "De arqueología musical. La música barroca y la Exposición Universal de 1889," in *Concierto barroco: Estudios sobre música, dramaturgia e historia cultural,* edited by Juan José Carreras and Miguel Ángel Marín, 289–307 (Logroño: Universidad de La Rioja, 2004); and a part of chapter 6 will appear as "New Media, Source-Bonding, and Alienation: Listening at the 1889 Exposition Universelle," in *Music, Culture, and National Identity in France, 1870–1939,* edited by Barbara Kelly (Rochester, NY: University of Rochester Press, forthcoming).

The publication of the book was supported generously by the College of Arts and Sciences at the University of North Carolina at Chapel Hill, the University Research Council of the University of North Carolina at Chapel Hill, and the Lloyd Hibberd Publication Endowment Fund or the American Musicological Society.

A.F.
April 2005

# Abbreviations

| | |
|---|---|
| B.H.V.P | Bibliothèque Historique de la Ville de Paris |
| DE | Annegret Fauser, ed., *Dossier de presse parisienne: Jules Massenet, "Esclarmonde."* |
| F-Pn | Bibliothèque Nationale de France |
| F-Po | Bibliothèque de l'Opéra |
| NGr2 | *Grove Music Online,* ed. Laura Macy, http://www.grovemusic.com. All articles were accessed before 31 August 2004. |

*Introduction*

# The Soundscape of the 1889 Exposition Universelle

The Exposition Universelle, which took place in the six months between 6 May and 6 November 1889 in Paris, was one of the major political, economic, and cultural events of the late nineteenth century in France. It attracted more than thirty million people to its wonders, and 61,722 exhibitors, as the government of France invited the world to come to Paris to show samples of its industrial products, natural resources, and cultural achievements.[1] The Exposition was located at the Champ de Mars, on the banks of the Seine, right in the center of the French capital. A spectacle to end all spectacles, the 1889 Exposition Universelle was an event of superlatives: the highest iron tower (figure I.1), the latest technology, the most exotic people, a maximum number of historic reconstructions, and the most diverse music ever heard. Surrounding the Eiffel Tower, an impressive array of buildings showcased the industries and crafts from countries as diverse as Bolivia and China; exhibitions in the Palais des Beaux-Arts presented paintings and sculptures from France and abroad; the Galerie des Machines was a temple to industrial progress, "a masterpiece of modern mechanics" containing "all the wonders of human activity."[2] Artists from all over the world came to Paris to perform at this event, whether inside the Exposition Universelle like the dancers and musicians from Java, or in other Parisian locations but loosely connected to the World's Fair, like Buffalo Bill's Wild West show, which was

---

1. Data taken from Dominique Brisson, *La Tour Eiffel: Tours et détours*, CD-Rom (Paris: arte Editions, 1997). For a short survey and evaluation of the 1889 World's Fair, see Pascal Ory, *L'Expo Universelle* (Paris: Éditions Complexe, 1989). The event is set in its historical context in Linda Aimone and Carlo Olmo, *Les Expositions universelles, 1851–1900*, trans. Philippe Olivier (Paris: Belin, 1993); and Winfried Kretschmer, *Geschichte der Weltausstellungen* (Frankfurt and New York: Campus Verlag, 1999), 121–31.

2. *Exposition de 1889: Guide Bleu du "Figaro" et du "Petit Journal" avec 5 plans et 31 dessins* (Paris: Le Figaro, 1889), 118: "un chef-d'œuvre de l'art mécanique moderne"; "toutes les merveilles de l'activité humaine."

Figure I.1. The Eiffel Tower and Fountain Coutain. Library of Congress, Prints & Photographs Division (reproduction number LC-USZ62-102634).

hired to add to the international attractions in and around the Exposition Universelle.[3]

But the fair was also designed to celebrate the centenary of the French Revolution of 1789. As a result, many a European monarch frowned upon the occasion. But while nations such as Britain, Italy, and Germany withheld official support, their governments encouraged private enterprise to represent their nations appropriately. For republics such as the United States, Argentina, and Brazil, however, the fair offered an perfect window to celebrate the republican ideal.[4] But 1889 was also a crucial year for other reasons.[5] Not only was it the centenary of the Revolution, but it also brought the Third Republic to the brink of collapse through a threatened coup d'état by the popular former Minister of War, General Boulanger, in January; the resulting political shifts over the year led to a major political realignment in 1890 that would finally stabilize the political and social landscape of France, both nationally and internationally, until it was again destabilized by the Dreyfus Affair. The Exposition Universelle became a major theater for these issues, reflecting and shaping a range of political and cultural concerns.

The Third Republic, although almost twenty years old in 1889, had been in crisis since the election in 1885, which shifted the majorities of moderate and conservative republicans in Parliament in favor of the radicals.[6] For the first time since 1870, the radicals had enough political weight to be included in government, and one of the ministerial posts given them was the Ministry of War, allocated to the *revanchiste* General Georges Boulanger (1837–91). Boulanger's strident, anti-German rhetoric was taken seriously enough by the German chancellor, Otto von Bismarck, to call up the reserves and enlarge the German army. This had French moderates sufficiently worried to get rid of the minister who, in turn, began a political campaign against the government. Starting out as a radical republican, Boulanger entered into secret negotiations with both the Bonapartists and the Royalists, and he also received support from the *Ligue des Patriotes*, a radical, right-wing organization.[7] Throughout 1888, Boulanger

3. On William F. "Buffalo Bill" Cody's linking of the Wild West Show to world's fairs, see Joy S. Kasson, *Buffalo Bill's Wild West: Celebrity, Memory, and Popular History* (New York: Hill and Wang, 2000), 71–75, 83–87.

4. Eric J. Hobsbawm, *Echoes of the Marseillaise: Two Centuries Look Back on the French Revolution* (New Brunswick, NJ: Rutgers University Press, 1990), 69–70.

5. Marc Angenot, *1889: Un état du discours social* (Longueil, Quebec: Éditions du Préambule, 1989).

6. Robert Gildea, *The Third Republic from 1870 to 1914* (London and New York: Longman, 1988), 16–23; Maurice Agulhon, *La République: L'élan fondateur et la grande blessure (1880–1932)* (Paris: Hachette, 1990), 64–78.

7. Zeev Sternhell, *La Droite révolutionnaire, 1885–1914* (Paris: Gallimard, 1997), 105–16.

toured France from one by-election to the next, winning seat after seat, only to resign and stand for election again. His association with the right became known but did little to diminish his popular appeal, and his support increased still further after he challenged the prime minister, Charles Floquet, to a duel and, to everybody's surprise, was wounded. On 27 January 1889, Boulanger won a by-election in Paris. On the night of his victory, a crowd "gathered at the Place de la Madeleine outside a restaurant where Boulanger met with political advisers in one room and with his mistress in another. 'To the Élysée! To the Élysée,' cried supporters, encouraging their hero to stage a coup d'état and march to the presidential palace a few streets away. But the general hesitated, the moment passed, and the republic survived."[8] Not only did it survive, but it went on the offensive. Under the leadership of the Minister of the Interior, Ernest Constans, the government developed enough evidence to accuse Boulanger of treason, but he made a dramatic escape to Brussels on 1 April 1889. Because Boulanger was an elected member of Parliament, his trial was for treason took place at the High Court of the Senate. It started on 8 August, and on 14 August he was found guilty and sentenced to deportation. By the end of 1889, Boulanger's support had fizzled out almost completely. He died two years later, committing suicide on the grave of his recently deceased mistress, Madame de Bonnemains (née Marguerite Crouzet).

Boulanger's base was distributed throughout France and her provinces, but the final act of the drama unfolded in the capital. In political terms, Paris was (and still is) a schizophrenic city, both the seat of government of France and its foremost and most populated metropolis. These two sides were not always in political alignment, and in 1889 the moderate national government was faced with a radical municipality: Parisians had, after all, voted Boulanger into the government at the beginning of 1889. During the Exposition Universelle, a third layer was added, with the fair constituted as a global village in the city. Both the nation and the city had designs on the Exposition Universelle, and while it served as a "garden" of the Republic, it was also a (temporary) district of Paris.[9] For both the city and the nation, however, it was a major event drawing national and international attention. The Exposition Universelle was touted—in the words of the *Guide bleu*—as a "gigantic encyclopedia, in which nothing was forgotten."[10]

8. Michael Burns, *Dreyfus: A Family Affair, 1789–1945* (London: Chatto & Windus, 1992), 77.

9. On the notion of the Exposition as a garden of the Republic, see Ory, *L'Expo Universelle*, 65.

10. *Exposition de 1889: Guide Bleu du "Figaro" et du "Petit Journal,"* 12: "une encyclopédie gigantesque, où rien n'a été oublié."

[This fair] shows us how, in 1889, man nourishes himself, dresses, furnishes, and speaks; through which scientific procedures he works to the satisfaction of his needs; it shows us the past history and the present state of the arts which ornament his life and of the sciences destined to make man happier, more intelligent, and better. . . . It shows, and it explains everything. Following the example of manufacturers who, every year, take stock in order to evaluate to the penny yesterday's returns and tomorrow's resources, one might say that all humanity has come in 1889 to take stock in Paris, between the Esplanade des Invalides and the Trocadéro.

. . . nous montre comment, à la date de 1889, l'être humain se nourrit, s'habille, se meuble et se parle; par quels procédés scientifiques il travaille à la satisfaction de ses besoins; elle nous montre l'histoire passé et l'état présent des arts qui ornent sa vie, et des sciences destinées à rendre l'homme plus heureux, plus intelligent et meilleur. . . . Elle montre et elle explique tout. A l'exemple des industriels qui font leur inventaire chaque année afin d'évaluer à un sou près leurs bénéfices d'hier et leurs ressources de demain, on peut dire que l'humanité toute entière est venue, en 1889, faire son inventaire à Paris, entre l'esplanade des Invalides et le Trocadéro.[11]

Humanity's current achievement was thus shown and celebrated in glorious detail at the Exposition Universelle. The fair also offered a significant retrospective of past developments, and even more than in the case of the previous Parisian world's fairs of 1855, 1867, and 1878. Indeed, retrospectives formed an important part of the Exposition's displays, whether related to France's past like the successful reconstructions of the Bastille or the medieval Tour de Nesle (built in 1190 by Philippe Auguste), or to human civilization in more general terms, most prominently in Charles Garnier's installation, History of Human Habitation, which was placed in close vicinity to the Eiffel Tower: "Was it chance, or was it premeditation? I do not know the answer, but the coincidence is piquant; given that the History of Human Habitation is right at the foot of the Eiffel Tower, a visitor can embrace with one glance the distance traveled by mankind."[12]

Furthermore, this microcosm in the heart of Paris offered not only an education in world achievements to its guests, but also the illusion of "authentic" encounters with other cultures, both historical and geographical.

11. Ibid., 12.
12. Ibid., 92: "Est-ce hasard, est-ce préméditation? Je l'ignore, mais la coïncidence est piquante; car, l'Histoire de l'habitation humaine se trouvant aux pieds de la Tour Eiffel, le promeneur peut embrasser, d'un coup d'œil, le chemin parcouru par l'homme. . . ."

Whether a visitor wandered into the History of Human Habitation to marvel at Charles Garnier's reconstruction of an Etruscan villa, or climbed the Eiffel Tower, the Champ de Mars represented a vast stage set to act out discovery and exploration. Indeed, the 1889 Exposition Universelle perfectly exemplifies Vanessa Schwartz's notion of the spectacle as a mass-performed reality show, where the audience participates in the creation of the display.[13] The Exposition Universelle represented a walled city within the city to be visited at leisure by both Parisians and travelers from the French provinces and from abroad. For some precious hours or even days, one could travel through worlds otherwise known only through books or journals. Guidebooks such as the *Guide Bleu du "Figaro" et du "Petit Journal"* or *Cook's Guide to Paris and the Universal Exhibition* facilitated the journey and directed visitors to those sections that were either particularly spectacular and thus a "must-see" (the Eiffel Tower, the reconstruction of the Bastille, the Galerie des Machines), or closest to the sightseer's interest.[14]

For those six months, Paris became truly the "capital of the nineteenth century," as Walter Benjamin so famously characterized her, embracing the entire world within her center. According to Henry Fouquier, "for many people, the Exposition was a veritable voyage around the world, only faster, less tiring, and cheaper than the one *Around the World in 80 Days* told by Jules Verne. . . . How many evenings have I spent like that, far from Paris but within Paris!"[15] This was a safe form of tourism except for blisters on tired feet, pickpockets, and in some rare cases, food poisoning. But contrary to the one-dimensional experience of reading travel literature and reports about famous explorers such as Stanley or Savorgnan de Brazza in newspapers, a visit to the Exposition was an experience that engaged all the senses. When walking along the rue du Caire, for example, with its donkeys, street vendors, and cafés, one could see, hear, touch, smell, and feel for oneself a small piece of Egypt. On the way to attractions such as the Galerie des Machines, *flâneur* Émile Goudeau was assailed by the music

13. Vanessa R. Schwartz, *Spectacular Realities: Early Mass Culture in Fin-de-Siècle Paris* (Berkeley, Los Angeles, and London: University of California Press, 1998), 10.

14. *Exposition de 1889: Guide Bleu du "Figaro" et du "Petit Journal"*; *Cook's Guide to Paris and the Universal Exhibition. Special Edition . . . Compiled under the Personal Superintendence of Thomas Cook & Son* (London: Thomas Cook & Son, 1889).

15. Henry Fouquier, "Autour de l'Exposition," in *L'Exposition universelle de 1889: Grand ouvrage illustré historique, encyclopédique, descriptif publié sous le patronage de M. le Ministre du Commerce, de l'Industrie et des Colonies*, ed. Émile Monod, 3 vols., 1:279–84 (Paris: E. Dentu, 1890), 280: "L'Exposition était pour bien des gens un véritable voyage autour du monde, plus rapide, moins fatigant et moins coûteux que le *Voyage en quatre-vingts jours* raconté par M. Verne. . . . Que de soirées j'ai passées ainsi, loin de Paris et à Paris même!" Similar remarks can be found in a variety of journal articles and books, such as Eugène-Melchior de Vogüe: "A travers l'Exposition," *Revue des deux mondes*, 1 July 1889, 186.

emanating from the Romanian cabaret.[16] Even inside the Galerie des Machines, where industrial products such as weaving-machines or pianos were shown, sound proved to be an overwhelming stimulus: "If you add to this the never-ending ticking, jingling, whirring, a hundredfold chatter in different languages, here the sound of an organ, there a piano chord, military music from the outside, the noise of the machinery from inside, then you have some slight impression of the first visit to the fair."[17] Indeed, sound counted among the most intriguing experiences of the 1889 Exposition Universelle, whether the uncanny sonorities of Thomas Alva Edison's gramophone in the Galerie des Machines, the intriguing music that the "exotic" people brought with them to the colonial exhibition of the Esplanade des Invalides, or for that matter, the more "classical" works performed at the Palais du Trocadéro and in the Opéra and the Théâtre de l'Opéra-Comique. Such was the uniqueness of the soundscape of the Exposition Universelle that writers and illustrators left a wide trail of documents chronicling both their sonic encounters and others' reaction to these sounds.[18] Music was so pervasive and inescapable that, as we read in a report from May 1889, it was perceived as being "everywhere, raging with equal violence at the bandstand of the gypsies, under the tents of the Arabs, in the picturesque shacks of Morocco and Egypt."[19]

The soundscape of the Exposition Universelle was woven from environmental noises and French bandstand music, from the musics of different

16. Émile Goudeau, "Une journée d'Exposition," *La Revue illustrée* 4 (1889): 211–16, 240–44, at 241: "Sur ma route, le Cabaret Roumain, d'où sortaient les sons exaspérés du *nainou* dans un accompagnement de lyre et de violons. C'est fini! je m'arrête là, dévoré par l'appétit de la musique."

17. B. Schulte-Smidt, *Bleistift-Skizzen: Erinnerungen an die Pariser Weltausstellung* (Bremen: Johann Kühtmann's Buchhandlung, 1890), 35: "Nimmt man dazu ein nie endendes rastendes Ticken, Klingen, Surren, ein hundertzüngiges Plaudern in verschiedenen Mundarten, hier Orgelton, dort Clavieraccorde, Militärmusik von draußen, Maschinengetöse von drinnen, so hat man einen schwachen Begriff vom Eindrucke des ersten Austellungsbesuches."

18. I borrowed the term "soundscape" from Reinhard Strohm's path-breaking battle cry to move beyond the silent historic document—whether written or iconographic—toward a historical ethnomusicology which assumes a sonic history incompletely reflected in our texts. See Reinhard Strohm, *Music in Late Medieval Bruges*, rev. ed. (Oxford: Clarendon Press, 1990), 1–9; see also Fiona Kisby, "Introduction: Urban History, Musicology and Cities and Towns in Renaissance Europe," in *Music and Musicians in Renaissance Cities and Towns*, ed. Fiona Kisby, 1–13 (Cambridge: Cambridge University Press, 2001); and Tim Carter, "The Sound of Silence: Models for an Urban Musicology," *Urban History* 29 (2002): 8–18.

19. Ch. G., "La Musique à l'Exposition," *L'Art musical* 28 (1889): 75: "Elle est partout, sévissant avec une violence égale, au kiosque des Tsiganes, sous la tente des Arabes, dans les baraques pittoresques du Maroc et de l'Égypte."

people—whether Romanian or Javanese—and the sounds of theater performances, from ceremonial music and dance music. Some of the sounds pervaded the open space; some were enclosed in theaters, concert halls, cafés; others became solitary experiences at the end of earphones. Many of these sonic events were left to chance, but others were carefully orchestrated to maximize impact and to further the goals of the fair. Listening to these sounds was an inescapable experience that characterized everyone's visit to the Exposition Universelle. The result comprised both sound-as-noise and sound-as-music.[20] Sound-as-noise at the Exposition Universelle was present at every moment: the voices of visitors, the sounds of the cafés and restaurants, shouts from street vendors, the neighing of horses and donkeys, machine noises, and snatches of music from various—and often simultaneous—sources. What startled visitors was not the presence of environmental sound as such, but its density and unique composition. This sonic phenomenon was not just an acoustic backdrop in the manner in which our habitual sonic environment recedes in our awareness. Through its disturbing concentration of unfamiliar sound objects, the underlying soundscape of the Exposition became an acoustic signifier of the event's specificity.

But when does noise become music? In the context of the soundscape of the Exposition Universelle, this was more than just a rhetorical or philosophical question. It was a concrete problem that pervaded much of the discussion heard at the fair, especially of non-Western music. The comment cited above that music was "raging with equal violence" all over the fairground indicates to what extent commentators responded to the incessant sonorous stimulus. Thus, the various musics at the Exposition Universelle brought to the fore aesthetic, psychological, and cultural concerns related to music, its meaning, and its consumption. The Exposition Universelle

---

20. My use of "noise" (as opposed to "music") is influenced by the concepts developed by Pierre Schaeffer and Jean-Jacques Nattiez rather than the economic model proposed by Jacques Attali. In this context, I take "noise" as a phenomenon of reception of sound objects (Nattiez's esthesic level), which is determined by the listening experience. Whether or not it is "noise," sound has to be identified and therefore presents a fascinating moment of perception where listening modes shift from objective hearing to subjective listening (Schaeffer's modes one and two). See Jean-Jacques Nattiez, *Music and Discourse: Toward a Semiology of Music,* trans. Carolyn Abbate (Princeton, NJ: Princeton University Press, 1990), 45–48; Pierre Schaeffer, *Traité des objets musicaux: Essai interdisciplines* (Paris: Éditions du Seuil, 1966). For a critique and further development of Schaeffer's listening modes, see Denis Smalley, "The Listening Imagination: Listening in the Electroacoustic Era," in *Companion to Contemporary Musical Thought,* ed. John Paynter et al., 2 vols., 1:514–54 (London and New York: Routledge, 1992), 515–20. Nicholas Cook's use of "listening" remains one-dimensional as one of "musical listening" (Schaeffer's mode three)—whether supported by musical knowledge or not—and is thus too limited for the present discussion. See Nicholas Cook, *Music, Imagination & Culture* (Oxford: Clarendon Press, 1992), 10–22.

became a laboratory both of musical perception and of modes of musical usage in late-nineteenth-century France. Aesthetic debates turned political at a very fundamental level; indeed, the politics of sound became tangible in presentation and reception within the townscape of the fair. Comparable to the body politic of societies, the "sound politic" of music at the Exposition Universelle was represented according to its place within late-nineteenth-century aesthetics and politics of music. Music's physical location within the fair became one form in which the sound politic could be seen embodied, not only with respect to the place as such, but also in the way in which listening modes were shaped through location. Townscape and soundscape were inextricably intertwined.

The grounds of the 1889 Exposition Universelle were in the heart of Paris—or at least, of bourgeois Paris, as situated in the western part of the city—and their location around the Champ de Mars inscribed the Exposition in the long tradition of Republican and Imperial celebrations and earlier fairs of the nineteenth century.[21] Like previous world's fairs, the 1889 Exposition represented a unique complex of buildings, streets, bridges, and other installations. One of its more prominent buildings, the Palais du Trocadéro, had already been built for the previous Exposition Universelle in 1878, but the majority of the buildings, including the Eiffel Tower, were erected specifically for the event. While almost all of the architecture was temporary, the most controversial structure, the Eiffel Tower, was to remain, both as a symbol of the fair and, increasingly, as a symbol of (modern) France.[22] Reading the physical appearance of the 1889 Exposition Universelle has therefore led to the use of various urban and architectural metaphors (for example that of a cathedral) to describe the underlying structure of the locality.[23] Yet such deep structures are too abstract in their immediate impact—in order to read the cathedral metaphor, a bird's-eye view or a map of the Exposition is necessary—to be a useful analytical tool in the quest for relating musical consumption at the Exposition (both individual and by groups) to its physical and cultural contexts. What had

21. Maurice Agulhon, "Paris: La traversée d'est en ouest," in *Les Lieux de mémoire*, ed. Pierre Nora, vol. 6: *Les France III: De l'archive à l'emblème*, 868–909 (Paris: Gallimard, 1984), 872.

22. Two fascinating readings of the Eiffel Tower and its structural and symbolic layers are Roland Barthes, "The Eiffel Tower," in *Rethinking Architecture: A Reader in Cultural Theory*, ed. Neil Leach, 171–80 (London and New York: Routledge, 1997); and Henri Loyrette, "La Tour Eiffel," in *Les Lieux de mémoire*, ed. Nora, 6:474–503.

23. Debora L. Silverman, "The 1889 Exhibition: The Crisis of Bourgeois Individualism," *Oppositions: A Journal for Ideas and Criticism in Architecture*, Special Issue: "City and Ideology: Paris under the Academy" (Spring 1977): 71–91; Michael Adcock, "The 1889 Paris *Exposition*: Mapping the Colonial Mind," *Context: A Journal of Music Research*, no. 21 (Spring 2001): 31–40.

far more influence on the presentation and reception of sound and music were the location and outfitting of various structures either fully or partially dedicated to music. The "palace of music," as the writer in *L'Art musical* called it, was the Trocadéro, which contained a very large and lavishly decorated concert hall, the location of official concerts and major musical competitions. Musical instruments were exhibited in a dedicated gallery, the Galerie Desaix, as part of an exhibition of manufacturing. The various cafés and restaurants had musical entertainments just as they did in Paris as a whole. In some cases, as in the Javanese village, the unusual aspect of performance transformed the space from a place of gastronomic enjoyment to one of cultural consumption. In others, the music and performances were perceived as part and parcel of the entertainment in a *café-concert* setting, for example in the Romanian or the Egyptian cafés. In other cases, again, theatrical settings—for example in the Théâtre Annamite—brought a transfer of the horizons of expectation from the Parisian stages to those of the Exposition. The Opéra and the Théâtre de l'Opéra-Comique also participated in the display, even though they were physically distant from the location of the fair. Special events, such as the performance of Augusta Holmès's *Ode triomphale en l'honneur du Centenaire de 1789* in the Palais de l'Industrie, added further layers to the dense web of musical contexts. All these performance contexts influenced the reception, even if—as the cases of the Romanian musicians and Javanese dancers reveal—the performances could also transgress the limitations of their institutional framing.

The sounds of the fair, however, vanished forever the moment they had died away. This is all the more ironic since the 1889 Exposition Universelle represented the moment when the existence of sound recording entered the mass consciousness in Europe. Edison's new gramophone was one of the most admired exhibits of the Exposition, surpassed in terms of number of visitors only by the Eiffel Tower.[24] Yet all we are left with is distorted reflections of these sonic events in texts—scores included—and images. This gap between historic sound and documentary trace leads directly into the heart of one of the most fascinating issues of historiography: the dichotomy of sensual immediacy and, more specifically, of our listening imagination on the one hand, and of the silence of historical documents and scholarly discourse on the other.[25]

24. Although early sound-recording devices were shown both in the 1878 Paris Exposition Universelle and the 1881 Exposition Internationale de l'Électricité, neither had a comparable impact on wider crowds of visitors. The problems related to the mediality of recorded sound have been addressed in recent scholarly work and form part of my discussion in chapter 6.

25. I am borrowing the term "listening imagination" with its various methodological implications from Smalley, "The Listening Imagination."

All too rarely do we question the business of history as one that engages generally only with silent traces of historic events (even most texts on twentieth-century issues focus on text and image alone), unless sound becomes specifically the topic of study.[26] So much have we embodied collectively the mediality of written and printed transmission that scholars are able to reduce such complex issues as private or public "spectacle" to the visual and written alone. In fact, Vanessa Schwartz never once hints at the sonic side of the various cultural practices of the "newly forming Parisian mass culture," which, for her, is characterized solely "by a shared visual experience of seeing reality represented."[27] However, even a cursory glance at newspapers, memoirs, or advertising posters from the late nineteenth century reveals sound as constituting an integral part of the consumption of Parisian spectacle.[28] In the case of the 1889 Exposition Universelle, silence might well have been the rarest commodity anyone but a deaf visitor could enjoy.[29] Oscar Comettant made this point in his report of a "concert as one has never had before," organized by Gustave Eiffel in his private apartment up on the third platform of the Eiffel Tower:

> From the moment that Miss Jenny Lefébure, one of our most brilliant, talented, and accomplished young pianists, sat down at the piano, there was a silence which was not one that simple mortals can obtain on earth. On the ground, in Paris, there is always a fog of noise which makes silence more or less sonorous. At the tip of the tower, when one is quiet, there is absolute silence. The doors had been closed to avoid drafts, and Miss Lefébure played this delicate and too-little-known inspiration by Liszt, which is called *Soupir*.

> Dès que Mlle Jenny Lefébure, une de nos jeunes pianistes les plus brillantes, les mieux douées, les plus instruites dans leur art, se fut assise au

26. See, for example, Alain Corbin, *Les Cloches de la terre: Paysage sonore et culture sensible dans les campagnes au XIXe siècle* (Paris: Éditions Albin Michel, 1994); James Johnson, *Listening in Paris: A Cultural History* (Berkeley, Los Angeles, and London: University of California Press, 1995). As Jonathan Sterne has observed, there "is a vast literature on the history and philosophy of sound; yet it remains conceptually fragmented" (*The Audible Past: Cultural Origins of Sound Reproductions* [Durham, NC, and London: Duke University Press, 2003], 4).

27. Schwartz: *Spectacular Realities*, 12. Similar problems are apparent in Jonathan Crary, *Suspensions of Perception: Attention, Spectacle, and Modern Culture* (Cambridge, MA, and London: MIT Press, 1999).

28. Ironically, Schwartz reproduces such documents as illustrations in her book. See, for example, the poster advertising the "dances and songs performed by the Japanese, Chinese and Javanese troupes" (*Spectacular Realities*, 175).

29. See, for example, the collection of comments about music's continuous presence at the Exposition Universelle reproduced in E. Douglas Bomberger, *"A Tidal Wave of Encouragement": American Composers' Concerts in the Gilded Age* (Westport, CT, and London: Praeger, 2002), 46.

piano, il se fit un silence qui n'était pas celui que peuvent obtenir à terre les simples mortels. A terre, dans Paris, il règne toujours comme un brouillard de son qui rend le silence plus ou moins sonore. A l'extrémité de la tour, quand on se tait, c'est le silence absolu. On ferma les portes pour éviter les courants d'air, et Mlle Lefébure joue cette délicieuse inspiration de Liszt, trop peu connue, qui s'appelle le *Soupir*.[30]

Indeed, the ear "is the most vulnerable sense organ. It cannot be closed or used selectively," and while "in Western culture . . . the visual and verbal are privileged as sources of knowledge, sound and music tend to slip around and surprise us."[31] Given that the soundscape of the Exposition Universelle was one that every visitor shared, its study thus offers a unique approach to a more complex understanding of the experience of spectacle in late-nineteenth-century France.

The presentation and reception of music at and around the Exposition Universelle mirrored, focused, and amplified cultural concerns in France in the late 1880s and contributed to the shaping of the performance of, and critical debate about, music in the subsequent decade. Several themes ran through the way in which music was presented and consumed in Paris in the context of the Exposition Universelle, whether it was music from the past—as in the case of the historical concerts organized by Louis Diémer— or the performance of Arab belly dancing. At the Exposition, almost all music was presented within a nationalist framework. In the concert series at the Trocadéro, programs reflected the countries of origin of the musicians: Russian music performed by Russians, French music by French, American music by Americans. Music from all corners of the world—whether Romania, Morocco, or Java—became acoustic representations of the performers' descent. The resulting tension between the notion of music as national and racial signifier on the one hand, and the ideal of musical universalism on the other were among the issues that influenced both the critical reception of music at the Exposition Universelle and subsequent debate about the place of music in changing worlds. The density of multiple performances within a square mile of each other, crammed into just half a year, provided a fertile laboratory setting for professional critics and lay writers alike to explore these issues in their reviews.

This subject was closely related to another key topic that came into focus during the Exposition: the concept of authenticity. Which cultural

30. Oscar Comettant, "Un Concert comme il n'y en a jamais eu," *Le Ménestrel* 55 (1889): 237.

31. Susan McClary, "The Blasphemy of Talking Politics during Bach Year," in *Music and Society: The Politics of Composition, Performance and Reception,* ed. Richard Leppert and Susan McClary, 13–62 (Cambridge: Cambridge University Press, 1987), 16.

artifacts were authentic (in the sense of genuine) and why? These questions were discussed with respect to both contemporary music and sounds of the past, not to mention those sonorities perceived as exotic. Beyond the matter of whether a piece or a performance was genuinely the music of a specific culture or era and thus neither imitation nor fake, critics also posed the question of whether the rendition of various sounds was "authentic" in the more narrow sense of performance practice, with respect not only to early music but also to folk music.[32] A third aspect of authenticity discussed in the French press related to the issue of fidelity and character of sound reproduction, triggered by the exhibition of Edison's gramophone and the transmission of operas through telephone lines.

Production and reception of sound at the Exposition Universelle also brought into relief the fundamental question of Self and Other, whether internally in terms of the juxtaposition of urban and pastoral spaces, or externally in the relationship between France, her colonies, and the rest of the world. Indeed, the Exposition was a space that could represent various aspects of a pastoral world.[33] The Exposition as a whole was understood by many French critics as an Arcadia within the confines of the most self-consciously urban environment of the time, the city of Paris. This utopian space, with its palaces for progress, its various national exhibits, and its retrospective exhibitions was more complete (because it was synthetic) than the world at large, creating a parallel world that represented the blueprint of a golden age of a future both technological and humanistic. At the same time, specific features of the Exposition—such as the *kampong javanais* with its straw huts, traditional crafts, and ostensibly happy and innocent people—re-created a natural and preindustrial paradise on the Esplanade des Invalides, where urbanites could observe innocence lost and dwell in an Arcadian stage set for a short moment in time. In both contexts music played an important role: sonic trace of past innocence and *primitivisme* on the one hand, sonic symbol of the music of the future on the other.

Thus the study of music at the Exposition Universelle allows a unique glimpse into the representation of, and discourses about, culture, and more specifically music, in late-nineteenth-century France. Because of its character as a centennial event, the fair merged ongoing cultural developments into a static representation during six months of dense cultural activity in the capital of France. But while it is a seductive subject of study, it also

32. David Lowenthal, "Authenticity? The Dogma of Self-Delusion," in *Why Fakes Matter: Essays on Problems of Authenticity,* ed. Mark Jones, 184–92 (London: British Museum Press, 1992).

33. On the heterogeneous definitions of "pastoral," see Paul Alpers, *What is Pastoral?* (Chicago and London: University of Chicago Press, 1996), 10–13; and Terry Gifford, *Pastoral* (London and New York: Routledge, 1999), 1–12.

presents significant problems for the music historian. Exceptional events such as the Exposition bring general trends into sharper relief, but they also distort more fluid and complex developments because of their need to fix cultural production in a single moment, whether an exhibition of paintings or a series of national concerts. Thus, while a "thick" description of 1889 Exposition can help uncover the complexities of cultural production and reception in late-nineteenth-century Paris, its narrow, rather than broad, focus denies access to the *longue durée* characteristic of institutionalized culture in any time or place. This project also raises questions about the materiality of musical, and music-historical, discourses: indeed a study of the music at the Exposition Universelle has to engage with the ephemeral character of its own object within a context that seeks to freeze its representation in exhibition form. Nevertheless, the 1889 Exposition Universelle represents a unique microcosm of the aesthetics, practice, and politics of music in late-nineteenth-century France. Whether opera or gamelan performance, whether gramophone or *musique d'occasion*, the sounds of the Exposition constituted a rich and varied counterpoint of the traditional and the unexpected, fitting for such a signal event.

*Chapter 1*

# Exhibiting Music at the Exposition Universelle

How to exhibit the music of France and abroad at the 1889 Exposition Universelle was a question that occupied the organizers of the fair very early on in its preparation, and it led to a variety of solutions, both in the official program and through private enterprise. From the outset, musicians had lobbied that a share larger than in any of the previous fairs should be reserved for music in 1889. With rising numbers of concerts in Paris, with new private music schools to cater to the greater need for teachers and performers, and with the increased manufacture of musical instruments, music was a growing field in 1880s France, both culturally and economically, echoing urban and industrial development. The government responded, in 1887, with the creation of a music commission for the Exposition, the Commission des Auditions Musicales, led by the director of the Conservatoire, Ambroise Thomas. Beside Ambroise Thomas as president, the Commission consisted of Léo Delibes as vice president and the pianist André Wurmser as secretary. Its sixteen members comprised, among others, Théodore Dubois, César Franck, Benjamin Godard, Charles Gounod, Jules Massenet, Ernest Reyer, and Camille Saint-Saëns.[1] The Commission was to ensure that music was "represented in the double aspect of composition and performance."[2] In addition, in the general categories of the fair's exhibits, "Class 13" was dedicated to musical instruments, sandwiched between Classes 12 (photography) and 14 (medicine and surgery), and grouped into the section "Education and Teaching—Materials and Processes of the Liberal Arts."[3] Within

1. See Elaine Brody, *Paris: The Musical Kaleidoscope, 1870–1925* (New York: George Braziller, 1987), 87, n. 35.

2. Alfred Picard, *Rapport général sur l'Exposition universelle internationale de 1889*, 10 vols. (Paris: Imprimerie nationale, 1890–91), 1:329: "que des auditions musicales seront organisées pendant la durée de l'exposition de 1889, et que l'art y serait représenté au double point de vue de la composition et de l'exécution."

3. *Exposition de 1889: Guide bleu du "Figaro" et du "Petit Journal" avec 5 plans et 31 dessins* (Paris: Le Figaro, 1889), 9: "Groupe II / Éducation et enseignement.—Matériel et procédés des arts libéraux."

the official structure of the Exposition Universelle, music was thus represented both aurally and visually, as an art and as a craft, and as belonging to
the past and to the future.

The Commission des Auditions Musicales comprised four subcommit-
tees: "musical composition" (which dealt with all art music); *orphéons* and
choral societies; brass and other bands; military music.[4] It organized a variety of performances and competitions to showcase French music and its
performance, and to engage in friendly rivalry with other nations. In particular, the five official orchestra concerts at the Trocadéro were meant to
display "the immense superiority" of France's composers.[5] Indeed, these
concerts "were going to correspond to a real exhibition of this art."[6] Other
official concerts included the performances by French municipal bands, by
children's choirs, and by *orphéon* societies. Foreign organizations were
invited to submit a bid for concert space to the Commission, and in the
end, orchestras, ensembles, and choirs from Belgium, Finland, Italy, Norway, Russia, Spain, and the United States were scheduled to perform at the
Trocadéro. A series of organ concerts by both French and international
organists rounded off the musical program there.

In keeping with the double axis of modern production and historical
retrospective at the Exposition Universelle, musical instruments were displayed in two locations. One was as part of the industrial exhibition in the
Palais des Arts Libéraux, where various manufacturers showed their latest
pianos, flutes, or harps in a gallery specifically dedicated to musical instruments. The other was an exhibition of historical instruments and instru-
ment-makers' workshops in the Histoire du Travail. (Also, musical artifacts
such as the autograph for Mozart's *Don Giovanni* appeared in the exhibition on the history of opera as part of a display of the history of theater in
France.) But musical performances, too, were part of the retrospective
effort. These included several "historic concerts" of early music, the centennial perspective of the five orchestra concerts, and a projected retrospective of six *opéras comiques* from the years of the First Republic.[7] Also part
of the Exposition, at least in the broader sense, were the premières of new
works at the Opéra and Opéra-Comique, discussed in chapter 2.

The Palais du Trocadéo represented the official exhibition space for
music performance at the Exposition (figure 1.1). Built for the 1878 World

4. Charles Darcours [Charles Réty], "La Musique à l'Exposition de 1889," *Le
Ménestrel* 55 (1889): 140–41, at 140.

5. Alfred Bruneau: "Musique," *La Revue indépendante*, August 1889, 203–11, at 204:
"ils affirment hautement l'immense supériorité de nos compositeurs."

6. "L'Exposition Universelle," *La Justice*, 28 May 1889, 3: "ce qui équivaudra à une
exposition réelle de cet art."

7. The retrospective of revolutionary *opéras comiques* is discussed in chapter 2.

Figure 1.1. The Palais du Trocadéro, view taken from the gardens towards the North-West. B.H.V.P., Dossier photographique *Divers XXI*, 15.

Fair and seating an audience of approximately 4,000 people, its Salle des Fêtes was the largest concert hall available in Paris and was proclaimed the "palace"—or even "official temple"—in which music would reside for the duration of the fair.[8] But despite its splendid decoration, it was an acoustic nightmare—"decidedly awful," according to Julien Tiersot.[9] His colleague Alfred Bruneau described the effect as sounds bouncing off the walls of an immense vessel, "thus producing innumerable echoes" which resulted in "dislocated harmonies" and "a disappearing melodic line."[10] The instrument best suited for the space, however, was the large Cavaillé-Coll organ whose sounds and repertoire were better adapted to the cavernous space of the hall than those of violins or voices.[11] Nevertheless, after a slow start in

8. Ch. G., "La Musique à l'Exposition," *L'Art musical* 28 (1889): 75; Bruneau, "Musique," 203.

9. Julien Tiersot, "Promenades musicales à l'Exposition," *Le Ménestrel* 55 (1889): 165–66, at 165: "Le Trocadéro est décidément mauvais!"

10. Bruneau, "Musique," 203: "En cet immense vaisseau . . . les sons se heurtent, s'embrouillent, s'aplatissent contre les murs et, produisant ainsi d'innombrables échos, apportent aux oreilles des harmonies disloquée au milieu desquelles s'estompe une ligne mélodique flottante et indécise."

11. Ernest Reyer, "Revue musicale," *Le Journal des débats*, 2 June 1889, 1–2, at 1; "Les Orgues," *Le Petit Parisien*, 20 June 1889, 3.

May, almost all of the concerts were packed—often sold out—and they were well received by their audience.

## *Musique française*

The five *Auditions officielles de Musique française* had two aims. The first was to present a centennial selection of French music akin to the retrospective of one hundred years of French art exhibited in the Palais des Beaux-Arts. The music was exclusively selected from works that had already been performed: there were no premières. The second objective behind the concerts was to feature the five major Parisian orchestras in a "performance exhibition."[12] Appendix 1A (p. 313) gives the dates and programs of these five concerts, whose music was selected in consultation between the Commission and the concert organizations. Three of the concerts—performed by the Concerts Lamoureux, the Concerts Colonne and the Société des Concerts du Conservatoire—were dedicated to symphonic and vocal concert repertoire; the other two—by performers from the Opéra and the Opéra-Comique—had extracts from operas from the previous hundred years on their programs.

The confinement to existing repertoire instead of new compositions shows a clear attempt to present a canon of selected works considered "French masterpieces." Some composers appeared on more than one program: Auber and Bizet—both dead composers with republican credentials—were present in no fewer than three of the five concerts. Even more to the point, the Société des Concerts and the Opéra each programmed extracts from Auber's *La Muette de Portici*, an opera on the subject of the Neapolitan rebellion against the Spanish Viceroy in 1647 whose revolutionary potential had become part of the work's republican appropriation during the nineteenth century.[13] The selection from *La Muette* comprised not only the overture, but also the patriotic duet "Amour sacré de la patrie."[14] In addition, the first concert of the series opened with Bizet's *Patrie!*, a concert-overture composed in 1874 which was inspired by the Franco-Prussian war of 1870 and which had become a patriotic staple of Third-Republic concert life.[15] Indeed, the program note for the concert referred specifically to Bizet's inspiration by "the misfortunes of the conquered and

12. Darcours, "La Musique à l'Exposition de 1889," 140.

13. Jane Fulcher shows that the opera's political impact as an agent in the July Revolution of 1830 should not be dismissed as a legend but taken seriously both as a historical account of the events in 1828–30 and an important case of reception history (*The Nation's Image: French Grand Opéra as Politics and Politicized Art* [Cambridge: Cambridge University Press, 1987], 11–46).

14. Johannès Weber, "Critique musicale," *Le Temps*, 23 Sep 1889, 3.

15. Winton Dean, *Bizet* (London: J. M. Dent & Sons, 1948), 112–14.

surrendered Fatherland, the anguish of the *année terrible*."[16] All the other composers whose works were performed on two occasions—in one of the orchestral concerts and in one of the operatic ones—were members of the Académie des Beaux-Arts, an institution founded by Cardinal Richelieu in 1635 to defend the values of French art and appropriated in this function by the Third Republic.[17] As for the rest of the programs, they included works created in a patriotic, republican spirit such as Charles Lenepveu's *Velléda* or Augusta Holmès's *Ludus pro patria*. Extracts from Paul and Lucien Hillemacher's *Loreley*, which won first prize in a competition organized by the city of Paris in 1882, represented a patriotic claim for those parts of the Rhineland lost to Germany in the Franco-Prussian War. Other composers with republican leanings included Reyer and Saint-Saëns. Whereas the majority of pieces stemmed from the second half of the nineteenth century, several were written earlier. One link with the First Republic, Cherubini's 1797 overture for *Médée*, was planned for performance by the Société des Concerts. It was replaced, however, with the overture for *Les Abencérages*, which dates from 1813, the end of the reign of Napoléon I. Other composers whose allegiances were not so clear-cut (Adam and Gounod, for example) were included in these programs due to their central place in the history of French music.

Few examples of concert programming in France in the late nineteenth century showed such obvious concern with the issue of creating a French canon of masterpieces. This becomes particularly clear with respect to the symphonic repertoire. All the selected pieces—apart from an extract from Félicien David's *Le Désert*—stemmed from the period after 1870, when French composers made a conscious effort to revive symphonic music as a matter of essential Frenchness, in contrast to the earlier periods, when making visible German influence (especially Beethoven's) would act as a mark of quality.[18] In particular, the concert by Colonne emphasized the

16. Program for the concert on 23 May 1889 by the Concerts Lamoureux, B.H.V.P., dossier "Actualités": "les malheurs de la Patrie vaincue et livrée, les angoisses de l'année terrible."

17. On the Académie des Beaux-Arts, see my "*La Guerre en dentelles*: Women and the *Prix de Rome* in French Cultural Politics," *Journal of the American Musicological Society* 51 (1998): 83–129.

18. On the revival of French symphonic music after 1870, see Angelus Seipt, *César Francks symphonische Dichtungen*, Kölner Beiträge zur Musikforschung, 116 (Regensburg, Bosse Verlag, 1981); Annegret Fauser, *Der Orchestergesang in Frankreich zwischen 1870 und 1920*, Freiburger Beiträge zur Musikwissenschaft, 2 (Laaber: Laaber-Verlag, 1994), 50–58 and 111–39; Brian Hart, "The Symphony in Theory and Practice in France, 1900–1914" (PhD diss., Indiana University, 1994); Annegret Fauser, "Gendering the Nations: The Ideologies of French Discourse on Music (1870–1914)," in *Musical Constructions of Nationalism: Essays on the History and Ideology of European Musical Culture, 1800–1945*, ed. Michael Murphy and Harry

decade prior to 1889, with only his trademark composer Hector Berlioz from the earlier part of the nineteenth century.[19] In contrast, music from operas and *opéras comiques* could draw upon a long tradition of French successes, which allowed for a broader selection. Indeed, the majority of operatic extracts predated 1870 and thus presented a sonic testimony to France's musical vitality during the whole nineteenth century—a true centennial exhibition. The ideological slant of this choice of program becomes particularly obvious through the exclusion of one of the most important composers of French nineteenth-century opera: Giacomo Meyerbeer. Whereas the Belgian César Franck lived in Paris for most of his life and the Italian Luigi Cherubini became a French citizen, and both could thus be appropriated as French composers, the German Meyerbeer, by the late 1880s, was perceived as essentially non-French and therefore unsuitable for the project of creating a canon of French music.[20]

While these five programs tell a story of their own, their reception among Parisian musicians and journalists was quite mixed. Indeed, any selection process for such a "veritable exhibition of our composers" was as much about exclusion as inclusion.[21] That the Société des Concerts du Conservatoire had restricted its program to composers who were members of the Académie des Beaux-Arts at the Institut de France was pointed out in several reviews as a method that favored established composers.[22] Similarly, the program for the Opéra concert favored composers who had been

White, 72–103 (Cork: Cork University Press, 2001); Ralph P. Locke, "The French Symphony: David, Gounod, and Bizet to Saint-Saëns, Franck, and Their Followers," in *The Nineteenth-Century Symphony*, ed. Kern D. Holoman, 163–94 (New York, Schirmer Books, 1997).

19. On Édouard Colonne and his programming strategies, see Jann Pasler, "Building a Public for Orchestral Music: Les Concerts Colonne," in *Le Concert et son public: Mutations de la vie musicale en Europe de 1780 à 1914 (France, Allemagne, Angleterre)*, ed. Hans Erich Bödecker, Patrice Veit, and Michael Werner, 209–38 (Paris: Éditions de la Maison de l'Homme, 2002).

20. Although Meyerbeer's Jewishness would soon become a further trait to be denounced negatively by nationalist rhetoric—turning him into a doubly suspicious composer in that context—anti-Semitic reasoning was not yet the issue that it would become during the Dreyfus affair, and the program did indeed contain works by Jewish composers such as Halévy. For the anti-Semitic rhetoric in late-nineteenth-century Meyerbeer reception, see Fulcher, *French Cultural Politics & Music: From the Dreyfus Affair to the First World War* (New York: Oxford University Press, 1999), 32; and Kerry Murphy, "Race and Identity: Appraisals in France of Meyerbeer on his 1891 Centenary," *Nineteenth-Century Music Review* 1, no. 2 (2004): 27–42.

21. "Les Théâtres," *Le Rappel*, 23 May 1889 / 6 Prairial an 97, 3: "une véritable exposition de nos compositeurs."

22. See, for example, Johannès Weber, "Critique musicale," *Le Temps*, 27 May 1889, 3; Charles Darcours [Charles Réty], "Notes de musique," *Le Figaro*, 26 June 1889, 6.

elected to the Académie des Beaux-Arts, save for extracts from Émile Paladilhe's opera, *Patrie!* The well-respected music critic Johannès Weber dedicated an entire column in *Le Temps* to the programs of the concerts, criticizing the whole enterprise as flawed. For him the exclusions were shocking: Henri Reber, although a member of the Institut de France, was represented by only one symphonic movement (rather than the two he deserved); the composer Louis Théodore Gouvy, whose symphonies Weber preferred to those of Saint-Saëns, was entirely absent. As for women composers, he reported that "only one was successful in conquering a place on the program, and that is Mlle Holmès, by whom one will hear a piece from *Ludus pro patria* next week."[23] Few other journalists were as outspoken as Weber, but the concerts did generate a discussion about who should or should not have been included, and furthermore, whether the pieces selected were the right ones to represent their creators. Journalists tallied the numbers of dead composers (twelve) versus living ones (twenty-eight), and scrutinized how much time each received.[24] Indeed, the reception of the concerts ranged from unmitigated praise—by the unnamed critic of *Le Rappel* and Charles Darcours, for example—to angry rejection.

The disagreement in the press over the five official concerts was certainly symptomatic of the aesthetic debates in late-nineteenth-century France. Only four years previously, Vincent d'Indy had ousted Camille Saint-Saëns as the president of the Société Nationale de la Musique. The fault lines between the Republican aesthetic of eclecticism on the one hand, and the Wagnerian nationalists on the other, were still visible in 1889, even though the Commission did include both César Franck and the young Vincent d'Indy on the programs.[25] But the weight clearly leaned toward the official line as represented by the state institutions of the Conservatoire and the Académie des Beaux-Arts. The critics exposed these fault lines, and, depending on their aesthetic position, either praised a well-chosen, canonic repertoire of French music or sharply criticized the selection for its lack of contemporary relevance. Canonicity was certainly more important for an eclectic aesthetic that defined progress as building on the past than for a self-consciously modernist one whose rhetoric of rupture emphasized presentism over historic legitimization. At least for some

23. Weber, "Critique musicale" (27 May): "Parmi les femmes compositeurs, une seule a réussi à conquérir une place sur un programme, c'est Mlle Holmès, dont on entendra, la semaine prochaine, un morceau de *Ludus pro patria*."

24. For example, Edmond Stoullig, "Musique," *Le National,* 28 May 1889, 2.

25. For an excellent summary of the aesthetic conflict, see Jann Pasler, "Paris: Conflicting Notions of Progress," in *Man and Music: The Late Romantic Era from the Mid-19th Century to World War I,* ed. Jim Samson, 389–416 (London: Macmillan, 1991).

critics, however, comfort could be found in the fact that both the occasion itself and the problematic acoustics of the concert hall allowed dismissal of these concerts as simply a manifestation of cultural politics associated with the Centenary celebrations. This discourse could be justified by the insignificance attributed in modernist aesthetic to "official art," and it side-stepped the sticky question of whether these programs did, in fact, represent a French music of the future.

A parallel series of organ concerts on the big Cavaillé-Coll organ of the Trocadéro was organized by Alexandre Guilmant (1837–1911), the resident organist of the Palais du Trocadéro, at the behest of the Commission. Of the fifteen planned organ concerts, thirteen took place in the end: eleven so-called "auditions" and two concerts with orchestra (Appendix 1B, p. 317). Most organists were French, but three were from abroad: Clarence Eddy (Chicago), Walter Handel Thorley (Blackburn, UK), and Filippo Capocci (Rome). The concerts were as much about showcasing the achievements of French organ builders through the example of the magnificent Cavaillé-Coll organ as about music. Indeed, as an article in *Le Petit Journal* put it, "the organ concerts are fashionable" because of an "infatuation with these simultaneously powerful and soft instruments."[26] In contrast to the five official concerts, the programs of the organ series were not limited to French composers, although all programs included some French music. Indeed, the choice seems to reflect mainly the individual organist's idiosyncrasies. Thus the program performed by Charles-Marie Widor on 3 July 1889 consisted of his own music (the organ symphonies no. 5 and no. 8), and the works of the composer he championed so famously, Johann Sebastian Bach.

But the official musical program had more to offer than these two series of concerts. Fanfares and brass bands, military bands, and male-voice and children's choirs had their place in the official musical performances. Two festivals of choral music were devoted to *orphéons* and other choral societies, and their programs contained pieces such as Massenet's "Chœur des Romains" from his opera *Hérodiade*, a nostalgic celebration of the fatherland. Between these two choral events, on Sunday, 16 June, Laurent de Rillé conducted a festival of school choirs from the Département de la Seine, where "850 children were chosen among the 8,000 in the schools from the *arrondissements* of Sceaux and Saint-Denis" to perform various choral pieces, starting with the *Marseillaise*.[27] Choral singing, especially in school

26. "Les Orgues," *Le Petit Parisien*, 20 June 1889, 3: "les concerts d'orgue sont à la mode"; "un engouement pour ces instruments puissants et doux à la fois."

27. Charles Darcours [Charles Réty], "Notes de musique," *Le Figaro*, 19 June 1889, 5–6, at 5: "850 enfants choisis parmi les huit mille que comprennent les écoles des arrondissements de Sceaux et de Saint-Denis."

education, was becoming a growing concern for the Third Republic's educators.[28]

The French defeat in 1870 had been perceived as the victory of a Prussia "that founded its force on the development of primary education and on the identity of army and nation."[29] Ernest Renan's observation of widespread popular education as a decisive element in Germany's victory became a national obsession in Third-Republic France, and French educational reforms after 1871 emphasized patriotic issues in their teaching programs.[30] Although music had already been introduced into primary education toward the end of the Second Empire in 1865, after 1870 it received a new Republican function of developing a national conscience in the school system. This was justified not only by educational ideals derived from Plato's *Republic* and Aristotle's *Politics*, but even more through music's ability to forge a sense of collective feeling by way of choral singing.[31] According to Bourgault-Ducoudray, music had an educating mission, creating "unity in the heart of a nation."[32] Choral singing was perceived as a "school of solidarity," even a "school of attention and discipline" for pupils and citizens who needed to give the same attention to their conductor "as soldiers to their colonels in a field of military maneuvers."[33] But choral singing achieved even more: "music educates both ear and voice, so important in a democracy; music teaches one to speak clearly—and to listen."[34] Plato's ideal republic, Aristotle's ideas of music's "ethos," the

28. Victor Wilder complains that even Belgium is more advanced in that field than France ("La Musique à l'Exposition," *Gil Blas*, 22 July 1889, 2).

29. Ernest Renan, "La Guerre entre la France et l'Allemagne" (1870), in *Qu'est-ce qu'une nation? et autres textes choisis*, ed. Joël Roman, 80–106 (Paris: Presses Pocket, 1992), 104: "La Prusse fonde sa force sur le développement de l'instruction primaire et sur l'identité de l'armée et de la nation."

30. Alexander Schmidt, "Deutschland als Modell? Bürgerlichkeit und gesellschaftliche Modernisierung im deutschen Kaiserreich (1871–1914) aus der Sicht der französischen Zeitgenossen," in *Jahrbuch für Wirtschaftsgeschichte* (Berlin: Akademie-Verlag, 1992), 234.

31. Louis-Albert Bourcault-Ducoudray, "L'Enseignement du chant dans les lycées," *La Revue musicale* 3 (1903): 725: "Luther a donc créé, avec un succès inouï, des occasions pour ses coreligionnaires d'exprimer le sentiment collectif religieux; en même temps qu'il rendait l'utilité de la musique évidente en l'appliquant à un but élevé et civilisateur, il renseignait l'Allemagne, une fois pour toutes, sur la fonction et la vertu du 'grand art,' et lui en inculquait à jamais l'amour et le respect."

32. Ibid., 727: "faire 'l'unité' dans le cœur d'une nation."

33. Jules Combarieu, "L'Étude du chant à l'école primaire," *La Revue musicale* 10 (1910), 314–17, 339–43, at 315: "elle est une école de solidarité"; "elle est une école d'attention et de discipline . . . [car l'attention] doit être entière, absolue, comme celle des soldats devant leur colonel sur un champ de manœuvre."

34. Ibid., 316: "la musique [chorale] faisant l'éducation de l'oreille et celle de la voix, si importante dans une démocratie; la musique apprenant à parler nettement,—et à écouter!"

glorious memory of the *chants révolutionnaires* in the Revolution of 1789, and the perceived success of choral practice in Germany formed the mainstays of an argument to give vocal music a new weight in French public education and music making.[35]

However, one of the high points of the Exposition's musical mass entertainments was the "grand festival given by 507 musical societies, representing seventy *départements*" in the gardens of the Tuileries on 8 July, with apparently 20,000 musicians in all.[36] The echo of Revolutionary mass celebrations was obvious, and the program contained not only the *Marseillaise* as the opening piece but also Charles Gounod's *Le Vin des Gaulois*; Jean-Philippe Rameau's "Paix charmante"; and to top it off, the trio from Rossini's *Guillaume Tell*, "Quand l'Helvétie est un champ de supplices," scored for five hundred singers per part.[37] In his lead article the following day, Jean Frollo made the connection explicitly: "The men of the Revolution attached great importance to music, even in the most tragic hours of History, and they dedicated a large part of their popular festivities to it."[38]

Thus the official concert programs achieved a variety of results: they contributed to the creation of a canon of French masterpieces exhibited in these concerts just as paintings were shown in the centennial retrospective of art. French choral singing and brass fanfares—although in themselves neither specifically Republican nor French—were appropriated for the political ends of Republican education and celebration, offering a showcase for new achievements in the popular instruction of children and working-class adults, and for military might, within the new Republic. Their colossal scale of the performances in 1889 created an openly acknowledged link to the mass celebrations during the First Republic, which had also taken place on the Champ de Mars.

35. Bourgault-Ducoudray unequivocally refers to both in his report "L'Enseignement du chant dans les lycées," 725: "Il lui faut, pour vivre, des sentiments réels, vivants, palpitants, qui aient besoin de se formuler et de s'épancher en un flot musical. En France, ces occasions n'ont jamais existé, ou du moins, si elles ont existé, c'est à une seule époque, pendant la première Révolution. En 1792, l'État voulut employer les arts et surtout la musique à exalter des sentiments 'réels,' comme le fit l'antiquité grecque."

36. "Le Festival des sociétés de musique," *Le Petit Parisien*, 9 July 1889, 3: "Un grand festival donné par 507 Sociétés musicales, représentant soixante-dix départements, a eu lieu hier soir dans le Jardin des Tuilleries." The number 20,000 is given in Jean Frollo, "Les sociétés musicales," *Le Petit Parisien*, 9 July 1889, 1.

37. Darcours, "La Musique à l'Exposition de 1889," 140.

38. Frollo, "Les sociétés musicales," 1: "Les hommes de la Révolution attachaient à la musique une très-grande importance, même aux heures les plus tragiques de l'Histoire, et ils lui faisaient une large part dans les fêtes populaires."

Figure 1.2. The Exhibition of Musical Instruments (Class 13) in the Galerie Desaix, Palais des Arts Libéraux. B.H.V.P., *Album Paris 4° 14*, 15.

But music was also part of the permanent displays of the Exposition. Instrument makers exhibited their products to the greater glory of France in the Galerie Desaix, which was part of the Palais de Arts Libéraux.[39] While harps, violins, flutes, and drums were all part of the exhibition, the most dominant instrument was the piano in all its shapes and forms: upright pianos, grand pianos, ornamented pianos (figure 1.2). This display and its broad coverage in the press clearly reflected patriotic intent, for piano manufacture in France had begun to slip behind by this time

39. See Constant Pierre's account of the exhibits in his *La facture instrumentale à l'Exposition Universelle de 1889: Notes d'un musicien sur les instruments à souffle humain nouveaux et perfectionnés* (Paris: Librairie de l'Art Indépendant, 1890). Pierre's book celebrates the achievements of French instrument makers even in the face of rising international competition. Thus for Pierre, the 1889 Exposition Universelle presented even more of a patriotic challenge to France's instrument makers than the one of 1878, but in the end, the quality of French manufacture triumphed over the rest of the world.

when compared with Great Britain, Germany, and even the United States. In contrast to the retrospective of musical instruments at the display of the Histoire du Travail, whose precious historic exhibits were off-limits to the visitors, the Galerie Desaix resounded with the music played on the various instruments, whether by specially hired musicians (often young female Conservatoire students) or the many amateur pianists who visited the exhibition.[40]

> While the venerable musical instruments shown in the galleries of the His-toire du Travail are mute, while no sound escapes the Italian clavichords from 1547, the harpsichords from 1678 and the piano of Marie-Antionette, what a racket, in contrast, in Class 13, where the modern instruments roar!

> Si les vénérables instruments de musique exposés dans les galeries de l'Histoire du travail sont muets, si aucun son ne s'échappe des clavicordes italiens de 1547, des clavecins de 1678 et du piano de Marie-Antoinette, quel tapage, en revanche, dans la classe 13, où mugissent les instruments modernes![41]

Indeed, the Galerie Desaix was described as "one of the most visited sec-tions of the Exposition as well as one of the most picturesque and noisy ones."[42] On the ground floor, the sounds of the organ competed with those of the piano, so that "the hymn melts into the waltz and the polka finishes with a fugue."[43]

While this merry mix of music characterized the sonic environment in the Galerie Desaix during the day, various French firms opened their doors to music lovers in the evenings with concerts given by artists of local or sometimes international fame, whether Cécile Chaminade, Louis Diémer, Catherine Kuhné, or Raoul Pugno. These concerts were organized regu-larly by the various exhibiting firms, in particular Érard and Pleyel, to show-case their instruments in the hands of capable players.[44] A high point was the performance on a new Érard piano in July by the Polish pianist Ignacy Jan Paderewski, who had become a darling of the French public in 1888.

---

40. "Les Instruments de musique," *Le Petit Journal*, 5 July 1889, 1: "les jeunes élèves du Conservatoire chargées de faire valoir les pianos de nos facteurs les plus réputés."

41. Ibid., 1.

42. "A travers l'Exposition," *Le Monde illustré* 33 (1889): 263: "Une des sections les plus fréquentées de l'Exposition comme aussi l'une des plus pittoresques et des plus bruyantes."

43. "Les Instruments de musique," 1: "l'hymne se fond dans la valse et la polka s'achève par une fugue."

44. "Chronique de l'Exposition," *Le Soir*, 19 June 1889, 2–3, at 2: "La galerie Desaix est envahie tous les soirs par un nombreux public mélomane. C'est que des concerts peu ordinaires y sont donnés par d'excellents artistes et au moyen des meilleurs instruments qui soient au monde."

Victor Wilder's review of the concert, however, concentrated more on the quality of the piano than on the performance itself:

> The other night, the virtuoso Paderewski let us hear the beautiful Érard, which is placed in the gallery of honor. It is a marvelous instrument which obeys the fingers, or better, the thoughts of the artist, with the docility of an intelligent being. This new piano joins to the exquisite softness of the old ones the vigorous sonority demanded by the large concert halls; but what surprised and charmed me above all was the sweet and transparent timbre, so to speak, of the upper octave, where until now one has always heard the dry clattering of wood.

> l'autre soir, le virtuose Paderewski nous a fait entendre le beau piano Érard, qui se trouve placé dans la galerie d'honneur. C'est un instrument merveilleux, obéissant avec la docilité d'un être intelligent, aux doigts, ou, pour mieux dire, à la pensée de l'artiste. Ce nouveau piano joint à l'exquise douceur des anciens, la sonorité vigoureuse exigée par les grandes salles de concerts; mais, ce qui m'a surpris surtout et charmé, c'est le timbre délicieux et transparent, pour ainsi dire, de l'octave supérieure, où, jusqu'à présent, on entendait toujours le clapotement sec du bois.[45]

If the official concerts of the Exposition were aimed at showcasing the achievements of composition and performance in France, the concerts and exhibition at the Galerie Desaix focused on the sonic and technical qualities of the musical instruments made in France, where visitors could feel "proud and happy" to see the "most varied specimens of these sonorous machines."[46] This French effort to showcase industrial achievement paid off in the allocation of prizes, for no other nation collected as many "grands prix" in Class 13 as the manufacturers from France, Érard and Pleyel included.[47]

## Archaeologies: Early Music at the Exposition

In contrast to the exhibition in the Galerie Desaix that linked the industrial progress of the French Republic with the manufacture of musical instruments, the impetus behind the retrospective endeavors related to music was one of both musical archaeology and historical realignment.[48] The

45. "La Musique à l'Exposition," *Gil Blas*, 23 July 1889, 2.

46. Auguste Boisard, "Chronique musicale: Les pianos à l'Exposition universelle," *Le Monde illustré* 33 (1889): 218–19, at 218: "on se sent heureux et fier"; "les spécimens les plus variés de ces engins sonores."

47. Arthur Pougin, "La Distribution des récompenses à l'Exposition Universelle," *Le Ménestrel* 55 (1889): 316–17.

48. See, for example, the account in Boisard, "Chronique musicale: Les pianos à l'Exposition universelle," and the article on the house of Pleyel under the rubric of "Les

players in this group were on the one hand official functionaries of the Republic, as for example Léon Pillaut, the curator of the Musée du Conservatoire. On the other hand, however, factions more in line with royalism such as the Société Philanthropique, a charity headed by Prince Auguste d'Arenberg, were also involved in the organization of retrospective events related to music. A more shadowy figure in these musical retrospectives was the disgraced General Boulanger. Not only did he appear rather prominently in the painting *La Soirée de clavecin* by Horace de Callias, which shows a salon recital by the renowned French harpsichordist Louis Diémer and which was exhibited in the 1889 *salon* (figure 1.3), but he also seems to have planned on attending all the performances of the retrospectives of late-eighteenth-century revolutionary *opéras comiques*, aligning himself with the musical culture of the eighteenth century.[49] As Katharine Ellis has shown, the music of the past could serve various and sometimes even opposite political sides throughout the nineteenth century, from royalism to republicanism, from ultramontanism to anticlericalism, and the same works could be appropriated by and reinterpreted for often conflicting causes.[50] The representation and reception of early music at the Exposition Universelle proved no exception.

Within the framework of the official retrospectives of the Exposition, historic musical instruments were shown in a specially dedicated room of the Histoire du Travail. According to Julien Tiersot, not only did the exhibition contain rare and precious pieces, but more importantly, it formed "a veritable museum of musical archaeology."[51] What made it so successful for Tiersot, however, was that its method of display was "very modern," including

Grandes Industries à l'Exposition Universelle," which has five illustrations of the piano factory, compared to a single one of Mme Roger-Miclos at the piano. See Destouches, "Les Pleyel," *La Revue illustrée* 4 (1889): 35–42.

49 Camille Le Senne, "La Musique et le théâtre au salon de 1889," *Le Ménestrel* 55 (1889): 164–65, at 164: "*La Soirée de clavecin*, d'Horace de Callias, nous montre M. Diémer au clavier; çà et là Chincholle, le général Boulanger, quelques autres mélomanes assez inattendues." For Boulanger's intention to attend the *Opéra-Comique* performances, see Emmanuel Chabrier's letter to Wilhelm Enoch, 12 April 1889 in Emmanuel Chabrier, *Correspondance*, ed. Roger Delage and Frans Durif with the contribution of Thierry Bodin (Paris: Klincksieck, 1994), 613: "Il paraît que Boulanger a retenu ses places pour toutes les représentations de 'L'Opéra-Comique au XVIIIe siècle' à l'Exposition."

50. Katharine Ellis, *Interpreting the Musical Past: Early Music in Nineteenth-Century France* (New York and Oxford: Oxford University Press, 2005).

51. Julien Tiersot, "Promenades musicales à l'Exposition," *Le Ménestrel* 55 (1889): 179–80, at 179: "un véritable musée d'archéologie musicale." The retrospective of musical instruments was examined in detail by Pierre in *La facture instrumentale à l'Exposition Universelle*.

Figure 1.3. Horace de Callias (d. 1921), *La Soirée de clavecin* (ca. 1889). Oil on canvas; location unknown; reproduced in *L'Illustration* 47 (1889): 354.

the reconstructions and reproductions that filled the gaps between the historic instruments represented.[52] Thus the exhibition of musical instruments from the past was yet more proof of intellectual and scholarly progress, given that "this taste for retrospective marks an advanced state of civilization in a people."[53] Tiersot celebrated in particular the reconstruction of medieval instruments by Léon Pillaut, based on sculptures and reliefs in gothic cathedrals such as Chartres and Amiens, those "documents left to us by the medieval sculptors."[54] The center of each room was dedicated to keyboard instruments—including the famous piano belonging to Marie-Antoinette—but there was also an intriguingly modern piece: an authentic, albeit "modern harpsichord," created by Érard in response to the large, "current enthusiasm for all that touches on things from times past."[55]

52. Tiersot, "Promenades musicales à l'Exposition," 179: "La méthode qui y a présidé est très moderne."

53. *Exposition universelle de 1889: Les expositions de l'État au Champ-de-Mars et à l'Esplanade des Invalides* (Paris: Imprimerie des Journaux officiels, 1890), 2:250, given in Pascal Ory, *L'Expo Universelle* (Paris: Éditions Complexe, 1989), 17: "ce goût du rétrospectif marque chez un peuple un état de civilisation avancé."

54. Tiersot, "Promenades musicales à l'Exposition," 180: "grâce aux documents que nous ont conservés les sculpteurs du moyen-âge."

55. Ibid.: "tant est grand l'engouement actuel pour tout ce qui touche aux choses du temps passé."

Like his fellow journalist from *Le Petit Journal*, Tiersot regretted that the instruments at the historic exhibition remained silent, but he then rejoiced in the attempt, within the parameters of the Exposition Universelle, to bring to life the sound of the past in two historic concerts organized by Louis Diémer. These two concerts were set within other musical activities evoking and invoking the past in the last two weeks of May and the first two weeks of June. In addition to Diémer's concerts, they comprised a concert of the choral society *La Concordia* featuring Handel's *Alexander's Feast*, two Italian chamber-music concerts, and a well-publicized performance of Handel's *Messiah*. These performances and their reception show paradigmatically how nationalist and musical concerns could intersect in intriguing ways with archaeological interests in uncovering musical roots and heritage.

By 1889, Baroque music, especially works by Handel and Bach, had a firmly established place in the repertoire. This was specifically the case for female pianists, whose gendered musical personas as interpreters rather than improvisers fitted all too well with the nineteenth-century development of a museofication of concert repertoire.[56] Thus it is no surprise to find Handel and Bach quite frequently in concerts performed by female pianists at the Galerie Desaix, such as the one given in the Érard series by Mme Depecker on 1 August 1889 where Schubert, Chopin, and Godard shared the program with an *Air varié* by Handel and a Gavotte by Bach.

However, these piano recitals in which Baroque music appeared as part of the current repertoire differed quite significantly from the early-music concerts that presented themselves self-consciously as retrospective. Indeed, even their titles betrayed a conscious effort to create a historical dimension for the musical repertoire by presenting so-called *musique ancienne* or *historique*. Toward the very beginning of the Exposition Universelle, on 25 and 31 May 1889, Parisians could hear two concerts of *Musique française ancienne et moderne*, followed by two of *Musique italienne ancienne et moderne* in early June. Both the French and the Italian concerts included contemporary and earlier music during each performance, but separated them into different sections.[57] This manner of splitting concerts into two halves was a familiar model that dated back to the 1860s.[58] Three months

56. Katharine Ellis, "Female Pianists and Their Male Critics in Nineteenth-Century Paris," *Journal of the American Musicological Society* 50 (1997): 353–85.

57. Malou Haine wrongly assumed that the programs of the two concerts were divided into a modern evening and an early-music evening; see Malou Haine, "Concerts historiques dans la seconde moitié du 19e siècle," in *Musique et Société: Hommages à Robert Wangermée*, ed. Henri Vanhulst and Malou Haine, 121–42 (Brussels: Éditions de l'Université de Bruxelles, 1988), 133.

58. Ellis, *Interpreting the Musical Past*.

later, on 9 September 1889, Alexandre Guilmant offered a *Concert historique d'orgue et de chant* which presented music from Andrea Gabrieli to Nicolas-Jacques Lemmens in self-consciously chronological order.

The two French concerts opened with chamber music by such composers as Camille Saint-Saëns, Edouard Lalo, and Charles-Marie Widor, followed by music by Marin Marais, Jean-Philippe Rameau, François Couperin, and other composers of the seventeenth and eighteenth centuries (Appendix 1C, p. 317). None of the Baroque pieces was unknown to Parisian audiences, and some of the works by Rameau and Couperin were even favorites from the Baroque repertoire played in many a *concert historique* over the past decades.[59] The greatest attraction of these two concerts, however, was the performance of the early pieces on "authentic instruments": a 1769 harpsichord built by Pascal Taskin, and reproductions of a viola da gamba, a viola d'amore, and a quinton.[60] Critics focused on the performance of the early pieces in their discussion of the concerts, passing over the modern section in cursory fashion. Two issues seem to have captured their attention: the use of early instruments and the nationalist meanings that could be ascribed to the enterprise.

According to the music critic Adolphe Jullien, the two concerts offered not only "the most attractive" but also the "most novel" works to be heard in the context of current music making.[61] These programs featured "exquisite pages of ancient music" and in particular that of Rameau, "the greatest French musician before Berlioz," even though—as Jullien complained—"he had to wait 150 years to be honored like that, with these small trifles of

---

59. Awareness of this repertoire dates back into the early nineteenth century, especially with the editions and performances of Aristide and Louise Farrenc and Amédée Méreaux. See Ellis, *Interpreting the Musical Past*.

60. E. Poulain de Cormon, "Séances de musique de chambre à l'Exposition Universelle de 1889," *Le Guide musical* 35 (9 Jun 1889), 5–6, at 6: "C'est sur des instruments authentiques que MM. Delsart et Diémer ont donné au Trocadéro leur première séance le samedi 25 mai." For a description of the Taskin harpsichord in Paris, see Martin Elste, "Nostalgische Musikmaschinen: Cembali im 20. Jahrhundert," in *Kielklaviere: Cembali, Spinette, Virginale,* ed. by John Henry van der Meer, Martin Elste, and Günther Wagner (Berlin: Staatliches Institut für Musikforschung Preußischer Kulturbesitz, 1991), 244–45. The instrument is now part of the Russell Collection of Early Keyboard Instruments in Edinburgh. It is described in detail with illustrations in the online catalogue of the collection, http://www.music.ed.ac.uk/russell/instruments/hd5jg176329/table.html (accessed 28 May 2004).

61. Adolphe Jullien, "Revue musicale," *Le Moniteur universel,* 17 June 1889, 2: "Savez-vous ce qu'il y a eu de plus intéressant, en fait de musique, au Trocadéro, de plus attrayant et surtout de plus nouveau? Ce sont deux séances de musique de chambre ancienne et moderne, organisées par MM. Diémer et Delsart, et dans lesquelles ces deux artistes, jouant en perfection du clavecin et de la viole de gambe, nous ont fait connaître de charmantes pièces de Rameau, de Couperin, de Marais."

intimate music, by two artists of taste without the sanction of an official committee."[62] Thus, for Jullien, Diémer and his colleagues had achieved what
the Commission des Auditions Musicales had failed to do, present the best
of French music, even if it was only miniatures reflecting a composer's
grandeur. Charles Darcours also emphasized the Baroque composers'
national importance by identifying them as "the true creators of French
music, the practitioners of an art singularly more national than the one we
possess today."[63] Darcours's jibe is aimed at modern French music influenced first by the Italians and then by Wagner, and thus in dire need of
regrounding in a rediscovered French tradition. As critics pointed out, however, this national art stemmed from the *Ancien Régime* and therefore from a
period well before the Revolution commemorated in the 1889 Exposition
Universelle.[64] In contrast to the retrospective of revolutionary *opéras comiques*
planned for early June, Diémer's concerts in fact celebrated a longer and
more inclusive past, which some critics, such as Poulain de Cormon, identified as belonging to a restrictive and exclusive aristocratic world—certainly
one whose musical recreation might have attracted General Boulanger.[65]

The instruments themselves became signifiers of pastness in these performances. The viols were "Italian" and thus fascinating, but as instruments
they were not necessarily worth that much critical attention. Indeed, the
major achievement of the concert's string players consisted in their ability
to play both modern and early instruments equally well in the same concert: violoncello and viola da gamba, viola and viola d'amore, violin and
pardessus de viole. This feat was accomplished by several outstanding
Parisian musicians, including harpsichordist Louis Diémer, cellist Jules
Delsart, and violist Louis van Waefelghem. In these two concerts, the competition was on between the early, "primitive" version of the instruments
and their more modern, progressive siblings.[66] However, Diémer's

---

62. Ibid.: "ces exquises pages de musique ancienne. Ce pauvre Rameau, le plus
grand des musiciens français avant Berlioz, aurait-il dû attendre cent cinquante ans
avant d'être ainsi remis en honneur, avec ces petits badinages de musique intime, par
deux artistes de goût et sans sanction d'aucun comité officiel?"

63. Charles Darcours [Charles Réty], "Notes de musique à l'Exposition," *Le Figaro*, 5
June 1889, 5–6: "les véritables créateurs de la musique française, les pratiquants d'un art
singulièrement plus national que celui que nous possédons aujourd'hui."

64. Jullien, "Revue musicale," 2: "le succès, il faut bien le dire, a été pour les vieux
maîtres du siècle dernier, tous antérieurs à l'année 1789 et qui, dès lors, ne rentrent
même pas dans l'Exposition centennale, telle qu'on l'a entreprise et réalisée pour les
productions des Beaux-Arts."

65. Poulain de Cormon, "Séances de Musique de Chambre," 5: "Au temps jadis la
musique beaucoup moins vulgarisée que de nos jours était renfermée dans un cercle
restreint et intime."

66. René de Récy [J. Trezel], "Chronique musicale: Les clavecinistes français à l'Exposition," *La Revue bleue*, 15 June 1889, 763–64, at 764. Six months earlier, Arthur Pougin

harpsichord, "this precious relic," had a different role, for the instrument's ownership created an intriguing link to musical modernity: the current owner (the grandson of the builder) was a well-known bass singer, Émile-Alexandre Taskin, who took the role of Phorcas in the latest operatic première: Massenet's *Esclarmonde*.[67] The instrument attracted the attention of the audience to the point that listeners went to the front after the concert to have it explained to them by Diémer.

More than any other instrument, the harpsichord became a symbol for this early and ever-so-French music performed in the two concerts.[68] In a review entitled "Les Clavecinistes français à l'Exposition," René de Récy explored the reasons why "the spirit of the harpsichord is the very spirit of the French eighteenth century" by declaring it the favorite musical "toy" of a period characterized by the art of Marivaux, Voltaire, and Boucher.[69] But this proved to be a double-edged issue: not only De Récy, but also Saint-Saëns, writing for the Republican journal *Le Rappel* equated the charm and the elegance of the instrument and its sonorities with feminine capriciousness, delicacy, and enervation, tying in also with the feminization of the eighteenth-century French court by Republican critics.[70] Thus these small pieces by Rameau and Couperin performed by Diémer could be only a partial reflection of the truly national music of that period, the *tragédie lyrique*.

---

praised such progress explicitly with respect to the same performers' virtuosity, See Arthur Pougin, "Concerts et soirées," *Le Ménestrel* 55 (1889): 31: "Tout ceci était fort intéressant non seulement au point de vue de la musique exécutée, qui vaut certes la peine d'être entendue, ne fût-ce que comme constatation de l'état de l'art il y a 150 ou 200 ans, mais aussi parce que cela nous faisait connaître des instruments aujourd'hui disparus et dont on ne peut se faire qu'une idée toute relative. C'est M. Van Waefelghem et M. Delsart qui nous ont rendu le viole d'amour et la basse de viole, et l'on peut assurer, sans crainte de se tromper, que ces excellents artistes, au jeu si remarquable et si pur, feraient pâlir les ombres des plus fameux virtuoses du XVIIIe siècle, les Forqueray, les Marais et autres, si ceux-ci pouvaient entendre leurs successeurs."

67. Poulain de Cormon, "Séances de Musique de Chambre," 5: "primitive"; "cette précieuse relique."

68. Érard and Pleyel had also manufactured new, "improved" harpsichords for the nineteenth-century consumer. See Edward L. Kottrick, *A History of the Harpsichord* (Bloomington and Indianapolis: Indiana University Press, 2003), 409–14. He points out (p. 414) that these new harpsichords found their way into new French compositions such as Jules Massenet's opera, *Thérèse* (1907), where Louis Diémer performed the off-stage harpsichord part.

69. De Récy, "Chronique musicale," 763: "Car l'esprit du clavecin, c'est l'esprit même du XVIIIᵉ siècle français."

70. Camille Saint-Saëns, "Le 'Rappel' à l'Exposition: Les instruments de musique," *Le Rappel*, 5 Oct. 1889 / 14 Vendémaire an 98, 1–2, at 2: "Et c'est délicieux! c'est bien l'instrument du boudoir, de la femme nerveuse et délicate, sur lequel on peut accompagner un chant discret, une mélodie murmurée dans l'oreille entre deux propos d'amour."

However, if understood as delicate miniatures pointing toward their larger forebears, they could become powerful symbols of a French historical lineage in music, especially given that the Italian-born Lully did not leave a *clavecin* legacy.[71] Not only did they refer to a past not yet tainted by foreign influence, they could also be seen as fundamental to current and future developments in French music. Not for nothing were the earlier pieces paired with works such as Diémer's Suite and Saint-Saëns's and Lalo's piano trios, all compositions distinctly in a traditionally French vein with respect both to their formal structure and to their historicizing references to the classical models so favored by the eclectic esthetics of anti-Wagnerian, Republican composers.

This lineage was, however, challenged by the programs of the two Italian concerts which started a week later (Appendix 1D, p. 319). The concerts represented a high point of the short season given by the Italian opera company, organized by the Italian publisher, Edoardo Sonzogno, in Paris at the Théâtre de la Gaîté from April to June. Besides works by Verdi, Rossini, and current Sonzogno composers, the programs contained some of the best-known pieces of early music in nineteenth-century France, especially Palestrina's madrigal "Sulle rive del Tebro," a favorite since Choron.[72] Another French favorite on the program was the Stradella aria "Pietà, Signore"—according to nineteenth-century sources probably a fake composed by Louis Niedermeyer—arranged as an "air d'église" for orchestra.[73] But the Italians also programmed a Gavotte for wind instruments by a certain Lulli (note the Italian spelling) and the overture for Cherubini's opera *Le due giornate* (note the Italian title for Cherubini's famous opera, *Les Deux Journées* [*The Water Carrier*], 1800).

The French press had a field day: Nicolet, from the newspaper *Le Gaulois*, demanded that "Lulli" and Cherubini be claimed for France rather than treated as Italian; so did Johannès Weber of *Le Temps*.[74] Weber also

---

71. Jullien, "Revue musicale," 2.

72. The correct title of the madrigal is "Alla riva del Tebro." On the French Palestrina reception (including "Alla riva del Tebro"), see Katharine Ellis, "Palestrina et la musique dite 'palestrinienne' en France au XIX$^e$ siècle," in *La Renaissance et sa musique au XIX$^e$ siècle,* ed. Philippe Vendrix, 155–90 (Paris: Klincksieck, 2000).

73. Ellis, *Interpreting the Musical Past,* Appendix. Both Katharine Ellis and Sarah Hibberd have recently floated another hypothesis that the author was probably François-Joseph Fétis.

74. Nicolet [Edouard Noël], "Courrier des Spectacles," *Le Gaulois,* 8 June 1889, 3: "Mais quoi! il nous semble que la France a quelque droit de revendiquer Cherubini et Lulli." Johannès Weber, "Critique musicale," *Le Temps,* 10 June 1889, 3: "Une gavotte me semble bien connue; elle est de Lully, dont le nom a été rendu à son orthographe italienne primitive. Il était Italien comme Meyerbeer était Allemand."

pointed out that performing early music demanded superior musical ability, letting it be understood that such excellence was lacking in the performances of the Italian musicians.[75] Moreover, in contrast to the French concerts, the Italian performance was entirely on modern instruments, and furthermore, according to Arthur Pougin, the Italians failed in their historical enterprise because they did not understand the nature of a historical concert, which should offer clear guidance in chronological and scholarly terms in the manner of the Parisian *concerts historiques*:

> The evening, which took on a kind of historical character because of the composition of its program, was divided into two parts, one devoted to early music, the other to entirely contemporary music. But from this [Parisian] standpoint, the structure of the program was defective and the program indications were insufficient. Indeed, rather than mixing everything, it would have been necessary for the early part to follow a rigorous and determined order, a chronological order, and to present, for example, Lully, Stradella, and Lotti, who belong to the seventeenth century, before Cimarosa and Padre Martini, who stem from the eighteenth. On the other hand, why not indicate on the program from which works the Gavotte by Lully and the "Ronde" by Cherubini were extracted? Such information would not have been superfluous to the public here, which likes to be informed in a full and effective manner.

> La séance, qui prenait une sorte de caractère historique par le fait de la composition de son programme, était divisée en deux parties, l'une consacrée à la musique ancienne, l'autre à la musique absolument contemporaine. Mais si l'on se place à ce point de vue, l'ordonnance de ce programme était défectueuse, et les indications étaient insuffisantes. Il eût fallu, en effet, pour la partie ancienne, au lieu d'entre mêler toutes choses, suivre un ordre rigoureux et déterminé, l'ordre chronologique, et nous faire entendre, par exemple, Lully, Stradella et Lotti, qui appartiennent au dix-septième siècle, avant Cimarosa et le Père Martini, qui relèvent du dix-huitième siècle. D'autre part, pourquoi ne pas indiquer sur le programme de quels ouvrages sont extraits la Gavotte exécutée de Lully, et la "Ronde" de Cherubini? Ces renseignements n'eussent pas été superflus pour le public, qui, chez nous, aime à être informé d'une façon certaine et complète.[76]

75. Weber, "Critique musicale," 3: "Le programme du premier concert embrassait une période de plus de deux siècles; mais l'exécution de l'ancienne musique n'est pas toujours facile, parce que les morceaux relativement simples exigent une interprétation très correcte, une diction expressive et juste sans la moindre exagération."

76. Arthur Pougin, "Semaine théâtrale," *Le Ménestrel* 55 (1889): 178–79.

No doubt Pougin would have liked the taxonomic program notes that were created for the later organ concert organized by Alexandre Guilmant, with names and dates of composers, their "school," and the titles of the pieces, all in chronological order. Guilmant's program ranged internationally from Andrea Gabrieli, Monteverdi, and Byrd, to Muffat, Buxtehude, Rameau, and Clérambault. Here, Lully's "Air du *Triomphe de l'Amour*" is indicated unequivocally as belonging to the "École française."[77] Guilmant represented both Lully and Rameau as composers of opera rather than church or keyboard music (incidentally, in both cases through bass arias), in marked contrast to their German contemporaries Muffat, Froberger, Buxtehude, and Bach. Guilmant's program fit therefore in the longstanding nineteenth-century concept of French Baroque music as secular—even in the context of an organ recital—which can be related to Paris's self-image as being a center for operatic production (both historically and currently) on the one hand, and, on the other, to the highly problematic relationship of the French to the "grand motet" as a heavy-handed and awkward genre of sacred music.[78] Guilmant's concert was lauded by the critics as a model for historical concerts with respect both to programming and to execution. Indeed, its success was such that Charles Darcours from *Le Figaro* predicted future concerts on the same model.[79]

All of these historical concerts were, however, overshadowed by the performance of one major work, Handel's *Messiah*, on 10 June 1889 in the Salle des Fêtes du Trocadéro for the benefit of the Société Philanthropique, under the patronage of the glamorous Comtesse de Greffulhe. The concert was so successful that hundreds of listeners apparently had to be turned away at the doors, even though ticket prices were steep.[80] A second performance—again at the Trocadéro—for the benefit of the orphanage of Biding (in Alsace-Lorraine) followed two months later, on 3 August.

The event was hailed as a "great and unique" opportunity to hear the "universal masterwork" of Handel.[81] As the society columnist of *Le Gaulois*

77. Program for the *9me Séance d'Orgue*, given by Alexandre Guilmant at the Salle des Fêtes of the Trocadéro, 9 Sept. 1889 (Collection of the B.H.V.P.).

78. While Palestrina, Stradella, and other Italian composers quickly became part of the sacred early-music repertoire during the nineteenth century, only few French sacred compositions were performed during the nineteenth century. The "grand motet" was problematic both for stylistic and religious reasons, given its link to the Gallican faction of the Catholic church. See Ellis, *Interpreting the Musical Past.*

79. Charles Darcours [Charles Réty], "Notes de musique à l'Exposition," *Le Figaro*, 2 Oct. 1889, 6.

80. Apparently, the proceeds topped 30,000 francs. See Marc Gérard, "Carnet Mondain," *Le Gaulois*, 11 June 1889, 2.

81. For a more detailed study of Handel in Paris during the 1870s, see Ellis, *Interpreting the Musical Past.* Fourcaud is one of the authors who called *Messiah* one of the masterworks of universal music (Louis de Fourcaud, "Musique," *Le Gaulois*, 9 June 1889, 2).

put it: "With the Exposition in full swing . . . the moment of the perform-ance could not have been better chosen."[82] Announced in the press from late May on, the performance received the treatment that the French press normally reserved for an operatic première. The last time that *Messiah* had been performed in Paris was fourteen years earlier, in a concert on 14 Janu-ary 1875 in the Cirque des Champs-Élysées, conducted by Charles Lam-oureux. Before the 1889 performance, numerous articles in the daily press introduced the audience to the piece, its history, and its background. French writer Victor Schœlcher's role as the most competent historian of Handel was extolled explicitly in several reviews as a national achievement.[83] Both the dress rehearsal and the performance received extensive reviews. Even society columnists informed their readers that "all the members of Parisian and for-eign high society, all the stalwarts of musical life had responded to the call of the Comtesse de Greffulhe, whose beauty is rivaled only by her generosity."[84]

The French translation of *Messiah* used in this performance was by the Wagnerian critic Victor Wilder, the score was the version by Mozart, and the work was cut mercilessly to two and a half hours. Some newspapers tried to convince their readers that the score was Handel's original uncut version, but most critics pointed out the changes. The performers included Gabriel Fauré at the organ, and soloists, singers, and orchestra musicians from the Opéra. The production was conducted by Auguste Vianesi, the music director of the Opéra. Among the singers were such favorites of the public as Blanche Deschamps and Rose Caron. But even with these well-known performers, music critics were hardly satisfied with the concert. Vianesi was blamed for the cuts as well as for a nonchalant attitude toward the demands of the score, which the journalist from *Le Matin* attributed to his Italian origins.[85] Vianesi,

82. Tout-Paris, "Bloc-Notes Parisien: Le 'Messie' à Paris," *Le Gaulois*, 30 May 1889, 1: "C'est en pleine Exposition. . . . Le moment ne pouvait donc être mieux choisi."

83. See, for example, "Le *Messie*," *Le Matin*, 10 June 1889, 3; Johannès Weber, "Cri-tique musicale," *Le Temps*, 13 Aug. 1889, 3. Like Victor Hugo, the writer and politician Victor Schœlcher (1804–93) lived in exile during the Second Empire for opposing Napoléon III's coup d'état. Between 1851 and 1871, he spent most of his time in Lon-don, where he amassed a vast collection of Handeliana and published his *Life of Handel*, in a translation by James Lowe, in 1857. His return to France was a national event.

84. Gérard, "Carnet Mondain," 2: "Tout le high-life parisien et étranger, toutes les notabilités du monde artistique, avaient répondu à l'appel de la comtesse de Greffulhe, dont la beauté n'a d'égale que la bonté." On the role of the Comtesse de Greffulhe as impressario, see Jann Pasler, "Countess Greffulhe as Entrepreneur: Negotiating Class, Gender, and Nation," in *The Musician as Entrepreneur, 1700–1914: Managers, Charlatans, and Idealists*, ed. William Weber, 221–55 (Blomington and Indianapolis: Indiana Univer-sity Press, 2004).

85. "Au Trocadéro," *Le Matin*, 11 June 1889, 2–3, at 3: "Peut-être pourrait-on lui reprocher un peu trop de cette fougue italienne qui pousse à précipiter certains mouvements, à diriger parfois un peu trop en *tempo rubato*; mais il serait injuste de mécon-naître l'énergie et le talent de l'homme qui a mené à bien une entreprise aussi colossale."

wrote Johannès Weber, was "a good Italian conductor, but it is a long way from an opera by Donizetti or Verdi to the oratorios of Bach or Handel."[86]

The anti-Italian discourse reflected in these reviews, but also in the reception of the Italian early-music concerts, had a long tradition in France. After 1870, it was upstaged by anti-German sentiment, but it had not vanished entirely and became stronger again in the 1880s.[87] Indeed, antagonism in France against Italian music and performers could be as fervent as its adulation by the so-called *dilettanti* who celebrated Piccinni, Bellini, and Rossini and their melodic bravura. Already in the times of Catherine de Medici, the Italian musicians imported by the Florentine queen were eyed with a suspicion that resurfaced periodically, whether in the reception of Cavalli's *Ercole amante* in 1662 or that of Italian *verismo* in the 1890s. If German music was charged with incomprehensibility, boredom, and noisiness, Italian music appeared superficial and was seen as characterized by an excess of melody.[88]

Vianesi's somewhat cavalier approach was contrasted with the French conductor Lamoureux's first and well-rehearsed performance of *Messiah* with the Harmonie Sacrée on 19 December 1873, which became the yardstick for several journalists' judgment of the 1889 performance.[89] Whether through personal experience or through anecdotal reference, the earlier performances lingered on in the collective memory of French musical circles. But even with all these faults in the 1889 rendering of *Messiah*, the power of Handel's music was seen as transcendent: the same journalist in *Le Matin* reported that the music produced a considerable effect on an audience not initially inclined to take the music seriously, but which then ended up listening in "religious silence" to the entire performance.[90] And

86. Weber, "Critique musicale" (13 Aug.), 3: "M. Vianesi est un bon chef d'orchestre italien, mais il y a loin d'un opéra de Donizetti ou de Verdi à un oratorio de Bach ou de Hændel."

87. Eugen Weber, *France: Fin de siècle* (Cambridge, MA, and London: Belknap Press of Harvard University Press, 1986), 134–35.

88. Jean Mongrédien shows that the notion of German music's proclivity to noisiness and over-complexity were already in place in 1801. See Jean Mongrédien, *La Musique en France des Lumières au Romantisme (1789–1830)* (Paris: Flammarion, 1986), 322. On anti-Italian discourse, see Hervé Lacombe, *The Keys to French Opera in the Nineteenth Century*, trans. Edward Schneider (Berkeley, Los Angeles, and London: University of California Press, 2001), 268.

89. Even though, according to Ellis (*Interpreting the Musical Past*), the performance was also based on an incomplete Mozart version, Lamoureux's performance was received as significantly more "authentic" than Vianesi's.

90. "Au Trocadéro," 2: "L'incomparable chef-d'œuvre de Hændel, dont le *Matin* a donné, hier, une rapide analyse a été exécuté, au Trocadéro, devant une salle comble, au milieu d'un religieux silence. . . . L'effet produit par le *Messie* sur le public un peu frivole qui avait tenu à se montrer hier au Trocadéro a été considérable."

music critics took the opportunity to discuss the possibilities of an "artistic education of the nation" by displaying masterpieces to Parisians, even those whose "stomach was debilitated by the whipped cream of modern *opéra comique* or the suspicious sweetmeats of operetta."[91]

The nationalist slant of the reviews is palpable: when Handel's life is told, the emphasis lies on his international and universal appeal to the sophisticated and "true public of taste."[92] Critics made a clear distinction between Handel the composer of justly forgotten Italian operas and Handel, the creator of *Messiah*, a universally valid oratorio which guaranteed his place in posterity.[93] In an almost knee-jerk reaction, critics returned to the shopworn but, by 1889, almost outdated juxtaposition of Bach the German and Handel the Universalist in their attempt to deflect any inkling of an equation between Handel and another German musical giant, Wagner.[94] An acerbic note by Victor Wilder shows that such precaution might still have been necessary. After accusing France of cultural protectionism, he emphasized that the "gallant Handel never, as far as I know, lacked respect for France or provoked the reactions of patriotic pettifoggers."[95] But denationalizing Handel allowed for a reception of such works through performance and study that could lead to renewed strength in the development of national French music. Indeed, because *Messiah* was read as a universal masterpiece, its performance could be fêted as a French achievement in the long race for musical superiority, for it showed the world that French musicians and audiences were not only performing French music past and present, but also music by great masters within a more universal canon.

Archaeology was not a new concept in 1889; nor was the performance of Baroque music or the practice of historical concerts. Even the use of "authentic" instruments, as they were called then and now, had begun a few years before.[96] A well-known but isolated early example is Chrétien Urhan's

---

91. Henry Bauer, "Les premières représentations," *Écho de Paris*, 12 June 1889, 3: "l'éducation artistique de la nation." Victor Wilder, "'Le Messie' de Hændel au Trocadéro," *Gil Blas*, 12 June 1889, 3: "notre estomac, débilité par les crèmes fouettées du moderne opéra comique ou les sucreries suspectes de l'opérette."

92. Ibid., 3: "le vrai public, celui qui ne demande qu'à s'instruire, dont le goût s'affirme sans cesse et dont les appétits sont de plus en plus exigeants."

93. A. Landely, "Le *Messie*," *L'Art musical* 28 (1889): 81–82, at 81.

94. See, for example, Landely, "Le *Messie*," 81; Fourcaud, "Musique," 2. From the early 1880s on (especially with the centenary of 1885), the tide begins to turn towards Bach as the great universal composer rather than Handel.

95. Wilder, "'Le Messie' de Hændel au Trocadéo," 3: "Et cependant le brave Hændel n'avait pas, que je sache, démérité de la France et provoqué la susceptibilité des marmitons patriotes!"

96. De Récy, "Chronique musicale," 763: "[M. Jules Delsart et ses collègues] nous ont rendu, aux costumes près, les célèbres concerts de La Popelinière." Ces concerts took place on 24 and 31 January 1889 and featured already some of the pieces and

performance on the viola d'amore in Meyerbeer's *Les Huguenots* in 1836, while, beginning in 1879, François-Auguste Gevaert initiated a series of concerts on "authentic instruments" at the Conservatoire in Brussels.[97] Nevertheless, the 1889 performances represent an important moment in the development of historical performance practice. Several issues came together, which both reflected and shaped these changes in repertory and musical approach.

The context of the 1889 Exposition Universelle was one in which the concept of historical retrospection was developed on the largest scale, both to celebrate and commemorate past achievements, and to validate new technical and artistic developments. Scientific and industrial accomplishments cannot be nationally specific in ways usually associated with language-based activities, and therefore in 1889, historic validation was possible only through a history of individual achievement embedded in the framework of French culture. This kind of legitimization based on the representation of national achievements throughout history allowed for claiming such developments as "French." In addition to the display of historic instruments in the Palais de Arts Libéraux, these concerts allowed the ears to participate in the historic re-creation: "This is indeed the right way to understand a retrospective exhibition."[98] Consequently, the concerts were programmed and received within the framework of nationalist ideologies. This becomes as clear in the Italian historical concerts, which included Lulli and Cherubini as theirs, as in the French concerts and the surrounding rhetoric. Not only did Parisian critics such as Arthur Pougin point to the superiority of French historical method, but Delsart and Diémer were also praised as virtuosos of the highest caliber. Thus, with respect to both the historic context and the present representation, the French concerts of "musique ancienne" were represented as beating the Italian ones hands down.

In such a historic perspective, Baroque music, whether by Rameau or by Handel, was felt to serve as a foundation for new developments in French music and French artistic taste. Such pedagogic understanding of early music had its roots in the early nineteenth century with Fétis and Farrenc.[99] After France lost the war with Germany in 1870, the ensuing crisis of

---

performers of the Exposition Universelle concerts six months later, including Rameau's *Pièces en concert*, Marin Marais's *Sarabande* for viola d'amore, and a *Vieille Chanson normande*, performed in both cases with great success by Fanny Lépine. However, the earlier concerts also featured works by Handel and Legrenzi, which had no place in the later programs of early French music.

97. Haine, "Concerts historiques," 124–27.

98. Julien Tiersot, "Promenades musicales à l'Exposition," 180: "Voilà la bonne manière de comprendre une exposition rétrospective."

99. Katharine Ellis, *Music Criticism in Nineteenth-Century France: "La Revue et Gazette musicale de Paris, 1834–1880"* (Cambridge: Cambridge University Press, 1995), 56–76.

national confidence led to an explosion of the rhetoric of heritage in France.[100] Retrospectives in the arts were thus not only a validation of progress but also, in Republican ideology in particular, the underpinning of a modern and national art. In the framework of an Exposition Universelle, the choice of repertoire performed in both halves of the *Musique française ancienne et moderne* concerts was therefore programmatic in itself: the concerts showcased musicians who were fluent in both musics, ancient and modern, and the new pieces in suite and sonata forms by Diémer, Saint-Saëns, and Lalo were heard in the context of their models.

Finally, such music was new and foreign in ways no longer possible with the symphony orchestra after the saturation of chromatic harmony in the late 1880s. While the rhetoric of the "newness" of early music can already be found in the writings of Hector Berlioz, the gist of the argument changed.[101] For Berlioz, early music was simply different from the usual fare performed at the concerts of the Conservatoire; for Tiersot and other critics, Baroque music was a hidden treasure that could open fresh doors in the search for "new" music. To perform Handel, musicians could no longer rely on a performance tradition but had to find the cryptographic key to interpret the scores.[102] Archaeology now was paired with almost militaristic spycraft in order to gain access to unknown territory. The "basse chiffrée," for example, thus became literally a cipher that needed decoding.[103] Hence modern technology and early documents came together in a treasure hunt. One such discovery was the new sound of authentic instruments, in particular Diémer's Taskin harpsichord. Here the discovery of the new sonorities in early music shows parallels to the sonic discovery of "other"

100. Avner Ben-Amos, "The Uses of the Past: Patriotism between History and Memory," in *Patriotism in the Lives of Individuals and Nations*, ed. Daniel Bar-Tal and Ervin Straub (Chicago: Nelson-Hall Publishers, 1997), 129–33. For general musical trends, see also Pasler, "Paris: Conflicting Notions of Progress."

101. Ellis, *Music Criticism*, 60.

102. Bauer, "Les premières représentations," 3: "Quand il s'agit d'Haendel, on ne saurait invoquer ni traditions, ni mouvements; les partitions du maître sont muettes, c'est une cryptographie délicate que chacun traduit un peu à sa manière et selon son tempérament."

103. Indeed, a few years earlier already, Camille Saint-Saëns had characterized the performing of Baroque oratorio as a "chimera," because the incomplete scores demand "restoration" and "reconstruction" for the reason that the performance tradition "was lost." "A mes yeux, l'exécution des ouvrages de Haendel et de Bach est une chimère. . . . Dans cette musique tout diffère de ce qu'on voit ordinairement. Pas de nuances, pas de coups d'archet; l'indication des mouvements est énigmatique ou fait défaut. La basse est chiffrée: du premier regard on voit qu'il faut restaurer, reconstruire" (Camille Saint-Saëns, "Les Oratorios de Bach et de Haendel," in *Harmonie et Mélodie* [Paris: Calmann-Lévy, 1885], 99–100). I wish to thank Katharine Ellis for this reference.

music at the Exposition Universelle, whether the gamelan or opera transmitted through the telephone. Musical novelty in 1889 consisted of sonic difference, and many commented on the fact that the *Concerts de musique française ancienne et moderne*, in particular, offered an intriguing archaeology of sound as an "exotic within."[104] Immediately after the Exposition Universelle, Louis Diémer, Jules Delsart, and Louis van Waefelghem capitalized on the new trend by establishing the Société des Instruments Anciens, probably the first standing early-music ensemble in the world.

## The Sounds of the Globe: National Concerts at the Trocadéro

New and unknown music, whether Russian or Finnish, could also be discovered in the concerts that foreign nations put on in the Trocadéro as part of the official series (see Appendix 1E, p. 321). By the middle of July, Charles Darcours characterized the performances at the Exposition as truly universal:

> At this moment, the Trocadéro is the musical center of the globe. One arrives from the countries of the world to be heard there, and the Salle des Fêtes has become a kind of Babel, where one sings in all languages and plays on all existing instruments and then some.

> Le Trocadéro est en ce moment le centre musical du globe. On vient s'y faire entendre de tous les pays du monde et la Salle des Fêtes est devenue une sorte de Babel où l'on chante dans toutes les langues, où l'on joue de tous les instruments existants, ou autres.[105]

Darcours alludes here not only to the competition, on 4 July, of folk music, both French and European, which brought sometimes unusual sounds, whether from the Auvergne or Romania, to Parisian ears (see chapter 5), but also to the series of sixteen foreign concerts organized by various national commissions to showcase the music of their countries. The programs had to be submitted by 1 April 1889 to the Commission des Auditions Musicales for approval, and the rules stated explicitly that they had "to produce in particular the music of their national authors, whether dead or alive."[106] The cost was assumed by the individual concert organizers, who also paid a 10 percent fee on receipts for the use of the hall.[107]

---

104. Early music as "exotic within" remains a form of its reception even in current musical life. See Kay Kaufman Shelemay, "Toward an Ethnomusicology of the Early-Music Movement," *Ethnomusicology* 45 (2001): 1–29.

105. Charles Darcours [Charles Réty], "Notes de musique," *Le Figaro*, 10 July 1889, 6.

106. Picard, *Rapport général sur l'Exposition Universelle*, 3:348: "produire particulièrement la musique de leurs auteurs nationaux morts ou vivants."

107. Ibid., 3:347.

## Russia

The series of these officially sanctioned, non-French concerts opened with two Russian programs on 22 and 29 June. The conductor, Nikolay Rimsky-Korsakov, and the concerts' organizer, the Russian publisher Belaïev, hoped to continue the success of the four concerts given by Nikolay Rubinstein at the previous Exposition Universelle.[108] But they did not count on the fact that none of the performers had the name recognition of such an international star, and the mere fact of playing new Russian music was not enough to attract an audience large enough to fill the Trocadéro—although the crowd of about one thousand spectators would still have matched the capacity of a Parisian concert hall such as that of the Conservatoire.

> In spite of a rather well-organized publicity these past days, the second Russian concert attracted barely more people than the first one, and nothing is as sad as when the vast hall of the Trocadéro is three-quarters empty. Why this indifference of music-lovers with respect to these two interesting performances, which lacked only the star on the poster who would attract the big crowds. Ah! If Rubinstein had been announced, for example!

> En dépit d'une réclame assez bien organisée en ces derniers jours, le second Concert Russe n'a guère attiré plus de monde que le premier, et rien n'est plus triste comme la vaste salle du Trocadéro aux trois quarts vide. Pourquoi cette indifférence des dilettantes à l'égard de deux séances intéressantes, auxquelles il ne manquait guère que la vedette d'affiche alléchant le gros public? Ah! Si Rubinstein, par exemple, avait été annoncé![109]

Charles Darcours blamed Russian music itself as the reason for the disappointing audience, stating his belief that it was better absorbed in small doses.[110] But while the audience was limited, it was nevertheless select and keen. Among the musicians applauding enthusiastically were Alfred Bruneau, Claude Debussy, Gabriel Fauré, André Messager, and Julien Tiersot.[111] Journalists were no less interested in the new music from Russia and published a good number of reviews, responding to the concerts'

---

108. In the 1878 Exposition Universelle, Nikolay Rubinstein conducted four concerts in September. See Elaine Brody, "The Russians in Paris (1889–1914)," in *Russian and Soviet Music: Essays for Boris Schwarz*, ed. Malcolm Hamrick Brown (Ann Arbor, MI: UMI Research Press, 1984), 159.

109. Edmond Stoullig, "Musique," *Le National*, 2 July 1889, 2.

110. Charles Darcours [Charles Réty], "Notes de musique," *Le Figaro*, 26 June 1889, 6: "le public faisait presque complètement défaut, parce que la musique russe ne doit pas, croyons-nous, être absorbée à dose extrême."

111. Stoullig, "Musique," 2; Bruneau, "Musique," 205–8; François Lesure, *Claude Debussy: Biographie critique* (Paris: Klincksieck, 1994), 105.

nationalist claims of representing what was truly "Russian" in music. Indeed, several critics speculated that Nikolay Rubinstein's works might have been excluded deliberately by Rimsky-Korsakov because they were too Germanic and thus not Russian enough, and most of the music performed could be read as producing a lineage of national music from Glinka to Glazunov.[112]

In their reviews, the French critics tried to define what was inherently Russian in the program, how it differed from French music, and whether it had anything to offer beyond its curiosity value. For Alfred Bruneau, the answer to the last question was obvious, for the Russian concerts daringly "screamed modernity" in ways to be emulated by French concert organizers.[113] What distinguished this modern Russian music was that it kept its "national color by the continuous use of folksong," while at the same time approaching French avant-garde by buying into the "shared vision of a mysterious and poetic beyond."[114] But what Bruneau put in positive terms, other critics formulated more ambivalently. Russian music was Other, even when it charmed "our occidental ears," and such musical alterity in the concert hall—rather than the Champ de Mars—needed addressing.[115] Thus two reception strands seem to become intertwined in this case: it is music allied with French concerns by rejecting Germanic models, but it is also exotic and therefore not quite where France was situated in the (French) hierarchy of national musics.

Indeed, relying on Russian folk melodies as musical material—a reliance inspired by the national proclivity towards the picturesque, the colorful, and the inventive—was seen as one of the points of difference from French contemporary music.[116] This was given as the reason for the Russians' favoring of "program music," itself a problematic and disputed concept in French musical aesthetics.[117] In these accounts, the Russians did not

---

112. The notion that Rubinstein was Germanic and thus not part of Russia's national musical heritage was first floated in France in a series of articles by Cesar Cui on the history of Russian music, published in the *Revue et Gazette musicale de Paris* between May 1878 and October 1880. See Ellis, *Music Criticism*, 177–78.

113. Bruneau, "Musique," 205: "hurlant la modernité."

114. Ibid.: "Tout en gardant sa couleur nationale par l'emploi contant des mélodies populaires, elle se rapproche de nous et elle nous ravit par la commune vision d'un au delà poétique et mystérieux."

115. Victor Wilder, "La Musique russe au Trocadéro," *Gil Blas*, 25 June 1889, 1–2: "nos oreilles occidentales sont charmées autant qu'étonnées."

116. See, for example, Balthazar Claes [Camille Benoît], "Chronique parisienne: Les deux concerts russes," *Le Guide musical* 35 (1889): 180–82; Darcours, "Notes de musique"; Adolphe Jullien, "Revue musicale," *Le Moniteur universel*, 29 July 1889, 2; Johannès Weber, "Critique musicale," *Le Temps*, 8 July 1889, 3.

117. On the French debates about program music, see Ellis, *Music Criticism*, 172–79; Fauser, *Der Orchestergesang in Frankreich*, 111–39; Seipt, *César Francks symphonische Dichtungen*.

create this genre; it was brought to Russia by none other than the French composer Hector Berlioz. While Berlioz was credited with adding sophistication to Russian orchestration techniques, he was also cited as a model for Musorgsky's *Night on a Bald Mountain*.[118] Save for their autochthonic folk music, Russian composers depended thus on Western (in particular, French) models for the creation of art music that could be taken seriously.

But the essentializing assessment of the Russian concerts saw pitfalls in the appropriation of these sophisticated Western models by composers from the East, especially since Russia was part not only of Europe, but also of Asia. Their national character might be suited to the writing of picturesque and descriptive music, but the Russians' "natural" penchant for exuberance led to long, incoherent pieces rather than concise and well-structured ones. The old notions of classic proportion and clarity raised their head as a measuring stick of musical quality in these reviews, even in those that are generally favorable. The length of Russian novels by Dostoyevsky and Tolstoy was thus seen mirrored in the excessive dimensions of Rimsky-Korsakov's *Antar*, the work otherwise most positively received in the press. What marked a composer as Slavic, according to the critics, was a lack of measure and control. Adolphe Jullien—whose review was generally supportive—criticized Glazunov's symphonic poem, *Stenka Razine*, as being flawed on two points, "lack of plan, excessive length."[119] Indeed Glazunov's piece represented

> all the essential qualities and the incontestable faults of the Russian musical school: a very clever and frequent use of popular motives, such as the song of the Volga boatmen, on which this entire musical tableau is built; a rare instinct for combining the strangest rhythms and for extracting from them effects of extraordinary violence and relief; an expressive and tender melancholy; a rare ability to describe through sounds all the episodes of a small imaginary drama; but also an exaggerated search of color, of the picturesque effect; a veritable abuse of developments or orchestral combinations; and above all, the absence of an underlying plan.

> les qualités essentielles et les défauts incontestables de l'école musicale russe: un emploi très habile et très fréquent des motifs populaires, comme le chant des bateliers du Volga, sur lequel est bâti tout ce tableau musical, un instinct peu commun pour combiner les rythmes les plus étranges et

---

118. For example, Claes ("Chronique parisienne," 181) dedicates an entire paragraph to Berlioz's "influence marquée" on the "style descriptif, et surtout l'instrumentation" of Russian music. His comparison between Musorgsky and Berlioz was positive, however, whereas Weber ("Critique musicale," 3) condemns *A Night on the Bald Mountain* as "que du Berlioz médiocre."

119. Jullien, "Revue musicale," 2: "manque de plan, excès de longueur."

pour en tirer des effets d'une violence et d'une relief extraordinaires; une mélancolie expressive et tendre; une habilité rare à décrire au moyen des sons tous les épisodes d'un petit drame imaginaire; mais aussi une recherche exagérée de la couleur, de l'effet pittoresque, un véritable abus des développements ou des combinaisons d'orchestre et surtout l'absence de plan général.[120]

Indeed, Jullien's review recalls the criticism of Romanticism leveled half a decade earlier at the one French composer associated with Russian music in this context, Hector Berlioz, except that now the general reproach against Romanticism's lack of formal control has been appropriated in a nationalist discourse influenced by nineteenth-century race theories as reflecting the character of a people.[121]

This assessment of modern Russian music in the French press corresponded to the general trends in the representation and reception of Russia at the Exposition Universelle as the "eternal Russia": a strange, barbaric, opulent, rich, and exotic country which at the same time was modern and full of industrial potential.[122] It was almost as if the musical experience at the Trocadéro was a sonic microcosm of the large-scale dichotomy of tradition and modernity shown at the fair, where a Russian *isba* (a small wooden cottage in the countryside) and a reproduction of the façade of the Kremlin contrasted with the exhibits of the Russian railroad and oil refineries.

In the end, the exoticism seemed more appealing. While Rimsky-Korsakov's concerts were too modern, even though picturesque, the four performances of Russian folk music by the "Russian national chapel," the *Slavyanskaya Kappella*, in September proved a major success because their colorful performance focused on what was the most traditional and thus least threatening repertoire. The visual aspect of the concerts corresponded to Parisian notions of Russian opulence. The program notes emphasized that the entire choir was being dressed in "unparalleled magnificence" with costumes that were "exact reproductions of those from the sixteenth and seventeenth centuries, copied from albums in the Kremlin of Moscow."[123] Even more splendid were the costumes and jewelry of

120. Ibid.

121. On nineteenth-century race theories and music, see chap. 4.

122. On the general trends of the reception and representation of Russia at the Exposition Universelle, see Laurence Aubain, "La Russie à l'Exposition Universelle de 1889," *Cahiers du Monde Russe* 37 (1996): 349–68, esp. 356–58.

123. "Concerts Russes de la célèbre chapelle nationale Dmitri Slaviansky d'Agréneff," Program Booklet (Paris: Maison Rapide, 1889), 1–8, at 6: "magnificence inouïe"; "la reproduction exacte de ceux des XVI$^e$ et XVII$^e$ siècles copiés sur des albums du Kremlin de Moscou."

Dmitri d'Agrenev, his wife, and his children, who stood in front of the choir during the performances in the manner of a tsarist Von Trapp family (figure 1.4). The programs were very cleverly designed. They started with an "epic poem," *Sviagator,* "singing about the famous hero of the eleventh century, Dobrynia Nikitich," which established a deep historic grounding of the performance in ancient times.[124] After that, the group performed a variety of folk songs, including the "famous song of the 'Volga boatmen,' which has become so popular among us that the public recognized and applauded it after the first measure."[125] "Vnis po matuchke po Wolgue," the song that had made Glazunov's symphonic poem *Stenka Razine* a semi-success at the Trocadéro in June, proved an unmitigated hit in its original guise as folk music. Indeed, sound and sight coalesced in this second series of Russian concerts to create a staged image of an eternal Russia, foreign enough to be picturesque and interesting, but contained in the framework of a concert at the Exposition. Theirs was not the disconcertingly savage modernity of the Rimsky-Korsakov concerts, but music performed by beautiful voices, including that of the conductor, who not only presented himself as being an aristocrat from an old Russian family—whose devotion to music was not a professional necessity but a nationalist cause—but who also looked vaguely familiar to the French audience because of his much remarked-upon resemblance to "our great poet, Théophile Gautier."[126]

### Scandinavia

In July, other choral concerts also caught the attention of Parisian audiences, shifting the interest from the Orient and the East to music of Northern Europe: "After the Orient, the North. After Russia, Sweden and, especially, Norway. How interesting they are, these people who have come late to artistic life, these alleged 'barbarians,' who seem to have so much to teach us, and with whom contact should rejuvenate us!"[127] While Russia was

124. Johannès Weber, "Critique musicale," *Le Temps,* 16 Sept. 1889, 3: "un poème épique chantant le célèbre héro du onzième siècle Dobrynia Nikitisch."

125. Charles Darcours [Charles Réty], "Notes de Musique," *Le Figaro,* 2 Oct. 1889, 6: "mais le plus grand succès de la troupe de M. d'Agreneff est toujours le fameux chant des 'Bateliers du Volga', devenu si populaire parmi nous que le public le reconnaît et l'applaudit dès la première mesure."

126. Jean de la Tour, "A travers l'Exposition," *Le Journal de Paris,* 22 Sept. 1889, 3: "le portrait de notre grand poète Théophile Gautier."

127. Balthasar Claes [Camille Benoît], "Chronique parisienne: La musique scandinave à l'Exposition," *Le Guide musical* 35 (1889): 196–97, at 196: "Après l'Orient, le Nord. Après la Russie, la Suède, et surtout la Norvège. . . . Comme ils sont intéressants, ces peuples tard venus à la vie artistique, ces prétendus 'barbares' qui auraient tant de choses à nous apprendre, et dont le contact devrait nous rajeunir!"

# CONCERTS  RUSSES

DE LA CÉLÈBRE CHAPELLE NATIONALE

## DMITRI SLAVIANSKY D'AGRÉNEFF

Figure 1.4. Title page of the program for the *Concerts russes*
(Paris: Maison Rapide, 1889).

often seen as dangerously exotic, Scandinavia evoked very different associations, described as a melancholic but nevertheless virile charm inspired by a landscape of fjords, lakes, and forests. Moreso than Russia, the Scandinavian North was unknown, rarely invoked in French music save such works as the *Rapsodie norvégienne* by Eduard Lalo, performed only a month previously at the official Trocadéro concert of the Orchestre Colonne. Some of its folk tales and poems were published in French translation by Xavier Marmier from the late 1830s onwards. The main Scandinavian composer known in France was Edvard Grieg, whose works figured regularly on the programs of the major French concert societies.[128] In contrast to Germany, Finland, Norway, and Sweden had not been tainted by recent wars against France, nor did they pose any immediate danger to her cultural supremacy since they were not seen as centers of musical creation.

Neither Finland nor Norway was an independent country at the time of the Exposition Universelle, and yet both were represented through exhibits and national pavilions as if they were. Norway would gain its independence from Sweden only in 1905; Finland was still a grand duchy under the rule of Russia. When the celebrated all-male Finnish choir, Muntra Musikanter from Helsinki University, arrived in Paris on 1 July 1889, the link between Finland and Russia was made explicit in the Press. Thus an article in *Le Petit Journal* declared that the Finnish, although under Russian rule, were not Russians in the full sense of the word, for the Russians "leave a great administrative autonomy" to their provinces—in complete contrast to the English and Germans, who "annex" them. "The Finnish have kept their character and customs of yesteryear."[129] Muntra Musikanter had the cachet of being popular with the Russian Imperial couple; indeed the choir was founded in 1878 as an elite ensemble to "perform regularly outside Finland, first and foremost in St. Petersburg."[130]

128. Darcours makes this point in his review of the Norwegian concerts. See Charles Darcours [Charles Réty], "Notes de Musique," *Le Figaro*, 31 July 1889, 6. On the relationship of Norway and France with respect to music, see Harald Herresthal and Ladislav Reznicek, *Rhapsodie norvégienne: Les musiciens norvégiens en France au temps de Grieg*, trans. Chantal de Batz (Caen: Presses Universitaires de Caen, 1994); Harald Herresthal and Danièle Pistone, eds., *Grieg et Paris: Romantisme, symbolisme et modernisme franco-norvégiens* (Caen: Presses Universitaires de Caen, 1996).

129. "Les Finlandais," *Le Petit Journal*, 7 July 1889, 3: "Mais la Russie, suivant un système tout à fait opposé à celui que suivent l'Angleterre et l'Allemagne en s'annexant des provinces, leur laisse une très grande autonomie administrative. . . . Aussi les Finlandais ont-ils gardé leur caractère et leurs mœurs d'autrefois."

130. Helena Tyrväinen, "Sibelius at the Paris Universal Exhibition of 1900," in *Sibelius Forum: Proceedings from The Second International Jean Sibelius Conference, Helsinki, 25–29 November, 1995*, ed. Veijo Murtomäki, Kari Kilpeläinen, and Risto Väisänen (Helsinki: Sibelius Academy, 1998), 115.

The visit to Paris of the Finnish choir was a triumph. Upon their arrival, they gave an impromptu concert which was fêted by the Parisian students as "a prelude to the successes that they have been called to achieve in Paris during the ten days that they will be staying among us."[131] On 4 July 1889, they gave a private concert in the offices of *Le Figaro*, performing, among other pieces, *Suomis Sång* by Fredrik Pacius, *Skål för kvinnan* by Karl Collan, *Olav Trygvanson* by Friedrich August Reissiger, and *Sångfåglarna* by Otto Jonas Lindblad.[132] The following day, *Le Figaro* published on its front page an article by Gaston Calmette which praised the choir's flawless performance of "all these mysterious melodies from the North," where one finds "the rustling of the wind and the roaring of the sea of this beautiful country."[133] By the time of their first concert, the Muntra Musikanter were on their way to becoming Parisian celebrities for the summer, and both concerts were very well attended. The audience included the wife of the president, Mme Carnot; the poet Jean Richepin; the singer Pauline Viardot; and, one of the journals observed, an unusually large number of women.[134] Such was their success that they had to add a good number of encores; indeed, one of the journalists reported that he had "rarely seen such enthusiasm in a concert hall. In their box, Jean Richepin and his wife applauded frenetically."[135]

As Helena Tyrväinen has observed, the choir performed a Scandinavian program which contained only some Finnish music: folk-song arrangements and choruses by Pacius, Collan, and Rikard Faltin. Most of the repertoire was by Swedish or Norwegian composers; the choice of Finnish music in nationalist terms was still limited and only just beginning to develop, with Jean Sibelius's signal *Kullervo* being composed three years later, 1892.[136] Reference to the repertoire was through texts more than

131. Georges Aubry, "Notes parisiennes: Muntra Musikanter," *L'Événement*, 6 July 1889, 2: "C'est le prélude des succès qu'ils sont appelés à remporter à Paris pendant les dix jours qu'ils doivent rester parmi nous."

132. See Helena Tyrväinen, "Suomalaiset Pariisin maailmannäyttelyiden 1889 ja 1900 musiikkiohjelmissa," *Musiikkitiede* 1–2 (1994): 31.

133. Gaston Calmette, "Les Étudiants d'Helsingfors," *Le Figaro*, 5 July 1889, 1: "toutes ces mélodies mystérieuses du Nord"; "le bruissement du vent et le mugissement des flots de ce beau pays."

134. "Les 'Joyeux Musiciens' Finlandais," *La Justice*, 7 July 1889, 3: "un nombreux public où les dames dominaient."

135. B. J., "Le Concert Finlandais," *La Justice*, 9 July 1889, 3: "J'ai rarement vu dans une salle de spectacle pareil enthusiasme. Dans une loge de face, Jean Richepin et sa femme applaudissaient avec frénésie."

136. Tyrväinen, "Sibelius at the Paris Universal Exhibition of 1900," 116. One important figure in the Finnish nationalist movement was the "father of Finnish music," Fredrik Pacius, whose choral works were part of the Parisian programs, including "Suomis Sång" and "Björneborgarnes Marsch." Pacius's opera *Kung Karls jakt* (1852) counted as a significant contribution to the development of a national tradition. See the

detailed descriptions of the music, although journalists did refer to the sizeable choruses and the variety of the program.[137] But what inspired them even more was the high standard of performance and the musical effects produced by the *a cappella* repertoire, which led both Adolphe Jullien and Albert Soubies to compare the Finnish choir with the French *orphéon* societies. The difference, Jullien concluded, was one of class: French *orphéon* members were workers and artisans; "the singers from the North occupy a higher social rank."[138] Indeed, while the Finnish singers were exotic in one sense, their musicianship had reached the pinnacle of Western musical achievement, and therefore they could serve as the rejuvenating force that Benoît had called them in his review cited above.

Less than three weeks after the visit of the Finnish choir, another group from Scandinavia continued blazing a trail for Northern music in Paris. Not a single seat was unoccupied at the concerts of the choir from Christiana (now Oslo), and the audience called for many encores.[139] Members of the press used very similar arguments in their discussions of the Muntra Musikanter when they reported on the Norwegian concerts, lauding the excellent performance of the choir and relating the music to a "national soul." In the opinion of the journalists, the Norwegians held their own in comparison to the students from Helsinki, but, as Charles Darcours put it, they had the advantage of a more appropriate repertoire because of having a clearer national identity:

> We would be thoroughly embarrassed if we had to manifest a preference between those marvelous choral societies: the Finnish students and the Norwegian singers; however, beside the performance, which is pure and beyond reproach in both camps, we believe that we have to congratulate the Norwegians on ownership of a personal repertoire, a national art.

> Nous serions fort embarrassés s'il nous fallait manifester une préférence entre ces deux merveilleuses Sociétés chorales: les étudiants finlandais et

unsigned article "Finland" in *Grove Music Online*, ed. Laura Macy, http://www.grovemusic.com. All articles were accessed before 31 August 2004. Reference to the dictionary is henceforth under the abbreviation *NGr2*.

137. Several reviews cited the text of one or two songs, including the "Björnebor-garnes Marsch" by Fredrik Pacius, which the journalist of *La Justice* equated with the *Marseillaise*. "Les 'Joyeux Musiciens' Finlandais," 3: "Écoutez ces vers. On croirait entendre la *Marseillaise*."

138. Adolphe Jullien, "Revue musicale," *Le Moniteur universel*, 18 July 1889, 2: "Mais voilà! ceux de la France sont des ouvriers, des artisans tandis que les chanteurs du Nord occupent un rang social plus élévé." Jullien's comparison with the French *orphéons* rather than society choirs such as *La Concordia* was probably prompted by the gender of the Finnish choir and the repertoire it performed.

139. B. J., "Les Concerts du Trocadéro," *La Justice*, 30 July 1889, 3.

les chanteurs norvégiens; toutefois, en dehors de l'exécution, qui est pure et sans reproche dans les deux camps, nous croyons devoir féliciter les Norvégiens d'avoir à eux un répertoire personnel, un art national.[140]

Like the Russians, the Norwegians were billed as performing "exclusively national music" in their concert, subsuming the Swedish pieces on the program under this nationalist umbrella.[141] Again the Northern landscape and its related melancholic charm were called upon in the description of the music's character. Selmer's *Charivari* thus "has a flavor of the soil," while the music in general consisted of "strange songs" "of soft melancholy and deep sentiment," but "almost always poetic."[142] In addition to the Norwegian choir, the orchestra of the Opéra-Comique—hired for the occasion—performed orchestral music by two Norwegian composers, Edvard Grieg and Johan Svendsen. In his extensive review of the concert, Charles Darcours recounted a piquant detail related to the composer Johan Selmer, whose earlier contacts with France were somewhat problematic. In 1871, as a thirty-year-old, he was active as a conductor of a Communard orchestra. When troops advanced from Versailles, he fled back to Norway, where he became an honored national composer in his home country. His piece *La Tempête* was the only newly composed work on the program, written especially for Paris.[143]

### United States

Between the Finnish and the Norwegian concerts, the Americans presented their national achievements in music with a concert at the Trocadéro on 12 July. The program was built not on the characteristic claim for folk music as representing national specificity, a ploy used by both the Russians with their emphasis on program music and the Scandinavians with their choral arrangements of folk melodies, but on works in the tradition of the cosmopolitan concert repertoire, including Edward MacDowell's second piano concerto and Arthur Foote's overture *In the Mountains*. In the

---

140. Charles Darcours [Charles Réty], "Notes de Musique," *Le Figaro*, 31 July 1889, 6.

141. Darcours, "Notes de Musique," 6: "exclusivement de musique nationale."

142. Claes, "Chronique parisienne: La musique scandinave à l'Exposition," 197: "a une saveur de terroir"; Fracasse, "Courrier de Théâtres," *Le National*, 31 July 1889, 4: "ces chants étranges"; B. J., "Concert norvégien au Trocadéro," *La Justice*, 28 July 1889, 3: "d'une mélancolie douce et d'un sentiment profond"; Edmond Stoullig, "Au Trocadéro," *Le National*, 30 July 1889, 4: "presque toujours poétique."

143. Darcours, "Notes de Musique," 6. On the Norwegian concerts in Paris, see Herresthal and Reznicek, *Rhapsodie norvégienne*, 165–69; Heinrich W. Schwab, "La Musique scandinave et les Expositions universelles parisiennes," in *Grieg et Paris*, ed. Herresthal and Pistone, 111–24.

context of a series of national performances, this strategy was rather risky. By now, the audience and critics would have expected more picturesque and less symphonic music that, with respect to America, would have echoed the sounds of the highly successful and oversubscribed Wild-West show of Buffalo Bill.[144] Indeed, what was perceived as autochtonic to the United States was not the urban musical practice modeled on Europe, but the music of the frontiers popularized not only by the Buffalo Bill show in Neuilly but also one that could be imagined as aligned with the travel reports by Alexis de Tocqueville or Gustave de Beaumont who tried to reach "the furthest frontiers of civilization," or with richly illustrated works such as Edmond de Mandat-Grancey's *Dans les Montagnes rocheuses* or his *La Brèche aux buffles: Un ranch français dans le Dakota.*[145] It is ironic that while the United States was vaunted as an heir to France in its pursuit of the republic, and while its technological achievements were without compare (as we shall see in connection with Thomas Alva Edison in chapter 6), it was denied access to a cultural sphere that, in the present context, might best proclaim its cultural credentials to the world—a tradition of national art and music.

As an event, the concert was successful. Present were not only dignitaries such as Mme Carnot, the president's wife, but also composers such as Bruneau, Chabrier, Lalo, and Massenet, and many of the notable music critics. But as Douglas Bomberger has shown, the French were less than impressed with the American composers and their music. As with the other national concerts, critics tried to identify what made this music specifically American. For Victor Wilder, "the art music of the Americans is like their nationality: an amalgamation of races whose fusion is not yet complete enough to constitute an irreducible type."[146] While the Russians were building their music on a deeply rooted national culture—strange but seductive—the Americans were seen as little more than inept imitators of European styles, and worst of all, those of Germany. Critics also referred to the Germanic antecedents of Grieg and Svendsen, but they had been

144. Douglas Bomberger makes this point in his well-documented chapter about the American concert in Paris, which contains a detailed analysis of the reception. The following paragraph is based on this chapter, but adds a more contextual reading relating the American concert to the other European ones, which is missing in Bomberger's analysis. See Bomberger, *"A Tidal Wave of Encouragement": American Composers' Concerts in the Gilded Age* (Westport, CT: Praeger, 2002), 45–64.

145. Jean-Baptiste Duroselle, *France and the United States: From the Beginnings to the Present*, trans. Derek Coltman (Chicago and London: University of Chicago Press, 1978), 71–75.

146. Victor Wilder, "La Musique américaine au Trocadéro," *Gil Blas*, 16 July 1889, 3–4, at 4: "L'art musical des Américains est comme leur nationalité, un amalgame de races, dont la fusion n'est pas assez complète pour constituer un type irréductible."

perceived as overcoming the model by infusing it with the "national senti-ment" of the North, an "originality" that was absent from the American concerts.[147] The racial theories that were employed when discussing German, Italian, Russian, or Norwegian music throughout the nineteenth century also shaped the understanding of the American music at the Expo-sition Universelle while revealing the danger of such discourse almost more powerfully than the racism shown in the case of non-Western music (see chapters 4 and 5). What the discourse about the American concert makes strikingly clear is that in music criticism, notions of racial purity were strongly linked with concepts of originality.[148]

Not only was the program seen as simply endearing or pretentious—depending on whether the critic was in a friendly mood or not—but the organizer of the concert, Frank van der Stucken, had committed the sin of bad taste when he distributed with the tickets and program a leaflet that lauded his contribution to the dissemination of French music in the United States. To the French, such presumption was a cause for ridicule, and journalists—Wilder and Jullien included—referred to the text in derogatory terms. Bad manners were among the few things that could not be easily forgiven in France, as many composers and performers had expe-rienced at their cost.[149] In contrast, journalists explicitly commented on the exquisite manners of the Finnish students.[150] Nevertheless, the American concert counted among the more interesting performances in the series, for it gave a glimpse into a musical culture related to one of Paris's heroes, Thomas Alva Edison. Journalists speculated about the future, when a musi-cal Edison would revolutionize American music.[151]

## Spain and Belgium

Two other countries joined the concert of nations at the Trocadéro: Spain and Belgium. The Spanish followed the folklore model in all their national concerts. The choral concerts on 20 and 24 August were a performance of "works by Spanish composers" and "folk songs from ancient European

147. Adolphe Jullien, "Revue musicale," *Le Moniteur universel*, 29 July 1889, 2.

148. How strongly the issues had entered racial theories can be seen in Gustave Le Bon's text on the psychology of people, first presented at the Colonial Congress of the 1889 Exposition Universelle. See the discussion in Jann Pasler, "The Utility of Musical Instruments in the Racial and Colonial Agendas of Late Nineteenth-Century France," *Journal of the Royal Musical Association* 129 (2004): 24–76, at 27.

149. Hervé Lacombe makes this point about Bizet and Wagner. See Lacombe, *The Keys to French Opera*, 38–40.

150. Georges Aubry, "Notes parisiennes: Muntra Musikanter," 2.

151. Bomberger, *"A Tidal Wave of Encouragement,"* 52, 54.

Iberia," creating a distinction with urban Spanish popular music as performed in many a *café-concert* in Paris. Like the ancient Russian or Finnish songs, those from Spain were billed as presenting the music of the "fatherland in this so solemn and important festival" to "the entire world."[152] Five days later, on 29 August, the *Grandes Fêtes espagnoles* that were enchanting all of Paris with their performances at the Cirque d'Hiver offered a concert-cum-dance show at the Trocadéro, which opened with three concert pieces played by the Union Artistico de Madrid and finished with dances performed by colorfully costumed ballerinas from the Grand Opera of Madrid. The last Spanish concert, on 20 September, was a medley of dances and other popular musics presented by a Basque choral society and its Estudiantina, whose program nodded to the host nation by way of choruses by Laurent de Rillé and Saint-Saëns, but which (save for the Belgian composer Gevaert's "Spanish" chorus, *Madrid*) was otherwise composed of manifestly Spanish works. The critic of *Le Figaro*, Charles Darcours, was particularly impressed by the excellent presentation of the choir and by the dancing musician (a "virtuose de fantaisie") "who somersaults with extraordinary speed while at the same time playing his tambourine which he hits with the fist, the elbow, the knee, the foot, the head, etc., while always maintaining his rhythm with astonishing precision."[153]

No such popular undercurrents were apparent in the Belgian concert, which was added to the series at the last minute as a benefit concert for the victims of an exploded gunpowder factory in Antwerp. The repertoire ranged from Grétry to Benoit, and the musicians were among the finest in Paris. Save for Jan Blockx's *Kermesse flamande*, the emphasis was on the Gallic side of Belgian culture, resulting in a concert more like that of a French province than that of a neighboring state. Reviews of the concert were sparse and no more positive than those of the French concerts. Indeed, for Victor Wilder, the Belgian program showed the same weaknesses of focusing on old repertoire rather than modern music and on favoring works composed by the official concert organizers.[154]

The organization and reception of this series of foreign concerts in Paris brought to the fore a variety of topics relating to musical idioms, national identity, and modernity. All three issues were associated particularly with program music. Judging from the reviews, it seems as if almost all Parisian

152. Concert advertisement, "Espagne: Orfeón Coruñès Numero 4," B.H.V.P., dossier "Actualités": "que represente á su patria en tan solemne è importante festival"; "al mundo entero."

153. Charles Darcours [Charles Réty], "Notes de Musique," *Le Figaro*, 2 Oct. 1889, 6: "qui cabriole avec une prestesse extraordinaire tout en jouant son petit tambour de basque qu'il frappe du poing, du coude, du genou, du pied, de la tête, etc., en maintenant toujours son rythme avec une étonnante netteté."

154. Victor Wilder, "Les Concerts belges au Trocadéro," *Gil Blas*, 1 Oct. 1889, 3.

critics shared some underlying concepts concerning music's representational properties. The way in which music was perceived as being able to reflect extrinsic content depended, however, on the critics' position. Some, such as Victor Wilder, supported a rather literal aesthetic of musical poetics, while others, among them Alfred Bruneau and Edmond Stoullig, relied on a more abstract conception of representation. The attribution of representational capacity to music had consequences for its reception within the framework of a concert series based a nationalist taxonomy to which the concert organizers had responded in the way the concerts were programmed. This taxonomy implied an unvoiced universality of musical language from which specific idioms could be distinguished. In the context of the 1889 reviews, this neutral level was the general repertoire performed during the Parisian Season: predominantly French and Italian operas, and German and French concert music.

Scholars such as Carl Dahlhaus and Marina Frovola-Walker have shown that discourse and musical creation are often divorced in the context of musical nationalism. While the mythology of national specificity could be rampant (especially in the context of Russian nation-building), the actual music rarely differed from contemporary, more cosmopolitan musical styles of composition.[155] Thus musical signifiers of nationalism were often extrinsic: program notes and titles, or motivic materials derived from well-known folk tunes. But even the use of folk melodies was not necessarily what made music intrinsically national, not even to the ears of a nineteenth-century critic. In the Finnish concert, the choir sang a folk song, "Serenade ved Strandbredden," arranged by Halfdan Kjerulf, that Adolphe Jullien recognized as the theme of Ophelia's ballad in Ambroise Thomas's opera *Hamlet*.[156] While in the opera the song added Northern *couleur locale* to the ballad of a Danish heroine, the opera's essentially French character was never in question. Similarly, the reviews of the American concert reveal that the critics identified an international style of composition that could be used regardless of a composer's nationality. Yet because of the way the concerts were set up, it was crucial that the national particularity of each country be singled out in the reviews. Except for making specific references to folk songs, the eternal fallback of nationalist signifying, especially when composer and folk song come from the same country, critics gave nonmusical reasons for describing generic musical elements as

---

155. Carl Dahlhaus, *Die Musik des 19. Jahrhunderts* (Laaber: Laaber Verlag, 1980), 32–34; Marina Frolova-Walker, "Against Germanic Reasoning: The Search for a Russian Style of Musical Argumentation," in *Musical Constructions of Nationalism*, 104–22.

156. Adolphe Jullien, "Revue musicale," *Le Moniteur universel*, 18 July 1889, 2: "le délicieux chant populaire: *Au bord de la rivière*, où M. Ambroise Thomas a puisé le thème de la ballade d'Ophélie."

nationally specific: the Russians wrote lengthy novels and long musical pieces; the Scandinavians inhabited wild landscapes and therefore had melancholic music; the Spanish liked to dance and thus produced vivacious compositions; the Americans were a melting pot of peoples and that was how they sounded. Such essentialist stereotyping is as old as discussions of national cultures, and can be found in French reports on Italian music in the sixteenth century, or German ideas about the French in the eighteenth. What distinguished these reviews in 1889 was their context, in which they responded to self-consciously nationalist frameworks. These are not discourses that try to engage with one foreign opera or composer; they provided a continuous commentary on institutionalized musical difference. Whether the pieces sound Russian or not is never the question in these reviews; it is only how they can be identified as sounding Russian that matters in the assessments of the critics. The underlying nationalist framework of the reviews itself is never put into question, but rather forms an aesthetic common place.

In this concert of nations, French music itself was no less nationally specific. Especially for avant-garde composers like Alfred Bruneau, French music was in competition with the world for the position of creative leadership. He warns his compatriots that the "movement of French art is one to which foreign schools give much more attention than one might think."[157] Others joined Bruneau in their criticism of the French concerts as being too canonic and not avant-garde enough to assure everyone of France's legitimate role as the world leader in musical terms. Thus, in his roundup of the concert series, the Wagnerian Victor Wilder compared the musical exhibition of France with the "marvelous" show of modern painting and found it sorely wanting.[158] While French painting had both a centennial and a decennial exhibition—one to show the historic dimension of French art, the other to look forward—the Commission des Auditions musicales was far more restricted in what it sought to achieve. It sacrificed the music of the future for that of the past, showcasing France as a nation whose musical culture had both depth and breadth. This was particularly important since France's superiority as a musical nation was at stake in the intense concert series of the Exposition summer. In the end, music from abroad

157. Before discussing the modern Russian music, Bruneau affirms the "immense superiority of our composers." Bruneau, "Musique," 205: "[le] mouvement de l'art français, mouvement dont les écoles étrangères se préoccupent beaucoup plus qu'on ne pense."

158. Wilder, "Les Concerts belges," 3: "Si l'on a réalisé des merveilles, au pavillon des Beaux-Arts pour la peinture, on a fait, au Trocadéro bien peu de chose pour l'art moderne par excellence." Other critics such as Charles Darcours and Louis de Fourcaud were equally underwhelmed with the place given in the French programs to more recent pieces.

was received first and foremost as picturesque and always lacking in substance when compared to that of France. The Russians might have been modern, but they lacked form and structure; the Finns and Norwegians might teach the French about poetic melancholy, but they were still the new kids on the block; the Americans were simply beginners; the Spanish were too Southern; and the Belgians occupied naught but a musical province of France. Even the Italians could not measure up. They did not organize an official "national" concert, but their early-music performance was nowhere near as sophisticated as that of the French. Conspicuously absent were the Germans. Whether by their own choice or discouraged by the organizers, France's archrival for musical superiority did not come to Paris in 1889 to spoil French pride.[159] The official musical setup of the Exposition Universelle may not have been as extensive as the one ceded to visual arts, but it ensured that the world witnessed (potentially) the triumph of *Ars Gallica*.

---

159. In 1900, Siegfried Wagner visited Paris just prior to the Exposition Universelle, but again German orchestras were absent from the official programs. According to Peter Lamothe, this fit with a generally noncompetitive approach of the German Empire during the 1900 Exposition. By contrast, the Austrians were musically represented with the Vienna Philharmonic Orchestra, conducted by Gustav Mahler. I am grateful to Peter Lamothe for this information.

*Chapter 2*

# Opera, Ballet, and the Politics of French Identity

The organizers of the official concerts of French music for the Exposition Universelle seemed mainly preoccupied with reappropriating the French musical past for the Third Republic, with respect both to compositions and to forms of music making. The leaders of Parisian cultural and political institutions, however, looked to new works as well as old to assert France's cultural glory. Indeed, the Théâtre de l'Opéra-Comique brought out a major French première with Jules Massenet's *Esclarmonde* on 15 May, right at the beginning of the Exposition. This was to be the only opera première for the duration of the Fair, and thus it was all the more significant.[1] But the Opéra-Comique also offered a series of widely advertised performances of late-eighteenth-century *opéras comiques* as a form of generic archaeology, as well as their regular performances of "classics" such as François-Adrien Boieldieu's *La Dame blanche* (1825) or Ferdinand Hérold's *Le Pré aux clercs* (1832). Furthermore, the hundredth performance of Edouard Lalo's *Le Roi d'Ys*, the previous year's major première, took place on 24 May 1889, and on 13 September there was the 400th performance at the Opéra-Comique of Georges Bizet's *Carmen* (1875).

In contrast to this artistic success story, the Théâtre de l'Opéra struggled for months under the embattled leadership of Eugène Ritt and Pierre Gailhard until they could finally present, on 26 June 1889, the première of Ambroise Thomas's ballet *La Tempête*. The rehearsals for Camille Saint-Saëns's new opera *Ascanio*, which was originally supposed to be the Opéra's great Exposition triumph to match the Massenet première of the Opéra-Comique, encountered mishap after mishap, and the work was not performed until almost a year later, on 21 March 1890. Thus, throughout the duration of the Exposition Universelle, the Académie Nationale de Musique did not offer a première of a new French opera, and to fill the house it had to rely instead on a ballet by the almost eighty-year-old doyen of French

1. See Appendix 2 for a day-to-day calendar of opera performances in Paris during the Exposition Universelle.

music and on repertoire performances of such operas as Charles Gounod's
*Faust* (1859) and *Roméo et Juliette* (1867), Giacomo Meyerbeer's *L'Africaine*
(1865) and *Les Huguenots* (1836), or Fromental Halévy's *La Juive* (1835).

Nevertheless, in financial terms, the Exposition Universelle was a
major economic asset for the opera houses and theaters throughout Paris.
Independently of their programming, they could count on the presence of
the more than thirty million visitors to the Exposition Universelle, many of
whom came from the French provinces and from abroad.[2] After all, a visit
to the world-famous theatres of the French capital was a "must" for any visitor to the Exposition. The demand was such that the Opéra, which usually
performed only four times per week, increased its frequency first to five
and finally, by the end of August, to six weekly performances (excluding
Sundays), while the Opéra-Comique filled their nightly presentations of
both recent and repertoire works without any problem.[3] Statistics compiled
after the event reveal that profits for the Opéra and Opéra-Comique were
36 percent and 33 percent higher in 1889 than in 1888.[4] Just as in 1878, the
Exposition boosted theater attendance in the city of Paris. Henri Lavoix
noted the consequences:

> The pessimistic forecasts from the theaters about the Exposition Uni-
> verselle have fortunately not materialized. It was feared that the Champ
> de Mars and the Esplanade des Invalides, the luminous fountains, the Eif-
> fel Tower, the "rue du Caire," the Arab cafés, and the Chinese and Viet-
> namese theatres would absorb the entire visiting population—however
> great in size it might be—without even counting the competition of Buf-
> falo [Bill] and the *toros* that arrived from all corners of Spain. Our poor
> theatres would be fatally abandoned next to such an exhibition. This was
> not so. . . . Paris, the real, everyday Paris, has a much higher resistance. It
> is in itself an exhibition and one of a different order; thus it had no
> difficulty fighting against all the attractions of the moment. For three

2. In April 1889, *Le Ménestrel* published the figures from 1878 to remind its readers
of the positive effects which the Exposition Universelle would have on cultural economy
in Paris. See "Nouvelles diverses: Paris et Départements," *Le Ménestrel* 55 (1889): 126. The
rising receipts were continuously tracked in the national press. See for example *Le
Figaro*'s regular column "Courrier des théâtres," as on 17 Aug. 1889, 4. The writer there
concluded that "le public, en effet, apporte aux théâtres plus d'argent que jamais."

3. Charles Darcours [Charles Réty] reported in the "Courrier des théâtres" of *Le
Figaro*, 25 Aug. 1889, 4: "A l'Opéra, l'affluence du public devient de plus en plus considérable, les cinq représentations par semaine ne suffisent plus, et, en présence des récla-
mations incessantes des personnes qui ne peuvent avoir de places, la direction a décidé
de donner une sixième représentation, le jeudi. A partir de cette semaine, l'Opéra
jouera donc tous les jours, sauf le dimanche."

4. Alfred Picard, *Rapport général sur l'Exposition universelle internationale de 1889*, 10
vols. (Paris: Imprimerie nationale, 1890–91), 3:289.

months, the Opéra has taken its fill of box-office receipts. Not that there are exceptional singers to attract the masses; no, it is just the Opéra with its repertoire. . . . *Faust, Roméo et Juliette, Le Cid, voilà* the true winners. . . . And the Opéra-Comique! It has been a long time since it had such good fortune. All repertoire receives the same reception, from *Esclarmonde*, yesterday's success, through *Carmen, Mignon,* to pieces that are half a century old. As you might guess, *La Dame blanche* is at the forefront. . . . What does it have for itself, this piece which is sixty-five years old and remains ongoing, impregnable in its eternal success? It is *La Dame blanche*, it is part of Paris.

Les prévisions pessimistes des théâtres au sujet de l'Exposition Universelle ne se sont pas réalisées, heureusement. Le Champ-de-Mars et l'Esplanade des Invalides, les fontaines lumineuses, la tour Eiffel, la rue du Caire, les cafés arabes et les théâtres chinois et annamites devaient absorber, si prodigieuse qu'elle fût, toute la population voyageuse, sans compter la concurrence de Buffalo et des *toros*, qui arrivaient de toutes les contrées des Espagnes. Nos pauvres salles de spectacle devaient être fatalement abandonnées, après une telle exhibition. Il n'en a rien été. . . . Paris, le vrai Paris, celui de tous les jours, a une résistance autrement grande. Il est à lui seul une exhibition et d'une bien autre importance; aussi ne lui a-t-il pas été difficile de lutter contre toutes ces attractions du moment. L'Opéra bat depuis trois mois le plein de ses recettes. Ce n'est pas qu'il ait des chanteurs hors ligne qui font courir la foule; non, il est simplement l'Opéra avec son répertoire. . . . *Faust, Roméo et Juliette, le Cid,* voilà les véritables triomphateurs. . . . Et l'Opéra-Comique! De longtemps, il ne s'était trouvé à pareille fête. Tout le répertoire y passe avec le même bonheur, depuis *Esclarmonde,* le succès d'hier, depuis *Carmen, Mignon,* jusqu'aux pièces qui datent depuis plus d'un demi-siècle. Vous pensez bien que la *Dame Blanche* est en première ligne. . . . Qu'a-t-elle donc pour elle, cette pièce qui compte soixante-cinq ans d'existence et qui reste sur la brèche, irrésistible dans son éternel succès? Elle est la *Dame Blanche*, elle fait partie de Paris.[5]

As Lavoix reveals, the relationship between the city and the Exposition was quite symbiotic, for the city itself and its cultural production became part of what was exhibited as French achievement, while at the same time, Paris was host to, and frame for, the Exposition, that competing city within the city that encompassed the world within its perimeter.[6]

---

5. M. Savigny [Henri Lavoix], "Les Théâtres," *L'Illustration* 47 (1889): 158.

6. On the notion of the *Exposition Universelle* as city in the city, see Annegret Fauser, "Die Welt als Stadt: Weltausstellungen in Paris als Spiegel urbanen Musiklebens," in *Musik und Urbanität*, ed. Christian Kaden and Volker Kalisch, 139–48 (Essen: Blaue Eule, 2002).

## Massenet's *Esclarmonde*: A French Answer to Wagner

On 15 May 1889, two apparently unrelated events coincided in Paris. In the morning, the Eiffel Tower was officially opened to the public; in the evening, the well-advertised first performance took place of the new masterpiece of France's best-known composer, Massenet's *Esclarmonde*. The Eiffel Tower celebrated French technical achievement and progress. The new opera was perhaps the most lavish production ever seen on the stage of the Opéra-Comique, and the opening night was packed with French and foreign dignitaries, including the presidential family:

> The Opéra-Comique has invited us this week to the first performance of the most important work to be prepared and mounted in Paris in the context of the Exposition Universelle. The appearance of *Esclarmonde* is a truly artistic event which will have a considerable impact on the entire world. And the hall at the Place du Châtelet was filled, for this solemn occasion, with an entirely exceptional public. Apart from the classical Tout-Paris of premières, we saw the most prominent personalities of the official world, of the arts, and of the foreign communities. The President of the Republic and Madame Carnot occupied, with their family, a large box that was specially fitted out for this occasion, and they showed the most visible signs of their enthusiasm for M. Massenet's beautiful score.

> L'Opéra-Comique nous a conviés, cette semaine, à la première représentation de l'ouvrage le plus important qui ait été préparé et monté à Paris en vue même de l'Exposition Universelle. L'apparition d'*Esclarmonde* est un véritable événement artistique qui aura un retentissement considérable dans le monde entier. Aussi la salle de la place du Châtelet était-elle, pour cette solennité, remplie d'un public tout-à-fait exceptionnel. En dehors même du classique Tout-Paris des premières, nous avons remarqué les notabilités les plus marquantes du monde officiel, du monde des arts et de la colonie étrangère. M. le président de la République et Mme Carnot occupaient, avec leur famille, une grande loge spécialement aménagée à cette occasion, et ont donné les marques les plus visibles de leur enthousiasme pour la belle partition de M. Massenet.[7]

Visitors and critics could not fail to understand *Esclarmonde's* quasi-official status as the great French musical creation for the Exposition, a high-profile response to the cultural challenges posed especially by Imperial Germany, symbolized in the figure of Richard Wagner. This was a "modern" work, dazzling like the Eiffel Tower, showing that France was at the forefront of artistic creation. The librettists, Alfred Blau and Louis de Gramont, in particular the latter, were known for their poetic skill, with

---

7. Damon, "Théâtres," *L'Univers illustré* 32 (1889): 326–27.

works performed in major Parisian theaters and opera houses. The composer, a member of the prestigious Académie des Beaux Arts, could look back on a series of such highly successful operas as *Le Roi de Lahore* (1877), *Hérodiade* (1881), *Manon* (1884), and *Le Cid* (1885). Last but not least, the première had the additional twist of introducing to Paris a young and beautiful singer with unusual vocal abilities: the American soprano Sibyl Sanderson. Her top notes, higher than any heard before, seemed the vocal equivalent of the Eiffel Tower's conquest of the skies, and more than one critic would write about the "Note-Eiffel de l'Opéra-Comique."[8]

The link between the Exposition and *Esclarmonde* was exploited by critics who tried to evaluate the opera's importance and meaning within this context. Whereas Maurice Lefèvre, in an article for the Italian *Il teatro illustrato e la musica popolare*, described the première as an event of particularly "solemn" proportions because "a cosmopolitan public comes together from all parts of the world,"[9] *La Justice*'s critic, Charles Demestre, pushed the link much further and described Massenet's opera as one of the most interesting parts of the Exposition. Among other successful features of the work, it managed to incorporate a multiplicity of medieval epics and Wagnerian operas into its libretto. Demestre's rhetoric mimicked that of the unveiling of a monument constructed for the Exposition, just like that of the Eiffel Tower:

> Yesterday, with solemnity and grandiose splendor, the opening of one of the most interesting parts of the Exposition Universelle took place. The president of the Republic inaugurated *Esclarmonde*, the gigantic opera built on the Place des Nations and whose unveiling Paris and her visitors have awaited with such lively curiosity. The list of marvels offered to foreigners is now complete, and thus all the slander of those who claimed that we would not be ready on Day One has been proven wrong. *Esclarmonde* is, together with its rival, the Eiffel Tower, the most immense work known to this day; it wins by several lengths over the Strasbourg cathedral and the *Nibelungen*. And it has the advantage over the Eiffel Tower in that it is itself an exquisite artwork. If it astounds us by its colossal dimensions, it also seduces us by the most delicate grace.

8. Auguste Vitu, "Chronique musicale," *Le Figaro*, 16 May 1889, in *Dossier de presse parisienne: Jules Massenet "Esclarmonde" (1889)*, ed. Annegret Fauser (Heilbronn: Musik-Edition Lucie Galland, 2001) [henceforth *DE*], 8. On Sanderson and Massenet, see Steven Huebner, *French Opera at the Fin de Siècle: Wagnerism, Nationalism, and Style* (Oxford: Oxford University Press, 1999), 73–81.

9. Maurizio [Maurice] Lefèvre, "Opere nuove: *Esclarmonda*," *Il teatro illustrato e la musica popolare* 9 (1889): 84–86, at 84: "Un'opera nuova del maestro Massenet che viene alla luce, è in ogni tempo un avvenimento artistico di un ordine elevato, ma, nelle circostanze particolari in cui si presenta *Esclarmonda*, alcuni giorni dopo l'aperture dell'Esposizione, nel momento in cui da ogni parte del mondo un pubblico cosmopolita accorre alla nostra chiamata, l'avvenimento assume le proporzioni d'una vera solennità."

Hier s'est faite avec une solennité et un éclat grandiose l'ouverture d'une des plus intéressantes sections de l'Exposition Universelle. Le président de la République a inauguré *Esclarmonde,* le gigantesque opéra édifié place des Nations, et dont Paris et ses visiteurs attendaient avec une curiosité si vive la révélation. A présent, la liste des merveilles offertes aux étrangers est au complet, et ainsi tombent les calomnies de ceux qui prétendaient que nous ne serions pas prêts au jour un. *Esclarmonde* est avec sa rivale la Tour Eiffel le plus vaste ouvrage connu jusqu'à ce jour; elle l'emporte sur le Munster de Strasbourg et les *Niebelungen* [*sic*] de plusieurs longueurs. Mais elle a l'avantage, sur la Tour elle-même d'être une œuvre d'art exquise. Si elle étonne par ses dimensions colossales, elle séduit par les grâces les plus délicates.[10]

But the reference to the Exposition also allowed comment upon the perceived problems of the opera (and the Exposition itself), as with, for example, Georges Saint-Mleux in his sarcastic "Chronique musicale." Here he compared *Esclarmonde* with the Eiffel Tower, both created to dazzle naive visitors from the countryside and abroad. Not even patriotism could make up for the aesthetic condemnation of this author, which contrasts with the much more chauvinist rhetoric in the previous reviews:

Finally! One climbs up the Eiffel Tower and one gives *Esclarmonde*! . . . Between those two coinciding events, there is more than a simple fortuitous connection, and where superficial observers see only some rather ridiculous coincidence, a wise person might find an interesting philosophical explanation based on the analysis of curious affinities. In fact—and one should not forget this viewpoint, as paradoxical as it may seem—*Esclarmonde* owes if not its birth then at least its current form to the same circumstances as the Eiffel Tower. Without the Exposition neither one nor the other would have its *raison d'être*, and herein lies the explanation for many of those things which at first sight appear so extraordinary in M. Massenet's score. The author of *Esclarmonde* wanted to *dazzle* the provincials and the foreign adventurers freshly arrived in Paris: he particularly wanted to create a work that was capable of bringing their money into the theater's coffers as well as his own. He has tried hard but in vain: he has taken ideas and procedures right, left, and center; he has overburdened his work with false gold and fake jewels, and he has succeeded in *exhibiting* this big contraption of sham gold, the latest *article de Paris.*

Enfin! l'on monte sur la Tour Eiffel et l'on joue *Esclarmonde*! . . . Il y a, entre ces deux événements coïncidents, plus qu'un simple rapprochement fortuit, et, là où les superficiels ne verront qu'un hasard assez ridicule, un

10. Charles Martel [Charles Demestre], "La Soirée d'hier: *Esclarmonde,*" *La Justice,* 16 May 1889; in *DE,* 22.

sage trouverait peut-être une explication philosophique intéressante, basée sur l'analyse de curieuses affinités. C'est que,—et il ne faut pas oublier ce point de vue, si paradoxal qu'il puisse paraître,—*Esclarmonde* doit, sinon sa naissance, au moins sa forme actuelle, au même concours de circonstances que la Tour Eiffel: sans l'Exposition ni l'une ni l'autre n'aurait plus sa raison d'être: et en ceci gît l'explication de bien des choses, au premier abord si extraordinaires, dans la partition de M. Massenet. L'auteur d'*Esclarmonde* a voulu *épater* les provinciaux et les rastaquouères frais débarqués à Paris: il a voulu surtout faire œuvre capable d'amener leur argent dans la caisse du théâtre et dans la sienne. Il s'est battu les flancs tant qu'il pu, il a pris à droite et à gauche des idées et des procédés; il a surchargé son ouvrage de dorures et de pierres fausses, et il a fini par *exposer* cette grande machine en toc, frais *article de Paris.*[11]

Ironically, Massenet's opera was neither commissioned for nor written for the opening of the Exposition Universelle. The name of the composer was already connected with the libretto, under its original name of *Pertinax,* as early as May 1886.[12] But by 1888, the opera had been accepted, with Sibyl Sanderson in the title role, for the 1889 season at the Opéra-Comique as the première that would be scheduled to correspond with the beginning of the Exposition.[13] The rehearsal period then proved to be a race against time, recorded, among other events, in regular installments in *Le Ménestrel.*[14] A massive public-relations campaign in the last couple of weeks before the première ensured that the attention of all Paris if not the Western world was focused on the opening night to witness the unveiling of a performance which was to showcase French achievement in all aspects of this splendid production (figure 2.1).

The première sparked a heated engagement with the new opera in the national press, centering on how *Esclarmonde* was to be judged in the

11. Georges Saint-Mleux, "Chronique musicale: *Esclarmonde* à l'Opéra-Comique," *La Musique des familles (Musique populaire)* 8 (1889); in *DE,* 180.

12. See Huebner, *French Opera at the Fin de Siècle,* 78. On the genesis of *Esclarmonde,* see also Patrick Gillis, "Genèse d'*Esclarmonde,*" *L'Avant-Scène Opéra,* no. 148 (September–October 1992): 22–33.

13. The possibility of a performance linked to the World's Fair was mentioned first in *Le Ménestrel* 55 (1888): 123: "Ce n'est pas tout. M. Paravey a profité de ce rapprochement avec M. Massenet [= engagement of Sibyl Sanderson] pour s'assurer d'une nouvelle partition da sa façon: *Pertinax,* sur un livret de MM. Alfred Blau et Louis de Gramont. Il ne s'agit nullement ici de l'empereur romain qui porte ce nom, mais bien d'un sujet emprunté à Shakespeare. C'est Mlle Sanderson, déjà nommée, qui en remplirait le principale rôle, et la pièce passerait au printemps prochain de l'Exposition. Car il y a des gens qui croient encore à l'Exposition."

14. See for example, the reports in *Le Ménestrel* 55 (1889), on 23 March (p. 91), 14 April (p. 115), 28 April (p. 134).

Figure 2.1. Paul Destez, "Théâtre de l'Opéra-Comique:
*Esclarmonde,*" *L'Univers illustré* 32 (1889): 328.

context of contemporary music theater in France, and whether it did indeed show to the world its greatest achievement at so crucial a moment. It was through these issues, rather than the more anecdotal references to the Champ de Mars, that *Esclarmonde*'s special place in the political context of the Exposition was explored. The unusually large space accorded to aesthetic and musical discussions in these reviews, especially those published in daily newspapers, reflected these concerns. Following a century-long tradition, nineteenth-century critics filled most of their accounts with the plot of a new piece, and then added a few summary remarks on the music and performance.[15] In the case of *Esclarmonde*, however, entire articles were devoted to aesthetic issues raised by the opera and by Massenet's music in particular.[16] The single question underlying almost everything written

15. An important study on the practices of the musical press in late nineteenth- and early twentieth-century Paris is James Ross, "Crisis and Transformation: French Opera, Politics and the Press, 1897–1903" (DPhil diss., Oxford University, 1999).

16. All in all, over 200 articles have come to my attention. I have published 35 of them in *DE*. Aesthetic issues were raised not only in the specialist music press, but also in daily newspapers such as *Le Figaro*.

about *Esclarmonde* was the issue of whether this high-profile opera did indeed represent "the new path" for French opera.[17] The yardstick against which to measure the answer was as ubiquitous as the question itself: had Massenet and his librettists found a route to overcome the challenge of Richard Wagner, the "Bismarck of Music?"[18]

Both supporters and adversaries of the opera hailed *Esclarmonde* as a turning point in the history of French opera, opening new paths for a generation of French composers who needed to find their own voices when faced with the challenge of Wagner. Even twenty years after the Franco-Prussian war, the German victory still lived on in the popular imagination as the greatest national defeat in French history. In that respect, 1889 was a crucial time, since after the death of Wagner and with the aging of Verdi the signs seemed favorable for France to become the leading musical nation of the Western world. German music, opera in particular, seemed exhausted (albeit still threatening with the ongoing performances of Wagner after his death), while Italian opera was dwindling away. During the 1880s and until the rise of Puccini in the late 1890s, the most important modern composer in the stable of the Italian music-publishing house of Ricordi was Massenet.[19]

*Esclarmonde* tells the story of a Byzantine empress and sorceress, Esclarmonde, who loves the French knight Roland de Blois, whom she had seen when he was in Byzantium for a tournament. The empress must remain veiled until her twentieth birthday, at which point another tournament will decide her future husband. When she learns that Roland de Blois is about to marry, she has him abducted to an enchanted island where she becomes his wife on condition that he will never ask her name or see her face, to which he agrees. After a night of passion, Esclarmonde sends him back to a Blois beleaguered by Saracens. She provides him with a magic sword which will make him invincible so long as he keeps his word, and she promises that she will see him every night wherever he is. Roland saves Blois and is

17. Georges Street, "Esclarmonde," *Le Matin*, 16 May 1889; in *DE*, 29.

18. The characterization of Wagner as the "Bismarck de la musique" was coined in the aftermath of the Franco-Prussian war and became part of the polemic surrounding Wagner reception in France. On Wagner reception in France, see Annegret Fauser and Manuela Schwartz, eds., *Von Wagner zum Wagnérisme: Musik, Literatur, Kunst, Politik*, Transfer: Die deutsch-französische Kulturbibliothek 12 (Leipzig: Leipziger Universitäts-Verlag, 1999); Huebner, *French Opera at the Fin de Siècle*.

19. Whereas Hartmann, and later Heugel, were Massenet's French publishers, Ricordi owned the rights for the Italian versions of a number of operas, including *Il Re di Lahore*, *Erodiade*, and *Esclarmonda*. These rights were not only important with respect to performances of Massenet's operas in Italy, but also for the entire world, given that many theaters in England, the United States, Germany, and other European countries often preferred the Italian version of French operas over the original when it was not translated into the vernacular.

offered the French king's daughter in marriage. He refuses without giving reasons, but the archbishop prises Roland's secret from him under the pretence of confession. Esclarmonde joins her husband/lover for the night. The archbishop enters the room and exorcises her. Roland tries to defend Esclarmonde, but the sword breaks. Rescued by spirits, Esclarmonde is brought before her father Phorcas, who declares that either Roland has to die or Esclarmonde must repudiate him. To save his life she chooses repudiation. Roland is devastated and wants to die honorably in combat, and just at that moment heralds announce the tournament for Esclarmonde's twentieth birthday. Roland wins the tournament and thus the hand of his beloved—this time officially.

The two librettists based *Esclarmonde* on a French medieval source, Denis Pyramus' tale narrating the love of the knight Parthénopeus de Blois and the fairy Melior. This epic was published in several editions during the nineteenth century, the most widespread being Georges Adrien Crapelet's version of 1834 in modern French.[20] Furthermore *Parthénopeus de Blois* figured in various literary histories published during the period, including Gaston Paris's educational *Littérature française au moyen-âge*, published the year before the opera's première.[21] Thus the librettists very cleverly chose a source which was a part, albeit minor, of the canon of French medieval literature without being as well known as the various tales of the *Table ronde*—problematical through their connection with Wagner—or the *Chanson de Roland* (although the renaming of Parthénopeus as Roland created a direct link to that particular epic). Therefore, the libretto offered a certain familiarity in terms of its place in French literature, while it gave greater leeway to the librettists with respect to their adaptation. But the adaptation of well-known literary works, especially classics such as Shakespeare's dramas, became increasingly subjected to the criticism of deformation if librettists took too much artistic freedom in relationship to the model. Cases in point were the librettos for Ambroise Thomas's operas *Mignon* and *Hamlet* whose original endings saw Mignon marry Wilhelm and Hamlet crowned the new king of Denmark. Later, these endings were modified to follow their literary sources more closely.

This aspect of the opera was not lost on the Parisian critics, who learned about the libretto's literary source most probably from the Opéra-Comique

20. I agree with Stephen Huebner that this version was most probably the source for the two librettists. We are supported in this by a nineteenth-century witness, Ernest Reyer, who refers to this link in his review in *Le Journal des débats* (19 May 1889, 1–2; in *DE*, 106–15), where he connects Alfred Blau and Georges Adrien Crapelet through their shared hometown Blois (*DE*, 106).

21. Gaston Paris, *Littérature française au moyen-âge* (Paris: Hachette, 1888).

through a detailed synopsis of the libretto included in the journalists' information packs for the first performance; this "analyse du livret" has not survived, but some of it can be reconstructed from almost identical passages in the reviewers' narrating of the plot.[22] Indeed, most critics started their reviews by identifying the medieval epic and discussing whether or not this kind of topic was appropriate for a French opera, even before they engaged with Blau and de Gramont's libretto and its setting by Massenet.

The issue at stake was the French response to Wagner's notion that subjects needed more than just entertainment value to be lofty music dramas. The widely popularized concept of medieval legends as carriers of eternal truths had become a trope in literary discussions of the late nineteenth century and were taken up, in almost knee-jerk fashion, in the majority of these reviews.[23] The critics' reaction was predictably uniform: given that such legends were steeped in the golden age of France's medieval glory, they offered a truly French subject without the pitfalls of more recent historical topics. At this specific point in time, when the radical Republic was moving toward a politically more inclusive realignment, such a neutral subject was particularly appropriate. Whereas Republican Rome, for example, represented a point of reference exclusive to Republican France, references to an idealized Middle Ages could be enjoyed by the French of all political allegiances.[24] The world of medieval knights, where manly qualities were defined not only by physical prowess but also by clear-cut moral values, represented thus both a lost utopia and a future to which to aspire. Wagner was seen as only one of the heralds of this golden past; others were French and included, for example, the architect Viollet-le-Duc or the philologist Paulin Paris, who edited the five-volume *Romans de la Table Ronde* (Paris: Léon

22. Explicit reference to this "analyse du livret" by the librettists can be found in Arthur Pougin's review for *Le Ménestrel* (*DE*, 171) and B. de Lomagne's [Albert Soubies] for *Le Soir* (*DE*, 82). We do not know much about the publicity strategies of opera houses in nineteenth-century Paris. However, the way in which the critics refer to this kind of information in the cases of both Massenet's *Esclarmonde* and Holmès's *Ode triomphale* leads me to suspect that this was a traditional ploy and not a one-time form of public relations. On the relationship between theater directors and the press, see Lesley Wright, "Leoncavallo, *La Bohème* and the Parisian Press," in *Nazionalismo e Cosmopolitanismo nell'opera fra '800 e '900: Atti del 3° Convegno Internazionale "Ruggero Leoncavallo nel Suo Tempo,"* ed. Lorenza Guiot and Jürgen Maehder, 165–80 (Milan: Sonzogno, 1998).

23. On French Wagnerism with respect to subject choice, see Jens Malte Fischer, "Singende Recken und blitzende Schwerter: Die Mittelalteroper neben und nach Wagner—Ein Überblick," in *Mittelalterrezeption: Ein Symposium*, ed. Peter Wapnewski, 511–30 (Stuttgart: Metzler, 1986).

24. On the idealized Middle Ages, see Annegret Fauser, "Die Sehnsucht nach dem Mittelalter: Ernest Chausson und Richard Wagner," in *Les Symbolistes et Richard Wagner—Die Symbolisten und Richard Wagner*, ed. Wolfgang Storch and Josef Mackert, 115–20 (Berlin: Edition Hentrich, 1991).

Techener, 1868–77). Such historical nostalgia offers an alternative rationale for the choice of *Esclarmonde*'s subject to that of purely Wagnerian tendencies, and political interpretations of the possible message of the opera's topic can be found in more than one review. Henry Bauer not only emphasized the masculine ideals of the Middle Ages in general, but contrasted them sharply with the decadence of Imperial Byzantium. This was a thinly disguised metaphorical reading of recent French history, when barbarous Prussians won over the decadent and Imperial Second Empire with its courtesans and interfering empress, and thus presented a reading of Massenet's opera through *Parsifal* in a twisted kind of way:

> The love of Esclarmonde for Roland, of the daughter of the effeminate and decadent civilization of Byzantium for the robust and valiant barbarian, is natural and human. . . . Esclarmonde's love for Roland is without doubt the link which unites an exhausted, disappearing race with the vigorous race that succeeds it in the world's empire.

> L'amour d'Esclarmonde pour Roland, de la fille de la civilisation efféminée et décadente de Byzance pour le barbare robuste et valeureux est naturel et humain. . . . L'amour d'Esclarmonde pour Roland est sans doute le lien qui unit une race épuisée qui disparaît à la race vigoureuse qui lui succède dans l'empire du monde.[25]

Critics even assured their readers that the bard Denis Pyramus' thirteenth-century version was but a late incarnation of an even older French epic, thus superior to the younger foreign (that is, mainly Germanic) tales that were all based on French texts anyway. The libretto's similarities with *Lohengrin* could thus be turned into a form of "plagiarism" on the German side, even though Wagner's opera had been composed some forty years earlier. Critics were usually quite explicit in their patriotic stance, as for example *Le Petit Parisien*'s Jean Frollo in a lead article on chivalric romances, where he concluded: "When France grew tired of [the romances], other countries welcomed them and modified them according to their own national character. Consequently, we came to admire 'foreign' tales whose basis was really French."[26] Even the simple choice of *Parthénopeus de Blois* as the

25. Henry Bauer, "Les Premières Représentations," *L'Écho de Paris*, 17 May 1889, in *DE*, 35.

26. Jean Frollo, "Les Romans de chevalerie," *Le Petit Parisien*, 20 May 1889, 1: "Quand la France en fut lasse, les autres pays les recueillirent, les modifièrent selon leur caractère national, et il arriva que, par une réaction, on admirât chez les étrangers des histoires dont le fonds était bien français."

literary source for *Esclarmonde* almost guaranteed that the opera, in its essence, would be truly French.

The debate about medieval sources for music dramas had been part of French Wagner reception since the 1860s, and it continued to be a pressing issue in the late 1880s. Until then, French librettists had not been seen as coming up with a text that could hold its own in a nationalist contest of operatic leadership.[27] For example, the subject of Eduard Lalo's *Le Roi d'Ys*, premièred at the Opéra-Comique the previous year, could not be appropriated for this specific search for national identity because its source was too "Northern" to be indisputably "French." Thus *Le Figaro's* eminent critic, Auguste Vitu, turned to Gallic literary history to ascertain *Esclarmonde's* position in French operatic history as one of the few librettos which did not undermine France's literary heritage:

> If one leafs through the catalogue of the seven or eight hundred operas performed in France in the last two centuries—whether based on mythology, history, or fairy tales—one is surprised by the small number of those which, among all these Greek, Roman, Italian, and Spanish subjects, were drawn from the nevertheless rich and varied body of our national literature. The poems of Ariosto, Tasso, Guilhem de Castro, Shakespeare, or Scandinavian, Germanic, Peruvian, Chinese, and Hindu legends, have successively tempted the eloquence of the librettists. But they passed by indifferently, without so much as a glance, the unexplored treasures of the French *romancero* and the multiple cycles which envelop, with sparkling fantasy, the sagas of glory and love.

> Si l'on parcourt le catalogue des sept ou huit cent opéras représentés en France dans le cours de deux siècles, mythologiques, historiques, féeriques, on s'étonne, parmi tant de sujets grecs, romains, italiens, espagnols, du petit nombre de ceux qui ont été puisés dans le fonds, cependant si riche et varié, de notre littérature nationale. Les poèmes d'Arioste, du Tasse, de Guilhem de Castro, de Shakespeare, ou les légendes scandinaves, germaniques, péruviennes, chinoises et indoues, ont successivement tenté la verve des librettistes. Mais ils passaient indifférents, sans y jeter un coup d'œil, près des richesses inexplorés du *romancero* français, aux cycles multiples enveloppant d'une étincelante fantaisie des épopées de gloire et d'amour.[28]

---

27. On the competitiveness of cultural debate see Michel Espagne and Michael Werner, "Deutsch-französischer Kulturtransfer als Forschungsgegenstand: Eine Problemskizze," in *Transferts: Les Relations interculturelles dans l'espace franco-allemand (XVIII<sup>e</sup> et XIX<sup>e</sup> siècle)*, ed. by Michael Werner and Michel Espagne (Paris: Éditions Recherche sur les Civilisations, 1988), 11–34.

28. Auguste Vitu, "Le Livret d'Esclarmonde," *Le Figaro*, 15 May 1889, 5.

Vitu counted up those few operas based on French legends that he was able to discover and came to a total number of six. His first could be traced back to the beginnings of French opera with Quinault's and Lully's *L'Amadis de Gaule*, and other works included Scribe and Meyerbeer's *Robert le diable* and *Le Lac des fées*, and Saint-Georges's and Halévy's *La Magicienne.*[29] Vitu then linked *Esclarmonde*, the seventh opera in this list, with both *Le Lac des fées* and *La Magicienne*, operas "that have for subject the love of a fairy and a simple mortal."[30] *Esclarmonde* was thus connected not only with Denis Pyramus' *Parthénopeus de Blois*, but also with another French epic, the *Lac de Graelan*, "the most precious legend left to us by Marie de France, the poetess of the thirteenth century."[31]

But *Esclarmonde* had even more to offer. After all, Denis Pyramus' tale was interpreted as a French version of the ancient legend of Amor and Psyche, and could thus be traced to ancient Greece, perceived as the cradle of human civilization ever since the Renaissance.[32] Indeed, the myth of Amor and Psyche was seen as one of those allegories "in which humanity always finds itself."[33] This apparently innocuous philological detail had more significance for the positioning of the opera's subject than immediately apparent, for ever since the times of François I, the concept of the "translatio studii"—that is, the idea of the progression of philosophy "through time and space until it reaches France" in the sixteenth century[34]—served as legitimizing the claim to France's superiority within the Western cultural nexus. This concept was based on the belief that cultures follow a necessary trajectory from primitive beginnings to decline. In the Paris of François I, the "home of the greatest cultural achievements was thought to have shifted from its origins in the East to Greece, Rome, modern Italy, and finally France as each old civilization became exhausted and corrupt."[35] By

29. *Amadis de Gaule* was a highly popular serial novel by Nicolas Herberay des Essarts, published in Paris from 1540 on.

30. Vitu, "Le Livret d'Esclarmonde," 5: "Les trois poèmes ont pour sujet les amours d'une fée avec un simple mortel."

31. Ibid.: "la plus précieuse légende que nous a laissée Marie de France, la poétesse du XIIIe siècle."

32. Critics who referred to the Greek legend include, for example, Camille Bellaigue, Alphonse Duvernoy, Paul Ginisty, Adolphe Jullien, Sâr Péladan, René de Récy, Albert Soubies, Edmond Stoullig, Auguste Vitu, and Victor Wilder (all in *DE*).

33. B. de Lomagne [Albert Soubies], "Théâtre," *Le Soir*, 17 May 1889; in *DE*, 80: "l'humanité s'y retrouve toujours elle-même."

34. Margaret W. Ferguson, "The Exile's Defense: Du Bellay's *La deffence et illustration de la langue françoyse*," *Publications of the Modern Language Association of America* 93 (1978): 280–81, given in Jeanice Brooks, "Italy, the Ancient World and the French Musical Inheritance in the Sixteenth Century: Arcadelt and Clereau in the Service of the Guises," *Journal of the Royal Musical Association* 121 (1996): 148.

35. Brooks, "Italy, the Ancient World and the French Musical Inheritance," 148.

the eighteenth century, this notion of cultural progression toward France had become a widely used commonplace underpinned by the new theories of environmental influence, especially through climate. Writers such as d'Espiard in his *Essais sur le génie et le caractère des nations* (1743) based their defense of France's cultural superiority on the amalgam of the new "scientific" ideas on climate with the older notion of the "translatio studii."[36] During the nineteenth century, the concept still retained an important place in aesthetic discussions and was developed still further, fueled by the Republican metaphor of France as the "new Rome" as much as by philological and archaeological work on Greek antiquity in French universities.[37] Thus the libretto of *Esclarmonde* could be legitimized doubly as belonging to both "golden ages" of humanity, ancient Greece and medieval France, and many critics had a field-day showing off their erudition when they discussed the literary pedigree of the libretto.[38] Indeed, the choice of Denis Pyramus' epic as a "truly French" source for *Esclarmonde* found wholehearted support in the French press, and was hailed as a way forward for French opera at the end of the nineteenth century.

The literary quality of the libretto, however, was an entirely different matter and caused extensive argument. The supporters of the opera—roughly half of the critics—praised not only the libretto's chivalrous spirit but also the elegance of the poetic adaptation and the deliciously youthful way in which the message of medieval heroism was developed in *Esclarmonde*.[39] For others, such as Henry Bauer, the opera fell short of the possibilities promised by the literary source. He was not alone in his disappointment with the librettists. Others joined him in denouncing the poem as "puerile," "convoluted," "sensualist without any moral message," too "fantasmagorical," and downright decadent.[40] Not only did the libretto lack moral messages—the quintessence of medieval legends—even worse, the opera showed Roland de Blois, the hero and a soldier at that, as the passive and thus feminized object in the

36. See Werner Oechslin, "Le Goût et les nations: Débats, polémiques et jalousies au moment de la création des musées au XVIIIe siècle," in *Les Musées en Europe à la veille de l'ouverture du Louvre*, ed. Edouard Pommier (Paris: Service Culturel du Louvre and Klincksieck, 1995), esp. 381–85.

37. See Edward Berenson, *The Trial of Madame Caillaux* (Berkeley, Los Angeles, and London: University of California Press, 1992), 103–17.

38. Several of these reviews, including those of René de Récy and Ernest Reyer, are reproduced in *DE*. On ancient Greece and medieval France as "golden ages" and their relation to opera, see Fauser, "Die Sehnsucht nach dem Mittelalter."

39. See, for example, the reviews of Simon Boubée (*La Gazette de France*, in *DE*, 116–23), Alfred Ernst (*La Paix*, in *DE*, 66–7) and Ernest Reyer (*Journal des débats*, in *DE*, 106–15).

40. See, in particular, Camille Bellaigue, "Revue musicale," *Revue des deux mondes* 59 (1889); in *DE*, 158–66.

games of an all-too-forward female of dubious morals.[41] The blame was thus not laid on the subject as such—whose qualities were often contrasted with the faults of the libretto—but on its decadent treatment in the hands of a modern poet, Louis de Gramont, and a Wagnerian librettist, Alfred Blau. Indeed, the discussion of the libretto mirrored pervasive French concerns of the late 1880s on such issues as decadence and morality.

Neither Louis de Gramont nor Alfred Blau was a librettist in the traditional vein of an Eugène Scribe or Jules Barbier. Whereas de Gramont was the author of decadent dramas and spicy novels, Blau had made his name with the "Wagnerian" opera *Sigurd*, set by Ernest Reyer and premièred in Brussels in 1884. Together, the two writers created an audacious, erotically charged, and decadent text for Massenet.[42] But this text was originally too audacious to pass muster in a state-funded institution in Republican France such as the Opéra-Comique. A comparison between earlier surviving versions and the final published libretto and score shows that lines that were too sexually evocative were toned down (whether during rehearsal or as a result of demands made by the state censor is not clear).[43] In the autograph manuscript and the proofs for the piano-vocal score, some of the original passages are still present.[44] These include, for example, Esclarmonde's sexually charged invitation to Roland after his betrayal:

| | |
|---|---|
| Regarde-le, ce corps . . . Où mouraient tes désirs apaisés. . . . | Look at this body . . . on which your quenched desires died. . . . |

This was replaced by the much safer:

| | |
|---|---|
| Regarde-le, ce corps . . . que ta faute a perdu sans retour! . . . | Look at this body . . . which your mistake has lost forever! . . . |

---

41. The role of soldiers in opera has been explored in Susan McClary, *Feminine Endings: Music, Gender, and Sexuality* (Minnesota and Oxford: University of Minnesota Press, 1991), 56–67; Steven Huebner, "*Carmen* as *corrida de toros*," *Journal of Musicological Research* 13 (1993): 3–29.

42. See Annegret Fauser, "'L'Orchestre dans les sons brave l'honnêteté. . .': Le rôle de l'élément érotique dans l'œuvre de Massenet," in *Massenet en son temps: Actes du colloque organisé en 1992 à l'occasion du deuxième Festival Massenet*, ed. Patrick Gillis and Gérard Condé, 156–79 (St. Étienne: Association du Festival Massenet, 1999).

43. The libretto for *Esclarmonde* is the only Massenet libretto missing in the collection of the Archives Nationales in Paris. I could not find any documents relating to the decisions of the state censor.

44. *Jules Massenet: Esclarmonde*, piano-vocal score (Paris: Hartmann & Cie, 1889), proofs with autograph annotations (private collection), 217. I am grateful to Patrick Gillis for sharing this information with me.

Other passages kept a certain erotic "frisson" when reworked before the première, but none retained the openly sexual references of the earlier version.[45]

Even so, the Opéra-Comique seemed to have felt compelled to distribute an expurgated version of the narrative for a bourgeois public, emphasizing Roland's military prowess, underlining the virtuous side of Esclarmonde's character—especially through her sacrifice—and sanitizing the sexual relationship between Esclarmonde and Roland by turning it into a mystical marriage. Both in the libretto itself and in the official synopsis, Esclarmonde is referred to as Roland's wife. Before their night of passion on the enchanted island, she offers herself as his wife ("Si tu m'acceptes pour épouse"), and the morning after Roland addresses her as his "chère épouse."[46] In addition, the hero's ultimate victory in the tournament—unaided by the magic sword provided by his seemingly all-too-decisive wife—and the portrayal of Esclarmonde as submissive, even in her apparently daring conquest of Roland, reflected the code of bourgeois morals not only of the Opéra-Comique's usual public but also of Republican France in general.[47]

These efforts at smoothing over what might have been too audacious or decadent for the Opéra-Comique were ignored by the press. As one might expect, the titillating elements became, on the contrary, exactly the points that were emphasized in the various reviews and examined in the light of the opera's performance context. Indeed, a closer look at the critics' reactions reveals that their evaluation of the libretto, either implicitly or explicitly, related the issue of the text's content and intrinsic literary value with the political and social meanings that it gained within an institutionalized operatic context. Here issues of morality and gender were as passionately discussed as the demands of clarity and verisimilitude and their necessity in an opera of the late nineteenth century. Such debates on dramatic structure were all the more important, since the "old mold" of French opera needed some manner of either justification or replacement in post-Wagnerian times. But the question was how much change was appropriate.[48]

Opinions were diametrically opposed. For the Wagnerian Louis de Fourcaud, the music critic for the highbrow *Le Gaulois*, "this fantasy" was in

45. Further examples are given in Fauser, " 'L'Orchestre dans les sons brave l'honnêteté . . .'."

46. Massenet, *Esclarmonde*, piano-vocal score, 91 and 107–9.

47. On Third-Republic moral attitudes, see Anne Martin-Fugier, *La Bourgeoise: Femme au temps de Paul Bourget* (Paris: Grasset, 1983).

48. Ernest Chausson, letter to Vincent d'Indy, April 1883, in Ernest Chausson, "Lettres inédites à Vincent d'Indy," *Revue musicale (numéro spéciale Ernest Chausson)* 1 Dec. 1925: 129: "vieux moule."

final analysis "hardly theatrical at all."[49] For Georges Street, the critic of the mass-daily *Le Matin*, the libretto possessed "rare clarity" and "first-class qualities":

> Notwithstanding the elegance of form which betrays the fine and delicate nature of the poet, Louis de Gramont, one must recognize at once that *Esclarmonde* breaks openly with the classical and solemn scenarios that are the foundation of all *opéra comique*. The librettists entered resolutely the new path of legend-opera; in adopting the form of musical fairy tale . . . they have chosen their heroes among the myths of poetic fantasy.

> Sans parler de l'élégance de la forme, qui trahit la nature fine et délicate du poète, M. Louis de Gramont, il faut reconnaître d'abord qu'*Esclarmonde* rompt franchement en visière avec les classiques et solennels scénarios qui sont la base de tout opéra comique. Les librettistes sont entrés résolument dans la voie nouvelle de l'opéra légendaire; adoptant la forme de la féerie musicale . . . ils ont choisi leurs héros parmi les mythes de la fantaisie poétique.[50]

The analysis of the libretto led Louis Besson in his review for *L'Événement* to ask the question of what theater was, in the final analysis. His answer echoed Wagner in an anti-Wagnerian rhetoric: theater for him was entertainment for the masses, not a scholarly exercise for the initiated few.[51] Here Besson echoed Fétis's criticism of Wagner as a "scientific composer" and poet, an expression that returned many times in the reviews of *Esclarmonde*.[52] Consequently the critics engaged in a complex argument: fairy-tale operas were seen as part of the tradition of *opéra comique*, and French legends offered a truly national choice of subject. Thus even while *Esclarmonde* might be suspiciously close to the plots of Wagnerian opera, it was nevertheless French through and through because of both its genre and origin. The old French genre of *opéra comique* had, well before Wagner,

49. Louis de Fourcaud, "Musique," *Le Gaulois*, 16 May 1889, in *DE*, 13: "Cette fantaisie, au fond, est très peu théâtrale."

50. Georges Street, "Esclarmonde," *Le Matin*, 16 May 1889, in *DE*, 29.

51. Louis Besson, "Critique musicale," *L'Événement*, 17 May 1889, in *DE*, 45: "Qu'est-ce que le théâtre en somme? Hélas! faut-il encore poser cette question? Va-t-on au théâtre comme on va écouter une conférence scientifique? La musique fait-elle partie du domaine abstrait des mathématiques? Le grand public répondra, et je serais heureux si, dans un plébiscite, la majorité donnait gain de cause, contre mes prévisions pessimistes, au musicien éclairé et éminent à qui nous devons déjà tant de délicieuses sensations. Cela prouverait que le public se forme et s'instruit et raisonne. Mais il ne faudra pas pourtant confondre le public avec les parasites et les mondaines névrosées, exhalant le ylang-ylang, qui, au seul nom de Massenet se pâment et s'écrient en respirant leur flacon!"

52. Katharine Ellis, "Wagnerism and Anti-Wagnerism in the Paris Periodical Press," in *Von Wagner zum Wagnérisme*, ed. Fauser and Schwartz, 51–83.

engaged with all the elements that the German composer declared as modern, whether medieval topics, legends, or the supernatural.

If the libretto was already raising questions about new paths for French opera, Massenet's music was scrutinized even more as to whether it could lead the genre out of the impasse in which French opera found itself in the wake of Wagnerism. While on the one hand, Wagnerian procedures were slowly seeping into European operatic language—whether through the use of leitmotifs, the reliance on musical prose, or increasing chromaticism—they were, on the other hand, so strongly related to Wagner the German that they raised immediate nationalist concerns. The question seemed to be: how much influence is too much to retain one's own national cultural identity? Massenet may have entered on a new path, but its origin was German.[53] Louis Besson's nationalist comment essentialized the issue, echoing countless stabs against German theater, whether by Mozart, Weber, or Wagner, over the course of the nineteenth century: "This theater has not been able to acclimatize itself in France thus far. It is of German essence—Will M. Massenet impose it? Time will tell."[54]

But unless he was shown as engaging with and—hopefully—overcoming Wagner, Massenet could not be celebrated as the savior of French music theater. His supporters described him as the leader of the "new school," adopting advanced musical techniques "without denationalizing himself" (Landely), applying the theories of Impressionism to music (Vitu), proving himself once again as the most gifted composer of France (Ernst), and achieving a step forward in renewing French opera (Besson).[55] Paul Ginisty, the critic of *Le Petit Parisien*, characterized Massenet's score as reflecting his "preoccupation with finding a formula, entirely French, which takes advantage of all that he can extract from the Wagnerian system, while staying in our tradition."[56] The Wagnerian critic Charles Malherbe dedicated a series of three articles to Massenet's exploitation of his eclectic adaptation and further development of Wagner's musical accomplishments, praising the fact that Massenet kept the truly French qualities of "clarity" and "simplicity" and thus showed himself as the only French composer "up to the task" of guiding the onward march of French music.[57]

53. Edmond Stoullig, "Les Premières," *Le National*, 17 May 1889, in *DE*, 63: "L'origine arrive en droite ligne de l'Allemagne."

54. Besson, "Critique musicale," in *DE*, 48: "Ce théâtre n'a pas pu s'acclimater en France jusqu'à présent. Il est d'essence germanique—M. Massenet l'imposera-t-il? C'est ce qu'il faut voir."

55. *DE*, 187 (Landely), 7 (Vitu), 69 (Ernst), 46 (Besson).

56. *DE*, 73: "mette à profit tout ce qui se peut tirer, pour rester dans notre tradition, du système wagnérien."

57. Malherbe, in *DE*, 221, 229.

Even Massenet's adversaries engaged lengthily with these issues, thus honoring him as a major French composer of the time even while criticizing him. The anonymous critic in *La Lanterne*, after offering praise of Massenet's talent and skill, declared that the musical structure of *Esclarmonde* represented a "negation of the theater, an antipode to lyric drama and opera."[58] But not only were his Wagnerian procedures in the score seen as dangerous; for several critics, such as Camille Bellaigue, the opera also "seemed to lack simplicity, unity, and elevation."[59] Such complexities identified Massenet as a "modern" composer, who adhered to the aesthetics of decadence. While for conservative critics such as Camille Bellaigue and Simon Boubée, too much of the Orient and too much sex infused the music of this medieval opera for it to be hailed as a model for future French music theater, the modernity of Massenet's sensual sound world was celebrated by other writers as Charles Demestre and Auguste Vitu. For Paul Ginisty, the première of *Esclarmonde* constituted an important date in France's music history, for Massenet had been able to align inspiration with science, the most modern combination possible in the arts.[60]

Not only its libretto and its music, but also its production turned *Esclarmonde* into a true exhibition piece during the Exposition Universelle. Its splendid staging, especially the "iconostasis" set for both prologue and epilogue (figure 2.1), showed the glamor of the French stage, and the electric projection of the royal hunt demonstrated its advanced abilities. Electricity was used to great effect, when the auditorium was suddenly plunged into darkness before the sudden lighting revealed the first tableau. The audience applauded the effect and called it "magic."[61] Thus the modern magic of electricity and the medieval magic of the sorceress Esclarmonde both played a significant part in the presentation of the work, reminding the audience of the magic of the Exposition. *Esclarmonde* could be advanced as proof that, in France, the highest form of musical composition—opera—was both alive and the most highly developed in Western culture. As such the opera was appropriate for the occasion, a "pièce de circonstance" much performed during the time of the Exposition, only to be dropped from the repertoire of the Opéra-Comique soon thereafter.

58. "Esclarmonde: Le nouvel opéra de M. Massenet," *La Lanterne*, 18 May 1889, in *DE*, 94: "La négation du théâtre, c'est l'antipode du drame lyrique et de l'opéra."

59. Bellaigue, "Revue musicale," in *DE*, 160: "L'œuvre de M. Massenet nous paraît manquer de simplicité, d'unité et d'élévation."

60. Ginisty, "Les Premières Représentations," in *DE*, 74.

61. Alphonse Duvernoy, "Revue musicale," *La République française*, 20 May 1889, in *DE*, 138: "Oui, c'est de la magie, de la sorcellerie."

## The Retrospective of Revolutionary *Opéras comiques*

*Esclarmonde*—called an "opéra romanesque" by its authors—was premièred at the Opéra-Comique. Although none of the critics tried to use the generic framework of traditional *opéra comique* to understand Massenet's work, the institutional performance context was often alluded to in the reviews. *Esclarmonde*, so Charles Demestre wrote, shocked "the friend of the old genre" because its authors were modernists.[62] But while *Esclarmonde* might or might not have been a step toward the future of French musical theater, the house also performed the traditional repertoire, whether Grétry's *Richard, Cœur de Lion* (1784) and Isouard's *Les Rendez-vous bourgeois* (1807) or Boieldieu's *La Dame blanche* (1825), and Adam's *Le Chalet* (1834; see Appendix 2, p. 331). The repertoire performed during the Exposition Universelle consisted of four major productions which played almost weekly, with others added to create variety from the historic repertoire. *Esclarmonde* had seventy-four performances, Bizet's *Carmen* (1875) and Ambroise Thomas's *Mignon* (1866) had twenty-six each, and Lalo's *Le Roi d'Ys* (1888) had twenty-five. Save for Victor Massé's *Les Noces de Jeannette* (1853) with eighteen performances, numbers for the other works remained in single digits. Audiences thus had a choice between the more avant-garde works by Massenet and Lalo or the traditional fare of the family theater.[63] Indeed, the program of the house catered to a wide variety of tastes.

The institution's choice of repertoire certainly focused on *opéra comique* as an "eminently national" genre. While the tradition of defining the genre as essentially French reaches back to the early years of the nineteenth century, it became commonplace after the Franco-Prussian War in 1870–71.[64] Thus, on the occasion of the Opéra-Comique's September concert (see Appendix 1A, p. 315), Georges Lefèvre, the critic of *Le Rappel*, commented

---

62. Charles Martel [Charles Demestre], "Courrier dramatique," *La Justice*, 20 May 1889, in *DE*, 124: "L'*Esclarmonde* de MM. Blau et de Gramont n'est pas pour consoler les amis du genre ancien ni rassurer l'amant de la *Dame Blanche*; les auteurs, très modernistes sur la scène même consacrée aux intrigues antiques, ont introduit un genre d'autant plus neuf qu'il est renouvelé des anciennes légendes."

63. The notion that the Opéra-Comique was the theater for families had become a commonplace, to the point that even specific pieces were associated with such social rites as marriage proposals. See, for example, the following observation in the popular novel by Henry Gréville, *Angèle* (Paris: Plon, 1883), 262: "Le *Chalet* et la *Dame blanche*! pour une jeune fille expérimentée, ce programme seul indiquait mariage, aussi sûrement que le dix de cœur, quand on se fait faire les cartes."

64. On the beginnings of French nationalist discourse about the genre of *opéra comique*, see Philippe Vendrix, "L'Opéra comique sans rire," in *Die Opéra comique und ihr Einfluß auf das europäische Musiktheater im 19. Jahrhundert*, ed. Herbert Schneider and Nicole Wild (Hildesheim, Zurich, and New York: Georg Olms Verlag, 1997), 31.

sarcastically on the equation of Frenchness and *opéra comique*: "Accordingly it is a well-known and settled issue to which we do not need to return. *Opéra comique* is a French genre."[65]

*Grand opéra* always had an undercurrent of cosmopolitanism, whereas *opéra comique* could be appropriated as a national operatic genre without too much difficulty. It had the appeal that its ancestry could be located in earlier French history, either in the glorious reign of Louis XIV or even so far back (in Fétis's, Weckerlin's, and Tiersot's rendering of the story) as the first proto-opera: Adam de la Halle's *Jeu de Robin et Marion*.[66] Indeed Tiersot, Bellaigue, and other writers of that period hailed *opéra comique* as a truly French genre because they could decipher its origins in both the *chanson populaire* and the vaudeville, that is, the musical language of the French "people." As Camille Bellaigue put it in 1887: "Through *opéra comique*, we can tie the new times to the old ones."[67]

While the formation of such ties to the past was part of the Opéra-Comique's longstanding strategy of repertoire-building, the retrospective of Revolutionary *opéras comiques* organized by the composer Paul Lacome d'Estanlenx (1838–1920) represented a very different enterprise. In this retrospective, a rarely discussed aspect of the all-encompassing, family-friendly genre was suddenly brought to the fore: *opéra comique* was not simply a popular genre of the people, but also a spectacle adopted throughout the period of the Revolution. Lacome originally planned a series that spanned the years 1790–95, "the most frenzied era of the Revolution," and he wanted to program works that "reflected the preoccupations of the public of the past."[68] This interrelationship between *opéra comique* and the

65. Georges Lefèvre, "Hommes et choses: Opéra-comique," *Le Rappel*, 12 Sept. 1889, 1: "Donc, c'est une chose entendue, convenue, sur laquelle il n'y a point à revenir. L'opéra-comique est un genre français."

66. "Adam de la Hale [*sic*]," in François-Joseph Fétis, *Biographie universelle des musiciens et Bibliographie générale de la musique*, 2nd ed., 8 vols. (Paris: Didot, 1860–65), 1:12–13; Jean-Baptiste Weckerlin, ed., *Ci commence le jeu de Robin et de Marion qu'Adam fit* (Paris: Durand & Schoenewerk, 1875); Julien Tiersot, *Histoire de la chanson populaire en France* (Paris: Librairie Plon/Au Ménestrel, 1889), 495. I wish to thank Katharine Ellis for the reference to Fétis. See also her *Interpreting the Musical Past: Early Music in Nineteenth-Century France* (New York and Oxford: Oxford University Press, 2005).

67. See Camille Bellaigue, *Un Siècle de musique française* (Paris: Librairie Ch. Delagrave, 1887), 6: "Nous pouvons, par l'opéra comique, rattacher aux temps anciens les temps nouveaux." On the continued actuality of this form of republican discourse with respect to *opéra comique*, see Jane F. Fulcher, *French Cultural Politics & Music: From the Dreyfus Affair to the First World War* (New York: Oxford University Press, 1999), 342–45.

68. Johannès Weber, "Critique musicale," *Le Temps*, 15 Jul 1889, 1: "datant de l'époque la plus agitée de la Révolution, c'est-à-dire des six années de 1790 à 1795, et reflétant les préoccupations du public d'alors." The original title is also cited by Weber.

Revolution was also suggested in the original title of the series, *L'Opéra comique pendant la Révolution, ou La Révolution dans l'opéra comique.* But in the course of negotiations with Louis Paravay, the director of the Opéra-Comique, and Jules Danbé, the house conductor, the program changed to focus on the years 1788–94. The proposed performance venue for the retrospective of revolutionary *opéra comique* was the Grand Théâtre de l'Exposition at the Champ de Mars. The series was advertised well in advance, even in foreign music journals such as *The Musical World*:

> Without doubt, the chief interest for musicians in the approaching Paris Exhibition will centre on the historical series of operatic performances which will be given, under the general title of "The Theatre during the Revolution." The performances will take place once weekly at the Grand Théâtre de l'Exposition, and be organised by MM. Lacôme, Paravey, and Danbé. The following is a complete list of the operas announced:

| | |
|---|---|
| 1788 | *Le Barbier de Séville,* translated into French by Framery. Music by Paisiello. |
| 1789 | *Raoul de Créqui.* Libretto by Monvel. Music by Delayrac [*sic*]. |
| 1790 | *La Soirée orageuse.* Libretto by Radet. Music by Delayrac [*sic*]. |
| 1791 | *Nicodéme* [i.e. *Nicodème*] *dans la lune.* Libretto by Le cousin Jacques. |
| 1792 | *Les Visitandines.* Libretto by Picard. Music by Deviene [i.e., Devienne]. |
| 1793 | *La Partie carrée.* Libretto by Hennequin. Music by Gaveau. |
| 1794 | *Les Vrais Sans-Culottes ou l'hospitalité Républicaine.* Libretto by Rezicourt. Music by C. Lemoine. |

"Le cousin Jacques", it will be remembered, was the *nom de plume* of Beffroy de Reigny, the author of several works which are characterised by Fétis as rubbish, deservedly forgotten. "Nicodéme [*sic*]," which is described as a "Folie en 3 actes, et en prose mêlée d'ariettes et de vaudevilles," was, however, very popular in its day, having been performed 191 times in 13 months.[69]

Relatively late in the game, it became clear that the stage of the Grand Théâtre de l'Exposition was too small for full-blown operatic productions, and instead of being held within a dedicated and concentrated series of afternoon performances at the Exposition Universelle, the *spectacles historiques*—as they became known—were incorporated into the regular schedule of the Opéra-Comique, to be performed every Friday evening for

---

69. "Foreign Notes," *The Musical World* 69 (1889): 241. (Beffroy de Reigny was the composer, not the librettist.)

seven weeks, starting on 27 June 1889 with Giovanni Paisiello's *Il barbiere di Siviglia* (in French). Nicolas Dalayrac's *Raoul, Sire de Créqui* and *La Soirée orageuse* were double-billed on 5 July. But on 12 July, the third historic spectacle, François Devienne's *Les Visitandines*, was replaced on short notice with Bizet's *Carmen*. The Opéra-Comique's logbook indicates that rehearsals for *Les Visitandines* continued until 15 July, but after that date, there is no further reference to the Revolutionary *opéras comiques* for the remainder of the year.[70] Adolphe Jullien probably hit upon the main reason in his article for *Le Moniteur universel* when he pointed out that the historic spectacles were not as lucrative as one of the Opéra-Comique's big hits such as *Carmen* or *Mignon*. But in that case, he suggests that "one should speak no longer of art, history, retrospective music, and one should confess frankly that the one and only aim in the view of whichever theater entrepreneur is to collect as much money as possible."[71] In addition, although I did not find any reference to it in the press, the embarrassment about the Terror in the context of commemorating 1789 might have contributed to the decision to abandon the series, and furthermore, there was simply no precedent for reviving these operas of the immediate post-Revolutionary period.

While the two retrospective performances at the Opéra-Comique may not have filled the theater at the place du Châtelet—which they were never meant to do in the first place—they did receive a warm welcome by the audience and engendered a fascinating debate in the press on the issues of retrospective, repertoire, and reception. In contrast to the concerts by Diémer and the performance of *Messiah* (see chapter 1), which were historic concerts in a more generic sense, the *opéra comique* retrospective was tightly linked to the Centenary theme of the Exposition. Thus, rather than fashioning a wider historic context of French music for contemporary consumption in the way one could interpret the aim of the five official concerts organized by the Commission des Auditions Musicales, these "so-called spectacles of the Centenary . . . associated our second national music theater with the memory of the Revolutionary period."[72] This seems to have triggered a far more self-conscious response from the journalists reviewing the performances for the Parisian press, given that the series was meant to reflect a specific historic moment from a centennial perspective. In an

70. *Journal de l'Opéra-Comique* for 1889, *F-Po.*
71. Adolphe Jullien, "Revue musicale," *Le Moniteur universel,* 12 Aug. 1889, 2: "qu'on ne nous parle plus d'art, d'histoire, de musique rétrospective et qu'on avoue franchement que l'unique et seul but visé par n'importe quel entrepreneur de spectacles est d'encaisser les plus d'argent possible."
72. "Les Théâtres," *Le Matin,* 28 June 1889, 3: "spectacles dits du Centenaire"; "associer notre second théâtre national de musique au souvenir de la période révolutionnaire."

unsigned article about the performance of Paisiello's *Il barbiere di Siviglia*, the music critic for one of the four big daily newspapers of Paris, *Le Matin*, addressed this historiographic self-reflexivity in a way that may even teach musicologists today a lesson about the perils of reception history.[73]

For the unwary reader, the article reads like one of the countless surveys published in newspapers, periodicals, and, occasionally, even in book form, that provide salient excerpts from competitors' articles on a specific political issue or an artistic première. For music, *Le Monde artiste*, for example, often sampled the press reaction to a specific première, as was the case for that of *Esclarmonde*, which was serialized over several issues.[74] Many a scholar has used such collections to bolster their interpretations of a specific opera. The critic for *Le Matin* introduces his selection of Parisian reviews of Paisiello's *Il barbiere di Sivigla* with a general remark about his endeavor to provide future historians of music and its criticism with some primary sources:

> We have tried to put together for the eyes of our readers the major reviews of our colleagues about Paisiello's *Barbiere* and the artistic attempt of the Opéra-Comique. The following extracts will serve those who will later write a history of contemporary music and criticism. At least that is our aim. Thus here is what the journals will say about the revival of the work by Paisiello.

> Nous avons cherché à mettre sous les yeux de nos lecteurs les principales critiques de nos confrères sur le *Barbier* de Paisiello et sur la tentative artistique de l'Opéra-Comique. Les extraits suivants serviront à ceux qui écriront plus tard l'histoire de la musique et de la critique contemporaines. C'est du moins le but que nous nous sommes proposé. Donc, voici ce que diront les journaux, à propos de cette reprise de l'œuvre de Paisiello.[75]

The subsequent extracts are cited as being from *Le Figaro*, *Le Gaulois*, *Gil Blas*, *Le Petit Journal*, *L'Événement*, *Le Temps*, and *Le Journal des débats*. "We could continue these citations," our critic writes, "but we should say a word about the interpretation, and we have only room to congratulate in summary fashion Messrs Fugère, Soulacroix, Fournets."[76] The cited review

73. According to the *Annales du Théâtre*, the regular music critic for *Le Matin* was Georges Street. See Edouard Noël and Edmond Stoullig, *Les Annales du théâtre et de la musique (1889)* (Paris: Bibliothèque Charpentier, 1890), 445.

74. *Le Monde artiste* 29 (1889): 314–15, 330–32, 345–47, 377–79.

75. "Les Théâtres," *Le Matin*, 28 June 1889, 3.

76. Ibid.: "Nous pourrons continuer les citations, mais il nous faut dire un mot sur l'interprétation, et il ne nous reste que la place de féliciter en bloc MM. Fugère, Soulacroix, Fournets."

segments represent salient moments of aesthetic judgment about Paisiello's opera, as for example the following:

> *Gil Blas.*—People are generally unaware that Paisiello's *Barbiere*, which inspired Rossini in such felicitous fashion, was originally, in the thought of its author, meant to be an *opéra comique*. If this project had no successor, it was uniquely because of the motives invoked by Wagner in support of his dramatic reform.
> *Le Petit Journal.*—It is with true restfulness that we have heard this charming work over whose so French and so national melodies our modern composers who speak continuously without saying anything—see Wagner, Lalo, and *tutti quanti*—would do well to meditate . . .
> *Le Journal des débats.*—If I may be permitted a personal remark, when *Sigurd* was presented at the Opéra, I protested energetically against the omission of the overture. Mr. Danbé has given us the overture of Paisiello's *Barbiere*. I am grateful to him.

> *Gil Blas.*—On ignore généralement que le *Barbier* de Paisiello, qui a si heureusement inspiré Rossini, devait être primitivement, dans la pensée de son auteur, un opéra comique. Si ce projet n'eut pas de suite, c'est uniquement pour les motifs qu'invoque Wagner à l'appui de sa réforme dramatique.
> *Petit Journal.*—C'est avec un véritable repos que nous avons écouté ce charmant ouvrage dont nos compositeurs modernes, qui parlent sans cesse pour ne rien dire—voyez Wagner, Lalo et *tutti quanti*—feront bien de méditer les mélodies si françaises et si nationales. . . .
> *Les Débats.*—Qu'on me permette un mot personnel. Lorsqu'on joua *Sigurd* à l'Opéra, je protestai énergiquement contre la suppression de l'ouverture. M. Danbé nous a rendu l'ouverture du *Barbier* de Paisiello. Je lui en sais gré.[77]

From the tone of the extracts, it seems as if the cited reviewers in question were the Wagnerian Victor Wilder (*Gil Blas*), the French nationalist Léon Kerst (*Le Petit Journal*) and the somewhat bitter composer, Ernest Reyer (*Le Journal des débats*), each relating the experience of Paisiello's opera to his own aesthetic position—a treasure trove indeed, but not quite the one the unwary and slightly distracted reader might have expected.

The cautious reader will have noticed one little word slipped into the article, the only giveaway, that this press summary was naught but a dazzling hoax, in which the author satirized his colleagues' mannerisms as reviewers, revealing a cynic assessment of Parisian music criticism and its perceived predictability. In his introduction, cited above, he referred to what

77. Ibid.

the journals "will say," not what they actually printed. But as a source for the music historian—for whom he had it intended anyway—this text is priceless. It documents a sharp awareness of the nuances of critical discourse within the network of Parisian critics, and an engagement with each other's ideas and writing. It also points to a sophisticated readership, even within mass journalism, who would not only be willing to follow such apparently esoteric exchanges but also be able to appreciate the subterfuge of the article itself and enjoy the intellectual challenge to the critic's colleagues. One of them, writing for the society column for *Le Moniteur universel* after the Dalayrac performance, actually played on notion of "restfulness" from the Léon Kerst hoax, praising the fact that the audience left the performance with "a much more rested spirit" than after listening to, for example, *Esclarmonde*.[78] More important, however, the "review" in *Le Matin* points to criticism's response to the centennial retrospectives by exposing the problems of the traditional critical discourse through the absurdity of the fake extracts. Two of the writers, the apparent Victor Wilder from *Gil Blas* and the even more absurd bombast attributed to the critic for *Le Gaulois* (presumably Louis de Fourcaud) use completely inappropriate Wagnerian frameworks to judge an eighteenth-century musical comedy. The impersonated Reyer's idiosyncratic self-reference is as pointless as the heavy-handed rejection of the female protagonist by the critic from *L'Événement* (Louis Besson) in terms of any serious assessment of this performance. And neither the technical description in the counterfeit *Le Figaro* (Auguste Vitu) nor the collection of bibliographic references in the fake extract from *Le Temps*—a parody of Johannès Weber's erudite reviews—say anything substantial about the piece. Through parody, the phony press profile published in *Le Matin* the day after the first of the Revolutionary *opéras comiques* was performed revealed how difficult it was to find appropriate parameters for the critical discourse on music that was no longer in the repertoire but part of a historical context brought back into the spotlight because of the centennial commemoration. Due to the centenary, journalists were faced with the notion of music-theater as the artistic reflection of a specific moment in the past, rather than engaging with a selection of repertoire that was simply "historical" in more general terms, as in the case of the Diémer's concerts.[79]

One of the main issues in the reviews was whether the selected repertoire of these "archaeological performances" (Bellaigue) did indeed reflect

78. Edyp, "Les Soirs de premières," *Le Moniteur universel*, 7 July 1889, 3: "on se sentait l'esprit beaucoup plus reposé, la tête beaucoup plus calme qu'après une représentation d'*Esclarmonde*, par exemple."

79. Katharine Ellis shows this difference in her new study, *Interpreting the Musical Past*, where the bicentenary celebrations of Rameau in Dijon set very different parameters than the resurrection of works such as Palestrina's madrigals.

the Opéra-Comique of that period in an appropriate way.[80] While the idea of a retrospective as such seemed ingenious to Adolphe Jullien, he wondered about the "singular fashion" in which the choice of works was made:

> Two of them, *Nicodème dans la lune* and *Madame Angot*, do not even belong to the repertoire of the Opéra-Comique, and the others, save for Dalayrac's *Raoul, Sire de Créqui* and Devienne's *Les Visitandines*, have only mediocre reputations. Finally, it is at least surprising that the most famous composers who worked for the Opéra-Comique during the Revolution shine through their absence. How about that! Nothing by Cherubini or Kreutzer, nothing by Méhul, nothing by Lesueur or by Berton?

> Il en est deux: *Nicodème dans la lune* et *Madame Angot*, qui n'appartiennent pas au répertoire de l'Opéra Comique et les autres, sauf le *Raoul de Créqui* de Dalayrac et *les Visitandines* de Devienne, sont de renom médiocre; enfin il est au moins surprenant que les plus célèbres des compositeurs ayant travaillé pour l'Opéra Comique pendant la Révolution brillent ici par leur absence. Eh quoi! rien de Cherubini ni de Kreutzer, rien de Méhul, rien de Lesueur ni de Berton?[81]

Another composer whose absence was lamented was Grétry.[82]

Some critics went still further, questioning the very nature of the enterprise. Johannès Weber wondered about the aim of the "historical spectacles," while the society columnist in the *Écho de Paris* found the series "much work for nothing," multiplying cost and effort simply to support the "archaeologico-lyrical zeal of Mr. Lacome."[83] But Weber's question about the sense behind the series aimed beyond the simple criticism of performing works from the past. His question was more fundamental: "Why does *Raoul, Sire de Créqui* constitute a historical spectacle and not Grétry's *Richard Cœur de Lion*, which predates it by four years?" He immediately answers his own question: "This is doubtless because *Richard* has remained in the repertoire, whereas no work by

---

80. Camille Bellaigue, "Revue musicale," *La Revue des deux mondes* 59 (1889): 446–64, at 464: "représentations archéologiques."

81. Adolphe Jullien, "Revue musicale," *Le Moniteur universel*, 1 July 1889, 2.

82. For further reviews criticizing the selection of composers or repertoire, see, for example, Arthur Pougin, "Semaine théâtrale," *Le Ménestrel* 55 (1889): 218–20; Victor Wilder, "Premières représentations," *Gil Blas*, 7 July 1889, 3; Charles Darcours [Charles Réty], "Beaux-Arts et Théâtres," *Le Journal illustré*, 14 July 1889, 218.

83. Johannès Weber, "Critique musicale," *Le Temps*, 8 July 1889, 3: "Je ne vois pas encore bien le but des 'spectacles historiques' comme dit l'affiche." Bicoquet [Maxime Boucheron], "Beaucoup de . . . besogne pour rien," *Écho de Paris*, 7 July 1889, 3: "zèle archéologico-lyrique de M. Lacôme."

Dalayrac has stayed."[84] By distinguishing between revival and exhumation, Weber's answer reflects a shift in the understanding of the role of the two national musical stages—the Opéra and the Opéra-Comique—as acting as both a place of creation and a museum for its great works from the past. As Katharine Ellis has shown, the notion of a museum—already well in place for the Comédie-Française with respect to the great classics by Corneille, Molière, and Racine—took hold only around 1880 with respect to opera.[85] However, Weber's differentiation between works of the repertoire—that is, classics in the sense of the Comédie-Française—and digging up long-dead works of the past adds another layer to this issue. His question grants the repertoire its history, while cautioning against mere exhumation as an exercise unlikely to provide the theatergoers with worthwhile examples from the past.[86] That the practice of the Comédie-Française was on critics' minds when engaging with the historical spectacles makes itself apparent in two ways: the seemingly innocuous use of the word "classiques" to describe the repertoire,[87] and the relating of the first work of the series, Giovanni Paisiello's *Il barbiere di Siviglia*, to the venerable theater where Beaumarchais's play was performed regularly.

Lacome's choice of Paisiello's work for a retrospective of Revolutionary *opéras comiques* was in fact highly problematic. It was an Italian *opera buffa*, premièred in St. Petersburg in 1780, performed in French in 1784 before the court in Versailles; it did not enter the repertoire of the Opéra-Comique until 16 March 1793, where, "in the middle of the Terror, Paisiello's opera still charmed its audience."[88] Why, asked Charles Darcours, would "the organizers of centennial representations consecrated to French *opéras comiques* open their series with a work by an Italian composer who never once wrote anything for France"?[89] If Lacome wanted to represent the year 1788 at the Opéra-Comique, he had plenty of choices

84. Weber, "Critique musicale" (8 July), 3: "Pourquoi *Raoul* constitue-t-il un spectacle historique et non pas *Richard*, de Grétry, qui lui est antérieur de quatre ans? C'est sans doute parce que *Richard* est resté au répertoire, tandis qu'aucun ouvrage de Dalayrac n'y est resté."

85. Ellis, *Interpreting the Musical Past.*

86. Weber, "Critique musicale" (8 July), 3: "Faut-t-il croire qu'il n'y a spectacle historique qu'autant qu'il n'y a eu exhumation?"

87. Bicoquet, "Beaucoup de . . . besogne pour rien," 3: "répertoire musical classique"; "Courrier des Théâtres," *Le Figaro*, 30 June 1889, 3: "une seconde représentation classique"; Simon Boubée, "Théâtres," *Le Gazette de France*, 30 June 1889, 1: "cette musique . . . qui rappelle la fraîcheur et la belle santé du style de nos écrivains classiques."

88. For the dates, see Arthur Pougin, "Semaine théâtrale," *Le Ménestrel* 55 (1889): 202–3; P. G., "Les Premières représentations," *Le Petit Parisien*, 29 June 1889, 3: "En pleine Terreur, l'opéra-comique de Paisiello charmait encore les spectateurs."

89. Darcours, "Beaux-Arts et Théâtres," 218: "pourquoi les organisateurs des représentations centennales consacrées à l'opéra comique *français*, ont inauguré leur série par l'ouvrage d'un compositeur italien, qui n'a jamais rien écrit pour la France."

among works by Berton, Dalayrac, and Grétry, so Arthur Pougin pointed out in his review.[90] Several of the reviewers did, however, come up with a nationalist argument for the choice of Paisiello's opera in such a retrospective. Almaviva's romance, "Je suis Lindor," was still used as incidental music at the Comédie-Française, and Paisiello's setting of *Le Barbier de Séville* convinced Beaumarchais to embrace instead of reject music in the theater.[91]

If the connection with Beaumarchais could provide a tenuous defense for the selection of Paisiello's *Barbiere di Siviglia*, the inclusion of Dalayrac was justified because he actually composed the works performed in the retrospective in Paris for the Opéra-Comique.[92] Nevertheless, several reviewers criticized either the selection of Dalayrac over the more preferred Grétry, Lesueur, and Méhul, or the choice specifically of *Raoul, Sire de Créqui* and *La Soirée orageuse* as not necessarily being Dalarayc's best operas. Nevertheless, the reviewers lauded the power of his romance of the Chevalier de Créqui and the enjoyment derived from the chanson "Un jour, Lisette allait aux champs." Given the parameters of performance, the reviewers interpreted the works in the context of *opéra comique* as national genre, lauding Dalayrac's works as "true expression of the French spirit and character."[93] For Adolphe Jullien, Berlioz's seal of approval was an important confirmation of Dalayrac's place in French music history: "When I listened to the sad romance of Raoul in his prison cell and the one that Craon sighs when he sees his last day begin, I thought about Berlioz's admiration for the tender and moving inspirations of Dalayrac."[94] "Charming," "tender," and "elegant" were words that permeated the description of Dalayrac's music in the reviews. But the two works had moments that were

90. Pougin, "Semaine théâtrale," 202.

91. On Beaumarchais' reaction, see A. Héler [Alphonse Leduc], "Le Barbier de Séville de Paisiello," *L'Art musical* 28 (1889): 95; Charles Martel [Charles Demestre], "Échos des Théâtres," *La Justice,* 28 June 1889, 3; Louis de Fourcauld, "Musique," *Le Gaulois,* 28 June 1889, 3. Simon Boubée points out that the romance "Je suis Lindor" "est connue de tout le monde" because it is performed traditionally at the Comédie-Française. See Boubée, "Théâtres," 1.

92. On the institution of the Opéra-Comique in the late eighteenth century, see Jean Mongrédien, *La Musique en France des Lumières au Romantisme (1789–1830)* (Paris: Flammarion, 1986), 87–106; Raphaëlle Legrand and Nicole Wild, *Regards sur l'Opéra Comique: Trois siècles de vie théâtrale* (Paris: CNRS Éditions, 2002), 59–92, 230–33.

93. Edyp, "Les Soirs de premières," 3: "l'expression vraie de l'esprit et du caractère français."

94. Jullien, "Revue musicale" (18 July), 2: "Quand j'écoutai la triste romance de Raoul dans son cachot et celle que Craon soupire en voyant luire son dernier jour, je pensais à l'admiration de Berlioz pour les inspirations tendres et touchantes de Dalayrac."

less than delightful: more than one critic found the scene where the jailor is made drunk by his own children quite tasteless, whereas *La Soirée orageuse* contained allusions to the parliamentary session of 4 February 1790, when the king swore the civic oath. This political reference was removed in an 1826 edition of *La Soirée orageuse*, but restored for the performance by Lacome.[95]

Lacome's interventions were not limited to such restorations. He also revised the orchestration for a full-size orchestra, and he rearranged the beginning of *Raoul, Sire de Créqui* by eliminating most of act 1 and adjusting act 2 accordingly. Such revisions were common in the editing and performance of earlier repertoire, whether in opera or in concert. Both Tiersot and Weckerlin had provided modern accompaniments in their editions of the medieval *Jeu de Robin et Marion*, Handel's *Messiah* was usually performed in the version by Mozart, and the French edition of Paisiello's *Le Barbier de Séville* was published in 1868 with a "new instrumentation" by Charles Constantin.[96] Yet in the context of this retrospective, the issue of "authenticity" suddenly raised its head again, and the question about Lacome's revisions became a matter of debate.[97] It was once again the erudite critic Johannès Weber who asked the uncomfortable question: "The poster informed us that the two operas by Dalayrac performed last Friday were 'restored by M. Lacome.' Why restored? They did not suffer any degradation; the orchestral scores survive in excellent condition, with complete dialogues and indications for the staging."[98] The critic for *Le Matin* on his part wondered slyly whether the addition of two cornets was a request by the last descendant of Dalayrac.[99]

For Lacome himself, restoration probably meant first and foremost the making available of works from the past to a contemporary public, as with his two editions of music published in 1878: *Les Fondateurs de l'opéra français*

---

95. Ibid.

96. *Le Barbier de Séville*, opéra en quatre actes, musique de Paisiello, traduit et arrangé d'après le texte de Beaumarchais et l'ancienne version française par Victor Wilder, instrumentation nouvelle et accompagnement de piano par Charles Constantin (Paris: Léon Escudier, 1868).

97. Critics raised similar questions about authenticity and adaptation after Adolphe Adam's revisions of Grétry, or the Lully performances in the 1870s. See Ellis, *Interpreting the Musical Past*.

98. Weber, "Critique musicale" (8 July), 3: "L'affiche nous a avertis que les deux opéras de Dalayrac repris vendredi dernier ont été 'restaurés par M. Lacome'. Restaurés, pourquoi? Ils n'avaient subi aucune dégradation; les partitions d'orchestre subsistent en excellent état, avec les dialogues complets et les indications scéniques."

99. "Les Théâtres," *Le Matin*, 6 July 1889, 3–4, at 4: "Mais pourquoi a-t-on introduit deux cornets à pistons dans l'instrumentation de Dalayrac? Auraient-ils été exigés par l'unique descendant du compositeur?"

and *Les Fondateurs de l'opéra-comique.*[100] While his volume of music by the founding fathers of *grand opéra* contained works by only three composers—Lully, Campra, and Destouches—his selection from *opéras comiques* was far broader, cementing a French history of music-theater. His starting point was not Adam de la Halle's *Jeu de Robin et Marion*, but the anonymous and marginally earlier *Aucassin et Nicolette*, an anonymous *chante-fable* "from the time of Saint Louis," which for him was the first French *opéra comique.*[101] After a hiatus in which Italian *intermedi* were fashionable in Paris, truly French *opéra comique* began with little-known composers of the mid-eighteenth century who remained almost anonymous among the masses. In contrast to the wave of Italian individualists, this "impersonality of its authors" (like that of *Aucassin et Nicolette*) offered new proof that *opéra comique* was a French genre *par excellence.*[102] The celebration of the authors' anonymity relates to ideas of folksong prevalent since the 1830s, with vocal music welling up from the Gallic masses, being the true expression of the French race.[103] But it is clear from Lacome's editions that he perceived this music in need of touching up if it was to survive the scrutiny of modern eyes and ears.

Both Victor Wilder and the anonymous critic of *Le Rappel* judged Lacome's revisions to the orchestration in positive terms. Paisiello's orchestration would have been "monotonous" and "arid" were it not for Lacome's "discreet" and "respectful" intervention on behalf of the composer to "avoid [the original work's] monotony for our ears that are used to modern polyphony."[104] Lacombe's choice, so the reviewer of *Le Rappel* said, was supported by a voice of the eighteenth century, that of Grétry, who had asked for the updating of his scores *expressis verbis*. Victor Wilder, who had been involved in numerous adaptations of earlier works for nineteenth-century Paris—Handel's *Messiah* and Paisiello's *Il barbiere di Siviglia* included—also mounted a defense of Lacome's revisions, pointing out that the innocent garb of Dalayrac's eighteenth-century music was no longer viable in the

---

100. Paul Lacome, *Les Fondateurs de l'opéra français: Transcriptions pour piano et chant* (Paris, Enoch Père et Fils, 1878); Paul Lacome, *Les Fondateurs de l'opéra-comique: Transcriptions pour piano et chant* (Paris, Enoch Père et Fils, 1878).

101. Lacome, *Les Fondateurs de l'opéra-comique*, ii–iii: "une production anonyme du temps de saint Louis. . . . Je n'hésite pas à saluer, dans le jeu d'*Aucassin et Nicolette*, le premier opéra-comique français."

102. Ibid., v: "Je vois donc une preuve nouvelle de la nationalité du genre de l'opéra comique chez nous, dans l'impersonnalité de ses auteurs."

103. On French folksong, see Jane F. Fulcher, "The Popular Chanson of the Second Empire: 'Music of the Peasants' in France," *Acta musicologica* 52 (1981): 27–37. See also chapter 5 below.

104. "Les Théâtres," *Le Rappel*, 29 June 1889 / 11 Messidor an 97, 3: "éviter sa monotonie pour nos oreilles habituées aux polyphonies modernes."

nineteenth century. Like his colleague at *Le Rappel*, he relied on the authority of Grétry:

> The two small scores were remounted by Mr. Lacome, who joins the skill
> of an excellent musician's hand with the taste of a delicate scholar. The
> task was perilous but necessary, because today, one can no longer present
> to the public a work by Dalayrac in its original clothing; it would mean
> exposing it in such a way that it would miss its effect, and would draw for
> itself, in a deliberate fashion, a welcome that would be at the very least
> somewhat restrained. There is, in any case, no impiety in restoring a
> painting that is flaking off or a crumbling building; this is done every day,
> and the overpious people who screech like a peacock every time one
> touches a work of art with one's fingertips are merely respectable fools. If
> the masters whom they defend with such zeal could speak, they would
> ask, I imagine, for a little less respect and a bit more love. For one of
> the masters, for Grétry, we have a written testimony, which clarifies the
> question.

> Ces deux petites partitions ont été rentoilées par M. Lacome, qui joint
> l'habilité de main d'un excellent musicien au goût d'un lettré délicat. La
> besogne était périlleuse mais nécessaire, car on ne peut plus, aujourd'hui,
> présenter au public un ouvrage de Dalayrac, dans son vêtement d'inno-
> cence; ce serait l'exposer à manquer son effet et lui préparer, de propos
> délibéré, un accueil tout au moins plein de réserve. Il n'y a, du reste,
> aucune impiété à retoucher une peinture qui s'écaille ou un édifice qui
> s'effrite; cela se fait tous les jours, et les gens trop pieux, qui poussent des
> cris de paon, chaque fois qu'on touche du bout du doigt à une œuvre d'art
> sont tout simplement de respectables niais. Si les maîtres qu'ils défendent
> avec tant de zèle pouvaient parler, ils leur demanderaient, j'imagine, un
> peu moins de respect et un peu plus d'amour. Pour l'un de ces maîtres,
> d'ailleurs, pour Grétry, nous avons un témoignage écrit, qui tranche la
> question.[105]

Wilder then quotes the passage by Grétry in which he invites musically sen-
sitive revisions when needed. That both the critic of *Le Rappel* and Wilder
had the same passage by Grétry at their fingertips when they felt the need
to defend the adaptation of earlier works to modern taste suggests a strong
element of collusion, or at least advance preparation. Presumably they had
anticipated that the centuries-old practice of musical revision—whether by
Mozart in the case of Handel, Mendelssohn in the case of Bach, or even
Lacome in the case of Dalayrac—was now becoming problematic. The
approach toward the historically informed performance of early music that
would characterize most of the twentieth century had clearly begun by

105. Wilder, "Premières représentations," 3.

1889, whether in the concerts by Diémer, performed on authentic instruments, or in the discourse about revision and Urtext.[106]

Lacome's series was an exceptional, politically motivated retrospective of specifically "French" musical theater, with the Opéra-Comique thus "participating in the Centenary" with its own "retrospective exhibition of works from the period of the French Revolution."[107] While any such retrospective defines the past from a specific moment of the present, it also shapes the perspective of this present in unique ways. More than one journalist began to wonder what kind of musical theater would be part of the next centenary that would look back to 1889. Indeed, as Charles Demestre put it: "I do not know whether many of our composers today will still be bearable at the next Centenary."[108] Such concerns over staying power were certainly addressed to the contemporary composers whose works were performed and premièred at the main houses in 1889, in particular Jules Massenet and Ambroise Thomas. Indeed, the latter's ballet, *La Tempête*, had its first performance at the Opéra the day before the revival Paisiello's *Il barbiere di Siviglia* at the Opéra-Comique.

## A Ballet for the Nation's Premier Stage: Ambroise Thomas's *La Tempête*

The première on 26 June 1889 of Ambroise Thomas's "ballet fantastique en trois actes," *La Tempête*, unveiled the only new work to be performed at the Opéra during 1889. This lack of new performances—in breach of the *cahier des charges*, the directors' contract with the French government—was cause for scandal. In his retrospective comment on the Opéra's achievements for 1889, Edmond Stoullig contrasted the financial success of the house during the year of the Exposition with the mediocrity of the artistic fare presented:

> The year of the Centenary will have been fruitful for the purse of the Opéra directors, but Art will not have fared as well. Messrs Ritt and Gailhard were

---

106. By the late nineteenth century, the key figure in the French restoration enterprise, Viollet-le-Duc, had become the subject of criticism, as for example by André Hallays in 1895, who called the architect with "his frenzy of restoration" a worse destroyer of churches than the Huguenots and the revolutionaries. Daniel D. Reiff, "Viollet le Duc and Historic Restoration: The West Portals of Notre Dame," *The Journal of the Society of Architectural Historians* 30 (1971): 17.

107. "Les Théâtres," *Le Rappel*, 29 June 1889 / 11 Messidor an 97, 3: "Le théâtre de l'Opéra-Comique a voulu prendre sa part dans les fêtes du centenaire et avoir aussi son exposition rétrospective d'œuvres de la période de la Révolution française."

108. Martel, "Échos des théâtres," 3: "Je ne sais si beaucoup de nos compositeurs d'aujourd'hui seront encore supportés au prochain Centenaire."

not prodigious with novelties; all in all, 1889 will have seen the hatching of a three-act ballet by Ambroise Thomas, *La Tempête*. Saint-Saëns's *Ascanio*, which has been in preparation since mid-1888, will see the light of day only in 1890. Despite the intense heat of the summer, despite the nightly distractions at the great fair at the Champ de Mars, the Palais Garnier did not stay empty for six months, even though the directorate had doubled the number of performances and in spite of often defective interpretations.

L'année du Centenaire aura été fructueuse pour la bourse des directeurs de l'Opéra, mais l'art n'aura pas été aussi bien partagé. MM. Ritt et Gailhard ne prodiguent pas les nouveautés; 1889 aura vu en tout l'éclosion d'un ballet en trois actes de M. Ambroise Thomas. *L'Ascanio* de M. Saint-Saëns, à l'étude depuis le milieu de 1888, ne verra le jour que dans le courant de 1890. Malgré la chaleur intense de l'été, malgré les distractions nocturnes de la grande kermesse du Champ de Mars, la salle de M. Garnier ne désemplissait pas pendant six mois, bien que la direction eût doublé le nombre des représentations et en dépit d'une interprétation souvent défectueuse.[109]

Eugène Ritt and Pierre Gailhard, the directors of the Opéra, were under heavy fire from the press for their distressing lack of artistic vision and quality, which were perceived as unsuitable for the premier music theater of the nation, whose image was being put in danger by their actions. Throughout the year of 1889, Henri Heugel, the owner of the music journal *Le Ménestrel*, harassed the two directors with almost weekly columns written under the pen name of H. Moreno. Other journalists followed suit, prompting the remark, in August 1889, that "the directorate of the Opéra continues to be in rather tense relationship with the majority of the newspapers, in particular Mr. Gailhard, who is clearly very little liked."[110] The accusations against Ritt and Gailhard were not minor: the "indescribable duet" of their directorship was a long tale of missed opportunities, with all major premières emigrating to Brussels. Their prospering "on the basis of worn-out repertoire without a singer of rank" was seen as leading to the destruction of the "national monument."[111] The Exposition was cited as one of the culprits supporting the two directors in their ways, for "indulgent provincials and foreigners" (figure 2.2) would attend just about anything, thus offering no incentive to better the

109. Noël and Stoullig, *Les Annales du théâtre et de la musique (1889)*, 1.
110. This extract from *Paris* is given in Arthur Pougin, "Semaine théâtrale," *Le Ménestrel* 55 (1889): 266–67, at 266: "la direction de l'Opéra continue à être dans des rapports assez tendus avec la plupart des journaux, surtout M. Gailhard, que l'on n'aime décidément bien peu."
111. Henry Bauer, "Les Grands Guignols: Les directeurs de l'Opéra et M. Ernest Reyer," *L'Écho de Paris*, 15 July 1889, 1: "duo inénarrable de MM. Ritt et Gailhard"; "ils prospèrent par un répertoire usé sans une chanteuse de rang"; "le monument national."

Figure 2.2. Mars, "Nos Provinciaux à Paris," *Le Journal amusant* 43 (1889): title page for 18 May 1889.

Below the caricature, the following dialogue explains this scene at the Opéra:

—Voyons, chère amie, je t'amène aux *Huguenots*, et tu ne cesse de dormir!

—Que veux-tu, Séraphin, probablement l'effet du chloral de Luther!

—See here, my dearest, I have taken you to *The Huguenots*, and all you do is sleep!

—What do you want, Seraphim, probably the effect of the Chloral by Luther!

quality of performances.[112] Indeed, as Edmond Stoullig put it, during the Exposition, one went to the Opéra "whatever the spectacle was."[113]

Journalists reproached Ritt and Gaillard for the defection of major stars such as Nellie Melba and Adelina Patti to better-managed houses, for the rejection of the new opera, *Salammbô*, by Ernest Reyer—which was now going to be performed in Brussels—and for the delay of the première of Camille Saint-Saëns's new opera, *Ascanio*.[114] The fact that *Ascanio* was not being premièred during the Exposition was, indeed, a major blow.[115] It was a work which would have fitted perfectly a nationalist rhetoric of the Académie Nationale de Musique, showcasing France as the cultural leader of Europe, if not the world. Saint-Saëns's new opera treated the subject of Benvenuto Cellini, set in the golden age of France during the reign of François I. It was a five-act *grand opéra*, fitting the mold of the French national genre and composed by one of the leaders of French music of the 1880s. Whether or not the work would have proven to be a major success, it could have been milked for nationalist propaganda just as with *Esclarmonde*. Instead, they were left with a three-act ballet. Maxime Boucheron related *La Tempête* rather sarcastically to the Exposition in his society column in *L'Écho de Paris* as proof that "not all new national products are to be found at the Champ de Mars," and that the Opéra followed the Eiffel Tower with the maxim: "always higher"—just like the summer temperatures, as Boucheron pointed out.[116]

*La Tempête* was loosely based on Shakespeare. Jules Barbier's scenario followed the mold of a "ballet d'action"—a "veritable ballet" in H. Moreno's words—telling the story of Miranda and her three suitors Ariel,

112. Arthur Pougin, "Semaine théâtrale" *Le Ménestrel* 55 (1889): 282–83, at 282: "des rengaines qu'on sert sans sourciller aux provinciaux et aux étrangers indulgents."

113. Edmond Stoullig, "Les Premières," *Le National*, 28 June 1889, 2: "on y vient du reste tous les soirs, et quel que soit le spectacle."

114. Ernest Reyer, *Salammbô*, opera in five acts, libretto by Camille du Locle after Flaubert, first performed at the Théâtre de la Monnaie, Brussels, 10 Feb. 1890; Camille Saint-Saëns, *Ascanio*, opera in five acts, libretto by Louis Gallet, Opéra, Paris, 21 March 1890.

115. The decision to postpone the première of *Ascanio* was taken in mid January, which led to the following sarcastic remark by Heugel about the opera directors' inability to secure a cast to perform the opera during the *Exposition*. See H. Moreno [Henri Heugel], "Semaine Théâtrale," *Le Ménestrel* 55 (1889): 19: "Alors qu'arrive-t-il? C'est que M. Camille Saint-Saëns, qui a eu l'imprudence d'introduire dans sa nouvelle partition d'*Ascanio* un rôle de contralto et un autre de ténor—a-t-on idée de pareille originalité!—voit son œuvre ajournée après l'Exposition; et encore *ajournée* est un euphémisme. Peut-être ne serait-elle jouée jamais. Car pourquoi y aurait-il plus d'artistes à l'Opéra après l'Exposition qu'avant? Ce n'est guère présumable, à moins d'un heureux changement de direction."

116. Bicoquet [Maxime Boucheron], "La Soirée parisienne," *L'Écho de Paris*, 28 June 1889, 3: "tous les nouveaux produits nationaux ne sont pas seulement au Champs de Mars"; "toujours plus haut."

Figure 2.3. Adrien Marie, engraving of the *Sommeil* scene in *La Tempête* at the end of Act 2, *Le Monde illustré*, 6 July 1889, 5.

Caliban, and Ferdinand.[117] The ballet opens with a sung prologue in which the soul of Miranda's mother implores God to protect her daughter. The plot of the three-act ballet eliminates Prospero—Miranda is an orphan—and reduces the action to fantastic dance scenes and the love story between Miranda and the shipwrecked Ferdinand. The composer, Ambroise Thomas, the doyen of French music and director of the Conservatoire, was seventy-eight years old at the time of the première, which for that reason alone made it a major event in the Parisian theater world. Rosita Mauri, the *étoile* of the ballet troupe, danced Miranda, and Ariel was performed by the talented Mlle Laus, freshly lured away from the Italian ballet troupe of the Excelsior (figure 2.3). The production of the new ballet was lavish, with a large, engarlanded ship brought on stage at the end of the ballet, which was meant to cause a sensation (figure 2.4). This ship delighted even the jaded reviewer of *Le Charivari*, in spite of himself, and it was hailed by almost all reviewers as one the major attractions of the performance.[118]

117. H. Moreno [Henri Heugel], "La Tempête," *Le Ménestrel*, 55 (1889), 201–2, at 201: "un véritable ballet."
118. Pierre Véron, "Théâtres," *Le Charivari*, 28 June 1889, 1–2, at 2.

Figure 2.4. Paul Destel, Final Tableau of *La Tempête*, *L'Univers illustré* 32 (1889): 408.

Like the première of *Esclarmonde* six weeks previously, that of *La Tempête* sparked a heated debate on the politics of French music and theater. However, while the press reception of *Esclarmonde* engaged with Massenet's work in a passionate but relatively fair way, the negative reviews of *La Tempête* went for the jugular in ways that were surprising even for the aggression levels of Parisian journalism. As with *Esclarmonde*, the journalists tried to assess the new ballet in a nationalist framework of post-Wagnerian music theater. But if *Esclarmonde* had incited a debate about French opera after Wagner, the discussion of *La Tempête* centered on ballet and its future as a national genre, for in addition to being the only new work of the season, *La Tempête* was also the first ballet premièred at the Opéra in three years, as Alfred Bruneau pointed out in his review.[119]

119. The last new ballet was André Messager's *Les Deux Pigeons* in two acts, libretto by Henri Régnier and L. Mérante, premièred at the Opéra on 18 October 1886. See Alfred Bruneau, "Musique," *La Revue indépendante* 12 (1889): 146–54, at 153. The article "Messager" in *NGr2* gives 8 Oct. 1886 as date of the première.

The issue of genre was at the center of the reviews. Thomas and Barbier's work had been announced as a "ballet of the future" but then proved to be more attached to the past:

> The new ballet has been created to satisfy all tastes. One sings in it, and one dances. One might believe oneself on the bridge at Avignon.[120] Unfortunately, the effects do not unite but superimpose themselves. Instead of a grand symphonic-choreographic-lyrical tableau, we are faced with a sequence of subjects treated more or less felicitously, quite pleasant in detail, but constituting a whole without homogeneity and without true grandeur. This ballet of the future, as it was announced, is the ballet-pantomime of the past in all its bourgeois manners.

> Le ballet nouveau a été crée pour la satisfaction de tous les goûts. On y chante et l'on y danse. C'est à se croire sur le pont d'Avignon. Le malheur est que les effets ne se combinent pas, ils se superposent. Au lieu d'un grand tableau symphonique-choréographico-lyrique, nous n'avons sous les yeux qu'une suite de sujets traités plus ou moins heureusement, assez agréables en détail, mais constituant un tout sans homogénéité et sans vraie grandeur. Ce ballet de l'avenir, ainsi qu'on l'annonçait, est tout bourgeoisement le ballet-pantomime du passé.[121]

*La Tempête* thus opened up a discussion about the past, present, and future of French ballet. Like many reviewers—for example Simon Boubée, Adolphe Jullien, and Léon Kerst—Alphonse Leduc characterized Thomas and Barbier's work as a ballet-pantomime in the manner of Adolphe Adam's *Giselle*, which was still a staple in the repertoire of the Opéra.[122] Others searched even further back in history and called upon the seventeenth century, with Campra's *Europe galante* or the works by Benserade, Lully, and Quinault as models.[123] Whether positive (Léon Kerst) or negative (Adolphe Jullien), these references to the ballet-pantomime and the *opéra-ballet* reveal that more was at stake than simply the performance of a new ballet, for

120. A reference to the children's song "Sur le pont d'Avignon, on y danse, on y danse."

121. A. Héler [Alphonse Leduc], "Théâtre national de l'Opéra: *La Tempête,*" *L'Art Musical* 28 (1889), 94–95, at 94.

122. Simon Boubée, "Théâtres," *La Gazette de France,* 1 July 1889, 1; Adolphe Jullien, "Revue musicale," *Le Moniteur universel,* 1 July 1889, 2; Léon Kerst, "Premières Représentations," *Le Petit Journal,* 28 June 1889, 3. On the ballet pantomime in France in the first part of the nineteenth century, see Marian Smith, *Ballet and Opera in the Age of Giselle* (Princeton, NJ: Princeton University Press, 2000).

123. Louis Besson, "Critique musicale," *L'Événement,* 28 June 1889, 3; Johannès Weber, "Critique musicale," *Le Temps,* 1 July 1889, 3; Victor Wilder, "Premières Représentations," *Gil Blas,* 28 June 1889, 2.

perhaps even more than in the case of *opéra comique*, ballet history was linked tightly to a national historiography of French music and theater.[124]

But while France could look back to a venerable history of ballet, the genre was at present in a deep crisis. The culprits, so the reviewers said, were the Italians. Their "muscular virtuosity" of figurative dance was replacing the venerable tradition of the more expressive French ballet, especially its pantomime.[125] Charles Demestre used the opportunity of his review of *La Tempête* to lament "the complete abandoning of the traditions of French dance in favor of Italian traditions." Expressive and true dance was being replaced by "ensemble movements of absolute regularity" and physical *tours de force*.[126] The question for the reviewers was whether *La Tempête* achieved a return to the "healthy traditions of choreography," and whether or not its clearly retrospective approach could serve as a model for future ballets.[127]

Opinions were sharply divided. Opponents of the work declared it a "flop" and "a marriage of foolishness between music and mime," a "banal" and "grey" composition.[128] The venerable Ambroise Thomas should never have consented to compose a ballet so late in his career, when he no longer had any ideas left, and the music was incoherent.[129] What, said the critic for *Le Matin*, had Shakespeare ever done to deserve such treatment?[130] The harshest accusations, however, were leveled at Jules Barbier's handling of Shakespeare. He was seen as denaturalizing the great English writer and disfiguring the play by eliminating all the complex issues and characters that made it interesting, starting with Miranda's father, Prospero.[131] In operatic adaptations of Shakespeare—most famously in Barbier's contribution to the librettos for Thomas's *Hamlet* and Gounod's *Roméo et Juliette*—the words of the playwright could be incorporated to give an aura of

124. Annegret Fauser, "Visual Pleasures—Musical Signs: Dance at the Paris Opéra," *South Atlantic Quarterly* 104, no. 1 (2005): 99–121.

125. Kerst, "Premières Représentations," 3: "virtuosité musculaire."

126. Charles Martel [Charles Demestre], "Courrier dramatique," *La Justice*, 1 July 1889, 1: "l'abandon complet des traditions de la danse française, en faveur des traditions italiennes"; "des mouvements d'ensemble d'une absolue régularité."

127. Kerst, "Premières Représentations," 3: "les saines traditions de la chorégraphie."

128. Henry Bauer, "Les Premières Représentations," *L'Écho de Paris*, 28 June 1889, 3: "C'est une chute"; "ce mariage de déraison entre la musique et la mimique"; Boubée, "Théâtres," 1: "quelque chose tout à fait banal"; Int . . ., "Les Soirs des premières," *Le Moniteur universel*, 28 June 1889, 3: "la grise partition du savant compositeur"; "Les Théâtres," *Le Matin*, 27 June 1889, 3: "sur la partition est répandue une teinte uniforme, grise, qui la rend d'un bout à l'autre monotone."

129. Weber, "Critique musicale," 3; Wilder, "Premières Représentations," 2.

130. "Les Théâtres," *Le Matin*, 27 June 1889, 3: "qu'est-ce que Shakespeare a bien pu lui faire?"

131. Besson, "Critique musicale," 3; Gaston Paulin, "Chronique parisienne," *Le Guide musical* 35 (1889): 182; Auguste Vitu, "Premières Représentations," *Le Figaro*, 27 June 1889, 3.

authenticity. Thus in Thomas's *Hamlet*, Michel Carré and Jules Barbier had based Hamlet's act 3 monologue on Alexandre Dumas *père*'s translation of "Être ou ne pas être." But a ballet—even one that incorporated pantomime such as *La Tempête*—had to rely on simplification. That the ballet's creators were aware of this conflict between the quality of Shakespeare's original and the literary reduction of the ballet scenario can be guessed from the ballet's proposed first title, *Miranda.*[132]

But even those who defended and supported the ballet had to deal with Barbier's changes to Shakespeare. Only a few, in particular Ernest Reyer, avoided the issue altogether and simply recounted the new plot without addressing the differences. Others—such as Louis de Fourcaud, Léon Kerst, and Henri Heugel—justified Barbier's changes as a function of the genre of ballet, even if it did harm to the original.[133] Prospero and the political conspiracy of his enemies, so Heugel said, had an important place in Shakespeare's play, "but, goodness me, what would all of that have to been doing in a ballet? I cannot see Prospero explaining to the audience, through pirouettes, his views on the government of people and other economic matters."[134] Thus Barbier's adaptation was successful, so the ballet's supporters argued, because it was appropriate for the expressive means of the genre.

According to Fourcauld, "a ballet is not exactly an easy work to conceive nor a convenient one to realize. One wants it to bring together very diverse and uncommon qualities. It has to present a relatively elementary plot so as to be understood by everybody, humane enough to interest even the sophisticated, poetic enough to give free rein to the composer, supple and varied enough so that dance and mime can find their place."[135] Fourcaud's view was that the authors had failed to do justice to this ideal. For the supporters of the production, however, Barbier and Thomas had met this challenging and complex goal, creating a work that highlighted the truly French

132. See, for example, Auguste Boisard, "Chronique musicale," *Le Monde illustré*, 6 July 1889, 11: "Les auteurs avaient résolu de l'intituler *Miranda*, du nom de l'héroïne de cette gracieuse fiction."

133. Ernest Reyer, "Revue musicale," *Le Journal des débats*, 30 June 1889, 1; Louis de Fourcaud, "Musique," *Le Gaulois*, 27 June 1889, 3; Kerst, "Premières Représentations," 3; Moreno, "La Tempête," 201.

134. Moreno, "La Tempête," 201: "Mais qu'est-ce que tout cela serait venu faire dans un ballet, grands dieux! Je ne vois pas Prospero expliquant au public, par des pirouettes, ses vues sur le gouvernement des hommes et autres matières économiques."

135. Fourcaud, "Musique," 3: "Un ballet n'est pas, précisément, une œuvre facile à concevoir ni commode à réaliser. On y veut une réunion de qualités très diverses et non communes. Il doit présenter une action assez élémentaire pour être compris de tout le monde, assez humaine pour intéresser même les raffinés, assez poétique pour donner carrière aux musiciens, assez souple et assez variée pour que la danse et la mimique y trouvent leur compte."

qualities of elegance, clarity, and simplicity. Ernest Reyer, who cited these classic attributes, observed that they could not be appreciated by those (young) critics corrupted by Wagnerian ideas. However, for him, Thomas had created an exquisite score, full of new ideas.[136] The observation that Thomas had produced fresh and youthful music runs like a leitmotif through almost all of the supportive reviews, countering the accusations of superannuation and fatigue leveled by the opponents of the work against the aging composer. Indeed, several reviewers credited Thomas and Barbier with developing a new, inspiring form of ballet, one that took the best of the French past and molded it into something new, combining dance, mime, and song, thus buying into the propaganda of future ballet based on traditional models.[137]

While Barbier and Thomas's ballet did not bring about "a revolution in the art of dance," it did engender some debate about the ballet of the future, for it brought the topic back into focus.[138] Pierre de Lano dedicated a front-page article in *L'Événement* to the question of how to rejuvenate ballet in France, which was "positively pitiable."[139] Influenced by Wagnerian ideas of music and expression, his solution anticipates what would make the fame of the *Ballets russes* twenty years later: a "dramatic art" characterized "on the one hand by the idea, and on the other by the décor—corresponding to the two extremes of Humanity: the Soul and the Senses."[140] For his part, Alfred Bruneau started his review with a fantasy about bringing back to life "the dead religion of the ancient Greeks under the imperious will of the all-powerful modernity," and "which was going to suppress the positivism of spoken language" with "synthetic gestures" joined to the expressive power of symphonic music. "And the modern ballet will be created."[141]

Fresh attempts at creating a modern ballet started soon after *La Tempête*, and within the framework of Wagnerian operas written for the Opéra rather than free-standing ballets. Indeed, during the 1890s, an innovative approach to the role of dance within French *grand opéra* led to the introduction of mimed allegorical ballets in operas such as Massenet's *Thaïs* (1894), Augusta Holmès's *La Montagne noire* (1895), and Alfred Bruneau's

136. Reyer, "Revue musicale," 1.

137. See, in particular, Moreno, "La Tempête," 201; Reyer, "Revue musicale," 1; "Les Théâtres," *Le Rappel*, 28 June 1889, 3.

138. Pierre de Lano, "Le Ballet," *L'Événement*, 2 July 1889, 2: "une révolution dans l'art de la Danse."

139. Ibid., 2: "Le ballet, en France, positivement, est pitoyable."

140. Ibid.: "Le ballet est un art dramatique. . . . Deux éléments bien distincts caractérisent, donc, le ballet: d'un côté l'Idée,—de l'autre, le Décor,—qui répondent à ces deux extrêmes de l'Humanité: l'Ame—les Sens."

141. Bruneau, "Musique," 147: "religion morte des vieux Grecs ressuscitée glorieusement sous l'impérieuse volonté de la toute-puissante modernité"; "supprimant la positivité du langage parlé"; "gestes synthétiques"; "Et le Ballet moderne sera créé."

*Messidor* (1897).[142] I would argue that rather than characterizing these and similar *fin-de-siècle* ballets as "some sort of compromise between the ideational demands of *drame lyrique* and the convention of the ballet," engendered by the institutional framework of the Opéra,[143] this use of dance may also have served a different purpose. As these two premières during the Exposition Universelle show, both French opera and ballet were undergoing a period of crisis and renewal under the influence (positive or negative, depending on the point of view) of Wagnerism. Repositioning the role of ballet-pantomime in French opera was a way of renewing the genre from the inside out, by keeping one of the key features of French opera in a way that linked it back to its origins in the seventeenth and eighteenth centuries, where allegorical figures populated the ballets of Lully, Destouches, and Rameau, and where dream sequences—such as the act 2 finale of *La Tempête* (figure 2.3)—counted among the more familiar balletic customs.[144] Neither *Esclarmonde* nor *La Tempête* stayed in the repertoire for long beyond the Exposition: Both premières were intimately linked to the World's Fair through their lavish productions aimed at impressing visitors and Parisians alike during the "great kermis," as the fair was so often called. But both premières gave new momentum to the continued discussions about the future of national music theater—which periodically surfaced in the reception of new works since the 1870s, as for example, with Lalo's ballet *Namouna* (1882), or Saint-Saëns's *Henry VIII*—at a time when centenary celebrations invited the French to locate their country's artistic production within a retrospective framework.

142. Huebner, *French Opera*, 109–10, 409–10. On *Thaïs* and the "Ballet de la Tentation," see Clair Rowden, ed., *Dossier de presse parisienne: Jules Massenet "Thaïs" (1894)* (Heilbronn: Musik-Edition Lucie Galland, 2000), xxi–xxxiii. The content of the "Ballet de la Tentation" is reproduced in Patrick Gillis, "Thaïs dans tous ses états: Genèse et remaniements," *Avant-Scène Opéra: Thaïs*, no. 109 (May 1988): 73–74.

143. Huebner, *French Opera*, 410. Huebner here follows the librettist rather than the composer, for Gallet himself referred to the "Ballet de la Tentation" as a compromise (Rowden, *Dossier de presse*, xxiii, n. 70).

144. The justification of ballet's extravaganza through dream sequences remained intact even in twentieth-century Broadway musicals such as Rodgers and Hammerstein's *Oklahoma!*.

*Chapter 3*

# The Republic's Muse: Augusta Holmès's *Ode triomphale*

As we have seen, the centenary year of the French Revolution was set to become a year of civic commemorations for the Third Republic. From the beginning, the 1889 Exposition Universelle itself was marked as a triumphant republican celebration in the face of political adversity, both internally and externally, and was poised to become "the greatest pacifist monument of Europe."[1] Indeed, the commemorative and thus historic aspect of the Exposition was more pronounced than in any of the earlier French fairs, and among its many retrospective exhibits—in addition to the musical ones discussed above—were the centenary exhibition of French paintings, Charles Garnier's "History of Human Habitation," and even a survey of erstwhile means, systems, and places of repression in France.[2] In 1889, France was constructing not only her future as a progressive republican nation, but also a past to go with it.

This past, however, was contested between various political groups, whether *Boulangistes*, *légitimistes*, moderates, or radicals. No other event in the history of modern France was as significant as the Revolution, whether it was vilified as the nadir of the nation's history or celebrated as its grandest era. But even in the case of those for whom the Revolution was a moment of glory, its historic location was disputed: for the moderate republicans, the liberalist year of 1789 represented the point in time to celebrate; for the radical republicans, 1792 was the key year because it was then that France became a republic; and for the socialists, 1793 was the year of regicide and the start of the Terror. The organization of the centenary celebrations proper thus turned into a disagreement over the specific commemoration dates. In the end, the moderate government won out over

1. Speech by President Sadi Carnot at the occasion of the banquet of French mayors, given in Eugène Clisson, "Le banquet des maires," *L'Événement*, 20 Sept. 1889, 1–2, at 1: "le plus grand monument pacifique de l'Europe!"

2. Pascal Ory, "Le Centenaire de la Révolution Française: La preuve par 89," in *Les Lieux de mémoire*, vol. 1: *La République*, ed. Pierre Nora (Paris: Gallimard, 1984), 541–42.

some of the more radical deputies and declared five dates as commemorative days for 1889, emphasizing the priority of 1789, yet aligning it subtly with the events of 1792: 5 May 1789 (the reopening of the Estates General); 20 June 1789 (the Tennis Court Oath); 14 July 1789 (the storming of the Bastille); 4 August 1789 (the abolition of privileges); and 21 September 1792 (the declaration of the Republic).[3] The commemorative chronology thus began with the royal act of recalling the Estates General, and ended with the Republic as the political system of modern France, a narrative that would allow the French president to declare in one of the commemorative speeches: "The Republic, gentlemen, one hundred years after 1789, the Republic has become France herself."[4] But things were more complicated, especially given that the politically far more radical City Council of Paris wanted a more populist slant on the celebrations and planned the addition of mass events: a large populist music festival of French *orphéon* societies on 13 July; a "brotherly" union of all the mayors of France on 18 August; and, to crown them all, a large-scale musical cantata evoking the "fêtes républicaines" of the 1790s on 11 September.[5] Save for the eve of 14 July, the other two dates seem to have been chosen for pragmatic reasons to fit around the already full summer schedule, even though the banquet of the mayors was close enough to recall the *fête* of 10 August 1793, when representatives from all over France were invited to Paris to celebrate the fall of the monarchy, even though the officially declared historical reference for the banquet were the events of 14 July 1790 (see below).

In this commemorative context, the Exposition Universelle formed the third point of a Parisian Centenary triangle between the Élysée Palace, the Champ de Mars, and the town hall. On the one hand, the Exposition produced some of its own commemorative projects such as the recreation of the storming of the Bastille on 14 July, while on the other, it served as a location that could be shared by both the national and the local Parisian governments, and where these governments' agendas could find expression in ways that were less openly politically charged than troop parades and rallies.

## Commemorations, Ceremonies, and the Exposition Universelle

The French state commemorated the abolition of privileges on 4 August 1789 with the *panthéonisation* of four revolutionary heroes. General Lazare

3. Ibid., 537. See also Robert Gildea, *The Past in French History* (New Haven, CT, and London: Yale University Press, 1994), 18–19.

4. Speech by Carnot at the banquet of French mayors, given in Clisson, "Le Banquet des maires," 2: "La République, Messieurs, cent ans après 1789, la République est devenue la France même."

5. Ory, "Le Centenaire de la Révolution Française," 540.

Carnot (the grandfather of President Sadi Carnot), General François Séverin Marceau, and La Tour d'Auvergne ("the first grenadier of the Republic") were three military leaders associated with the victories of year II (1793); the fourth, Deputy Jean Baudin, died in 1851 while resisting the coup d'état of Prince Louis-Napoléon.[6] In contrast to the state funeral of Victor Hugo in 1885—the last time a Republican hero had been laid to rest in the Panthéon—this ceremony honored men of military action, three of whom had died in battle defending either the First or the Second French Republic. Now they were being entombed in the Panthéon as patron saints for the defense of the Third, replacing Ste Geneviève, the patron saint of Paris to whom the Panthéon was originally dedicated as a church.[7] In the place of her statue, a new monument was built for Louis Lazare Hoche and Jean Baptiste Kléber (two further key revolutionary generals), whose foundation stone was laid by the president during the ceremony (figure 3.1). The Panthéon was no longer Parisian but Republican, and the program behind this choice of heroes for the 1889 ceremonies underlined this message, as Ben-Amos has shown, for these revolutionary military heroes "clearly combined in their deeds republicanism and patriotism. They fought both against the monarchists from within and the foreign powers—notably the Prussians—from without, and most of them were of humble origin."[8] The Republican implication of the substitution of revolutionary military leaders for Ste Geneviève was underlined not only by a military parade during the festivities, but also by a concert of military music in the Palais de l'Industrie within the Exposition Universelle.

Two of the bodies—Carnot and La Tour d'Auvergne—were repatriated from Munich and Magdeburg. One had died in exile during the Royalist restoration, while the other was killed defending France against Prussia. The efforts of repatriation were followed in the press, and when the coffin of the war hero, La Tour d'Auvergne, arrived at the train station of Nancy on 2 August, it was greeted by six thousand spectators to the sounds of drum rolls and the *Marseillaise*.[9] During the ceremonies of 4 August, the military bands of various regiments served to support the solemn mood of the occasion with drum rolls and "funeral pieces," including the "grave

6. Avner Ben-Amos, *Funerals, Politics, and Memory in Modern France, 1789–1996* (Oxford and New York: Oxford University Press, 2000), 96, 206–9.

7. The Panthéon was consecrated and deconsecrated on several occasions, beginning in 1791 when Ste Geneviève was renamed Panthéon by the Marquis de Villette. Its last conversion from church to national necropolis was effected at the occasion of the state funeral for Victor Hugo. See Klaus Bußmann, *Paris und die Ile de France* (Cologne: DuMont, 1980), 246–47.

8. Ben-Amos, *Funerals, Politics, and Memory*, 206.

9. "Nos grands hommes au Panthéon," *Le National*, 4 Aug. 1889, 2.

# RÉPUBLIQUE FRANÇAISE
LIBERTÉ — ÉGALITÉ — FRATERNITÉ

## Commissariat Général des Fêtes du Centenaire

# FÊTES DU 4 AOUT 1889

**A 9 heures et demie du matin**

PLACE DU PANTHÉON, CÉRÉMONIE DE LA TRANSLATION AU PANTHÉON DES RESTES DE

## CARNOT, MARCEAU, LA TOUR D'AUVERGNE ª & BAUDIN

Pose de la première Pierre d'un Monument commémoratif élevé au Panthéon

**EN L'HONNEUR DE**

## HOCHE & DE KLÉBER

## DÉFILÉ DES TROUPES DE LA GARNISON DE PARIS

SUR LA PLACE DU PANTHÉON

**A 8 heures du soir**

## GRAND FESTIVAL

### Des Musiques Militaires Françaises

AU PALAIS DE L'INDUSTRIE

**ENTRÉE : 3 FRANCS PAR PERSONNE**

**A 9 heures et demie du soir**

## EMBRASEMENT DES HAUTEURS DE PARIS

Montmartre, Belleville, Buttes-Chaumont, Réservoir de Montsouris,
Parc de Montsouris, Réservoir de Ménilmontant, Sommet de la Colonne de la Bastille,
Sommet de la Tour Eiffel.

En souvenir de la Nuit du 4 Août 1789, date de l'abolition des Privilèges.

Paris, le 27 Juillet 1889.

*Le Commissaire général des Fêtes,*

**A. ALPHAND.**

IMPRIMERIE CENTRALE DES CHEMINS DE FER. — IMPRIMERIE CHAIX. — RUE BERGÈRE, 20 PARIS. — 19167-7-9.

Figure 3.1. Program for the national celebrations of 4 August 1889.
B.H.V.P., *Dossier d'Actualités.*

accents of Chopin's funeral march" during the procession.[10] After the subsequent dedication of the monument to Hoche and Kléber, the band of the elite Garde Républicaine performed the *Marseillaise*, closing the ceremony to the sounds of the national anthem.

The military theme was even more prominent in the evening festivities at the Exposition Universelle, in a monster concert given by 1,173 musicians from various French regiments and military schools.[11] The ceremonies of 4 August fell during the middle of the state visit of the Shah of Persia. While he did not attend the Panthéon ceremony, he was present at the military concert that opened with both national anthems, the *Marseillaise* and that of Persia. At least 10,000 people were in the audience at the beautifully decorated Palais de l'Industrie, listening to a concert that comprised works by contemporary French composers such as Massenet, Victorin Joncières, and Émile Jonas, as well as the "Marche religieuse" from Gluck's *Alceste* and overtures by Auber (*La Muette de Portici*) and Beethoven (*Egmont*). The final program differed significantly from the one published in February 1889, which included Saint-Saëns's *Hymne à Victor Hugo* of 1881 and extracts from Verdi's *Aida*.[12] But it seems that the changes in program were motivated by aesthetics rather than ideology. The final one was well chosen to show off the musical qualities of the performers, and "the sublime *Marche religieuse* from *Alceste*, full of soft nuances, produced no less profound an effect than the dashing overture of *La Muette de Portici*."[13] Although it was not stated publicly, the military monster concert was part of the response of the Commission des Fêtes du Centenaire to address the concerns of the municipality of Paris: "the organization of a solemnity that has a simultaneously patriotic and popular character which recalls the grand festivities of the first Revolution."[14] Its location in a building on the Champ de Mars was triply significant: not only was it part of the Exposition Universelle, but the Champ de Mars

---

10. Fernand Xau, "Au Panthéon," *L'Écho de Paris*, 6 Aug. 1889, 2: "les graves accents de la *Marche funèbre* de Chopin"; "Nos grands hommes au Panthéon," *Le National*, 6 Aug. 1889, 2: "Plusieurs morceaux funèbres exécutés par diverses musiques militaires et des roulements des tambours voilés de crêpe ajoutaient à l'effet."

11. The number is derived from "Le festival de Musiques militaires," *Le National*, 4 Aug. 1889, 2; and Charles Darcours [Charles Réty], "Notes de Musique," *Le Figaro*, 7 Aug. 1889, 6.

12. Charles Darcours [Charles Réty], "La Musique à l'Exposition," *Le Ménestrel* 55 (1889): 140–41.

13. Darcours, "Notes de Musique," 6: "La sublime marche religieuse d'*Alceste*, toute dans les nuances de la douceur, n'a pas produit une sensation moins profonde que la pimpante ouverture de la *Muette*."

14. *Fêtes du Centenaire/Commission de Contrôle/Séance du 8 Juin 1889/Procès-verbal* (Paris: Imprimerie Chaix, 1889), 3: "l'organisation d'une solennité ayant un caractère à la fois patriotique et populaire rappelant les grandes fêtes de la première Révolution."

was also the place of revolutionary mass celebrations and was adjacent to the École militaire. Furthermore, the Palais de l'Industrie itself had strong associations with the working and artisan classes, and the *orphéon* movement.

These multiple references of the Champ de Mars and of the Palais de l'Industrie also came in handy at the next major event in August, the banquet of French mayors. This event was initiated by the municipality of Paris (originally against the wishes of the national government) to recall the events of 14 July 1790, where thousands of delegates from all corners of France had come together on the Champ de Mars to be addressed by Louis XVI as representatives of the new French Federation at the first anniversary of the storming of the Bastille.[15] The banquet made its point: "Never, in fact, since 14 July 1790, nor in any country, could one see a similar spectacle: the entire nation assembled at one place."[16] So that the mayors were not in conflict with their municipal duties during the local centenary festivities of 14 July 1889, the banquet in Paris was set to take place on 18 August.[17] In all, 11,182 mayors accepted the invitation by the municipality of Paris to join a parade from the Hôtel de Ville along the rue de Rivoli, then passing from the royal symbol of the Louvre to the Palais de l'Industrie at the Champ de Mars.[18] The parade drew a large crowd of spectators, with close to 25,000 just on the Place de l'Hôtel de Ville.[19] But only at its end were the mayors joined by President Carnot, who had remained conspicuously absent from the municipal event in the streets of Paris.

Ceremonial music accompanied the procession. Indeed, the sounds of the *Marseillaise* were the signal of its beginning. The organizers had placed military bands at strategic intervals among the almost 12,000 people in the procession, far enough away from each other to avoid sound bleeding over, but close enough to frame the procession musically. In addition to the *Marseillaise*, their repertoire consisted of military marches. But the mayors themselves contributed to the music by singing revolutionary songs such as Étienne Nicolas Méhul's *Chant du Départ.*[20] When the President of the Republic joined the mayors and several thousand other guests at the banquet in the Palais de l'Industrie decorated with tapestries and the emblazoned arms of the City of Paris, he did so, again, to the sounds of the

---

15. Ory, "Le Centenaire de la Révolution Française," 540.

16. Émile Chautemps, toast to the banquet of mayors on 18 August 1889, given in Clisson, "Le Banquet des maires," 1: "Jamais, en effet depuis le 14 juillet 1790, ni dans aucun pays, pareil spectacle ne s'était vu: la nation entière assemblée en un même lieu."

17. Olivier Ihl, *La Fête républicaine* (Paris: Gallimard, 1996), 210–11.

18. The number was published in "Le Banquet des maires," *Le Gaulois*, 17 Aug. 1889, 2; and "Le Banquet des maires: Les 11,182 convives," *Le National*, 18 Aug. 1889, 2. Ihl underestimates it as "près de neuf mille" (*La Fête républicaine*, 210).

19. A. Possien, "Le Banquet des maires," *L'Écho de Paris*, 20 Aug. 1889, 2.

20. Clisson, "Le Banquet des maires," 1.

*Marseillaise.* At the sounds of the anthem, the 15,000 guests were seized by "an admirable spirit of vibrant patriotism," thanks to the "superb music of Rouget de Lisle."[21] More music was provided during the banquet by the Garde Républicaine and civil music societies, but as the correspondent for *L'Écho de Paris* admitted, it could barely be heard over the noise of conversation and cutlery.[22] At the end of the banquet, the *Marseillaise* was played again, and then the mayors went to see the Eiffel Tower, "whose illumination, as an exception, continued until midnight."[23]

In all of these festivities, the music of the *Marseillaise* played a central role in the Republican ritual. This is reflected in the French press coverage of the Centenary and other celebrations of the summer and fall. In order to underline the festive character of the event, reporters would refer in general terms to marches and other music that were played at occasions such as the parades for 14 July, the *panthéonisation* of 4 August, or the banquet of mayors on 18 August. But each time the national anthem was performed, it is mentioned specifically in a large number of newspaper reports. Since its institution as the anthem of the Third Republic in 1879, the *Marseillaise* had become the musical symbol of the nation.[24] During the six months of the Exposition which covered also the main events of the Centenary, the *Marseillaise* was played at a significant number of official occasions in addition to being heard regularly at bandstand concerts and on the Edison phonograph. The acoustic signature of the Republic was thus ever-present during these months, in particular between 14 July and 21 September. A satire by the columnist of *Le Gaulois* played on its omnipresence in both Paris and at the Exposition. Trying to escape the sounds of the *Marseillaise* proved impossible, and he heard it everywhere: played on the bandstands by firemen, performed on the Javanese *angklung* and on the Spanish guitar, and even whistled by a passing African.[25] Thus the sonic symbol of the Republic was as present as any visual object, but because ears cannot be closed in the way eyes can be averted, its impact was far more direct and inescapable.

21. Possien, "Le Banquet des maires," 2: "Un admirable élan de patriotisme vibrant semble avoir gagné les quinze mille assistants énervés encore par la superbe musique de Rouget de Lisle."

22. Ibid., 2.

23. V.-F. M., "Les Fêtes de l'Exposition," *L'Exposition de Paris*, 3–4 (1889): 286–87, at 286: "la Tour Eiffel, dont l'embrasement se prolonge exceptionnellement jusqu'à minuit."

24. The introduction of the *Marseillaise* as the French national anthem in 1879 was cause for major controversies split along political lines, and the anthem remained controversial until the 1890s. See Eric J. Hobsbawm, *Echoes of the Marseillaise: Two Centuries Look Back on the French Revolution* (New Brunswick, NJ: Rutgers University Press, 1990), 69–76; Maurice Agulhon, *La République de Jules Ferry à François Mitterand, 1880 à nos jours* (Paris: Hachette, 1990), 24.

25. Un Petit Parisien, "L'Exposition à coté: La 'Marseillaise' partout," *Le Gaulois*, 7 Aug. 1889, 1.

While music played a large role as festive framework and ritual object in the centenary festivities, none of the pieces performed at these events was actually composed for the occasion. But on 11 September 1889, again in the Palais de l'Industrie, the centenary celebrations of the French Revolution at the Exposition Universelle finally reached their musical climax with the presentation of Augusta Holmès's *Ode triomphale en l'honneur du Centenaire de 1789*. Like the banquet of the mayors, this *représentation monstre* was organized by the city of Paris and was received as commemorating the revolutionary mass celebrations of the Champ de Mars. The committee for the centenary celebrations pulled out all the stops to turn it into a memorable event.[26]

## A Revolutionary Spectacle in the Palais de l'Industrie

From the outset, the Commission des Fêtes du Centenaire had planned the performance of a cantata to celebrate the revolution with a "chant séculaire" at the occasion of the prize-giving; this "chant séculaire" would unite all the exhibitors at the Palais de l'Industrie on 30 September to receive their honors in the presence of the French president. The title of the cantata was to be *Quatre-vingt-neuf* ("Eighty-nine"), and there was to be a competition for both the text and the music. Led by Théodore de Banville, a jury of seventeen writers, including Jean Richepin, François Coppée, and Ludovic Halévy, unanimously nominated a text by the folklorist poet Gabriel Vicaire.[27] The next step was a second competition in late February 1889, whose jury was led by Ambroise Thomas. Twenty-five scores setting Vicaire's text were submitted, but the jury decided not to award a prize because none of the submitted cantatas was considered worthy; the last possible candidate was excluded because he used the *Marseillaise* in his setting, an anachronism, given that Rouget de Lisle's hymn was composed three years after 1789.[28] To save the situation, the head of the Commission des Fêtes du Centenaire, Jean Charles Alphand, tried to convince Charles Gounod to compose the work, but the eminent composer declined and proposed one of his protégés, Palicot, with the suggestion of using a different text or at least of amending Vicaire's text in such a way that it was suited to musical composition.[29]

26. "L'Ode triomphale: Représentation monstre," *Le XIXe Siècle*, 12 Sept. 1889, 1.

27. Charles Darcours [Charles Réty], "Notes de Musique," *Le Figaro*, 3 July 1889, 6. The full text of Vicaire's cantata is reproduced in *L'Exposition de Paris* 1–2 (1889): 115.

28. "Paris et Départements," *Le Ménestrel* 55 (1889): 86. On the issue of the anachronistic cantata, see Johannès Weber, "Critique musicale," *Le Temps*, 30 Sept. 1889, 1.

29. Ferdinand Xau, "L'Histoire d'une cantate," *L'Écho de Paris*, 22 July 1889, 1–2. No details of Gounod's suggestions are known.

This caused a tempest in a teapot: the members of the literary jury accused the musicians of poetic incompetence, while the composers pointed to the poets' lack of musical understanding. The literary jury let it be known that Vicaire's text was selected unanimously by the chief representatives of France's writers. François Coppée could have not made his point more clearly: "True verses, verses that are verses, never do suit musicians. I have worked for some of them, I know what it is like."[30] On the front page of *Gil Blas*, Paul Arène reported a dialogue with Gabriel Vicaire, in which the cantata's author realized his mistake of writing beautiful verses for incompetent composers, while Lepelletier, on the front page for *L'Écho de Paris*, attacked Gounod for his refusal and wondered why neither the well-known masters Massenet and Saint-Saëns nor younger composers such as Raoul Pugno, André Messager, or Emmanuel Chabrier "were able to give our generation its fitting hymn to peace."[31] The rebuttal from the side of the musicians came in the voice of the music critic Johannès Weber, who compared "writers adjudicating musical issues" to the "insanity of the blind being made to judge colors."[32] He then dissected the cantata almost line by line in order to show not only its questionable literary value—the opening, he claimed, simply plagiarized Dante's *Divina commedia*—but also its unsuitability to composition, not least because of "a tirade of twenty-four alexandrines," in which "images, metaphors, and hyperboles are overabundant without saying much." Weber concluded that Vicaire "is a very distinguished folklorist, but I am forced to say that he understands nothing about music; no more, indeed, than the seventeen *littérateurs* who crowned him."[33]

In addition, there was the question of procedure. If a cantata was to be selected by competition, the musicians had no right, the poets claimed, to circumvent the system and try to commission a cantata by Gounod. Nor should the Commission des Fêtes du Centenaire (led by Alphand) and the commission for the Exposition (directed by Georges Berger) have supported so questionable a practice. Even worse for the proponents of the competition, the Commission des Fêtes du Centenaire eventually chose to perform, at great cost and as an event of its own, a work that had not been

---

30. Xau, "L'Histoire d'une cantate," 2: "Jamais de vrais vers, des vers qui sont des vers, ne conviennent aux musiciens. J'ai travaillé pour quelques-uns, je sais ce que c'est."

31. Paul Arène, "Et Cette Cantate?" *Gil Blas*, 28 June 1889, 1; R. Lepelletier, "La Cantate," *L'Écho de Paris*, 29 June 1889, 1: "capables de donner à notre génération l'hymne de la paix qui lui convenait?"

32. Weber, "Critique musicale" (30 Sept.), 1: "l'insanité qu'il y a de rendre les aveugles juges des couleurs et les littérateurs juges des questions musicales."

33. Ibid., 1: "cette tirade de vingt-quatre alexandrins"; "Les images, les métaphores, les hyperboles y surabondent sans dire grand'chose"; "[Vicaire] est un folkloriste très distingué, mais je suis forcé de dire qu'il n'entend rien à la musique, pas plus que les dix-sept littérateurs qui l'ont couronné."

entered into either of the competitions, while for the awarding of the prize on 30 September, Alphand and Berger selected a program mostly of well-tried repertoire pieces, framing the event with the *Marseillaise* instead of the originally planned cantata. This program contained, among other pieces, the *Marche héroïque* by Camille Saint-Saëns; Benjamin Godard's *Lux* with words by Republican icon Victor Hugo; various extracts from works by Hector Berlioz, Charles Gounod, Jules Massenet, and Ambroise Thomas; and—to add insult to injury—a work specially written for the occasion, *Fanfares* by Léo Delibes.[34]

It is not entirely clear when Augusta Holmès (1847–1903), an Irish-born French composer successful on the Paris concert stage, became involved in the centenary celebrations. Her original idea for an "intellectual and artistic spectacle" seems to have been developed in December 1888 as a *Fête de la République pour le 14 juillet 1889*.[35] By February 1889, Holmès had finished a first version of the libretto, and she began to compose the work in April.[36] She entered into negotiations with Alphand after the jury's rejection of the Vicaire cantata settings and after Gounod had declined the commission, probably by the end of March.[37] Alphand recounted the story in an interview with a journalist from the daily newspaper, *L'Éclair*, on the day of the dress rehearsal: "What to do? It was then that a municipal counselor introduced to me Mme Augusta Holmès, whom I did not know. Mme Holmès told me that she had composed, with the Centenary of the French Revolution in mind, a triumphal ode."[38] In late spring,

34. "Courrier de l'Exposition," *Le Figaro*, 26 Sept. 1889, 1.

35. Chamillac, "L'Ode triomphale d'Augusta Holmès," *La Revue illustrée* 4 (1889): 203–6, at 204: "un spectacle intellectuel et artistique." Several newspaper and journal articles refer to December 1888 as the date of inception; so does Gérard Gefen in his *Augusta Holmès, l'outrancière* (Paris: Belfond, 1987), 193. The three-page outline for the *Fête de la République* is undated and kept in the dossier of Augusta Holmès, "Fêtes du Centenaire de la République," *F-Pn*, Réserve ThB 56 (2) C.

36. The manuscript libretto is dated "février 1889" at the end of the text, on p. 19; farther down on the page, Holmès noted "Musique commencé en Avril." See Augusta Holmès, "Fêtes du Centenaire de la République," *F-Pn*, Réserve ThB 56 (2).

37. This is confirmed by Holmès in an interview with *Gil Blas*, where, however, she changes the moment of the work's inception by several months to March. See R. Ch., "Au Palais de l'Industrie," *Gil Blas*, 6 Sept. 1889, 3: "Ce ne fut qu'après que ce concours eut complètement échoué qu'elle a eu l'idée de son Ode." The end of March is the time indicated in the article "Le Triomphe de la République," *Le Journal illustré*, 15 Sept. 1889, 290–91, at 290.

38. "L'Ode de Mme Holmès," *L'Éclair*, 13 Sept. 1889, 1–2, at 2: "Que faire? C'est alors qu'un conseiller municipal me présenta Mme Augusta Holmès, que je ne connaissais pas. Mme Holmès me dit qu'elle avait composé, en vue du centenaire de la Révolution française, une ode triomphale."

she performed her work on the piano for members of the Commission des Fêtes du Centenaire, after which negotiations must have started with the stage designers of the Opéra-Comique, Lavastre and Carpezat, and the conductor, Édouard Colonne.[39] The Commission des Fêtes du Centenaire voted on 8 June to perform her cantata on 5 September as part of the official celebration, allocating 300,000 fr. to cover the cost of three free performances in the Palais de l'Industrie.[40] For Holmès, it was a dream come true: "It seems as if I am walking in a fairy tale and that it is not real."[41] She finished the full score of the *Ode triomphale* on 15 August 1889, and the work was premièred four weeks later, after a slight delay, on 11 September.[42]

The performance was a grand affair. The Palais de l'Industrie had been redecorated at great cost, including new electric chandeliers, to contain space for 22,000 spectators and a gigantic stage—45 m. (148 ft.) high, 60 m. (197 ft.) wide and 50 m. (164 ft.) deep—which served also for the final prize-giving festivities on 30 September. The medallion on top of the proscenium prominently displayed the monogram "RF" for "République Française" (figure 3.2). The lavish stage set by Lavastre and Carpezat showed an altar to the Republic, surrounded by "four tripods burning incense" with stairs and platforms leading up to it.[43] A golden curtain was suspended above the altar, and the backdrop represented forests, mountains, and cities in the distance. A large, split curtain modeled on Bayreuth was to open over the stage, while imposing velvet draperies in front of the proscenium created the effect of sacred unveiling, a familiar iconographic topos dating back to the Renaissance.[44] One dress rehearsal (on 10 September) and three free performances (on 11, 14, and 16 September) were planned, with the first performance dedicated to President Carnot, who,

39. For the audition, see Chamillac, "L'Ode triomphale d'Augusta Holmès," 204. The budget and report contain references to both the stage designers (including a proposal for the decoration) and the conductor; see *Fêtes du Centenaire . . . Procès-verbal*, 6, 8.

40. *Fêtes du Centenaire . . . Procès-verbal*, 8–9.

41. Letter by Augusta Holmès to "Maman Aillard," given in Nancy Sarah Theeman, "The Life and Songs of Augusta Holmès," PhD dissertation, University of Maryland, 1983, 141: "Il me semble que je marche dans un conte de fées et que ça n'est pas vrai." Holmès also refers to the performance opportunity as a "dream" in Edmond Stoullig, "Les Premières," *Le National*, 13 Sept. 1889, 3.

42. Augusta Holmès, *Ode triomphale en l'honneur du Centenaire de 1789*, autograph score, dated "15 août 1889," *F-Pn*, Département de la Musique, Ms. 6693.

43. Augusta Holmès, *Ode triomphale en l'honneur du Centenaire de 1789*, printed libretto (Paris: Imprimerie Chaix, 1889), 4: "quatre trépieds où brûlent les parfums."

44. At least two journalists make explicit reference to Bayreuth as the model. See G. de Boisjoslin, "Revue musicale," *L'Observateur français*, 16 Sept. 1889, 2: "le théâtre est fermé par deux rideaux qui, comme à Bayreuth, s'ouvrent par le milieu"; Adolphe Mayer, "Notes musicales," *Le Soir*, 13 Sept. 1889, 4: "A huit heures et demie, le rideau se découvre d'un seul coup, à la manière du rideau au théâtre de Bayreuth."

Figure 3.2. Augusta Holmès, *Le Triomphe de la République,* engraving of stage set,
published as *Supplément au n° 79, L'Exposition de Paris 1889,*
vols. 3-4 (Paris: Librairie Illustrée, 1889).

however, did not attend. It is unclear whether he was absent for similar reasons to those which led him to avoid the parade of the mayors, which—like
Holmès's *Ode triomphale*—was too strongly linked with the radical Republic,
or whether there were simply scheduling conflicts. In the spirit of Republican civic education, the second performance was offered to schoolchildren
from the region of and around Paris, while the third one was a popular performance for the masses.[45] A fourth, paying performance was added for 18
September for the benefit of the victims of a catastrophic explosion in
Antwerp, where a gun-powder factory had exploded and destroyed parts of
the city (figure 3.3).

There were 1,200 performers, comprising 900 singers and 300 instrumentalists. The *Ode triomphale* was a large-scale choral work with an alto solo
(sung by Mathilde Romi).[46] After a fanfare-style opening, processions of
winemakers, harvesters, workers, mariners, soldiers, scientists, artists,
youth, and children entered the stage, each led by an allegorical figure

45. On the educational impetus of Republican festivities, see Ihl, *La Fête républicaine,*
271–96.

46. It is not clear whether Holmès selected the voice type because of her own vocal
register or whether she banked in her portrayal of La République on the less gendered
register of the alto when compared with a high soprano.

# FÊTES DU CENTENAIRE DE 1789

## Représentation Extraordinaire

DE

# L'ODE TRIOMPHALE

DE

## Augusta HOLMÈS

### *Au Bénéfice des Victimes de la Catastrophe d'Anvers*

**MERCREDI 18 SEPTEMBRE 1889**, à 8 h. 1/2 du soir

#### AU PALAIS DE L'INDUSTRIE

Avec le Concours de M<sup>me</sup> Mathilde ROMI, Contralto-Solo

*DES SOCIÉTÉS CHORALES*

| | |
|---|---|
| Les Amis de la Rive Gauche | Directeur : M. AUDONNET. |
| Le Choral des Amis Réunis | M. VINARDI. |
| Le Choral de Belleville | M. JOUVIN. |
| Le Choral Chevé de Belleville | M. FAUVELLE. |
| Le Choral Chevé Polytechnique de Montmartre | M. DUPERRON. |
| Le Choral du Louvre | M. BASLAIRE. |
| L'École Galin-Paris-Chevé | M. AMAND CHEVÉ. |
| Les Enfants de Paris | M. DELHAYE. |
| La Lyre de Belleville | M. BESANÇON. |
| L'Union Chorale Française | M. LEQUIN. |
| L'Union Chorale Néerlandaise | M. CAHEN. |
| Des Enfants des Écoles de la Ville de Paris | |

Et des Chœurs de l'Association Artistique du Châtelet.

*Orchestre et Chœurs :* **1,200** *Exécutants, sous la Direction de*

# M. Édouard COLONNE

### Chef des Chœurs : M. ALFRED FOCK.

Décors par **MM. Lavastre** et **Carpezat**.

Mise en scène de M. BAUGÉ. — Costumes par M. BIANCHINI. — Accessoires par M. HALLÉ.

---

PRIX DES PLACES : Orchestre. **10** fr. — Parquet, **5** fr. — Tribunes, **3** fr.

**ON TROUVE DES BILLETS :** A la Légation de Belgique, rue Bizet, 6. — Au Ministère des Affaires Étrangères. — A la Présidence du Conseil des Ministres, au Ministère du Commerce, de l'Industrie et des Colonies, rue de Grenelle, 101. — A la Direction générale des Travaux de l'Exposition Universelle, avenue de Labourdonnais, 22. — A la Direction générale de l'Exploitation de l'Exposition Universelle, avenue de Labourdonnais, 16. — A la Direction générale des Finances de l'Exposition Universelle, avenue de Labourdonnais, 18. — Au Commissariat général Belge, à l'Exposition Universelle.—A la Préfecture de la Seine (Pavillon de Flore, Palais des Tuileries).— A la Préfecture de Police.— A l'Hôtel de Ville. — Dans les Agences des Théâtres et chez les Éditeurs de Musique.

LES PORTES DU PALAIS SERONT OUVERTES A 7 H. 1/2.

*Le Commissaire général des Fêtes,*

**A. ALPHAND.**

9-89  2094 bis. — Paris, Typ. Morris père et fils, rue Amelot, 64.

Figure 3.3. Program for the fourth, extraordinary representation of Augusta Holmès's *Ode triomphale*, 18 September 1889. B.H.V.P., *Dossier d'Actualités*.

modeled on a Roman god or goddess such as Ceres, Apollo, or Minerva, a logical choice given the notion of republican France as the "new Rome" and thus as the modern continuation of the great republic of antiquity (table 3.1). As they entered, each chorus celebrated France's industries, fertility, and achievements. Towards the end, a figure with long blonde hair, veiled in black and in chains, came in slowly and moved to the altar. After the calls of the assembled singers, the golden curtain over the altar was rent in two, revealing the female incarnation of La République (figure 3.4):

> She wears an azure-colored peplum, a white tunic, and the Phrygian cap, circled by a crown of golden ears of grain. The [Masonic] star sparkles on her forehead. A sheathed sword hangs from her belt. With one hand, she leans on a royal scepter; in the other, she holds an olive branch. The people fall on their knees.

> Elle porte le péplum d'azur, la tunique blanche et le bonnet phrygien cerclé d'une couronne d'épis d'or. L'étoile [maçonnique] brille sur son front. Un glaive au fourreau pend à sa ceinture. D'une main, elle s'appuie sur le sceptre souverain; de l'autre, elle tient des rameaux d'olivier. Le peuple tombe à genoux.[47]

In the subsequent dialogue between La République and the full chorus, the previously distinct groups were united as "the people" of France. To the words "Glory to you, daughter of Glory," the (silent) veiled figure tore off her chains and veil—"like Jeanne d'Arc by Schiller," writes Weber[48]—and appeared clothed in the colors of France. The veiled figure, so Holmès said in an interview, was the "universal Republic, to whom the French Republic gave her freedom."[49]

As Jann Pasler has shown, much of Holmès's rhetoric in the *Ode triomphale* was influenced by nationalist concepts of the revolutionary right.[50] Holmès "promoted white and blonde women as the ideal of French society," following the lead of Paul Déroulède's *Le Livre de la Ligue de patriotes* (1887).[51] Her sailors call on "France la blonde" for their protection before

---

47. Holmès, *Ode triomphale*, libretto, 17. Holmès's manuscript [*F-Pn*, Réserve ThB 56 (2)] contains the attribute "maçonnique" which was left out of the published description.

48. Johannès Weber, "Critique musicale," *Le Temps*, 16 Sept. 1889, 2: "La figure voilée arrache ses chaînes, comme la Jeanne d'Arc de Schiller."

49. R. Ch., "Au Palais de l'Industrie," 3: "la figure voilée était la République universelle à qui la République française a donné sa liberté." Weber ("Critique musicale," 16 Sept.) refers to an "officious note" ("note officieuse") that indicates the same.

50. Jann Pasler, "The Ironies of Gender, or Virility and Politics in the Music of Augusta Holmès," *Women & Music: A Journal of Gender and Culture* 2 (1998): 21–23.

51. Ibid., 22.

Figure 3.4. Detail from Paul Mervart, "Représentation de l'*Ode triomphale* de Mme Augusta Holmès au Palais de l'Industrie," *L'Univers illustré* 32 (1889): 601.

Table 3.1. Sequence of entries in Augusta Holmés, *Ode triomphale en l'honneur du Centenaire de 1789.*

| No. | Group and Allegorical Figure[a] | Incipit |
| --- | --- | --- |
| 1 | Les Vignerons (Wine Growers) Bacchus/Wine | "Evohé! Soleil! Evohé!" |
|  | Les Moissonneurs (Harvesters) Ceres/Harvest | "Evohé! Soleil! Evohé!" |
| 2 | Les Soldats (Soldiers) Mars/War | "L'arme au bras, l'épée à côté" |
|  | Les Marins (Soldiers) Neptune/Ocean | "Sur les flots gris de l'Océan" |
| 3 | Les Travailleurs (Workers) [double chorus] Mercury/Work and Industry | "Tope, frère! et dis-moi ton nom!" |
| 4 | Les Arts (Arts) Apollo/Genius | "Peuple, lève les yeux vers la Lyre immortelle" |
|  | Les Sciences (Sciences) Minerva/Reason | "Du fond de l'Océan jusqu'au delà des astres" |
| 5 | Les Jeunes Gens (Young Men) Eros/Love | "Vers Elles!" |
|  | Les Jeunes Filles (Girls) Psyche/Youth | "Je rêve qu'un soleil très doux" |
| 6 | Les Enfants (Children) [double chorus] walking on with wild beasts chained by flowers and flower-covered swords | "Nous venons saluer notre chère mère chérie" |
| 7 | All choral groups together | "A travers les cités et les sombres forêts" |
| 8 | La République, joined by Le Peuple (the People) | "O peuple, me voici" |

[a]The costumes of the allegorical figures were modeled on the iconography of Roman gods. Originally, Holmès called them by their antique names, but then changed them into allegorical figures.

their colonialist promise to conquer the world for her.[52] Holmès's vocabulary incorporated nationalist, Christian, and Masonic symbolism, creating a work of religious undertones, a solemn celebration of the Republic which tried to be many things to many people.[53] Christian references are used right from the beginning when the Eucharistic wine/blood and bread/flesh become the signs of the French soil and people, thus aligning the *Ode* with the "France Catholique" of a Maurice Barrès or, later, Paul Claudel.[54] What might seem blasphemous at first was, in fact, an attempt to elevate the Republican rite towards one of sacred dimensions. La Patrie was to have her own cult and one that had its roots in the Christian rite:

| LES VIGNERONS | THE WINEMAKERS |
|---|---|
| Ce vin, c'est le sang | This wine is the blood |
| Chaud et rubescent | Hot and turning red |
| De la terre qui nous fit naître! | From the earth which made us! |

| LES MOISSONNEURS | THE HARVESTERS |
|---|---|
| Ce pain, c'est la chair | This bread is the flesh |
| Du sol trois fois cher, | Of the three-times cherished soil |
| Que le soc déchire et pénètre! | That the plow tears and penetrates! |

| LES DEUX CHŒURS | THE TWO CHORUSES |
|---|---|
| Forts et rénovés | Strong and renewed |
| Mangez et buvez, | Eat and drink, |
| Fils du Rire et de la Vaillance, | Sons of laughter and valor, |
| Le pain et le vin | The bread and the wine |
| Sans qui tout est vain, | Without which all is vain, |
| La chair et le sang de la France![55] | The flesh and the blood of France! |

52. Holmès, *Ode triomphale*, libretto, 8.

53. Ihl distinguishes between various strands of Republican festivities in the early years of the Third Republic and their relationship to previous religious structures. See Ihl, *La Fête républicaine*, 75–87.

54. On the "France Catholique," see Pierre Birnbaum, "Nationalisme à la française," in *Théories du nationalisme: Nation, nationalité, ethnicité*, ed. Gil Delannoi and Pierre-André Taguieff, 125–38 (Paris: Éditions Kimé, 1991). Paul Claudel and Arthur Honegger's staged oratorio, *Jeanne d'Arc au Bûcher* (1938), is a prominent later example of the alignment of wine and bread with the soil of France, here clearly linked to a regional symbolism, with bread representing the wheat-growing North and wine the grape-growing South. For the Masonic references of the *Ode*, see Ory, "Le Centenaire de la Révolution Française," 558.

55. Holmès, *Ode triomphale*, libretto, 6–7.

The religious overtones become more obvious just before the appearance of La République as all unite in a prayer-like call, after which lightning accompanies her unveiling. Her speech is composed predominantly in classic alexandrines:

TOUS

> Apparais, déesse, apparais!
> Viens! approche! Sois là! Surgis
>   dans la lumière!
> Ton peuple t'invoque à genoux!
>
> O terrible, ô clémente, ô
>   triomphante, ô fière.
> O République, apparais-nous!

LA RÉPUBLIQUE

> O peuple, me voici! du haut de
>   l'Empyrée
> Où je règle à jamais tes destins
>   glorieux
> Je viens à ton appel, et, de
>   flamme entourée,
> J'apparais à tes yeux.

ALL

> Appear, goddess, appear!
> Come! Approach! Be here!
>   Emerge in the light!
> Your people calls you on their
>   knees!
> O terrible, o clement, o
>   triumphant, o proud.
> O Republic, appear to us.

LA RÉPUBLIQUE

> O people, here I am! From
>   the heights of the heavens
> Where I rule forever your
>   glorious destiny
> I come at your call, and
>   surrounded by flames
> I appear to your eyes

Christian allusions continue throughout. Thus in her address to the French people, La République paraphrases biblical passages such as, for example, Matthew 11:28 ("Come unto me, all ye that labor and are heavy laden, and I will give you rest."), which here receives a particular slant through her incorporation of the Proudhonian concept of "justice" which replaces "égalité" in her elaboration of the three principles of republican liberty, fraternity, equality. She finishes with a reference to the absolutist formulation of "L'État, c'est moi" after the evocation of the apocalyptic trumpets. La République has taken the place of Louis XIV:

> Venez à moi, vous qui souffrez
>   pour la justice!
> Pauvres, déshérités, martyrs,
>   suivez ma loi;
> Il faut que le clairon terrible
>   retentisse. . . .
>       La Justice, c'est moi![56]

> Come to me, you who suffer
>   injustice!
> Poor, disinherited, martyrs,
>   follow my law;
> The terrible trumpet must
>   resound. . . .
>       I am Justice!

56. Ibid., 18.

The patriotic message of Holmès's *Ode triomphale* was overwhelming, and the 22,000 French spectators in the Palais de l'Industrie reacted to the piece with almost the mass hysteria of a political rally:[57] "A cry of triumph greeted this apparition [of La République] and frenzied applause broke out while the choral masses celebrated in unison the freed and regenerated 'Patrie.' The public was in a fever with patriotic enthusiasm."[58]

Holmès's setting underlines the often hymn-like character of the text while taking into account both the probably limited abilities of her choirs and the large space in which the music would be sung. Thus most of the choruses are homophonic, using changes in register rather than complex polyphonic textures to generate musical interest, and leaving the creation of timbral differentiation to the much more sophisticated nature of the orchestral parts. La République's long alto solo towards the end opens with triads in the style of fanfares before moving into a chant-like recitation. Sacral, organ-like incantations in the orchestra are followed by more triadic lines in martial rhythms. In this solo, Holmès uses all the signifiers of regal and divine music developed from Gluck to Berlioz, also with a reference to Wagner's "Nothung" motive. Its key signature, B major, carried meaning as signifying light in the circle of Holmès's teacher, César Franck.[59] The ending of the *Ode* in E-flat major, on the other hand, may well refer back to the Masonic elements in Mozart's *Die Zauberflöte*. Musically, Holmès's *Ode* is indeed laden with references, whether to Mozart, Berlioz, or Wagner. The most important musical intertext, however, is truly Revolutionary: François-Joseph Gossec's 1792 "scène," *Offrande à la Liberté*. In several self-serving interviews with newspapers, Holmès herself established the link to these Revolutionary spectacles:

> My ode, Mademoiselle Holmès answered, is quite simply the apotheosis of the Republic and of France in 1889. On the model of the great festivities which the original Revolution offered its people, I wished that in 1889, the year of the centenary celebration, the people could also see, in the shape of an immense spectacle, an imposing allegory of the republican idea.

> Mon ode, nous a répondu mademoiselle Holmès, est tout simplement l'apothéose de la République et de la France de 1889. A l'instar des

---

57. While there are no specific data on the national composition of the audience, newspaper reports emphasized that the audience consisted of mainly French citizens and commented on the political intent behind the invitations.

58. V.-F. M., "Les Fêtes de l'Exposition," 267: "Un cri de triomphe a salué cette apparition et des applaudissements frénétiques ont éclaté, pendant que les masses chorales célébraient à l'unisson la Patrie délivrée et régénérée. L'assistance était enfiévrée d'enthousiasme patriotique."

59. On Franck's notion of key signatures, see Angelus Seipt, *César Francks symphonische Dichtungen*, Kölner Beiträge zur Musikforschung 116 (Regensburg: Bosse Verlag, 1981).

grandes fêtes que la première révolution offrit au peuple, j'ai voulu qu'en 1889, année de la célébration du centenaire, le peuple pût également voir, sous forme d'un immense spectacle, une allégorie imposante de l'idée républicaine.[60]

Throughout the nineteenth century, the composer most associated with these great festivities of the first Republic was, indeed, Gossec, mainly because of his oft-played orchestration of the *Marseillaise*.

## Gossec the Revolutionary

While the career of François-Joseph Gossec (1734–1829) spanned almost a century—from the *Ancien Régime* to the Restoration, including the First Republic, the Consulate, and the First Empire—after his death, he was (and still is) most associated with the musical festivities of the Revolution, in particular because of his collaborations with Marie-Joseph Chénier (1764–1811), the brother of André Chénier and poet of the Revolutionary song "Chant du départ."[61] So strong were the associations that the nineteenth-century historian, Auguste Challamel, could write: "The Revolution can be compared to a grand opera with words by Marie-Joseph Chénier and music by Gossec."[62] Gossec's best-known revolutionary work, however, was the *Offrande à la Liberté*, his musical dramatization of the *Marseillaise*, staged at the Opéra on 20 September 1792 with choreography by Pierre Gabriel Gardel.[63] It was followed a year later by another key piece, *Le Triomphe de la République*, with words by Marie-Joseph Chénier.

Gossec and Gardel's *Offrande à la Liberté* proved a major success. Not only was the piece performed over one hundred times during the First

---

60. R. Ch., "La Représentation de l'*Ode triomphale* de mademoiselle Holmès," *Gil Blas*, 6 Sept. 1889, 3.

61. Dominique Lauvergnier makes the point for the twentieth century in her article "François-Joseph Gossec: Compositeur dramatique," in *Fêtes et musiques révolutionnaires: Grétry et Gossec*, ed. Roland Mortier and Hervé Hasquin, 61–89, Études sur le XVIIIe Siècle 8 (Brussels: *Éditions de l'Université de Bruxelles*, 1990), 61.

62. Quoted without bibliographical attribution in Jean-Louis Jam, "Marie-Joseph Chénier and François-Joseph Gossec: Two Artists in the Services of Revolutionary Propaganda," in *Music and the French Revolution*, ed. Malcolm Boyd, 221–35 (Cambridge: Cambridge University Press, 1992), 221: "La Révolution peut être comparée à un grand drame lyrique, paroles de Marie-Joseph Chénier, musique de Gossec."

63. On the creation and reception of the *Offrande à la Liberté*, see M. Elizabeth C. Bartlet, "Gossec, l'*Offrande à la Liberté* et l'histoire de la *Marseillaise*," in *Le Tambour et la Harpe: Œuvres, pratiques et manifestations musicales sous la Révolution, 1788–1800*, ed. Jean-Rémy Julien and Jean Mongrédien, 123–46 (Paris: Éditions du May, 1991). I wish to thank David Charlton for bringing this text to my attention.

Republic, but it was also given in 1848 and was known during the Third Republic. Interest in this Revolutionary repertoire grew especially in the later 1880s, with the approach of the Centenary, when the City of Paris commissioned Constant Pierre to collect and catalogue hymns, odes, and other Revolutionary material.[64] In 1887, he found a cache of unpublished works "by the founders of the Conservatoire," which enabled him to publish a significant body of Revolutionary works ten years after the Centenary, in 1899.[65] Both *L'Art musical* (15 Jan. 1888) and *La Musique des familles* (19 Jan. 1888) announced proudly that Pierre's find contained pieces unknown to scholars such as Julien Tiersot—known to insiders as his fiercest rival—and contained works by Gossec, Méhul, and Lesueur.[66]

In 1889, Parisians could hear some of Chénier and Gossec's work during the inauguration of the statue of Jean-Jacques Rousseau on 3 February 1889, including the *Hymne à Jean-Jacques Rousseau* and the *Hymne à la Liberté*[67] sung by the choir of the École Galin-Paris-Chevé, which also participated in the performance of Holmès's *Ode triomphale* (figure 3.3).[68] Pierre's rival Tiersot seems to have been involved in the selection of the pieces for the Rousseau celebration, choosing those that, in his opinion, were appropriate for the celebration of a Revolutionary fête.[69] Indeed, in an article published later, in July, commenting on the musical selections for the Centenary, he complained of the absence of works by composers such as Gossec, Méhul, and Lesueur for the celebration of 14 July and other centenary events, specifically citing Gossec's *Offrande à la Liberté*, "which summarizes in a concise tableau the decorative tendencies (sometimes touching the grandiose), the love of declamatory forms and theatrical pomp, as well as the patriotic exasperation of the years when the fatherland was in danger."[70]

64. Gefen, *Augusta Holmès*, 192; Karen Henson, "In the House of Disillusion: Augusta Holmès and *La Montagne noire*," *Cambridge Opera Journal* 9 (1997): 238.

65. Constant Pierre, *Musique des fêtes et cérémonies de la Révolution française* (Paris: Imprimerie nationale, 1899), x: "hymnes et chants composés par les fondateurs du Conservatoire."

66. Report in *La Musique des familles (Musique populaire)* 7 (1888): 7: "Notre collaborateur, M. Constant Pierre, vient de découvrir plusieurs chants exécutés aux fêtes nationales de la première République, pour la plupart inconnus aux historiens de la musique sous la Révolution, MM. Aug. Challamel, G. Chouquet, J. Tiersot. Parmi les plus importants, nous citerons: l'*Hymne à la liberté*, et le *Chant du 14 juillet* de Gossec; le *Chant du Retour*, de Chénier et Méhul; l'*Hymne pour la Patrie*, de Beauvarlet-Charpentier, la *Fête de l'Agriculture*, de Vogel et le *Chant pour l'anniversaire du 21 janvier*, de Lesueur." See also *L'Art musical* 27 (1888): 7. I am grateful to Alicia Levin for finding these citations for me.

67. "Paris et Départements," *Le Ménestrel* 55 (1889): 46–47.

68. "La Statue de Jean-Jacques Rousseau," *Le National*, 5 Feb. 1889, 3.

69. Reference to Tiersot is made in several newspaper articles, most explicitly in Eugène Clisson, "J.-J. Rousseau au Panthéon," *L'Événement*, 5 Feb. 1889, 2.

70. Julien Tiersot, "Promenades musicales à l'Exposition," *Le Ménestrel* 55 (1889): 227–29, at 228: "l'*Offrande à la Liberté*, de Gossec, qui résume en un tableau concis les

Gossec's *Offrande à la Liberté* opens with sharply punctuated fanfares in B-flat major, followed by a Citoyen's warning of imminent dangers to the Republic.[71] After a first section based on the revolutionary chanson "Veillons au salut de l'Empire," the scene moves to a dramatization of the *Marseillaise* evolving around the altar of Liberty. As Elizabeth Bartlet has shown, Gossec's setting emphasized the sixth strophe of the *Marseillaise*—"Amour sacré de la Patrie"—which thus became the centerpiece of subsequent patriotic manifestations.[72] Gossec turned the sixth strophe and the ensuing refrain into an augmented coda for the entire piece, accompanied by a full orchestral setting in an archaic style.[73] Before this final chorus, a "religious dance" underlined the procession of adults and children of both sexes dressed in white who bring flowers to, and burn incense around, the statue of Liberty. This dance is a slow and melodious variation of the *Marseillaise*, in C major and with an ornamented clarinet solo.[74]

Both the text and the music of Holmès's *Ode triomphale* make reference to Gossec's *Offrande à la Liberté*. Like Gossec, Holmès opens the piece with punctuated fanfares in B-flat major, and ends it with a large apotheotic chorus celebrating the glory and victory of Liberty. She took up Gardel and Gossec's idea of processions towards the altar of the statue of Liberty, including soldiers, women, and children bringing flowers and burning incense at the statue's feet. But Holmès refers also to Gossec and Chénier's later revolutionary piece, *Le Triomphe de la République* from 1793.[75] From the latter stems the idea of revealing an incarnation of the Republic (following

tendances décoratives, atteignant parfois au grandiose, l'amour des formes déclamatoires et des pompes théâtrales, ainsi que l'exaspération patriotique des années où la Patrie était en danger."

71. François-Joseph Gossec, *Offrande à la Liberté: Scène composée de l'Air Veillons au Salut de l'Empire et de la Marche de Marseillois* (Paris: Imbault, 1792). An exemplar of this score is preserved in the British Library (shelf mark: H.1980.ff.(2)). A modern edition by M. Elizabeth C. Bartlet is planned for *Art and Revolution: The Paris Opéra's Contribution to Fêtes and Tableaux Patriotiques during the 1790s*, Recent Researches in the Music of the Classical Period (Madison, WI: A-R Editions).

72. Bartlet, "Gossec, l' *Offrande à la Liberté* et l'histoire de la *Marseillaise*," 128.

73. Ibid., 126–27. Bartlet describes the style as signaled by homophonic texture, suspensions (especially 4–3) and chords generally presented in root position.

74. Scenic description in score, François-Joseph Gossec, *Offrande à la Liberté*, 15: "Danse religieuse / Des adorateurs de la Liberté, des Enfants des deux sexes vêtus de Blanc apportent des Parfums pour Brûler autour de la Statue de la Liberté pendant le C[oupl]et suivant."

75. *Le Triomphe de la République, ou le camp de Grand-Pré, divertissement lyrique, en un acte; représenté par l'Académie de Musique, le 27 janvier, l'an deuxième de la République Française. La Musique est du Citoyen Gossec, Les Ballets, du Citoyen Cardel* [*sic*] (Paris: Baudoin, Desenne & Bailly, [1793]). Exemplars of the libretto and the setting are preserved in the British Library (shelf marks: R.399 (II); H.453).

the imploring calls of the French citizens) who addresses the French both on stage and in the audience as their just ruler.

Holmès's openly acknowledged references to Gossec's Revolutionary spectacles were picked up in the reviews of her *Ode triomphale*, as, for example, in *Le Voltaire*:

> Mlle Augusta Holmès, creator of both the poem and the music of the *Triomphe de la République* [*sic*], has conceived her work following the simple and grandiose plan originally imagined by Gossec, when, in 1792 at the Opéra, he dramatized each strophe of the *Marseillaise* in a lyric scene, *L'Offrande à la Liberté*, and, with the help of Gardel, the *maître de ballets*, had women, children, soldiers, and old men file in front of the statue of the Republic—which was standing, armed, in the center of the stage—while swearing to conquer and die for the defense of the invaded country.

> Mlle Augusta Holmès, ouvrière à la fois du poème et de la musique du *Triomphe de la République*, a conçu son œuvre d'après le plan naïf et grandiose imaginé jadis par Gossec, alors que, en 1792, à l'Opéra, dans une scène lyrique intitulée l'*Offrande à la Liberté*, il dramatisa chacune des strophes de la *Marseillaise*, et avec le concours de Gardel, le maître de ballets, fit défiler devant la statue de la République, debout et armée au milieu de la scène, les femmes, les enfants, les guerriers et les vieillards, jurant de vaincre et de mourir pour la défense du pays envahi.[76]

This journalist—like several others—confused the title of Gossec's 1793 work with that of Holmès. Indeed, *Le Triomphe de la République* floated around as an unofficial name for the *Ode triomphale*, also linking Holmès's composition to the next Republican event, the inauguration of the monument entitled *Le Triomphe de la République*, on 21 September 1889, the anniversary of the declaration of the First Republic, on the Place des Nations.[77] In a similar way in which the altar carried the figure of the Republic in Holmès's *Ode triomphale*, the monument by Jules Dalou was crowned by a female figure carrying the flame of freedom. Thus Holmès's work was received not only as a major celebratory piece in itself, but also as a bridge between the Revolutionary festivities of the eighteenth century

---

76. H. C., "Le Triomphe de la République: Le poème et la partition," *Le Voltaire*, 13 Sept. 1889, 1–2, at 1.

77. The monument was inaugurated by President Carnot, with the *Marseillaise* prominently featured in the ceremony. See, for example, the reports by Eugène Clisson, "Le Triomphe de la République: Inauguration du monument," *L'Événement*, 23 Sept. 1889, 2; Fernand Xau, "Le Triomphe de la République," *L'Écho de Paris*, 23 Sept. 1889, 2. Jann Pasler refers to *Le Triomphe de la République* as an earlier name of Holmès's *Ode triomphale*, but none of the sources that I was able to consult supports this claim. See Pasler, "The Ironies of Gender," 21.

and the unveiling of the new monument to the Republic ten days after the première of the *Ode triomphale*. Save in the case of those journalists who had political reasons for despising the Revolution, Holmès's intertextual references to the Revolutionary festivities in general, recalling the "marvelous old celebrations" at the Champ de Mars, and Gossec's *Offrande* in particular, were pronounced a positive aspect of the *Ode triomphale*.[78]

## Singing the Republic

With no première in sight either at the Opéra or the Opéra-Comique, Holmès's lavishly staged work was the closest there was to a major musical event at the beginning of the new season. Some journalists, such as Victor Wilder, returned to Paris especially to attend the affair. After all, the forty-two-year-old Augusta Holmès was one the more successful composers of her generation, with works performed regularly all over Paris, and one of her pieces was even part of the official concerts of the Exposition Universelle (see Appendix 1A, p. 314). The *Ode triomphale* was her first staged production and thus worthy of the attention of the music critics of Paris. The journalists however, were rather unhappy with the way they were treated. In the major Parisian theaters, the press had special privileges and were offered the best seats so that their coverage would be likely to be positive. But Berger and Alphand placed their political friends close to the stage and relegated the press to the back, where the acoustics were rather poor. Because of an overzealous employee, Wilder was even thrown out of the performance, while Francisque Sarcey, the eminent theater critic of *Le Temps*, was seated in the last row.[79] It speaks volumes for the high esteem in which Holmès was held at the time that the journalists rose above such bad treatment and wrote fair and usually laudatory reviews of the work, unless there were political reasons to do otherwise.

Politics did, indeed, color the press reception of the *Ode triomphale* in significant ways. Not surprisingly, the anti-republican press became vitriolic: the conservative and Catholic *L'Autorité* called it a credo of the new religion for republican freethinkers, where only Robespierre was missing, sneering over a quotation attributed wrongly to Holmès's *Ode*: "Certainly music, over the years, has always accompanied stupid words, but in this

---

78. Damon, "Théâtres," *L'Univers illustré* 32 (1889): 597–98, at 597: "ces merveilleuses fêtes antiques"; for positive references to the allusion to Gossec, see *Le Matin*, 12 Sept. 1889; *L'Éclair*, 12 Sept. 1889; *Le National*, 13 Sept. 1889; *Le Soir*, 13 Sept. 1889; *Le Temps*, 13 Sept. 1889; *Le Voltaire*, 13 Sept. 1889; *La Bataille*, 14 Sept. 1889.

79. "Gazette des coulisses," *La Bataille*, 14 Sept. 1889, 3.

case, Madame Augusta Holmès, author of the *Ode*, has had to exert herself strenuously but in vain to find an inspiration for the following silliness: 'Human knowledge has devalued the Christian tradition.' "[80] The *légitimiste Journal de Paris* criticized the *Ode* for celebrating the controversial Republic instead of using the occasion of a national event to include all French citizens in a festivity dedicated to industrial achievement throughout France, if not the world.[81] The monarchist and ultramontane *L'Univers* took issue with the religious overtones in the *Ode*, denouncing it as a parody of religious ceremony, an odious sacrilege adoring the goddess Reason.[82]

Similarly, journalists writing for the republican and socialist press kept close to the party line. *La Bataille* celebrated the *Ode* as the apotheosis of France and the glorification of the Republic; the *Écho de Paris* referred to the work's epic spirit, in particular in the vibrant strophes of Liberty (as this critic called La République); and the *Petit Parisien* opened its lead article with the sentence, "Never has a solemnity been more imposing, more brilliant, and more magnificent than this representation of the *Ode triomphale en l'honneur du Centenaire de 1789*, for which Mlle Augusta Holmès wrote the poem and the music."[83] Celebrating the *Ode* as a patriotic and truly French work, the republican press devoted much space to a description and evaluation of the piece and its reception. Both poem and music were examined in detail and with as much attention as an opera to see how Holmès achieved her "formidable task: to sing the Republic."[84] Journals praised her music as adequate to the task because she had simplified her normally more complex musical style for this mass spectacle without compromising artistic standards. The emotional content and quality of the music were described as being an important element in the overall experience. *Le Rappel* applauded the "male voice" of the "redeeming Republic" (gendering the speech as nobly masculine, even though sung by an alto),

---

80. Destrelle, "L'Ode," *L'Autorité*, 14 Sept. 1889, 2: "Certes, la musique s'est, de tout temps, accommodée de paroles stupides, mais, pour le coup, Mme Augusta Holmès, auteur de l'*Ode*, a dû se battre furieusement les flancs pour trouver une inspiration sur cette niaiserie: 'La science de l'homme a démonétisé la tradition chrétienne.'" This sentence can be found neither in the autograph nor the printed version of either libretto or score.

81. "A travers l'Exposition; L'Ode triomphale de l'Exposition," *Journal de Paris*, 15 Sept. 1889, 3.

82. Auguste Roussel, "Leur Religion," *L'Univers*, 13 Sept. 1889, 1.

83. "L'Ode triomphale," *Le Petit Parisien*, 13 Sept. 1889, 1–2, at 1: "Jamais solennité n'a été plus imposante, plus éclatante et plus magnifique que cette représentation de l'Ode triomphale en l'honneur du Centenaire de 1789, dont Mlle Augusta Holmès a écrit le poème et la musique."

84. Charles Martel [Charles Demestre], "La Soirée d'hier," *La Justice*, 12 Sept. 1889, 3: "cette tâche formidable: chanter la République."

and *Le Voltaire* went as far as to describe the final chorus as "a patriotic 'hosannah.' "[85]

A variety of journals debated whether the final chorus of the *Ode triomphale* should have followed Gossec's model by being a rendition of the *Marseillaise*, or whether Holmès should at least have quoted its melody. For some, her final chorus was too close to the sounds of the British national anthem, "God Save the Queen," and thus smacked of *légitimiste* undertones.[86] Not only that, but any British connection would still have been unwelcome for patriotic reasons. Victor Wilder wished for a piece in a more popular style akin to the *Marseillaise*, as did Léon Kerst from *Le Petit Journal.* The reporter from *La République française* hoped for the *Marseillaise* itself as the final musical statement, while, conversely, the journalist from *Le Voltaire* congratulated Holmès for having resisted the urge to include it.[87] Alphand and Berger, in the end, sided with the journalist of *La République française* and, for the third, popular performance, they tacked on the *Marseillaise*—"saluted by a triple salvo of applause"—at the end of the performance of the *Ode triomphale.*[88] Republican politics had won the day over artistic concerns.

Indeed, the musical Centenary celebrations added another Republican edge to the commemoration of the events of 1789 that related it to, and reinforced, the message of the solemn events in the Panthéon on 4 August 1889. If the latter ceremony at the Panthéon reminded the citizens of the Third Republic that the First Republic was based on the blood and suffering of patriotic soldiers, Holmès's cantata celebrated the glory and victory of liberty as a signpost towards universal republicanism led by France. Instead of the overt political and nationalist rhetoric in the speeches during the banquet of mayors on 18 August and the inauguration of the monument to the Republic on 21 September, Holmès's cantata shifted the discourse from party politics into a unifying cult of France and Republicanism, fusing all ages and all professions into one people. That she aimed at moving the cantata away from the specifics of political events

---

85. Émile Marsy, "Les Théâtres," *Le Rappel*, 13 Sept. 1889, 3: "la République rédemptrice apparaît! Sa mâle voix, en une large mélopée, appelle les hommes à la concorde"; A. D., "Le Triomphe de la République: *L'Ode triomphale*," *Le Voltaire*, 13 Sept. 1889, 1: "un 'hosannah' patriotique."

86. See, for example, Martel, "La Soirée d'hier," 3: "J'aurais aimé moins entendre le *God save the Queen*"; Le Souffleur, "Les Premières," *La République française*, 12 Sept. 1889, 3–4, at 4: "faisant penser au *God Save* cher au 'loyalistes' anglais."

87. Victor Wilder, "Premières représentations," *Gil Blas*, 13 Sept. 1889, 3; Léon Kerst, "Premières représentations," *Le Petit Journal*, 13 Sept. 1889, 3; Le Souffleur, "Les Premières," 3–4; H. C., "Le Triomphe de la République: Le poème et la partition," 2.

88. "Courrier des Théâtres," *Le Figaro*, 15 Sept. 1889, 3: "saluée par une triple salve d'applaudissements."

becomes clear in her substituting one veiled figure for the two that were in her original draft.[89] In this draft, two women had represented Alsace and Lorraine, lost to imperial Germany in 1870; now the one figure was the "universal Republic." Whether this change was requested by the commission or was Holmès's own revision, it turned the *Ode triomphale* away from the specific political concerns of *Revanchisme* and into a more universal ceremony ringing in the more conciliatory years of the *Ralliément* between the Conservatives and the moderate Republicans in the early 1890s, before the Dreyfus Affair would bring new strife. In that sense, Holmès's decision to avoid all reference to the *Marseillaise* and instead write a choral hymn in a more solemn character reflected the political realignments that were taking place during the time of the Exposition Universelle. Indeed, of all the centenary celebrations in 1889, that of Augusta Holmès was not only the most lavishly produced—save the Exposition itself—but surely also the one most in tune with the political developments of late 1889.

## The Republic's Muse

If the journalists were divided along political lines in their assessment of the *Ode triomphale*, they were more unified in their keen interest in the sex of the author of such a large-scale work. Some of the journalists celebrated Augusta Holmès as a "Republican Muse,"[90] while other writers wondered whether her sex was not a clever ploy by the organizers. The British writer for *The Musical Times* reported with some cynicism:

> The Republic having been always symbolized by a female figure, it was obviously appropriate as well as chivalrous on the part of the Municipal Council of Paris to entrust to a lady the composition of the ode "Le triomphe de la République," which, with all magnificence of scenic pomp, was performed at the Palais de l'Industrie, on Wednesday, the 11th ult.[91]

But in the eyes of her fellow composer, Alfred Bruneau, she was a veritable heroine: her bypassing of the cantata competition represented a truly

---

89. Holmès, "Fêtes du Centenaire de la République," *F-Pn*, Réserve ThB 56 (2)C.

90. L'Angely [Adolphe Brisson], "Fêtes du Centenaire," *L'Estafette*, 13 Sept. 1889, 1–2, at 2: "la grande Muse républicaine"; Camille Saint-Saëns, "L'Ode triomphale," *Le Rappel*, 23 Sept. 1889 / 2 Vendémiaire an 98: "la République française a trouvé ce qu'il lui fallait: une Muse."

91. "Hoods and Falsehoods," *The Musical Times* 30 (1889): 590–94, at 591. See also Balthasar Claes [Camille Benoît], "Chronique parisienne," *Le Guide musical* 35 (1889): 220–21, at 220: "en choisissant une femme, on introduisait un élément d'intérêt et un piquant particuliers, choses dont l'art officiel a toujours eu grand besoin."

brilliant victory for artistic freedom and independence against state-sponsored bureaucracy. Bruneau concludes: "We owe to her delicate and feminine ardor the final collapse of one of the barriers built in hatred of our art by all-powerful mundanity."[92]

Questions of feminine delicacy and musical virility, which pervaded the discourse on women's contribution to French musical life in general, were particularly in the foreground in the discussions of so public and substantial a work as the *Ode triomphale*. Its performance within the Exposition Universelle and its unique character—a centenary celebration—made it a highly unusual work in terms of Paris's musical institutions. The wholly atypical nature of the piece—in terms of genre, location, and (female) composer—prompted an unusual degree of attention in the press. Indeed, it was probably because of these extraordinary circumstances that the *Ode triomphale* could become such a personal triumph for Augusta Holmès, placing her in the national and international spotlight in ways none of her earlier works had done. The notoriety she gained from it surely facilitated the acceptance of her opera, *La Montagne noire*, for performance at the Opéra six years later, in 1895. But this operatic première in the leading musical institution in France—only the fifth stage work by a woman composer performed there, after Élisabeth Jacquet de la Guerre's *Céphale et Procris* (1694), Mlle Duval's *opéra-ballet Les Génies* (1736), Mme Dévismes's *Praxilète ou La Ceinture* (1800) and Louise Bertin's *Esméralda* (1836)—had a very different outcome, bringing about the nadir of Holmès's impressive career.[93] All the same, 1889 proved a key year for her public image, for her contributions to the revolutionary festivities of the Centenary aligned her with the French Republic as one of her official composers. Overnight, Holmès had become herself a Marianne figure, leading the Republican arts to victory and glory.[94]

This created a conflict between the feminine imagery of Muse and Marianne on the one hand, and the virility associated with large-scale official art on the other. As Jann Pasler has shown, Holmès herself actively masculinized her appearance through her severe clothing in the mid-1880s—indeed, one reviewer of the dress rehearsal described Holmès's

92. Alfred Bruneau, "Musique," *La Revue indépendante*, Nov. 1889, 500–502, at 502: "Nous devons à son ardeur délicate et féminine le définitif écroulement d'une des barrières édifiées en la haine de notre art par la toute-puissante routine."

93. On the reception of *La Montagne noire*, see Henson, "In the House of Disillusion," 257–60. Henson (p. 261) rightly points out that Holmès rallied herself after the defeat at the Opéra. However, the lack of success of *La Montagne noire* tarnished the luster of her star in French public opinion.

94. In an explicit reference to Marianne in an article in *Le Figaro* (30 Aug. 1889) on the preparations for the performance of the *Ode*, the symbol of the French republic and Augusta Holmès are fused: "Marianne n'aura pas à se plaindre."

Figure 3.5. Paul Mervart, "Augusta Holmès," *L'Univers illustré* 32 (1889): 593.

"semi-masculine suit" as the "chic of virility so fashionable with certain women artists" (figure 3.5)—yet her behavior during the première was decidedly feminine, playing on French notions of honorable woman-hood.[95] Holmès's balancing act between femininity and masculinity is

95. Pasler, "The Ironies of Gender," 6. "L'Ode triomphale," *L'Éclair*, 12 Sept. 1889, 1–2, at 1: "un costume semi-masculin"; "ce chic de virilité si fort à la mode chez certaines

reflected in the press accounts of the performance and may have been one of the keys to her success: she was a serious composer, but also a well-bred woman.

Rare were reviews such as the one in *Le Petit Parisien*, which made no specific allusion—save through her name and the pronouns "she/her"—to the composer's sex, and instead engaged with the *Ode triomphale* in much the same way as any such work might have been covered in the French press.[96] For most journalists, it was an issue to be dealt with. Sometimes a play on words could draw attention to Holmès's femininity, as when Victor Wilder characterized her work as a revolutionary *sans-culottide*, "using the term without reference to the sex of the delightful and excellent artist"— which, of course, he then just had.[97] But save for one reviewer in *La Vie Parisienne*, who wrote, "Stick with doves and roses, Mademoiselle," critics were careful about how they handled the subject.[98] As the composer of the Republic's centenary music, she had to be taken seriously instead of being dismissed as simply a stereotypical "woman composer" of salon music and other delicate works.[99] Journalists employed several strategies to declare her the exception to the rule.

In some cases she was clearly a Marianne figure—even though she was not named as such—who saved the honor of French music. Edmond Stoullig claimed that "without the powerful conception of a truly gifted woman such as the author of *Lutèce* and *Les Argonautes*, we would doubtless have had some additional nautical celebration or fireworks; but music—and that would have been a pity—would not have been represented at the Centenary."[100] For others, her musical style was masculine, turning her into a male

femmes artistes." On French concepts of womanhood see Anne Martin-Fugier, *La Bourgeoise: Femme au temps de Paul Bourget* (Paris: Grasset, 1983).

96. Paul Ginisty, "L'Ode triomphale," *Le Petit Parisien*, 13 Sept. 1889, 1–2.

97. Victor Wilder, "Premières représentations," *Gil Blas*, 13 Sept. 1889, 3: "L'ode triomphale de mademoiselle Holmès est une *sans-culottide*, soit dit sans faire allusion au sexe de l'aimable et excellente artiste." Ingeborg Feilhauer cites another reference to the *sans-culottides* in the course of her discussion of the *Ode triomphale*. See Feilhauer, "Augusta Holmès (1847–1903): Biographie—Werkverzeichnis—Analysen" (master's thesis, University of Heidelberg, 1987), 62.

98. X., "Choses et autres," *Le Vie parisienne*, 27 (1889): 517: "Restez aux colombes et aux roses, mademoiselle."

99. On French notions of "woman composer," see Annegret Fauser, "Zwischen Professionalismus und Salon: Französische Musikerinnen des *Fin de siècle*," in *Professionalismus in der Musik*, ed. Christian Kaden and Volker Kalisch, 261–74 (Essen: Blaue Eule, 1998). See also Florence Launay, "Les Compositrices françaises de 1789 à 1914" (PhD diss., Université de Rennes 2, 2004), 40–85, 128–82.

100. Edmond Stoullig, "L'Ode triomphale," *Le National*, 11 Sept. 1889, 2: "Ainsi, sans la puissante conception d'une femme vraiment douée comme l'auteur de *Lutèce* et

composer. Thus Pougin deliberately gendered her male rather than describing her as a "musicienne": "I say expressly 'one of the *musiciens*' because the very vigorous, sometimes very powerful talent of Mlle Holmès gives, in an entirely exceptional way, short shrift to the qualities that women usually bring to the activity of musical composition."[101] "Virile" was one of the catchwords used to characterize Holmès and her music: Bicoquet called her a "women of powerful and virile talent," echoed by Hughes Imbert (writing of her "totally virile" talent), and sections of the *Ode triomphale* were declared as possessing "'virility'—if it is permitted to use this word in the case of Mme Augusta Holmès."[102] Her achievements were related to those of Hector Berlioz, one of the few French composers who had written similarly colossal works in recent history, with his Requiem and his *Symphonie funèbre et triomphale.*[103] Holmès's Wagnerian style and her doubling as poet and composer contributed to the masculine credentials and to her exceptional role in contemporary French music. Thus she is praised as the only composer— and a woman at that—in a capital with thousands of poets (read Vicaire) and hundreds of musicians (none of whom was able to set the cantata) who was a musician-poet in the vein of Homer, Berlioz, and Wagner.[104]

But Holmès was a woman and as such susceptible to feminine ways of action. She might have been a "servant to Wagner," but as a woman she was bound to be capricious and thus betray him with another man, cuckolding

des *Argonautes*, nous eussions eu sans doute quelque fête nautique, quelque feu d'artifice en plus; mais la musique—et c'eût été dommage—n'eût pas été représentée au Centenaire."

101. Arthur Pougin, "Semaine théâtrale," *Le Ménestrel* 55 (1889): 290–92, at 290: "Je dis expressément 'l'un des musiciens' parce que le talent très vigoureux, parfois très puissant de Mlle Holmès tranche d'une façon tout exceptionnelle avec les qualités que les femmes apportent d'ordinaire à l'exercice de la composition musicale."

102. Bicoquet, "La Soirée parisienne," *L'Écho de Paris*, 13 Sept. 1889, 3: "la femme au talent puissant et viril"; Hughes Imbert, "Ode triomphale," *La Musique des familles (Musique populaire)* 8 (1889): 386–89: "Le talent d'A. Holmès est absolument viril"; "L'Ode de Mme Holmès," *L'Éclair*, 13 Sept. 1889, 1: "de la 'virilité'—s'il est permis d'employer ce mot quand il s'agit de Mme Augusta Holmès."

103. H. C., "Le Triomphe de la République," 1: "Mlle Augusta Holmès a écrit une partition colossale, de dimension matérielle, et qui est peut-être ce qu'il y a été composé de plus considérable depuis Berlioz, son *Requiem* et sa *Symphonie funèbre et triomphale.*"

104. Chamillac, "L'Ode triomphale d'Augusta Holmès," 204: "Depuis Homère, qui s'accompagnait sur la lyre en chantant les exploits de ses héros, jusqu'à Wagner et à Berlioz . . . ce furent toujours de rares personnalités artistiques, d'une incontestable élite, qui sut allier le don de Poésie au don de la Musique. . . . Il faut une puissance d'organisation miraculeuse; or, dans notre Paris où l'on compte les poètes par milliers et les musiciens par centaines, il ne se trouve guère qu'un seul compositeur-poète hors ligne, et ce compositeur-poète est une femme, Mlle Augusta Holmès."

the German composer with the French Gounod or Massenet.[105] Her shift in musical style for the *Ode triomphale*, which privileged a more traditionally French idiom over the more Wagnerian complexities she usually favored, were thus represented as changes in sexual relationships that turned Holmès into the promiscuous mistress of great men instead of a responsible composer in her own right. But her fickleness aside, she was a charming woman, which is why her (temporary) grandeur could also be perceived as a clever feminine trick rather than artistic achievement. Charles Darcours thus compares the *Ode triomphale* to an enlarged photograph that would have been better off being reduced in size.[106] In the end, however, Holmès herself behaved in as womanly a manner as only a well-bred society lady would do: she refused for some fifteen minutes to be called on stage to take her bow, only accepting this personal honor when the audience threatened to destroy the decoration of the hall. On stage, she burst into tears before receiving a kiss from Jean Charles Alphand, to the great delight of the spectators.[107] Holmès may have dressed like a man, composed like a man, and organized the performance like a man, but in the final analysis, so her critics implied, she proved to be a mere woman.

Six weeks after the première of the *Ode triomphale*, Julien Tiersot drove the point home in a sarcastic report in which he compared the seemingly weak efforts of a Tahitian woman composer at the Colonial Exhibition with Holmès's contribution to the centenary celebrations: "this composer with her olive and chocolate coloring is a woman, no more and no less, than Mme Augusta Holmès. I could, at least for the sake of its curiosity value, give a transcription of this Tahitian *ode triomphale*, but it would have been too long for this review, and I also could not catch it in its entirety."[108] The Tahitian composer, like Holmès, composed "official" music—and not very

105. Two critics play on Holmès's unfaithfulness to Wagner. See "L'Ode de Mme Holmès," *L'Éclair*, 13 Sept. 1889, 1; and Gérôme, "Courrier de Paris," *L'Univers illustré* 32 (1889): 594–95, at 594.

106. Charles Darcours [Charles Réty], "Notes de Musique," *Le Figaro*, 18 Sept. 1889, 6: "Vous avez devant les yeux une charmante image: le photographe arrive et braque son objectif: il va l'agrandir ou la réduire à volonté. L'œuvre de Mme Augusta Holmès a été agrandie outre mesure, tandis qu'elle n'avait rien perdu au rapetissement."

107. For a detailed report of the scene, see, for example: "Ode triomphale," *Le Matin*, 12 Sept. 1889, 1; "Au jour le jour," *Le Temps*, 12 Sept. 1889, 3; Edmond Jacques, "Musique," *L'Intransigeant*, 13 Sept. 1889, 2; "Spectacles et concerts," *Le Soir*, 13 Sept. 1889, 2. On Alphand's role in republican ceremonies, see Ihl, *La Fête républicaine*, 262–65.

108. Julien Tiersot, "Promenades musicales à l'Exposition: Les Nègres," *Le Ménestrel* 55 (1889): 331–32, at 331: "Et ce qu'il y a de plus singulier, c'est que ce compositeur au teint d'olive et de chocolat est une femme, ni plus ni moins que Mlle Augusta Holmès. Je

good at that—which was neither historically correct nor autochtone (because influenced by European psalm settings). Given Tiersot's generally careful assessment of music, his clear link between what he perceived as the most primitive of musical arts—that of black musicians—and the woman composer of the day leaves little doubt that Holmès (because she is a woman) should be counted among the musical savages. With this comparison he played on nineteenth-century race theories that equated blacks and women.[109]

Saint-Saëns similarly played on exotic references when he wrote what on the surface seems like a laudatory article about the composer of the *Ode triomphale*, starting with reminiscences of her as a "young Venus" who inspired her surrounding admirers in the salon world of the 1860s and 1870s. But then, he recalls, she became fanciful and "developped a passion for Kali, the Indian Venus, the goddess of love and death," improvising exotic music at the piano. After discovering in an art exhibition a statue of Kali that was colored blue from head to toe rather than corresponding to French ideals of beauty, Holmès became an "ex-priestess" of the goddess and went on to write such works as the *Ode*.[110] Saint-Saëns's ambiguous public homage to a woman crowned her a Muse because there was no (male) God to compose the cantata. It was followed by a homage-poem in alexandrines, sent to Holmès privately in November.[111] While praising her beauty and talent, he played nevertheless on another trope of femininity, that of woman's closeness to nature: Holmès is like the forest moved by great winds, the cicada inspired by the sun. Logic, rationality, construction, and learnedness, however, are conspicuously absent from his—and as far as he is concerned, her—vocabulary.[112] Her talent (Saint-Saëns withholds the word "genius"—albeit in the sense of "spirit" rather than "brilliance"—to

pourrais, au moins à titre de curiosité, donner cette ode triomphale taïtienne; mais, en outre que ce morceau est trop développé pour le cadre restreint de ces études, je n'ai pas pu l'avoir d'une façon absolument complète."

109. On the equation of blacks and women in French nineteenth-century thought, see William B. Cohen, *The French Encounter with Africans: White Responses to Blacks, 1530–1880* (Bloomington and London: Indiana University Press, 1980), 236–45.

110. Saint-Saëns, "L'Ode triomphale": "Elle se prit un jour d'une belle passion pour Kali, la Vénus indienne, la déesse de l'amour et de la mort . . . voici l'ex-prêtresse de Kali."

111. Ibid.: "Il fallait plus qu'un homme pour chanter le centenaire; à défaut d'un dieu impossible à rencontrer, la République française a trouvé ce qu'il lui fallait: une Muse."

112. On the gendering of nature and culture, see Marcia J. Citron, *Gender and the Musical Canon* (Cambridge: Cambridge University Press, 1993), esp. 44–54.

characterize the fatherland) is gendered as nature-based, even when she roars like a tiger:

A Augusta Holmès

L'Irlande t'a donnée à nous. Ta
    gloire est telle
Qu'un double rayon brille à ton
    front: Astarté,
Aussi belle que toi, ne savait
    qu'être belle.
Sapho qui t'égalait n'avait pas ta
    beauté.

Tu chantes, comme vibre une
    forêt superbe
 Qu'agite la fureur des grands
    vents déchaînés;
Comme aux feux de midi la
    cigale dans l'herbe;
Comme sur un récif les flots
    désordonnés.

Ton talent réunit la force à la
    souplesse,
Et d'une défaillance il n'a pas à
    rougir;
Si tu peux gazouiller comme en son
    allégresse
L'oiseau des champs, tu sais
    comme un tigre rugir.

La République, l'Art et l'Amour
    ont ensemble
Mêlé leurs voix, guidés par ta
    puissante main.
Cette main qui jamais n'hésite
    ni ne tremble,
Que la lyre soit d'or ou qu'elle
    soit d'airain.

Tout un peuple a chanté l'Hymne
    de délivrance,
Vignerons, matelots, artisans,
    laboureurs,

To Augusta Holmès

Ireland has given you to us. Your glory
    is such
That a double ray shines on your fore-
    head: Astarte,
As beautiful as you, knew only how to be
    beautiful.
Sappho, your equal, could not rival your
    beauty.

You sing as a superb forest would vibrate

When the fury of great unleashed winds
    move it;
Like the cicada in the grass in the heat
    of noon;
Like the jumbled floods on a reef.

Your talent unites force and agility.

And never does a fault cause you to
    blush;
While you can chirp like the bird in the
    fields
In its delight, you know how to roar like
    a tiger.

The Republic, Art and Love mixed
    together
Their voices, guided by your powerful
    hand.
This hand which never hesitates or
    trembles,
Whether the lyre is made of gold or ore.

The whole people has sung the Hymn of
    delivery,
Winegrowers, sailors, artisans, workers.

| | |
|---|---|
| Artistes et savants, parure de la France, | Artists and philosophers, the gems of France, |
| Les guerriers, les enfants qui leur jettent des fleurs. | The soldiers, the flower-throwing children. |
| | |
| A ta flamme allumée en brillante spirale | Alighted at your flame in a brilliant spiral, |
| La flamme des trépieds sur tous les fronts à lui, | The flame of the tripods on all of its fronts, |
| Et nous avons trouvé dans l'Ode Triomphale | And we have found in the *Ode triomphale* |
| Pour le grand Centenaire un chant digne de lui. | For the great Centenary a song worthy of it. |
| | |
| La Patrie adorée, au tout puissant génie | The adored fatherland with its all-powerful genius |
| Te presse avec amour sur son cœur glorieux. | With love clasps you at its glorious heart. |
| Sois par nous acclamée et par elle bénie, | Be acclaimed by us and blessed by it, |
| Et puisse ton étoile illuminer les cieux! | And may your star illuminate the heavens! |
| Cadix, 7 novembre 1889<br>C. Saint-Saëns | Cadiz, 7 November 1889<br>Camille Saint-Saëns[113] |

Saint-Saëns's poem, with its references to the Centenary, the Republic, and "la patrie adorée," turned Holmès into a priestess of France, a role well in line with both the subservient role of women and the quasi-religious nature of Holmès's own *Ode triomphale.*

While, on the surface, the political reception and the issue of Holmès's gender seem to have precious little to do with each other, they are, in fact, intimately linked on a more structural level. If the Republic as a nation was to be celebrated in ritual form, taking the renascent and competing modes of festivities of the 1870s to a new level of realigned homage, then the new cult needed someone to "attend" it. A male author would have been too much of an individualist creator, whereas a woman could be fused with the symbolic figure of Marianne. Indeed, the role of Marianne as a symbol of the French Republic slowly rose to prominence in the late 1880s, and

113. Camille Saint-Saëns, "A Augusta Holmès," manuscript poem, *F-Pn*, Département de la Musique (shelf mark: *l.a. Saint-Saëns 75*). A pencil note on the poem indicates that it was found in the papers of Augusta Holmès after her death.

Holmès fitted the mold perfectly.[114] She was no shrinking violet but a battle-experienced composer in the middle of her career. Devoted to the cause of France, she and her music could easily be co-opted to serve as a modern Marianne whom—as Saint-Saëns put it in the last stanza of his poem—"the adored fatherland with its all-powerful genius,/With love clasps . . . at its glorious heart." After the performance of the *Ode triomphale*, it was the ceremonial master of the Republican festivities, Jean Charles Alphand, who embraced Holmès, the handmaid of the Republic.

114. Maurice Agulhon has dedicated two volumes to the changing fate of Marianne in the context of modern France. See especially his second volume, *Marianne au pouvoir: L'imagerie et la symbolique républicaines de 1880 à 1914* (Paris: Flammarion, 1989).

*Chapter 4*

# French Encounters with the Far East

Although the various concerts, opera performances, and centennial festivities of and around the 1889 Exposition Universelle contributed to the unparalleled presence of music at a World's Fair, it was the music of cultures perceived as "Other"—whether European folk music or more exotic species from the Near and Far East—that most excited visitors and commentators alike. Romanians, Hungarians, Arabs, and Gypsies enriched the sonic landscape of the many restaurants and cafés scattered along the Champ de Mars, while sounds never heard before by (most) European ears, such as those of the Javanese gamelan and the Vietnamese Theater, brought new thrills to the listening experience of the Exposition by providing a new soundtrack for the by now all-too-familiar exoticisms of prints, novels, theater, and popular entertainment. These sounds, in particular those that pervaded the colonial exhibition of the Esplanade des Invalides, generated sonic encounters of the "Other" that redrew the boundaries of musical experience both of musicians like Claude Debussy and of the wider Exposition audience. Listeners whose musical experience of the East thus far was one created by the imaginary world of European exoticism now came face to face with "the real thing," usually for the first time. The two sonic worlds proved irreconcilable. This gap between the imagined and the real became one of the main threads of the sonic perception and reception of non-Western music during the 1889 Exposition Universelle. The music of other cultures was often too unfamiliar to be enjoyed comfortably as mere sonic background to the sampling of local foods in cafés. Visitors also encountered the jarring reality of sounds that accompanied the spectacle of the exotic, and began listening actively to these "new" and exotic musics that had come from afar to the Exposition Universelle on the banks of the Seine. The reactions were not always positive.

## Musical Exoticism and the Listening Imagination

It is difficult to gauge the listening imagination and sonic experience of European listeners in the late 1880s from the vantage point of the early twentieth-first century. But although we can neither recreate the sonic horizon of expectation for an imagined 1889 listener, nor listen ourselves to music with 1889 ears (an issue discussed further in chapter 6), we can nevertheless rely on circumstantial evidence that may allow us to evaluate to some degree these European encounters with the musical "Other."[1] It is safe to assume that the language of tonal Western music was an experience shared by most nineteenth-century Europeans, whether through singing in primary-school education or in church; by exposure to military bands, barrel-organs, or music in popular entertainment such as fairs and *cafés-concerts*; or through participation in choral societies or municipal bands. Furthermore, the musical horizons of the middle and upper classes enclosed the ubiquitous piano and its repertoire, supplemented by the traditional visits to the opera house and concert hall.

Within the middle-class experience of music, musical exoticism was located mainly in piano pieces, songs and *romances*, symphonic poems, operas, and operettas.[2] Songs such as "La Captive" by Hector Berlioz (1832) and operas such as *Lakmé* (1883) by Léo Delibes, plus the title-pages of sheet music—as for example that for Loïsa Puget's "La Bayadère" (figure 4.1)—and opera posters since the 1850s, offered all the trappings of literary and visual exoticism. The actual music, however, rarely transgressed the boundaries of nineteenth-century European tonality and musical forms. Musical signifiers of generic exoticism provided *couleur locale* as surface ornamentation in the form of characteristic melodic turns with augmented seconds, the use of modal or pentatonic scales in the musical foreground, the pervasiveness of dance rhythms such as the *habañera*, and the employment of unusual instruments (e.g., saxophone and percussion) over generally lush instrumentation.[3] In opera, exotic moments contained in the plot could provide the justification for musical excess, but only within Western musical bounds, whether in the use of sensuous orchestration and unabashedly melodic voluptuousness (as in Jules Massenet's "Le Paradis d'Indra" in *Le Roi de Lahore,* or Camille Saint-Saëns's "Bacchanale" in *Samson et Dalila,* both 1877), or in musical representation of sexual excess, as for example Herod's masturbatory "Vision fugitive" in Massenet's *Hérodiade* (1881) or Thaïs's striptease in "Les Amours d'Aphrodite" in the eponymous opera (1894).[4] Here the safe and official setting of operatic

1. See also my "Alterity, Nation and Identity: Some Musicological Paradoxes," *Context: A Journal of Music Research,* no. 21 (Spring 2001): 1–18.

2. On musical exoticism see the bibliographies in Ralph P. Locke, "Exoticism" and "Orientalism," in *NGr2.* See also Gerry Farrell, *Indian Music and the West* (Oxford: Clarendon Press, 1997).

3. See the classic article by Ralph P. Locke, "Constructing the Oriental 'Other': Saint-Saëns's *Samson et Dalila,*" *Cambridge Opera Journal* 3 (1991): 261–302.

4. Clair Rowden, *Republican Morality and Catholic Tradition in the Opera: Massenet's "Hérodiade" and "Thaïs"* (Weinsberg: Musik-Edition Lucie Galland, 2004). See also Gilles

# LA BAYADÈRE.

Figure 4.1. Title page of Loïsa Puget's song "La Bayadère"
(Paris: J. Meissonnier, 1839).

convention allowed the inclusion of materials that, in other contexts, might have gone beyond the limits of bourgeois acceptability. Indeed, the musical exoticism of Massenet and his fellow composers could be paralleled with the often sexually evocative paintings of a Jean-Léon Gérôme or Henri Regnault, whose academic treatment of the subjects permitted their exhibition in the official *salons* despite their strong erotic overtones.[5]

Travel, military campaigns, and ethnographic musical research added further layers to the musical exoticism of nineteenth-century France. Thus "exotic" works could receive additional kudos through the inclusion of authentic materials in the same way that Eugène Fromentin's paintings were validated by way of his travels to the Middle East.[6] In opera, local and/or historical authenticity in the stage sets had been a tradition since the 1820s, when stage designers were widely expected to undertake a ritual research trip either to an actual location or into the archives.[7] In music more generally, such signifiers of authenticity usually consisted of the inclusion of one or several exotic melodic fragments into an otherwise undisturbed Western structure.[8] Félicien David's *ode-symphonie, Le Désert* (1844), famously integrated musical elements such as the *Chant du muezzin* that the composer had collected during his stay in the Middle East.[9] After that, many a musician went to the Maghreb for travel and

de Van, "Fin de Siècle Exoticism and the Meaning of the Far Away," *Opera Quarterly* 11, no. 3 (1995): 77–94, in particular for his discussion of exoticism as metaphor of desire (pp. 78 and 92).

5. It is not by chance that Ralph Locke selected images from both painters to illustrate his article "Constructing the Oriental 'Other.'" On Gérôme, see Gerald M. Ackerman, *Jean-Léon Gérôme: Monographie révisée, catalogue raisonné mis à jour* (Courbevoie: ACR, 2000).

6. Sylviane Leprun, *Le Théâtre des Colonies: Scénographie, acteurs et discours de l'imaginaire dans les expositions, 1855–1937* (Paris: Éditions l'Harmattan, 1986), 78–83. For further discussion of this issue, see chapter 5, pp. 216–41.

7. Van, "Fin de Siècle Exoticism and the Meaning of the Far Away," 80; Nicole Wild, "Eugène Lacoste et la création de *Henry VIII* à l'Opéra de Paris en 1883," in *Échos de France et d'Italie: Liber amicorum Yves Gérard*, ed. Marie-Claire Mussat, Jean Mongrédien, and Jean-Michel Nectoux, 213–32 (Paris: Buchet/Chastel, 1997).

8. On "authenticity" and its problematic use in the context of music, see the collection edited by Nicholas Kenyon, *Authenticity and Early Music* (Oxford: Oxford University Press, 1988). The concept is explored with respect to the early-music movement, but similar issues come to the surface in the context of "authentic" non-Western music and its appropriation in European concert repertoire. See also Jann Pasler, "Reinterpreting Indian Music: Albert Roussel and Maurice Delage," in *Music-Cultures in Contact: Convergences and Collisions*, ed. Margaret J. Kartomi and Stephen Blum, 122–57 (Basel: Gordon and Breach, 1994).

9. Ralph P. Locke, "Cutthroats and Casbah Dancers, Muezzins and Timeless Sands: Musical Images of the Middle East," in *The Exotic in Western Music*, ed. Jonathan Bellman (Boston: Northeastern University Press, 1998), 126–33.

relaxation (Camille Saint-Saëns in particular), where they could hear Arab music first hand. Closer to the 1889 Exposition Universelle was Louis-Albert Bourgault-Ducoudray's exotic symphonic poem, *Rapsodie cambodgienne* (1882), which became a much-performed staple of the French concert repertoire. Bourgault-Ducoudray had previously visited Indochina on a cultural mission, and his orchestral work was received as presenting "musical souvenirs" from this voyage to his audience in the manner of a travel writer presenting his impressions to a Parisian readership, who consumed such tales eagerly, whether in the form of illustrated reports in journals such as *L'Illustration* or in book form. This was reinforced by the inclusion, in the score, of the program associated with the piece, describing a rural water festival, *Khénh Préavossa* (*La Fête des eaux*), in the manner of travel reports.[10]

This form of artistic appropriation of non-Western musical material for the purpose of creating a more "authentic" musical experience intersected with scholarly endeavors starting in the second half of the eighteenth century. While reference to earlier and non-Western musical cultures formed an obligatory part of the fledgling discipline of music history, expeditions such as Napoléon's campaign in Egypt spearheaded the collecting and analyzing of instruments and of transcriptions of indigenous musics.[11] Journals such as *L'Illustration* contributed to this cache of "authentic" knowledge through their visual representations of exotic musicians. Accompanying texts, however, normally avoided any specific reference to the sonic side of the image.[12] Musical (rather than visual) knowledge remained the purview of a relatively small group of musicians and music historians. Music histories for a general audience rarely included the type of information on non-Western music that a more specialized reader might have found in, for example, Joseph-Marie Amiot's *Mémoire sur la musique des Chinois* (1779) or Juste-Adrien de La Fage's *Histoire générale de la musique et de la danse* (1844).[13] These more

10. Louis-Albert Bourgault-Ducoudray, Preface to the full score of *Rapsodie cambodgienne* (Paris: Au Ménestrel, n.d.).

11. See Philip V. Bohlman, "The European Discovery of Music in the Islamic World and the 'Non-Western' in 19th-Century Music History," *Journal of Musicology* 5 (1987): 147–63; Philippe Vendrix, *Aux Origines d'une discipline historique: La musique et son histoire en France aux XVIIe et XVIIIe siècles* (Liège: Bibliothèque de la Faculté de Philosophie et Lettres de l'Université de Liège, 1993); Tom Cooper, "French Empire and Musical Exoticism to the End of the Nineteenth Century" (PhD diss., Liverpool University, 1998).

12. Thumbnail-size images of all musical illustrations in *L'Illustration* between 1843 and 1899 are given in Robert H. Cohen et al., *Les Gravures musicales dans l'Illustration, 1843–1899* (Quebec: Les Presses de l'Université Laval, 1982–83).

13. Joseph-Marie Amiot, *Mémoire sur la musique des Chinois, tant anciens que modernes* (Paris, 1779; reprint, Geneva: Minkoff, 1973); Juste Adrien de La Fage, *Histoire générale de la musique et de la danse* (Paris: Au Comptoir des Imprimeurs Unis, 1844). See also Philip V.

specialized publications did, however, alert their readers to the gap between the fantasy world of musical exoticism and the actual music of the exotic Others, offering windows to those different musical worlds and their sounds.

Indeed, the reality check at the 1889 Exposition Universelle proved to be somewhat unsettling for many a listener who had become accustomed to the exoticist sounds of composers such as Massenet. Musical exoticism thus provided the referential framework against which the actual music of the "Other" could and would be judged. When confronted with Arab music accompanying the Egyptian belly dancers at the Exposition Universelle, for example, the journalist for *La Vie parisienne* exclaimed:

> Those who dream somewhat, who have fabricated for themselves an ideal Orient through the conventional lens of artists, are really disappointed. Hey! Is this the dance of the Egyptians? Could it be such rude spectacles that the potentates of the crescent-moon relish in the secrecy of their harem? . . . How far from the smallest oriental ballet in the Opera, how vulgar, how unlike the descriptions of writers or the striking images of the painters are these obscene calls of girls moving rhythmically to a barbaric motive, the precise opposite of those accents that our Western musical language applies to express the infinite voluptuousness of the flesh. . . .

> Ceux qui rêvent quelque peu, qui se sont fabriqué un Orient idéal à travers l'optique conventionnelle des artistes, éprouvent une déception véritable. Hé quoi! C'est cela, la danse des almées? C'est à ces grossiers spectacles que les potentats du Croissant se délectent dans le mystère des harems? . . . Combien éloignés du moindre ballet oriental à l'Opéra, combien vulgaires, combien différentes des descriptions d'écrivains ou des fulgurantes toiles de peintres sont ces obscènes appels de filles rythmés sur un motif barbare, antipode des accents que nos langues musicales d'Occident appliquent à l'expression des voluptés infinies de la chair. . . . [14]

Bohlman, "Representation and Cultural Critique in the History of Ethnomusicology," in *Comparative Musicology and Anthropology of Music: Essays on the History of Ethnomusicology*, ed. Bruno Nettl and Philip V. Bohlman, 131–51 (Chicago and London: University of Chicago Press, 1991); Annegret Fauser, "Gendering the Nations: The Ideologies of French Discourse on Music (1870–1914)," in *Musical Constructions of Nationalism: Essays on the History and Ideology of European Musical Culture, 1800–1945*, ed. Michael Murphy and Harry White, 72–103 (Cork: Cork University Press, 2001); Fauser, "World Fair— World Music: Musical Politics in 1889 Paris," in *Nineteenth-Century Music Studies*, ed. Jim Samson and Bennett Zon, 179–223 (London and Aldershot: Ashgate, 2002).

    14. Ibrahim, "A l'Exposition: La danse du ventre," *La Vie parisienne* 27 (1889): 333.

The entire article plays with the contrast of civilized West and barbaric East (at least as far as shown in the Exposition Universelle), whose crassness destroyed any mythologizing concept a Westerner (Parisian) might have developed of the Orient. This evaluation—neither ironic nor unique— reflects value judgments that were common in musical aesthetics during the nineteenth century. Models of progress—whether linear or circular— located the highest achievement in music in contemporary Europe. Earlier and non-Western musics were but primitive and preliminary forms in a historical process tending toward greater sophistication.[15] In terms of such an aesthetic model, the exotic as mediated through Western musical language was superior to the original. Thus Egyptian music would not only have sounded barbaric to this Parisian's ears; it also fulfilled its role as an exhibit of the cultural inferiority of non-Western music when compared to the ballets at the Opéra. Indeed, one of the recurring themes of the encounter with the musical Other is that of comparison, whether negative, as in the extract above, or positive, as in the case of Debussy's evaluation of Vietnamese music. By relating it to what was familiar, the encounter with music from a different culture seemed to have been enabled while, at the same time, being contained.

Prior to the 1889 Exposition Universelle, picturesque and exotic music would be heard only on rare occasions—in particular, during the 1867 and 1878 Expositions Universelles, where Gypsy bands were all the rage—and in some *café-concert* performances. They were certainly not widely accessible.[16] Sometimes music formed part of the exhibits of African tribes in the Jardin d'Acclimatation (which began in 1877), but it seems to have been received as primitive African sounds on drums rather than as music in the emphatic sense of Western aesthetics.[17] Such spectacles put music in a "natural" environment of tribal life, in contrast to the *café-concert* performances of the 1889 Exposition Universelle. Furthermore, these sporadic events represent mainly Parisian entertainment. Exotic music rarely found its way to French (or European) ears in general, save for occasional touring events and locally specific chance encounters with "Others," for example in port cities such as Marseilles.

15. Jann Pasler, "Paris: Conflicting Notions of Progress," in *Man and Music: The Late Romantic Era from the Mid-19th Century to World War I*, ed. Jim Samson, 389–426 (London: Macmillan, 1991).

16. See Zeynep Çelik, *Displaying the Orient: Architecture of Islam at Nineteenth-Century World's Fairs* (Berkeley, Los Angeles, and Oxford: University of California Press, 1992), 23–29.

17. On the exhibitions of African and other "exotic" people, see Nicolas Bancel et al., eds., *Zoos humains: De la Vénus hottentote aux Reality Shows* (Paris: La Découverte, 2002). See also Timothy Mitchell, "Orientalism and the Exhibitionary Order," in *Colonialism and Culture*, ed. Nicholas B. Dirks, 289–317 (Ann Arbor: University of Michigan Press, 1995).

Therefore the majority of listeners in 1889 would probably never have had any prior contact with non-Western music, and musical concepts of the Orient would have been shaped through exoticism in opera, song, and concert in the form of surface color within the framework of a familiar tonal language. To be sure, a treacherous familiarity with apparently exotic art had been fanned through decades of cultural consumption by an increasingly large middle class that collected sheet music and read travel novels such as Jules Verne's *Le Tour du monde en 80 jours* (1873) or Pierre Loti's *Madame Chrysanthème* (1888).[18] But even educated musicians had difficulties adjusting their ears to the reality of the exotic sound world, as becomes clear in Camille Saint-Saëns's attempts to engage with the "atrocious" sounds of the Vietnamese Theater.[19] Thus the reception of non-Western music can be broadly characterized as one shaped by the embodiment of Western music through musical and cultural practice whether on the part of listeners or of professional musicians.[20]

## Music and Race in French Nineteenth-Century Musicography

Julien Tiersot's well-known opening gambit for his reports about music at the Exposition Universelle, which were serialized in *Le Ménestrel* between May and November 1889, encapsulates these issues:

> Rome is no longer in Rome; Cairo no longer in Egypt and Java no longer in the East Indies. All of that has come to the Champ de Mars, on the Esplanade des Invalides, and to the Trocadéro. Thus, without leaving Paris, we have the leisure to study for the next six months, at least in their exterior manifestations, the practices and customs of the most distant peoples. And since music is one of the most striking manifestations of them all, none of the exotic visitors of the Exhibition have let themselves forget it. Without speaking of the large concerts of orchestral music, vocal music, and organ music which were just opened at the Trocadéro, we find, in the various sections of the Exposition Universelle, many opportunities to study the different musical forms specific to those races who understand art in a

---

18. On the popularity of travel topics in fin-de-siècle novels and its relating to newspaper reports, see Anne-Marie Thiesse, *Le Roman du quotidien: Lecteurs et lectures populaires à la Belle Époque* (Paris: Le Chemin Vert, 1984).

19. Camille Saint-Saëns, "Le *Rappel* à l'Exposition: Les instruments de musique," third part, *Le Rappel*, 10 Oct. 1889 / 19 Vendémiaire an 98, 1–2: "[L]a véritable musique chinoise est atroce à nos oreilles, mais quand on prend la peine de l'étudier, elle offre un grand intérêt, qui fait ici [in Vietnamese music] défaut."

20. I employ the term "embodiment" with respect to music in the anthropological sense outlined by Christian Kaden, *Des Lebens wilder Kreis: Musik im Zivilisationsprozeß* (Kassel: Bärenreiter-Verlag, 1993).

very different fashion from ours; and even when these forms should be considered by us as characterising an inferior art, we nevertheless have to pay attention to them, because they show us new aspects of music, and are probably infinitely closer to the origins of our art that, today, is so complex and refined.

Rome n'est plus dans Rome; le Caire n'est plus en Égypte, ni l'île de Java dans les Indes orientales. Tout cela est venu au Champ de Mars, sur l'Esplanade des Invalides et au Trocadéro. De sorte que, sans sortir de Paris, il nous sera loisible pendant six mois d'étudier, au moins dans leur manifestations extérieures, les us et coutumes des peuples les plus lointains. Et la musique étant, entre toutes ces manifestations, l'une des plus frappantes, aucun des visiteurs exotiques de l'Exposition n'a eu garde de l'oublier. Sans parler des grands concerts d'orchestre, de musique vocale, d'orgue, etc. dont la série vient de s'ouvrir au Trocadéro, nous trouvons dans les diverses sections de l'Exposition universelle mainte occasion d'étudier les formes musicales propres à des races chez lesquelles l'art est compris d'une façon très différente de la nôtre; et lors même que ces formes devraient êtres considérées par nous comme caractériser un art inférieur, il n'en faudrait pas moins leur prêter attention, car elles nous montrent des aspects nouveaux de la musique, et, très vraisemblablement, sont infiniment plus proches des origines que notre art aujourd'hui si complexe et si raffiné.[21]

As with many other nineteenth-century French writers and musicians— among them Ernest Renan, Gustave Flaubert, and Léo Delibes—Tiersot's world was a racist one, and music serves racism very well indeed.[22] After all, so the contemporary reasoning might go, music is an art which is semantically fluid and which can be seen as a universal language that allows access to truths more essential than those corrupted by the specificity of words. If translation was needed it was one from a medium of rhythmically

21. Julien Tiersot, "Promenades musicales à l'Exposition," *Le Ménestrel* 55 (1889): 165–66, at 165.
22. Popular, political, and scholarly racism and racialism in nineteenth-century France have been addressed extensively in the literature. While the distinction between racialism and racism seems sophisticated on the surface, I would, however, question the use of a terminology based on intent, for the distinction is hopelessly trapped in the vicious circle of intentional fallacy. See, for example, the following monographs: William B. Cohen, *The French Encounter with Africans: White Responses to Blacks, 1530–1880* (Bloomington and London: Indiana University Press, 1980), 210–48; Tzvetan Todorov, *On Human Diversity: Nationalism, Racism, and Exoticism in French Thought*, trans. Catherine Porter (Cambridge, MA, and London: Harvard University Press, 1993); Reina Lewis, *Race, Femininity and Representation* (London and New York: Routledge, 1996); Meyda Yeğenoğlu, *Colonial Fantasies: Towards a Feminist Reading of Orientalism* (Cambridge: Cambridge University Press, 1998).

organized pitch into words, not from one language into another. Music as "universal language" was, and is, a concept dear to Western philosophy and aesthetics.[23] Its historical pedigree can be traced from Plato and Boethius to François-Joseph Fétis, Eduard Hanslick, and beyond, with recent incarnations in such texts as Roger Scruton's controversial *The Aesthetics of Music*.[24] The key French figure for anchoring tonality, and therefore harmony, in "natural" laws was Jean-Philippe Rameau, and while his ideas were contested in specific areas—in particular the notion of a "corps sonore"—his writings offered a theoretical foundation of music in laws of nature, instituting a teleology toward (modern) art-music of the West.[25]

Such concepts had been explored in countless European music histories of the nineteenth century—popular and erudite—which contrasted the dynamic progress of Western art music with the static world of exotic sound.[26] In these music histories, anecdotal narratives of musical events

---

23. For a short survey, see Klaus-Jürgen Sachs, "Musiktheorie," in *Die Musik in Geschichte und Gegenwart*, 2nd ed., ed. Ludwig Finscher (Kassel and Stuttgart: Bärenreiter and Metzler, 1994–), 6 (1997), Sachteil, cols. 1714–35, at col. 1722. These notions of music as a developing universal language can be found in almost every theoretical text in the late nineteenth century, as for example in Camille Saint-Saëns, *Harmonie et Mélodie* (Paris: Calman-Lévy, 1885), 13–14. Even in recent semiotic discussion, the topic of universal elements of music remains a burning issue. See, for example: Jean-Jacques Nattiez, "The Universals of Music," in *Music and Discourse: Toward a Semiology of Music*, trans. Carolyn Abbate (Princeton, NJ: Princeton University Press, 1990), 62–68.

24. Roger Scruton, *The Aesthetics of Music* (Oxford: Clarendon Press, 1997). See also A. E. Denham, "The Moving Mirrors of Music: Roger Scruton Resonates with Tradition," *Music & Letters* 80 (1999): 411–32. By self-consciously limiting his discussions to Western art, Karol Berger shows how notions of "what is music" are conditioned by cultural frameworks, even in universalist claims. See Karol Berger, *A Theory of Art* (New York and Oxford: Oxford University Press, 2000), esp. 28–39. This contrasts with, in particular, the work of John Blacking, whose ethnomusicological research lead him to propose a musical universalism of "man." See John Blacking, *How Musical is Man?* (London: Faber & Faber, 1976), esp. 3–31.

25. On Rameau, see Thomas Christensen, *Rameau and Musical Thought in the Enlightenment* (Cambridge, MA: Harvard University Press, 1993); Joel Lester, "Rameau and Eighteenth-Century Harmonic Theory," in *The Cambridge History of Western Music Theory*, ed. Thomas Christensen, 753–77 (Cambridge: Cambridge University Press, 2002). Rameau's reception in the nineteenth century is addressed in Renate Groth, *Die französische Kompositionslehre des 19. Jahrhunderts*, Beihefte zum Archiv für Musikwissenschaft 22 (Wiesbaden: Franz Steiner, 1983); and, more specifically with respect to Fétis, in Thomas Christensen, "Fétis and Emerging Tonal Consciousness," in *Music Theory in the Age of Romanticism*, ed. Ian Bent, 27–56 (Cambridge: Cambridge University Press, 1996).

26. Glenn Stanley, "Historiography," in *NGr2*; Pasler, "Paris: Conflicting Notions of Musical Progress"; Katharine Ellis, *Music Criticism in Nineteenth-Century France: "La Revue et Gazette Musicale de Paris" (1838–1880)* (Cambridge: Cambridge University Press, 1995). On French music history, see also John Haines, "Généalogies musicologiques aux origines

were gradually replaced by a locating of history within the "art work" itself, thus cementing progress within the realm of the absolute.[27] Indeed, starting with Fétis, music history in France began to be understood as "an ideal process unfolding rationally according to universal laws, which it was the task of historians to identify and elucidate."[28] Music history thus allowed tracing the progress through time towards current or (in the case of Wagner or d'Indy) future music.

However, throughout the nineteenth century (and well into the twentieth), music was understood as an art that was not equally distributed among cultures, a given that Fétis acknowledged in 1868, in the opening paragraph of his *Histoire générale de la musique*:

> The history of music is inseparable from the appreciation of the special abilities of the races that have cultivated it. This, in essence ideal, art exists only through man, who creates it and to whom nature gave only sound and time. From whatever perspective one examines the musics spread over this world, from the most rudimentary song to the most grandiose and complex works, one cannot but notice that it is the product of human abilities, which are distributed unequally among peoples as well as among individuals.

> L'histoire de la musique est inséparable de l'appréciation des facultés spéciales des races qui l'ont cultivée. Cet art, étant essentiellement idéal, n'a d'existence que par l'homme qui le crée, et à qui la nature a fourni d'autres éléments que le son et le temps. Sous quelque aspect qu'on examine les productions musicales répandues sur toute la terre, depuis le chant le plus rudimentaire jusqu'aux œuvres les plus grandioses et les plus complexes, on n'y aperçoit autre chose que le produit des facultés humaines, lesquelles sont distribuées inégalement aux peuples comme aux individus.[29]

Here the racist theories of a Paul Broca or an Ernest Renan—both of whom correlated racial with genetic difference in their writings— intersected with music theory. Racial difference was seen as engendering

d'une science de la musique vers 1900," *Acta musicologica* 73 (2001): 45–76. For earlier layers in the process of creating music history in France, see Vendrix, *Aux Origines d'une discipline historique*.

27. That this process is closely linked with the development of the "work concept" in music and the raise of "absolute music" is no surprise and has been addressed by various authors. Key texts in the critical debate are Carl Dahlhaus, *The Idea of Absolute Music*, trans. Roger Lustig (Chicago: University of Chicago Press, 1989); and Lydia Goehr, *The Imaginary Museum of Musical Works* (Oxford: Clarendon Press, 1992).

28. Christensen, "Fétis and the Emerging Tonal Consciousness," 37. On Fétis's notion of history, see also Ellis, *Music Criticism in Nineteenth-Century France*, 33–45.

29. François-Joseph Fétis, *Histoire générale de la musique depuis les temps les plus anciens jusqu'à nos jours*, 6 vols. (Paris: Firmin-Didot, 1869–76), 1:i.

cultural and musical difference, and Fétis, the most influential Franco-phone writer on music between 1830 and 1880, conceived of a direct relationship of cause and effect between race and musical product.[30] It is worth remembering in this context that by the mid nineteenth century, harmonic and structural complexity had become fetishized as the highest achievement in musical composition, in particular with the reception of middle- and late-period Beethoven through composers of the generations of Berlioz, Saint-Saëns, and d'Indy.[31] Thus Fétis declared that "music, if considered with respect to the relationships of sounds, is not a simple sensation: it is, on the contrary, complex to the point of excess."[32] The creation and understanding of such complexity was, however, limited to those races—in Renan's words—"who have in common, and are alone in possessing, the sovereign characteristic of beauty."[33] For Renan as for Fétis, these abilities were the prerogative of Aryan races alone.

Fétis started his music history with a taxonomy of race-related musical abilities in which he contrasted the European and the "savage":[34]

The inhabitants of Europe and of the colonies founded by them have, in general, the necessary aptitude to seize the tonal relationship between certain tone series. This aptitude is developed through the habit of listening to music, which is perfected by study, because the law of progress is inherent in the nature of this race. Through it, they possess the ability to sing in tune and to vary the forms of their song. Savage populations also possess the psychological organization through which one perceives the sensation of sound and which allows one to grasp the relationship between the sounds, so that one does not mix up the intonations and is aware of their differences; but these sensual and intellectual operations are much more limited for them, because of the inferiority of their cerebral configuration.

Les habitants de l'Europe et ceux des colonies fondées par eux ont, en général, l'aptitude nécessaire pour saisir les rapports de tonalité de certaines séries de sons; aptitude qui se développe par l'habitude d'entendre de la

---

30. For a detailed examination of the reciprocal influences of a musician and a race theorist, see the case of Richard Wagner and Joseph Arthur comte de Gobineau in Eric Eugène, *Wagner et Gobineau: Existe-t-il un racisme wagnérien?* (Paris: Le Cherche Midi, 1998).

31. Marcia J. Citron, *Gender and the Musical Canon* (Cambridge: Cambridge University Press, 1993).

32. Fétis, *Histoire générale*, 1:11: "La musique, considérée dans les rapports des sons, n'est pas une sensation simple: elle est au contraire complexe à l'excès."

33. Quotation given in Todorov, *On Human Diversity*, 109.

34. The Fétisian savage is not the "noble savage" of Rousseau, but a racially different Other in the tradition of Comte and Hegel as a member of a "people without history." On Comte, Hegel, and Fétis, see Rosalie Schellhous, "Fétis's 'Tonality' as a Metaphysical Principle: Hypothesis for a New Science," *Music Theory Spectrum* 13 (1991): 230–31.

musique et que l'étude perfectionne, parce que la loi du progrès est inhérente à la nature de cette race. C'est par elle qu'ils possèdent la faculté de chanter dans des rapports de justesse tonale et de varier les formes de leur chant. Les populations sauvages ont aussi l'organisation physiologique par laquelle on perçoit la sensation du son et qui permet de saisir les rapports des sons entre eux, de manière à ne pas confondre les intonations et d'avoir conscience de leurs différences; mais ces opérations sentimentales et intellectuelles se font en eux dans des limites plus étroites, à raison de l'infériorité de leur formation cérébrale.[35]

While—as humans rather than animals—"savages" and other races share some degree of musical sentiment, Fétis continued, they are limited by "the inferiority of their cerebral configuration." In the subsequent discussion of the musical abilities of various races, Fétis's perception of the relationship between race and culture reflects the common ground of both Renan's and Gobineau's anthropologies in that he relates cultural ability to skin color in a similar fashion to their racial hierarchies.[36] The darker the skin, Fétis claims, the lower the natural ability for music, which leads to his conclusion "that the creation of the true art of music was limited to the white race, a mission which could not be fulfilled by the black or yellow races."[37] Africans in particular, Fétis argues, are lacking in their musical abilities and are far

35. Fétis, *Histoire générale*, 1:12. Fétis refers here to the Europeans who settled in the United States and Australia, for example, not the indigenous inhabitants of those regions.

36. Renan's notion that only white races possess beauty and culture cited above is expressed repeatedly by Gobineau as well, for example in his first chapter of the *Essai sur l'inégalité des races humaines* (1853): "Toute civilisation découle de la race blanche, aucune ne peut exister sans le concours de cette race." The quotation is given in Alain Ruscio, *Le Credo de l'homme blanc* (Paris: Éditions Complexe, 2002), 30. The relationship between Renan and Gobineau was complex, given that they shared in a similar discourse. Already in 1859, Gobineau accused Renan of plagiarism in a letter to Alexis de Tocqueville, claiming that "les orientalistes, comme M. Renan, dans son livre sur l'origine du langage . . . copient des chapitres de mon livre sur les races et ont le plus grand soin du monde d'ignorer mon nom." Citation given in *Richard et Cosima Wagner—Arthur Gobineau: Correspondance (1880–1882)*, ed. Eric Eugène (Saint-Genouph: Librairie Nizet, 2000), 57n. Gobineau repeated the same accusation twenty-two years later in a letter to Richard Wagner (ibid., 57–58).

37. The section in which Fétis relates race and music (often in great detail), spans pages 1–183 of the first volume. Quotation from Fétis, *Histoire générale*, 1:119: "J'ai dit qu'il était réservé à la race blanche de créer l'art véritable de la musique, mission que n'ont pu remplir les races noires et jaunes." Fétis—if mentioned at all in texts on comparative musicology—receives an astoundingly positive evaluation, as if his anthropological enquiries were value neutral. See, for example, Joep Bor, "The Rise of Ethnomusicology: Sources on Indian Music c. 1780–c. 1890," *Yearbook for Traditional Music* 20 (1988): esp. 60–61. Philip Bohlman echoes Bor's assessment in his "The European Discovery of Music in the Islamic World," 156.

Figure 4.2. "Tambours de la danse des nègres," in François-Joseph Fétis, *Histoire générale de la musique depuis les temps les plus anciens jusqu'à nos jours,* 6 vols. (Paris: Firmin Didot, 1869–76), 1:35.

too easily excited by the rhythms of the drums, all the more because the sounds engender physical (and therefore the most primitive) reaction to music in the form of dance (figure 4.2).[38] Rhythmic dominance, simple melodic formulas, and absence of complexity were other descriptors, which,

38. See, for example, Fétis, *Histoire générale,* 1:29, where he claimed about Africans: "Suivant la loi de capacité musicale, basée sur la conformation du cerveau, la conception des rapports d'intonation des sons ne peut exister que dans les limites les plus étroites chez une race si peu favorisée de la nature." In a footnote on the same page, Fétis rejects Gobineau's claim that "un des caractères de la race noire est une certaine disposition pour les arts." In order to empower art (and in particular music) rather than science as the ultimate

in the context of European aesthetics, had negative value. (Not for nothing was it the harmonically static but rhythmically provocative "Les Augures printaniers" in Stravinsky's *Sacre du printemps* that caused the famous scandal in 1913.) While Fétis showed Africans generally as people with limited musical ability, he used music to distinguish between various groups; indeed cannibals apparently were the least musical group, "with no more than three notes" at their disposition.[39] Fétis was neither the first nor the only author to formulate this kind of racist music theory; but because they were integrated in a major and widely received nineteenth-century work of music theory, Fétis's notions of music, culture, and race were the foundation on which the majority of his contemporaries and subsequent generations based their judgment of music both Western and non-Western.[40]

Fétis's concepts were based on French anthropological theories of the mid-nineteenth century, in particular those of Paul Broca, which tried to show that humans were polymorphous and races therefore genetically different.[41] Indeed, towards the end of his life, in 1867, Fétis presented a study, "On a New Form of Classification of Human Races According to Their Musical Systems," to the Société d'Anthropologie. Fétis's account of the close relationship between anthropology and musicology received the support of Broca during the subsequent debate.[42] According to Fétis,

signifier of civilized achievement, Fétis needed to demonstrate that the ability for culture was the major distinction between races and therefore the most important signifier for racial superiority. I would contend that Fétis's argument was not only an attempt to inscribe the history and theory of music within the horizon of knowledge of mid-nineteenth-century France, but to validate music as the most important expression of human achievement in the rivalry of scholarly subjects in French academic discussions. Given that music was continuously under threat to be perceived as a feminized "art d'agrément," such forms of legitimization were part of the ongoing project of masculinizing French music. On the French feminization of the Oriental Other since the enlightenment (especially Diderot and Montesquieu), see Madeleine Dobie, *Foreign Bodies: Gender, Language, and Culture in French Orientalism* (Stanford, CA: Stanford University Press, 2001). On the project of masculinizing French music, see Fauser, "Gendering the Nations."

39. Émile Haraszati, "Fétis fondateur de la musique comparée: Son étude sur un nouveau mode de classification des races humaines d'après leurs systèmes musicaux," *Acta musicologica* 4 (1932): 102.

40. Katharine Ellis, "François-Joseph Fétis," in *NGr2*.

41. For a short introduction into the early history of French anthropology and ethnography, see Claude Blanckaert, "On the Origins of French Ethnology: William Edwards and the Doctrine of Race," in *Bones, Bodies, Behavior: Essays on Biological Anthropology*, ed. George W. Stocking, 18–55, *History of Anthropology* 5 (Madison: University of Wisconsin Press, 1988). See also the discussion of anthropology and ethnography in Cohen, *The French Encounter with Africans*, 232–36.

42. Harasazti, "Fétis fondateur de la musicologie comparée," 98. The study's title in French is "Sur un nouveau mode de classification des races humaines d'après leurs systèmes musicaux."

specific scales and instruments were restricted to individual racial groups, and close examination of their music would allow for anthropological conclusions about races and their connections and differences.

In contrast to these anthropologists, however, ethnographers started from a strongly monogenetic position, which maintained the Enlightenment concept that human difference was not genetic but, rather, a result of climate and other environmental conditions. Racial and cultural superiority were perceived as a result of favorable contexts and stages of development.[43] As Claude Blanckaert has observed, ethnographers were religiously orthodox in their belief in creation and were "actively involved in social and moral questions in the old sense. At the moment in which, through the work of Gobineau and his zealots, a polymorphous racism was being objectified in a biopolitical mythology . . . 'ethnography' was set up as a discipline in marked hostility to 'anthropology.' It presented itself as a culturalist counter-model, a 'science of nationalities' which sought, among other goals, to fight against ignorance of the 'science' of political agents."[44] While anthropologists were closer to new Darwinian concepts of evolution, the more conservative Catholic ethnographers believed firmly in the creation of man as God's image and therefore as inherently the same.

If Fétis's concepts of music and race were indebted to the anthropologists, other writers—especially those related to Christian institutions such as the École Niedermeyer or the Schola Cantorum—based their observations and judgments on more universalist ethnographic concepts of race. One salient example is Félix Clément, whose *Histoire de la Musique depuis les temps anciens jusqu'à nos jours* (1885) shows the contrast with Fétis's musical anthropology and yet also demonstrates Fétis's continued influence on French musicography.[45] In his introduction, Clément distanced himself from "anthropological theories" that had "let him [Fétis] astray" and stated instead:

> All the divisions and subdivisions in the taxonomy of human races that one tries to establish so laboriously will not invalidate the fact that all men, without exception, possess the same senses and that the sense of hearing has given them that of sound; as for the results, they can only be related to the degree of culture and civilization that on can observe here and there.

43. On eighteenth-century notions of national difference, see Werner Oechslin, "Le Goût et les nations: Débats, polémiques et jalousies au moment de la création des musées au XVIIIe siècle," in *Les Musées en Europe à la veille de l'ouverture du Louvre*, ed. Edouard Pommier (Paris: Service Culturel du Louvre and Klincksieck, 1995), esp. 381–85. I wish to thank Matthias Waschek for bringing this article to my attention.

44. Blanckaert, "On the Origins of French Ethnology," 48.

45. Félix Clément, *Histoire de la Musique depuis les temps anciens jusqu'à nos jours* (Paris: Librairies Hachette et Cie, 1885).

Toutes les divisions et subdivisions qu'on s'évertue à établir dans le classe-ment des races humaines n'infirmeront pas ce fait que tous les hommes sans exception sont doués des mêmes sens; que celui de l'ouïe leur donne celle du son; quant aux résultats, ils ne peuvent être qu'en rapport avec le degré de culture et de civilisation que l'on constate ça et là.[46]

Clément criticized modern science's concept that music (like language) was spontaneous and instinctive (and thus genetically conditioned) because that theory obscured the true, divine nature of music. If certain people such as the Zulus did not take advantage of the gifts they received from God, it did not mean automatically "that they received these abilities in a smaller dosage than other men."[47] Differences in music thus reflect different customs, not different genes.[48] Clément's views were founded not only on the divine world order that created both man and music but also on the widespread notion of music's universalism, which he introduces in his preface—"musicians have a unique privilege in this world, that of using a universal language"—and to which he refers throughout his his-toric account.[49] But Clément's notion of music as universal is music as he knows it: that of Beethoven or Rossini. Throughout his account, he shows how other musics are, in effect, only variations of the eternal laws of har-mony. And while his aesthetic and ethnographic concepts were diametri-cally opposed to those of Fétis, Clément's historiography remained indebted to his illustrious predecessor not only with respect to the order of his historical account but also in terms of musical descriptions of non-Western musics, which could be close to Fétis's to the point of simple paraphrase.[50]

46. Ibid., 3.

47. Ibid., 5: "Le faible parti que certaines peuplades ont tiré des facultés données par le Créateur ne doit pas faire conclure que ces facultés leur aient été octroyées à plus faible dose qu'aux autres hommes."

48. Ibid., 6: "La culture, la transmission des connaissances acquises, le progrès, la civilisation en un mot, ont manqué aux peuples qui n'ont qu'une musique rudimen-taire, mais non les éléments de cet art. Ne nous attardons pas à chercher dans le bégayement de cette langue des types originaux et mêmes intéressants, je ne sais quelle saveur âpre et quels effets pittoresques; loin de là, on ne doit s'attendre qu'à une défor-mation des éléments naturels, à des cris sauvages remplaçant les sons appréciables, à des articulations grimaçantes, à des mouvements précipités et uniformes, convulsifs et désor-donnés, au lieu de danses harmonieuses, variées et réglées; déformation de la nature analogue à celle que ces malheureux pratiquent sur leurs corps et sur leurs visages."

49. Ibid., i: "Les musiciens jouissent d'un privilège unique au monde, celui de se servir d'une langue universelle."

50. See, for example, Fétis's and Clément's descriptions and implied value judg-ments of oriental song in Fétis, *Histoire générale*, 1:295, and Clément, *Histoire de la Musique*, 84.

Thus the anthropologist/ethnographer divide was founded more on articles of faith than on scientific observation, with the same data leading to
directly opposite conclusions.

In the absence of sound—contrary to other artifacts, music could not
be collected and exhibited in museums—written accounts, images, instruments, and transcriptions provided by travelers were the only sources of
information for the writers of music histories. Amiot's 1779 *Mémoire sur la
musique des Chinois,* for example, remained a much-used source until the
end of the nineteenth century; it was consulted and exploited by both Fétis
and Clément. Prior to the phonograph, transmission of musical information was limited to means of representation familiar from the Western
repertoire with its privileging of common-practice tonality. Like many
other such histories, Fétis's and Clément's books contained transcriptions
of indigenous musics in staff notation that could be played on the piano.
Therefore musical encounters with non-European musics were possible
only by reference to Western notation (and therefore its systems of music
theory) and instruments, and Fétis, at least, seems to have been aware of
that some of the original might be lost in translation (figure 4.3). Thus
Bourgault-Ducoudray called on scholars to learn non-Western musical
notation in order to contribute to the Orientalist project in the introduction of his 1877 study, *Études sur la musique ecclésiastique grecque: Mission musicale en Grèce et en Orient*:

> The main aim of this book is to facilitate the study of oriental music—far too
> neglected thus far—to people from the Occident. . . . We would strongly
> encourage musician-archeologists who are attracted by this kind of studies to
> translate the greatest number of oriental songs (both religious and secular)
> into European notation. They would be rendering a tremendous service to
> both science and art.

> Le principal but que nous nous proposons en publiant ce livre est de
> faciliter aux occidentaux l'étude de la musique orientale, trop négligée
> jusqu'ici. . . . Nous conseillions vivement aux musiciens-archéologues qui
> se sentiraient attirés vers ces études, de traduire en notation européenne
> le plus grand nombre possible des chants orientaux (chants religieux et
> chants profanes). En le faisant, ils rendront à la science et à l'art un service
> éminent.[51]

That this process of translation—whether in music, art, or literature—
was part of the colonial project has been explored extensively since Edward

---

51. Louis-Albert Bourgault-Ducoudray, *Études sur la Musique ecclésiastique grecque:
Mission musicale en Grèce et en Orient, janvier–mai 1875* (Paris: Librairie Hachette, 1877), vii.

Figure 4.3. "Chinese Air Translated into European Notation," in François-Joseph Fétis, *Histoire générale de la musique depuis les temps les plus anciens jusqu'à nos jours,* 6 vols. (Paris: Firmin Didot, 1869–76), 1:60.

Said first drew attention to its role in *Orientalism* (1978).[52] But these translations also offered glimpses into a world of music which would have otherwise remained exclusively within either the orientalist imaginary of the visual, or the musical banality of exotic signifiers in works such as *Lakmé.* Even with all their racist problems, de La Fage, Fétis, and Clément pointed towards a musical Other who was human, who existed, and whose cultural artifacts warranted if not respect then at least attention. Yet these musicographic texts were at the heart of imperialism in that they prepared their readers for a world translatable into European systems of empire.[53] They proposed a taxonomy of all known music of all mankind that could and would be reflected in such events as the 1889 Exposition Universelle in fashions similar to other enterprises such as the "History of Human Habitation" in both representation and reception.[54] Texts such as Fétis's were a repository of contemporary knowledge of the Other—as fraught as it may be—and they became the foundation for those musical encounters at the Exposition Universelle that went beyond the simple comparison of operatic dream (or music-hall performance) and the sonic reality of picturesque and exotic music displayed at the fair. But given that nineteenth-century music theory was a discipline that was hierarchical in

52. Edward W. Said, *Orientalism: Western Conceptions of the Orient* (London: Penguin Books, 1991), esp. 123–66. For the use of music in the colonialist project, see the bibliographies of the articles "Ethnomusicology," "Exoticism," and "Orientalism" in *NGr2.*
53. Edward W. Said, *Culture and Imperialism* (London: Vintage, 1994).
54. Mitchell, "Orientalism and the Exhibitionary Order."

the same manner as contemporary anthropological and ethnographic writings, the reception of the various musics reflected more than just concepts of racial and cultural difference. The hierarchy shown at the Exposition Universelle was double: one, absolute, between Western music and the rest; the other, relative, within this remainder of musics.

## The Location of Exotic Music at the 1889 Exposition Universelle

Picturesque and exotic musics were located in two areas of the Exposition Universelle (figures 4.4 and 4.5). The first was on the right when entering the Champ de Mars along the Avenue de Suffren, where sovereign foreign countries such as Bolivia, China, Morocco, Romania, and Spain had their pavilions and—in some cases—associated cafés (the Moroccan and the Egyptian exhibitions were immediately adjacent to—and contrasted with—the Galerie des Machines, from which one would turn into the rue du Caire, a fantasy of "old Cairo" complete with donkeys and coffee bars). The second was in the colonial exhibition at the Esplanade des Invalides, where pavilions representing French colonies and protectorates as well as those of some other exotic nations, in particular Java, surrounded the central Palais des Colonies much like a medieval village would its cathedral.[55] The layout of the colonial exhibition created "four different ethnic 'neighborhoods'—Arab, Oceanic, African, and Asian," the quarters "divided into streets and alleys, each named after a colony or protectorate."[56]

The particularly prominent space allocated to the presentation of the French colonies bears significant witness to France's attempt to stand up as colonial power in comparison to her arch-rival, Britain.[57] This political agenda was transparent even to the authors of popular tourist guidebooks such as *Cook's Guide to Paris*, which makes it clear that the French were somewhat lacking as colonialists compared with a Victorian Britain that saw

55. On the ideological concepts behind the spatial layout of the Exposition Universelle, see Debora L. Silverman, "The 1889 Exhibition: The Crisis of Bourgeois Individualism," *Oppositions: A Journal for Ideas and Criticism in Architecture*, Special Issue: "City and Ideology: Paris under the Academy" (Spring 1977): 71–91. The exotic pavilions are discussed in Caroline Mathieu, "Invitation au Voyage," in *1889: La Tour Eiffel et l'Exposition Universelle*, ed. Caroline Mathieu, 102–29 (Paris: Éditions de la Réunion des Musées Nationaux, 1989). I have addressed the layout of the colonial exhibition in my "Die Welt als Stadt: Weltausstellungen in Paris als Spiegel urbanen Musiklebens," in *Musik und Urbanität*, ed. Christian Kaden and Volker Kalisch, 139–48 (Essen: Blaue Eule, 2002).

56. Silverman, "The 1889 Exhibition," 75.

57. On the problematic relationship of Britain and France, see Eugen Weber, *France: Fin de siècle* (Cambridge, MA, and London: Belknap Press of Harvard University Press, 1986), 105–10.

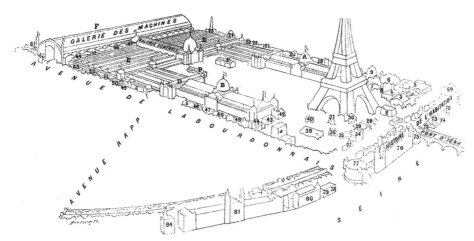

Croquis du panorama du Champ-de-Mars et du Trocadéro (Voir la légende explicitive ci-contre).

Figure 4.4. View of the Exposition Universelle at the Champ de Mars, *L'Illustration* 47 (1889): 347.
The view shows the outlines of the buildings on the Champ de Mars. The constructions on the right (nos. 3 to 25) represent the majority of national pavilions. The Egyptian exhibit is no. 24, the rue du Caire no. 25.

herself as the bearer of culture to the "uncivilized" world.[58] From what the Exposition displayed of the industry of Cambodia and Tahiti, the *Cook's Guide* concluded that, in contrast to Britain, France's colonizing endeavors did not reach so far as bringing the benefits of civilization to their overseas territories. In contrast to Britain's Raj, France's empire was not yet advertised as an enterprise of taking cultural and political "progress" to the rest of the world. The doctrine of the *mission civilisatrice* became official only later, in the mid- to late 1890s.[59]

> Next to the Tonquin Pavilion comes the Exhibition of Cambodian Industry, another picturesque construction, containing, however, little to interest European visitors. The same may be said of the Pavilion of Tahiti. All these exhibits are intended to show France to the world in the light of a colonising power. The idea is pretty fancy; but, as a matter of fact, the

58. With respect to British encounters and enmeshment with Indian music and music theory in the nineteenth and early twentieth centuries, see Farrell, *Indian Music and the West*, esp. chapter 2: "Indian Music, Notation and Nationalism in the Nineteenth Century" (45–76).

59. On the *mission civilisatrice*, see Alice L. Conklin, *A Mission to Civilize: The Republican Idea of Empire in France and West Africa, 1895–1930* (Stanford, CA: Stanford University Press, 1997).

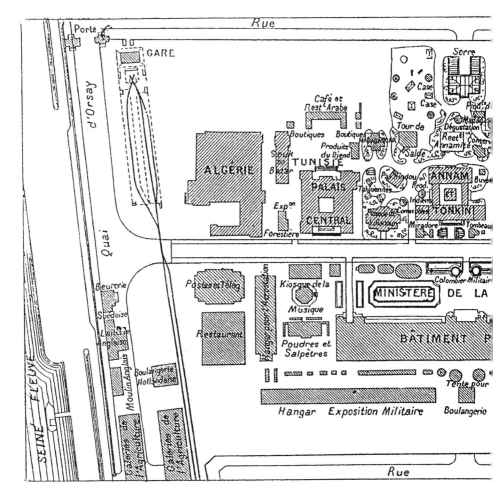

Plan de l'Exposition des Co

Figure 4.5. Map of the Exposition des Colonies at t

colonising influence of France rarely extends beyond the range of her cannon. The French are a homesick nation. If they leave their country for foreign parts, it is always with the idea of gaining money to be spent in a little villa in some part of la Belle France.[60]

60. *Cook's Guide to Paris and the Universal Exhibition. Special Edition . . . Compiled under the Personal Superintendence of Thomas Cook & Son* (London: Thomas Cook & Son, 1889), 107.

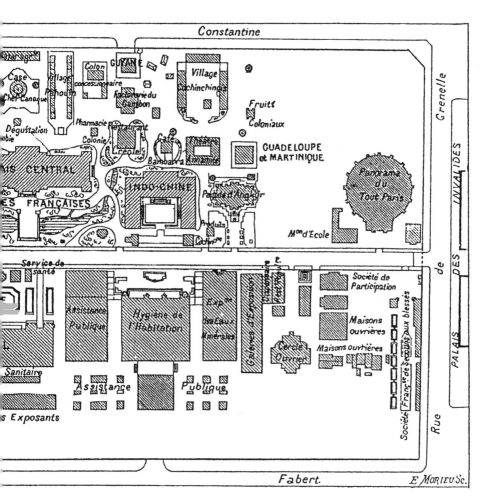

à l'esplanade des Invalides.

planade des Invalides, *L'Illustration* 47 (1889): 347.

Indeed, Louis Henrique, the special commissioner for the colonial exhibition, confirmed the colonialist project ridiculed by the writer of *Cook's Guide to Paris* by declaring proudly that "we want to show the colonies to France."[61] At the end of the Exposition Universelle, Henrique could state that his mission was a major success, for the positive reception of the colonial exhibition both

61. "Nous voulons montrer les colonies à la France." Quotation given in Silverman, "The 1889 Exhibition," 90.

through visitors and the French press contributed to the growing popular support of the still disputed colonizing effort of Third-Republic France.[62]

In this spatial taxonomy of foreign nations as either sovereign or colonized, music played a fascinating and revealing role. In fact, almost all so-called picturesque music, including French and European folk music, was to be found in the pavilions and restaurants of the Champ de Mars, whereas all exotic music from Africa and the Far East was located in the colonial exhibition.[63] The music that shared both spaces was Middle Eastern: while Moroccan and Egyptian music could be enjoyed in the Champ de Mars, Algerian and Tunisian musicians performed in the colonial exhibition. Thus Middle Eastern music, the exotic music best known to Europeans and closest to Europe, was located symbolically between the sovereign and the colonized nations, acting as a mirror for the long and complex relationship of France with the Middle East as possible but not always actual colonies.[64]

At the 1889 Exposition Universelle, such cultural differences became visible and audible in the various music performances. Western music had its "palace" with the Trocadéro.[65] As we have seen, the various concert series not only offered self-consciously "national" repertoires by visiting orchestras from Russia, Spain, and the United States, but also involved, in the case of France, an attempt at presenting works that would form a canon of national masterworks past and present. This was complemented by a range of musical retrospectives, in particular the two *Concerts de musique française ancienne et moderne* discussed in chapter 1. Thus Western art music

62. See Edward Berenson, "Unifying the French Nation: Savorgnan de Brazza and the Third Republic," in *Music, Culture, and National Identity in France, 1870–1939*, ed. Barbara Kelly (Rochester, NY: University of Rochester Press, forthcoming).

63. None of the sources that I encountered mentions any music performed in the exotic pavilions of the Champ de Mars, including China, Siam, Japan, or India. None of the drawings and photographs shows any musicians, not even in the Indian restaurant where music would have been most likely. Japan would capitalize on the 1889 craze for exotic music in the 1900 fair with their show of kabuki theater, whose main attraction was the actress, dancer and musician, Sada Yakko. See Lesley Wright, "Music Criticism and the *Exposition Internationale Universelle* of 1900," *Context: A Journal of Music Research*, no. 21 (Spring 2001): 19–30.

64. I am using the geographical term "Middle East" in its broadest sense to include Islamic North Africa as well as the Arabian Peninsula and Persia. On the creation and inscription of cultural meaning into physical spaces, see the contributions to Pierre Nora, ed., *Les Lieux de mémoire* (Paris: Gallimard, 1984), in particular Maurice Agulhon, "Paris: La traversée d'est en ouest," in vol. 6: *Les France III: De l'archive à l'emblème*, 868–909. Indeed, even the location of "high" and "low" culture, French and non-Western music within the geography of the Exposition reflects the geographic layout of politics and culture sketched by Agulhon.

65. Ch. G., "La Musique à l'Exposition," *L'Art musical* 28 (1889): 75.

at the Exposition also had a history, visibly in such exhibits as Charles Nuitter's history of the theater (including the autograph manuscript of Mozart's *Don Giovanni*), and audibly in these historic concerts. Aesthetic value judgment and representation within the context of the exhibition correlated closely in this case.

Picturesque music in the sense of French and European folk music seemed to hold a middle ground. It migrated between the Champ de Mars and the Trocadéro, between open air and concert hall, between *café-concert* and *concours* (see chapter 5). Exotic music, on the other hand, was mainly located in the sphere of the colonial exhibition, either as an anthropological by-product, for example in the case of the Sudanese village, or as entertainment in the *café-concert.* There it was consumed with the samples of local beverages, whether hot chocolate and beer from the island of Java, or coffee from the Middle East. Music formed part of the exotic spectacle, and more often than not, it was associated with exotic dance (figure 4.6). In particular, the performance location of Middle Eastern music in the Arab cafés—both in the Champ de Mars and in the colonial section—might well have served as a sonic signpost, pointing Middle Eastern culture away from the Champ de Mars towards the colonial section where, in due course, both Morocco and Egypt would indeed wind up. These exotic sounds were certainly not received as concert music worthy of attention, but, rather, as a noisome sound track for an exotic spectacle.[66]

But here the story becomes even more fascinating: while the visual side of the exotic spectacle remained confined within the context of the Fair's *variété* entertainment, music was able to break out of these boundaries and demand to be noticed. It escaped both physically, for it could be heard beyond the boundaries of the *cafés-concerts* and often quite loudly, and—in the case of Far Eastern music—it also began to escape aesthetically.[67] While the sounds were unfamiliar and often even disturbing, they nevertheless captured attention. Contrary to the sights, which could be subsumed under the Parisian experience of exoticism in vaudeville, concert, and opera as a performance of exotic dancers (familiar through exotic costumes, albeit quite different in their movements), the sound of the spectacles clashed with horizons of expectation formed through decades of musical exoticism. On the more sinister side, such sonic experience could

66. On the confinement of "exotic" music in the consumer context of the *café-concert,* see Çelik, *Displaying the Orient,* 23–29; and Leprun, *Théâtre des colonies,* 70–78.

67. Music's power to transgress physical limitation has been addressed in recent studies on reception of music in the context of urban environment or, more localized, in convents. See Fiona Kisby, ed., *Music and Musicians in Renaissance Cities and Towns* (Cambridge: Cambridge University Press, 2001); and Tim Carter, "The Sound of Silence: Models for an Urban Musicology," *Urban History* 29 (2002): 8–18.

Figure 4.6. The Algerian *café-concert* at the 1889 Exposition Universelle, photograph by Prince Roland Bonaparte. Bibliothèque nationale de France, Collection of the Société de Géographie, cliché We 327(1). Used by permission.

be interpreted in an entirely negative way and thus justify racial and colonial politics by being perceived as reflecting "primitive" cultural dispositions; for example, accounts of performances of the *Théâtre Annamite* often referred to the sounds being like those of animals, and Arab music was qualified as "caterwauling" or worse and thus reflecting racial deficiency.[68] On the more positive side, however, listeners started to engage with the unfamiliar sounds in a process of "active listening" (*écoute réduite*), which may not have been entirely disinterested, but which did show respect for the Other's art.[69] Claude Debussy was but the most famous of these listeners, and in his writings he later referred to the two Far Eastern spectacles on display: the Vietnamese Theater and the Javanese gamelan. Indeed, these musical engagements with the Far East became key experiences for the young composer and widened his sonic horizon in ways that the exclusively visual of Parisian *japonisme* and the musical exoticism of works such as Bourgault-Ducoudray's *Rapsodie cambodgienne* could not provide. Encounters with the Exotic Others at the 1889 Exposition Universelle became most prominently those with the least familiar and most sensational to the French at the time: the music, dance, and theater of Java and Vietnam.

## The *Kampong javanais*

"Come to the Javanese village, the *Kampong*, with me," Camille Benoît invites his readers. "There, four very young women, dressed up like goddesses, dance a symbolic ballet accompanied by the sounds of the gamelan"[70] (figure 4.7). The Tout-Paris of writers, painters, and musicians joined the crowds of visitors who gathered, day in and day out, in the small *café-théâtre* (which seated 100–150 people) situated within the Javanese village. Here they consumed Dutch beer, sorbets, Van Houten hot chocolate, and the performance of the dancers.[71] Within just a few weeks, the four

68. Frantz Jourdain, "L'Exposition algérienne," *L'Exposition de Paris* 1–2 (1889): 146–47, at 147: "effroyable charivari."

69. The issue of modes of listening will be developed further in chapter 6. On modes of listening, see Denis Smalley, "The Listening Imagination: Listening in the Electroacoustic Era," in *Companion to Contemporary Musical Thought*, ed. John Paynter et al., 2 vols., 1:514–54 (London and New York: Routledge, 1992).

70. Balthasar Claes [Camille Benoît]: "Chronique Parisienne: La Musique à l'Exposition," *Le Guide musical*, 9 June 1889, 3–4, at 3: "Entrez avec moi au village javanais, au *Kampong*. Là, aux sons du *Gamelang*, quatre toutes jeunes femmes, parées comme des idoles, dansent un ballet symbolique."

71. L. Archinti, "Le Giavanese," *Parigi e l'Esposizione Universale del 1889*, no. 32 (Oct. 1889): 249–50, at 249: "In un angolo c'è una tettoia capace di contenere da 100 a 150 persone con un palco scenico in fondo."

Figure 4.7.  The four Javanese dancers (Wakiem, Seriem, Taminah, and Soekia).
B.H.V.P., Dossier photographique *Divers XXI*, 364.

*tandak* became celebrated stars of the Exposition, their dance a spectacle
not to be missed. All in all, 875,000 visitors came to see them.[72] Writers and
photographers observed their every step and created a trail of documents
that records this fascination while offering some information about the
nature of these performances and their reception.

The *kampong javanais* constituted a world in itself: a fenced-in re-
creation of a Sundanese village, guarded by a large portal flanked by two
minarets (figure 4.8). A pastoral idyll, it offered a pre-industrial paradise
where women crafted batiks and men wove straw hats. Just over sixty men,
women, and children from Sunda and Java lived and worked in the village
built at the end of the Exposition des Colonies, right next to the temple
from Angkor.[73] Like any other pastoral construct, the Javanese village
depended on the dual opposition between city and country, artifact and

72. Alfred Picard, *Rapport général sur l'Exposition universelle internationale de 1889*, 10
vols. (Paris: Imprimerie nationale, 1890–91), 3:285.
73. Chazal lists sixty-three names based on the photographic records of Prince
Roland Bonaparte. See Jean-Pierre Chazal, " 'Grand Succès pour les Exotiques': Retour
sur les spectacles javanais de l'Exposition Universelle de Paris en 1889," *Archipel* 63
(2002): 134–36.

Figure 4.8. Exposition Universelle, Paris, 1889: Exposition Coloniale, Entrance of the Javanese village, photograph. B.H.V.P., Dossier photographique *Divers XXI*, 65.

nature, presenting a glimpse into an exotic Arcadia while containing the Other within the primordial natural space. The placement of the *kampong javanais* at the fringes of the fairground also ensured a certain sonic isolation, which was denied to most other musical performances. (Visitors to the Creole restaurant, for example, could enjoy simultaneously the performance of "La Paloma" inside the restaurant and the sounds of the Vietnamese Theater drifting over.[74]) Thus the village represented an enclave of calm in terms not just of visitors but also of sonic intrusions.

Musical sound formed the visitors' first encounter with Java, even beyond the parameters of the village, in the guise of the *angklung*, whose players literally guided the spectators from the entrance of the compound to the place of the performance, a centrally located pavilion with bamboo columns. The tuned bamboo sticks of the *angklung* thus provided a transition from the Western metropolis into the carefully enclosed pastoral world within which the illusion of traveling into a new culture could be sustained

74. See B. Schulte-Smidt, *Bleistift-Skizzen: Erinnerungen an die Pariser Weltausstellung* (Bremen: Johann Kühtmann's Buchhandlung, 1890), 75: "Mein Gefährte erwartet mich schon längst im Café Créole und hat unterweilen stark Bresche in die *hors d'œuvre* geschlagen. Hier geht's hoch her! Die Musik spielt in rauschenden Tönen "La Paloma," und vom nahen Annamitentheater dringt die winselnde, schneidende Tanzbegleitung herüber."

(figures 4.9a and 4.9b). The audience's physical and aesthetic trajectory was carefully orchestrated. Once the spectators were installed at the tables with their drinks, the sounds of the gamelan replaced those of the *angklung* and announced the beginning of the show. An illustrated program informed "temporary visitors to the mysterious kingdom of Javanese dance" that they were about to witness the most exquisite performance of the entire Exposition (figure 4.10).[75] On the small stage, Wakiem, Seriem, Taminah, and Soekia were already seated in front of a row of marionettes (used in separate performances of Sundanese marionette theater). The four dancers, aged between thirteen and seventeen, ignited the fantasies of the Parisian audiences: they were perceived as nubile courtesans from the "harem of a sultan," the Solonese prince Mangkunêgara VII.[76] As the gamelan began the first piece, the four *tandak* rose slowly and began the courtly dance. Their dance represented an episode of the Javanese epic *Damarwulan*, in which the hero tries to rescue two captive princesses from his enemy, Menakjinggâ.[77] The dance from the princely court of Surakarta was performed in the characteristic formation of four *tandak* to the accompaniment of the Sundanese gamelan, including a singer.[78] Chazal speculates that the dance may have been in the style of *langêndrian*, a fashionable court entertainment in late-nineteenth-century Java.[79] The

75. Jean Kernoa, "La Danse," *1889 / Exposition Universelle / Java / Programme Explicatif Illustré* (Paris: n.p., 1889), 4: "le visiteur de passage au royaume mystérieux de la danse javanaise."

76. Tout-Paris, "Les Vieilles Lunes de Java," *Le Gaulois*, 2 June 1889, 1–2, at 2: "ces danseuses de cour, empruntées au harem d'un sultan." Judith Gautier, *Les Musiques bizarres à l'Exposition de 1900* (Paris: Société d'Éditions Littéraires et Artistiques, 1900), 5: "ces hiératiques bayadères, échappées du harem."

77. Several newspaper accounts of the Javanese dances, including the one cited in the previous footnote, and the program refer to the plot of the dance as stemming from the epic *Damarwulan*. For a short summary, see Chazal, "'Grand Succès pour les Exotiques,'" 114–15.

78. For an introduction to Javanese dance and music, see "Indonesia," in *NGr2*.

79. Chazal, "'Grand Succès pour les Exotiques,'" 115. See also R. Anderson Sutton, Endo Suanda and Sean Williams, "Java," in *The Garland Encyclopedia of World Music*, vol. 4: *Southeast Asia*, ed. Terry E. Miller and Sean Williams (New York and London: Garland Publishing, 1998), 654: "During the late 1800s, two genres of dance-drama with sung dialogue arose among the nobility and lesser courts in central Java: *langen driyan* (formerly *langen driya*) and *langen mandra wanara*. Both are thought to have been developed by one highly talented individual, R. M. A. Tandhakusuma, a Solonese master of dance who spent time in Yogyakarta in the late 1800s. In contrast to other genres of drama in Java, these rely on written texts, requiring the singer-dancers to memorize their lines. *Langen driyan* (from *langen* 'entertainment' and *driya* 'heart,' 'sense') presents episodes from the story of the mythical eastern Javanese hero Damar Wulan. Though known in a musical-narrative version in Yogyakarta (as *langen driya*), it has become the quintessential performance genre at the Mangkunegaran court, where it is normally performed by an all-female cast of dancers singing their lines."

LES JOUEURS DE ANG-KLONG (ORCHESTRE POPULAIRE) ALLANT CHERCHER LES DANSEUSES.

Figure 4.9a. "Les Joueurs de *Ang-Klong* (orchestre populaire) allant chercher les danseuses," in *L'Exposition Universelle* 1 (1889): 162.

Figure 4.9b. The pavilion for the Javanese dance (building on the left), in *L'Exposition Universelle* 1 (1889): 163.

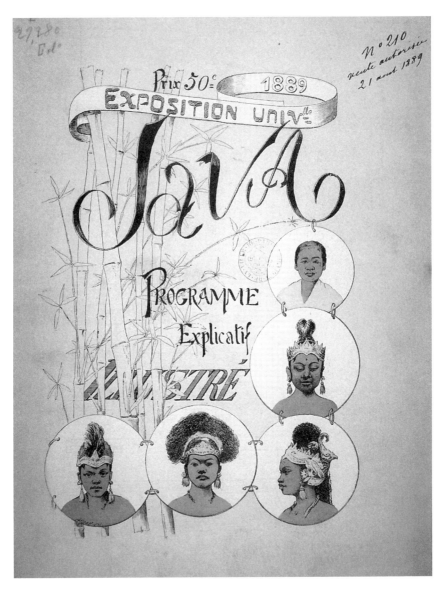

Figure 4.10. *1889 / Exposition Universelle / Java / Programme Explicatif Illustré*
(Paris: n.p., 1889), title page.

splendid costumes and jewels, the careful makeup, the controlled poses both before and during the dances, together with the young age and exotic beauty of the dancers, created a spectacle which kept the audience spellbound, while "the foam of the beer withered and the sorbet melted under distracted spoons," as Judith Gautier would recall some eleven years later.[80] Her (estranged) husband, the writer Catulle Mendès, tried to capture the dancers and their movements in a *rondel* that used most of the images derived from nature and mythology that were associated with the *tandak*:

|  |  |
|---|---|
| Les Javanaises[81] | The Javanese |
| Elles dansent, sacerdotales, | They dance, sacerdotally, |
| Avec de menus airs d'oiseaux, | In their minute, bird-like manner, |
| Et leurs mains sur l'or des réseaux | And their hands over the gold web |
| Semblent des ailes digitales. | Seem like fingered wings. |
|  |  |
| A des gravités de Vestales | Has one to the Vestal's gravities |
| A-t-on promu des Los, des Zos? | Promoted the Lo, the Zo? |
| Elles dansent, sacerdotales, | They dance, sacerdotally, |
| Avec de menus airs d'oiseaux. | In their minute, bird-like manner. |
|  |  |
| Selon un rite aux lois fatales | Moving their small, boneless bodies |
| Mouvant leur petit corps sans os, | Following a rite of fateful laws, |
| Ainsi que serpentent les eaux | In the way waters slither |
| Et comme ondulent les crotales | And rattlesnakes undulate |
| Elles dansent, sacerdotales. | They dance, sacerdotally. |

But in the end, it was not the poets who were the most attentive audience, as an anonymous writer observed:

> Painters and musicians are the most excited. Every day, one can see *dessinateurs* and water-colorists who use [the dancers] as models during the performance. As for the musicians, they are struck by the unfamiliar rhythms and bizarre sonorities of the two orchestras, which play in the background and at one side of the stage.

> Peintres et musiciens sont surtout les plus empressés. Chaque jour, l'on voit des dessinateurs et des aquarellistes qui les prennent pour modèles pendant la représentation. Quant aux musiciens, ils sont frappés par les

---

80. Gautier, *Les Musiques bizarres à l'Exposition de 1900*, 5: "où la mousse de bocks se fanait, où des sorbets fondaient sous les cuillers distraites."
81. Catulle Mendès, "Les Belles du monde," *L'Écho de Paris*, 18 Sept. 1889, 1.

rythmes inusités et les sonorités bizarres des deux orchestres qui jouent au fond de la scène et dans l'une de ses côtés.[82]

The dance of the *tandak* was followed by a "danced pantomime."[83] This more popular dance from Sunda was performed by the fifteen-year-old Elles from Parakan Salak (a Sundanese tea plantation near Sukabumi) and a partner (unidentified), both in everyday Javanese dress (figure 4.11). In press accounts of this dance, Elles is usually characterized as a "bajadère" (*ronggeng*), a public dancer of dubious morals, who makes her living through performances such as the present one, of a dance of seduction. What seemed to have impressed the audience among other things, however, were the moments of silence and static pose that marked the high points of the dance: "The orchestra—the gamelan—plays more and more softly and hesitantly—and finally becomes mute. Man and woman stand opposite each other, bent backwards, the eyes half closed, fingertips pressed against the chest, knees and hips trembling. The music begins again: nothing but a long, mourning sound, growing and fading; almost without changing her pose, the *bajadère* flees, stepping backwards, the man following her. . . . "[84] After that second dance, the show was over. The musicians exchanged the instruments of the gamelan for those of the *angklung* and guided the audience away, so that the next group of visitors could take their place. It was an efficient and well-organized spectacle, offered repeatedly throughout the afternoon to the visitors of the *kampong*.

The dance of the four *tandak* was received as a stylized, aristocratic, and rarefied expression of an ancient art, and within the controlled environment of a colonial exhibition, the audience could revel in a ritual of subjugation to exotic beauty, which was reflected over and over again in programs, letters, and newspaper columns. The focus, however, was on the splendor of the four *tandak*, not on Elles, the everyday performer. The exotic world of the Javanese spectacle became a place to which one could escape from the modern Paris in search of a world of exquisite primitivism.

82. "Échos de Paris," *L'Événement*, 27 Aug. 1889, 1.

83. Émile Michelet, "Autour de l'Exposition," *Paris illustré*, 6 July 1889, 475–76, at 476: "Aux danses succède une pantomime dansée."

84. Schulte-Smidt, *Bleistift-Skizzen*, 68: "Das Orchester—das Kamelong—spielt immer leiser, immer zögernder—endlich verstummt es ganz. Da stehen Mann und Weib sich gegenüber, zurückgebogen, die Augen halb geschlossen, die Fingerspitzen gegen die Brust gepreßt, Knie und Hüften in zitternder Bewegung. Die Musik setzt wieder ein: nichts als ein langer, schwellender und verhauchender Klagelaut; fast ohne ihre Stellung zu verändern flieht die Bajadere, rückwärts schreitend, von dannen, und der Mann folgt ihr, die weitgespreizten Finger in tastender, suchender Bewegung vor sich hinstreckend und dabei einen eigenthümlichen, miauenden Ton ausstoßend, fast wie das Fauchen des Wildkaters."

Danse javanaise.

Figure 4.11. Exposition Universelle, Paris, 1889: Exposition Coloniale, Sundanese Dancers (Elles and partner?), *La Revue illustrée* 4 (1889): 44.

The imagined timelessness of the Far East became an antidote to the struggle for progress in metropolitan Paris.[85] Words such as "dream," "symbol," and "hieratic idol" became obligatory ingredients of the press reception, which in turn conditioned the audience's attitude in a feedback loop. One went to the *kampong javanais* to experience "penetrating and unknown sensations" and "to breathe a new air impregnated with exotic perfume."[86] The gamelan provided the acoustic backdrop for an exotic pastoral with its "strange and confused harmony. Whisperings, murmurs, the rustling of a tree in the wind, raindrops . . . nothing but the sounds of nature, and a

---

85. Timelessness and stagnation were habitually associated in French nineteenth-century anthropology with cultures from the Far East, especially those perceived as "old": India and China. See, for example, La Fage, *Histoire générale de la musique et de la danse*, 2:608. On the philosophical underpinning for such constructs and their resonance in twentieth-century philosophy, see Kerwin Lee Klein, "In Search of Narrative Mastery: Postmodernism and the People without History," *History and Theory* 34 (1995): 275–98.

86. Kernoa, "La Danse," 3: "On éprouve des sensations pénétrantes et inconnues. On y respire comme une atmosphère nouvelle toute imprégnée de parfums exotiques."

melody that is always beyond reach."[87] The fact that the four dancers came from the princely court of Surakarta only added to the fantasy of catching a glimpse of a hidden world of mysterious exotic beauty, even if, as the symbolist writer Joris-Karl Huysmans observed in truly Parisian fashion, these goddesses had dirty feet. . . . [88]

Indeed, every detail of the spectacle—whether on stage or behind the scenes—was scrutinized in press accounts. Life in the *kampong* was shared with the entire world, including the death and funeral, in early July, of Aneh, one of the musicians.[89] The four dancers lived the life of tabloid celebrities: every move of these "living Gustave Moreaus" was described in the newspapers, while the illustrated press ran articles with lavish pictures.[90] A favorite topic was the grooming of the four *tandak*, to which selected journalists were admitted, creating an exotic shade of the Parisian *foyer de la danse*, where for over half a century dancers were exhibited to the gaze of admirers and (possible) "protectors."[91] And when the four *tandak* went to town, the theaters they visited made sure that the public knew in advance about the additional attraction in the hall: "In full gala costume, the Javanese dancers . . . will attend the Théâtre de la Gaîté tonight."[92]

The spectacle itself received the same treatment by journalists as would a major production in one of the Parisian theaters, and the music obtained surprising coverage in the press reports after the "première" in late May.

87. Judith Gautier, "Les Danseuses javanaises," *Le Rappel*, 27 May 1889 / 8 Prairial an 97, 1: "Oh! L'étrange et confuse harmonie! Des rumeurs, des murmures, un frisson d'arbres dans le vent, de gouttes de pluie sur des grandes feuilles rudes, des caquetements [*sic*] d'oiseaux, une cascade lointaine, l'écho sourd et rythmique des lames dans une grotte marine. Rien que des bruits de la nature, une insaisissable mélodie."

88. See François Lesure, *Claude Debussy: Biographie critique* (Paris: Klincksieck, 1994), 105.

89. For the announcement of the death, see Georges Grison, "Courrier de l'Exposition," *Le Figaro*, 5 July 1889, 3. The report of the funeral—which appeared in identical wording in various newspapers—was probably a press release from the organizers. The fullest account appeared in the column "L'Exposition," *Le Rappel*, 8 July 1889, 2.

90. Letter from Henry Lerolle to Ernest Chausson, dated June 1889, in *Ernest Chausson: Écrits inédits*, ed. Jean Gallois (Paris: Éditions du Rocher, 1999), 214: "Ce sont des Gustaves Moreau vivants."

91. For two of the many examples, see: Marcel Édant, "La Toilette des danseuses javanaises," *Le Figaro*, 20 July 1889, 1–2; and Émile Michelet, "Autour de l'Exposition," *Paris illustré*, 14 Sept. 1889, 655–58.

92. Georges Boyer, "Courrier des Théâtres," *Le Figaro*, 2 Oct. 1889, 6: "Les danseuses javanaises, accompagnées de leurs gentilles camarades soudanaises, iront ce soir, en costume de gala, au théâtre de la Gaîté." The "Courrier de Théâtre"–type columns offer normally a mixture of reports and advertising, the latter (if not both) subject to payment by the theaters mentioned in the column. See James Ross, "Crisis and Transformation: French Opera, Politics and the Press, 1897–1903" (DPhil diss., Oxford University, 1998), 13.

Traditionally, only opera criticism would put a similar focus on the music, although plot and *mise-en-scène* received significantly more prominence even there.[93] In reviews of vaudeville and similar attractions, the musical side of the show remained further in the background. In the case of the *kampong javanais*, however, music seemed to have suffused the experience to such an extent that it could not but pervade the accounts in newspapers. These accounts allow us to trace what Parisian writers perceived as the distinctive qualities of Javanese music.

In contradiction to most Western spectacles, here the musicians themselves were part of the show. They guided the audience into the theater. They were sitting visibly on the stage and were part of the exotic ambience. Their instruments were unusual and ornamental in ways few Western instruments of the nineteenth century could rival (save, perhaps, the harp and artisan-built pianos).[94] Most drawings and engravings of the Javanese spectacle show the musicians playing their unusual instruments, and even caricatures—always a sign that an event had caught the imagination of a wider audience—represented the gamelan players and their music (figures 4.12a and 4.12b). Yet not only their music and instruments, but also their posture, their clothing, and their expressions were scrutinized: "The Sundanese beat on all the instruments, some with a serious face, others already half-ironically."[95]

Journalists—themselves rarely musicians—tried to explain to their readers what this music was like. In the unsigned column in *Le Petit Journal*, we read of the gamelan as "a grouping of instruments of wood and brass, kinds of rudimentary pianos with a nasal and monotonous sound, which are supported by a cello with two strings and a drum made from the bark of a coconut tree."[96] Gustave Geffroy described the gamelan as an orchestra

93. On the "formula" of nineteenth-century opera criticism, see Hervé Lacombe, *The Keys to French Opera in the Nineteenth Century*, trans. Edward Schneider (Berkeley, Los Angeles, and London: University of California Press, 2001), 68.

94. While the gamelan used in the *kampong* was most probably a smaller ensemble, it nevertheless featured *bonang, gambang*, gongs, *jenglong*, drums, and *rebab*. Whether the ensemble had *sarons* and a *tarumpet* is not clear. See Chazal, " 'Grand Succès pour les Exotiques,' " 122–23. The splendor of the painted and carved wood-work and of the shiny brass gongs formed part of the spectacle. The visually more spectacular "gamelan de Cirebon," which had been offered to the French in 1887, could be admired in the Palais des Expositions Diverses (Ibid., 120).

95. "Chronique de l'Exposition; Le kampong javanais," *Journal des débats*, 28 May 1889, 3: "Des Sundanais [*sic*] tapent sur tous ces instrumens [*sic*], les uns au visage sérieux, les autres déjà à demi-ironiques."

96. "Curiosités de l'Exposition: Un kampong javanais," *Le Petit Journal*, 29 May 1889, 1: "réunion d'instruments de bois et de cuivre, sorte de pianos rudimentaires aux sons nasillards et monotones, soutenus par un violoncelle à deux cordes et par un tambour en écorce de cocotier."

Figure 4.12a. Engraving of Javanese dancers, in *L'Exposition Universelle* 1 (1889): *Supplément no. 27.*

Figure 4.12b. Caricature of gamelan players, *La Caricature*, 20 June 1889, 195.

that comprised a violin, drums, gongs, and harmonicas, while G. Lenôtre was reminded of pastoral cowbells in the Alps.[97] The apparently nasal grain of the singer's voice represented a strange form of vocal production that the audience had not expected, and it was greeted at first with merriment.[98] The sonorities of the *angklung*, on the other hand, seem to have found easier resonance with the Parisian audiences as a soothing sound of nature.

Only a few musicians, though, left any specific descriptions of the sonorities at the *kampong*. Julien Tiersot, whose interest in non-Western music was just emerging at this time, tried to offer transcriptions and explanations of the music, while Louis Benedictus arranged his renderings for piano in a lavishly illustrated music album, *Les Musiques bizarres de l'Exposition*, published by Hartmann in August 1889.[99] Some sparse information about the music can be gleaned from these sources.

As Chazal has shown convincingly, the gamelan that accompanied the dances was most probably a gamelan *salendro* from Bandung.[100] Thus the

---

97. Gustave Geoffroy, "Chronique," *La Justice*, 30 May 1889, 1: "Un violon conduit le tapage sourd des tambours, des gongs, des harmonicas." G. Lenôtre, *Voyage merveilleux à l'Exposition Universelle de 1889* (Paris: Duquesne et fils, n.d.), 31: "Écoutez ce bruit bizarre, assez semblable à celui que produisent les clochettes des troupeaux des Alpes: c'est le *gamelang*, nom général donné à l'orchestre javanais. . . ." This volume is based on Lenôtre's contributions to *Le Monde illustré*.

98. Gautier, "Les Danseuses javanaises," 1: "Quand la voix humaine se mêle au concert, inattendue, nasillarde, sans s'inquiéter de l'accord, le public s'égaye un peu."

99. Julien Tiersot published his regular column, "Promenades musicales à l'Exposition," in *Le Ménestrel* between 26 May and 20 Oct. 1889. These were reprinted as *Promenades musicales à l'Exposition* (Paris: Fischbacher, 1889). Louis Benedictus, *Les Musiques bizarres de l'Exposition* (Paris: Hartmann & Cie, 1889). Richard Muller discusses these two sources to some extent in his article "Javanese Influence on Debussy's *Fantaisie* and Beyond," *19th-Century Music* 10 (1986): 157–86. In his sources for *Vani-Vani*, he neglects, however, the version offered in the program for the *kampong javanais*. Furthermore, he misreads Benedictus's *Danse javanaise* as a version of *Vani-Vani* (166–67), for which there is no evidence. In contrast, I propose that Benedictus is offering a version of the first dance from the *langêndryian*, which is supported to a certain extent by the analysis in Jürgen Arndt, *Der Einfluß der javanischen Gamelan-Musik auf Kompositionen von Claude Debussy* (Frankfurt/Main: Peter Lang, 1993), 63–64. The publication date for Benedictus' volume is confirmed by a publication of one piece in *Le Figaro*, 16 Aug 1889, in which the imminent release of the volume was announced.

100. Chazal, " 'Grand Succès pour les Exotiques,' " 125–26. For a brief introduction into the music of the gamelan (and in particular the Sundanese gamelan), see Anderson Sutton, Suanda, and Williams: "Java," 630–728. See 701 and 703: "A Sundanese gamelan usually consists of a core group of metallophones (*saron*), horizontal gong-chime sets (*bonang*), vertically suspended gongs (*go'ong*), and a set of barrel drums (*kendang*). Other features, including xylophones, aerophones (flutes or oboes), a bowed lute, and vocalists, are included according to the type of ensemble. . . . *Gamelan saléndro* includes metallophones, gong chimes, gongs, drums, a bowed spiked lute, and a vocalist."

performance at the Exposition was one that offered dances from both Central and Western Java accompanied by an ensemble that originated in Sunda. While on the surface this combination of performance styles might seem incongruous, princely marriages and trade between the two Javanese provinces had ensured that music of either origin was known in the other province and that musicians were fluent in both styles. I would therefore side with Ernst Heins in his speculation that "in those days Sundanese gamelan players could, with some adaptations, meaningfully perform Javanese music (and sing Javanese *tembang macapat*)."[101] Chazal's conclusion that the musicians played Sundanese popular music while the *tandak* danced an unrelated dance from Central Java is unfounded and rather problematic because the scenario of musical unprofessionalism painted by Chazal is uncomfortably close to declaring the Javanese performers as musically unfit and technically limited from a modernist European perspective.[102]

As for the repertoire, we can find some hints in the sources. Both Kernoa, in his 1889 program note for the spectacle, and Tiersot mention *Vani-Vani* as a popular Sundanese melody that (might have) accompanied the dance of Elles and her unknown partner in a congruently Sundanese performance in which the *rebab* played a less prominent role than *bonang*, *saron*, and *gambang*.[103] Tiersot mentions a second title in his description of the Javanese dances: *Feuille d'or* or *Dahonn-Maas*, which may have been a Sundanese popular song (example 4.1).[104] The musicians he interviewed in June 1889 played this piece to him as an illustration for the gamelan *salendro*. It seems, however, that the music that accompanied the *langêndriyan* is reflected in the untitled, more extensive transcriptions of fragments of the performance earlier in Tiersot's text and in Benedictus's version of the *Danse javanaise* for piano (examples 4.2 and 4.3 [Ex. 4.3 is found at the end of this chapter, pp. 207–15]). Benedictus's and Tiersot's transcriptions reveal strong similarities in that they represent a melodic line whose contours include a falling fourth, a major second, and a third. In Western terms—given that these transcriptions were rendered as tonal pieces—both start and focus on the supertonic and keep reaching the third below, with a

101. Ernst Heins, email communication to the "Indonesian Performing Arts List" (gamelanlistserv@dartmouth.edu) from 6 Nov. 1998. I am grateful to Catherine Falk for communicating this email exchange to me.

102. Chazal, " 'Grand Succès pour les Exotiques,' " 126.

103. Julien Tiersot, "Promenades musicales à l'Exposition," *Le Ménestrel* 55 (1889): 260: "La musique de ces danses ne diffère pas sensiblement de celle des précédentes, si ce n'est peut-être qu'elle admet moins de recherches et de complications dans son développement. De même, les thèmes ont généralement moins de relief, et la personnalité du *rebab*, l'instrument mélodique par excellence de l'orchestre javanais, y disparaît le plus souvent devant celle des instruments frappés, *bonang, saron* et *gambang*."

104. Ibid., 259. I wish to thank Sarah Weiss for pointing out the similarity of *Feuille d'or* to Sundanese popular songs.

a. Melody of *Feuille d'or (Dahonn-Maas)*, played by *rebab*.

b. Ornamentation of melody in *rebab* part.

Example 4.1. Transcription of *Feuille d'or (Dahonn-Maas)*, performed by the game-lan in 1889 in Paris, from Julien Tiersot, "Promenades musicales à l'Exposition," *Le Ménestrel* 55 (1889): 260.

a. Beginning of the piece, melody played by *rebab*.

b. Beginning of melody line (sung?), starting slowly.

c. Melodic fragment played by *rebab* and *bonang-ageng*, with *saon-barong*, low *bonang*, and gongs.

d. Ornamentation of high-pitched *bonang* over the melody.

Example 4.2. Transcriptions of the gamelan performances for *langêndriyan* in 1889 in Paris, from Julien Tiersot, "Promenades musicales à l'Exposition," *Le Ménestrel* 55 (1889): 236.

rhythmic shift from duplets to triplets and the inclusion of similar sixteenth-note ornaments. In both renderings, the texture gradually becomes rhythmically more complex, and the registers spread out more widely.

It is far too easy to dismiss, as does Richard Muller, Benedictus's mediation of the dance as an inadequate and simplistic representation of

e. Faster development performed by *bonang, rebab, sarong-barong, gambang, bonang, gongs,* "sorte de sistre," and drum.

Example 4.2. (Continued)

the gamelan performance at the Exposition, while trusting Tiersot's more "ethnomusicological" one.[105] A closer look at Benedictus's version (example 4.3) offers some fascinating insights into the way in which a pair of Parisian ears might have heard the dance and what, in its course, Benedictus found striking. His *Danse javanaise* emphasizes those traits of gamelan music to which newspaper accounts drew their readers' attention: the slow build-up of the dynamic curve; the abrupt and unprepared ending of the piece on loud (*fortissimo*) beats; the cyclic structure of gamelan music which halts at the end of a cycle and then begins anew (see the fermatas in mm. 11, 17, 45); the percussive quality and the increasing density of the texture. Through the depression of the pedal at the beginning, the relatively simple harmonic language receives an aura of non-Western tuning, especially through the close dissonances in the top registers at the beginning (mm. 1–9) and the increasing presence of the sixteenth-notes (mm. 32–43, 66–79). Between the latter two passages, a rhythmically more challenging section (*Tempo 1° ma più mod*[to], mm. 46–65) reflects the interlocking rhythmic strata of the gamelan performance. It is to be played "très rythmé," the pedal still depressed. Thus Benedictus created a representation of the sonic surface, offering some approximation to the timbral experience of the gamelan performance and mirroring the static, unpredictable and cyclic nature of the music that accompanied the dancers while echoing the faintly familiar melodic fragments of the performance. Benedictus's transcription permitted his audience to take a small piece of sonic memory of the Javanese spectacle back into the Parisian and provincial *salons* and drawing rooms at a time when recordings were not yet an alternative.

Musicians and dilettantes alike were fascinated both by the spectacle of the Javanese dance and by the music that accompanied it. It was, as Saint-Saëns put it, "a dream music which had truly hypnotized some people."[106] This subsumed the experience in the *kampong javanais* under one of symbolist art, where exquisitely adorned "savage marionettes" came to life to the sounds of a mesmerizing and strange music.[107] While literary and painterly images from Flaubert's *Salammbô* to Moreau's *Salomé* offered a framework of

105. See, for example, Muller, "Javanese Influence on Debussy's *Fantaisie* and Beyond," 167. For an uncritical eulogy of Tiersot's ethnomusicological credits, see Jean-Paul Montagnier, "Julien Tiersot: Ethnomusicologue à l'Exposition Universelle de 1889. Contribution à une histoire française de l'ethnomusicologie," *International Review of the Aesthetics and Sociology of Music* 21 (1990): 91–100.

106. Camille Saint-Saëns, "Le 'Rappel' à l'Exposition: Les instruments de musique," *Le Rappel*, 10 Oct. 1889 / 19 Vendémiaire an 98, 1–2, at 2: "C'est de la musique de rêve dont quelques personnes ont été réellement hypnotisées."

107. Maurice Guillemet, "Sadisme à l'Exposition: III. Au Kampong," *Gil Blas*, 19 Aug. 1889, 3: "De les regarder longtemps, marionnettes sauvages dont nous ignorons la psychologie, incite à une hypnotisation douce." See also Henri Lavedan, "Les Petites Javanaises," *La Revue illustrée* 4 (1889), 43–48, at 45.

exotic fantasies into which the dancers could be inscribed, the sonic reality of the music transgressed—albeit gently and in dream-like fashion—the confines of exoticism and forced an encounter with "an unknown music."[108] But even if it might have broken down forms of exoticist consumption by drawing attention to a positive and powerful force, this was music framed by the pastoral context of the pre-industrial Javanese village, thus marginalized as the sounds of an idealized primitive, albeit intriguing, past.

## The *Théâtre Annamite*

The exquisite experience in the *kampong javanais* contrasted with the lively and noisy performances in the Vietnamese theater, which were nevertheless perceived as the "archi-comble de l'archi-exotisme."[109] Starting in early June, a troupe of thirty-four actors and musicians performed every day in a theater that held about five hundred spectators and whose components had been brought over from Saigon (figure 4.13). The inside décor of the hall, with its rich colors and carvings, was sumptuous, and like the Javanese dancers, the Vietnamese actors stunned the Parisians with the splendor of their costumes, which, as one commentator put it, would make any Parisian belle envious (figures 4.14a and 4.14b). These performances drew almost as much attention as the Javanese dances, even though their reception turned out differently. In particular, hearing the actual sounds of music from Indochina proved to be quite a shock to Parisian and other Westerner listeners, who had come to associate music from this area—if with anything at all—with the sounds of Bourgault-Ducoudray's *Rapsodie cambodgienne*. The "charivari annamite," as it quickly became known, met with a complete lack of understanding at best, and with in most cases a ferocious rejection. Yet it seems as if the apparent "hideousness" of the performance became a major part of the exotic attraction of the Vietnamese theater, which was perceived as a spectacle of the grotesque rather than of the exquisite.

The *Théâtre Annamite* opened with a gala performance for the press on 5 June 1889. Until the closing of the Exposition on 6 November, the troupe normally ran eight daily performances, five in the afternoon and three in the evening.[110] The theater charged admission to the shows, with

108. Michelet, "Autour de l'Exposition" (July), 475: "On entend une musique inconnue."

109. Émile Goudeau, "Théâtres de l'Exposition," *La Revue illustrée* 4 (1889), 2:171–74, at 171: "L'archi-comble de l'archi-exotisme, c'est de se plaire au Théâtre Annamite, c'est d'ouïr, sans broncher, durant de longues heures, les extraordinaires miaulements de l'acteur principal."

110. Arthur Pougin, *Le Théâtre à l'Exposition Universelle de 1889: Notes et descriptions, histoires et souvenirs* (Paris: Librarie Fischbacher, 1890), 91. The shows took place at 1:30 P.M., 2:30 P.M., 3:30 P.M., 4:30 P.M., 5:30 P.M., 8:00 P.M., 9:00 P.M., and 10:00 P.M.

Figure 4.13. Unsigned photograph of the Théâtre Annamite. B.H.V.P., *Paris Album 4° 14.*

prices ranging between 50 centimes and 5 francs, and—according to Pougin—gained at least 230,000 francs during these six months.[111] Between 306,000 and 480,000 people came to watch the spectacle.[112] But while the obsession of both writers and music historians with the Javanese dancers uncovered information about their background and their performance, the group of Vietnamese actors remained much more anonymous. The four Javanese dancers had acquired star status and were treated as such. The Vietnamese actors and musicians blended into their group and were rarely mentioned as individuals.

Nevertheless, we encounter a few details about the performers and their performances in the press reports, which might help us to uncover some information about the spectacle beyond the ubiquitous characterization as "charivari." It is possible that the director of the *Théâtre Annamite*

111. Ibid., 91. Compare this sum with the income of the Opéra and the Opéra-Comique during the same period discussed in chapter 2 (p. 60).

112. Picard, *Rapport général sur l'Exposition universelle internationale de 1889*, 3:285. The report distinguishes between 306,271 paying visitors and, according to the police chief, 482,545 visitors in all.

Figure 4.14a. Photograph of Vietnamese actors in costume. B.H.V.P., *Paris Album 4° 14.*

Figure 4.14b. Unsigned photograph of three Vietnamese actors in costume, B.H.V.P., *Paris Album 4° 14.*

*Ngu-Hô* was Nguyễn Trọng Trì, one of the writers who contributed to the stabilization and revitalization of classical theater in late-nineteenth-century Vietnam.[113] The company itself was from Saigon, and the facilitator of the theater's visit to the Exposition was probably Georges Marx, who was then involved with the daily newspaper *Saïgon républicain*.[114] The descriptor of *Théâtre Annamite* apparently referred to the repertoire performed, which seems to have been in the style of theater from around Huế.

Indeed, all the indications in the reports of the première and in later newspaper coverage point towards the fact that the 1889 audience was treated to a form of classical Vietnamese theater (*hát bội* or *tuồng*): the descriptions of the performances, the images of stage and costumes, the episodes, the forms of dialogue and song, and the musical ensemble that accompanied the actors all fit the characteristics of the genre. Pougin identified four different episodes: *Le Roi de Duong, Nuy-Ho* (*Cinq tigres mandarins*), *Vo-Haû*, and *Lé Hué* (*La Rose*).[115] Hippolyte Lemaire, who paraphrased the program notes in his article, offered a Vietnamese title for *Le Roi de Duong* as *Ly-Tieng-Vuong*.[116] Few people in the audience, however, knew anything about *hát bội* or about its music, and the program booklet was all

113. Pougin spells his name as Nguyen Dông Tru. Given differences in pronociation and spelling in French and English (which extends to the transliteration of Asiatic languages), the slight deviation in spelling may indicate the same person (*Le Théâtre à l'Exposition Universelle de 1889*, 91). My identification of this writer is, however, based upon conjecture rather than unshakable proof. See Pham Duy, *Musics of Vietnam* (Carbondale and London: Southern Illinois University Press and Feffer & Simons, 1973), 116–17. See also Phong T. Nguyễn, "Vietnam," in *The Garland Encyclopedia of World* Music, vol. 4, *Southeast Asia*, ed. Terry E. Miller and Sean Williams (New York and London: Garland Publishing, 1998), esp. 490–93.

114. "Exposition Universelle: Le Théâtre Annamite," *La Justice*, 24 May 1889, 2–3.

115. Pougin, *Le Théâtre à l'Exposition Universelle de 1889*, 97. Johannès Weber identifies the third piece as *Yo-Haû*, "Suite du *roi de Duong*, épopée mêlée de chant"; see "Feuilleton du *Temps*: Critique musicale," *Le Temps*, 19 Aug. 1889, 3.

116. Hippolyte Lemaire, "Théâtres," *Le Monde illustré*, 15 June 1889, 398–99, at 399: "Voici, d'après le programme, le scénario de la pièce représentée qui s'appelle *Ly-Tieng-Vuong*, c'est à dire *le Roi de Duong*. C'est l'histoire d'une conspiration qui rappelle, dans ses grandes lignes, le *Macbeth* de Shakespeare. La Scène se passe dans le pays de Chau. Chien-Ou, beau-frère du roi et son vassal, a invité à une grande fête son auguste parent: Il médite un attentat contre la personne sacrée du roi. Mais celui-ci est prévenu par les fidèles ministres qui l'accompagnent et qui ont deviné les projets de l'hôte déloyal. Ly-Tieng-Vuong s'enfuit à travers les rizières, où il pense se noyer et où un de ses mandarins trouve la mort. Chien-Ou envoie une armée à sa poursuite. Le roi est cerné et les régicides mettent le feu aux prairies infinies. Un autre mandarin du roi périt encore dans l'incendie. Mais le fils adoptif de Ly-Tieng-Vuong, ne voyant pas revenir son père, a aussi rassemblé des troupes et accourt au devant de lui. Les deux armées se rencontrent: la bataille s'engage, terrible, acharnée et finit par un massacre général. La victoire est

the information there was about the spectacle.[117] Critics worried repeatedly that the meager information about the dramas, their music, and their meaning could not be verified, for almost none of the Vietnamese spoke French and vice versa.[118] This lack of understanding, however, did not seem to diminish the attraction of the spectacle as the summit of exoticism at the Exposition.

Critics compared the spectacle to pantomimes or to performances of the *commedia dell'arte*.[119] This form of reception might be one key to understanding the success of the Annamite spectacle, for although the Vietnamese Theater was alien to its Parisian audience, the spectators had a framework of theatrical reference within which the colorful, gestural performances of the *Théâtre Annamite* could be read. Reviews reflected this by alluding to the pantomimes at the Cirque Olympique and other venues, to the character Pierrot at the Théâtre des Funambules, or to Harlequin.[120] What the audience saw were performers with grotesquely painted faces, quite unusual costumes, and exaggerated gestures, who moved about the stage in jumps or strange steps, easily a subject of caricature (figure 4.15). Although the visual side of the *Théâtre Annamite* was alien in its specificity, the general context of seeing grotesquely madeup actors bouncing on the stage and miming a story was familiar to European pantomime audiences. Even the vocal production of the actors—which was described invariably as shouting, yelling, and screaming—was not completely out of context. While in Vietnamese culture *hát bội* counted among the most venerable theatrical genres, it was received at the Exposition as exotic popular pantomime and stood thus even less chance at being taken seriously.

The music that accompanied the production was too strange to allow for a reception similar to that of the Javanese gamelan, whose tuning and scale

restée avec les troupes du roi. Ly-Tieng-Vuong est sauvé et il rentre triomphalement dans sa capitale, au milieu de l'allegresse générale."

117. Thus far I have been unable to locate the program booklet which is referred to by critics and which is cited in Anik Devriès, "Les Musiques d'extrême Orient à l'Exposition Universelle de 1889," *Cahiers Debussy*, 1 (1977): 37.

118. See, for example, Francisque Sarcey, "Chronique," *Le XIX Siècle: Journal républicain*, 11 June 1889, 1: "Le diable c'est que l'on ne peut vérifier aucune de ces assertions, ces-gens là [*sic*] ne parlant point français." According to Pougin, the director of the troupe spoke some French, and Tiersot managed to interview one of the musicians with the help of a translator (Julien Tiersot, "Promenades musicales à l'Exposition," *Le Ménestrel* 55 [1889]: 195).

119. See, for example, "Chronique théâtrale," *Le Temps*, 10 June 1889, 1–2, at 2: "On m'assure que la pièce est jouée sur scénario: c'est une *comedia* [*sic*] *dell'arte.*"

120. See, for example, the unsigned column "A l'Exposition: Ouverture du Théâtre Annamite—Un art étrange," *Le Matin*, 6 June 1889, 2.

Figure 4.15. Lucien Menvet, "Le Théâtre annamite à l'Exposition," *Le Courrier français illustré: Littérature + Beaux-Arts + Théâtres + Médecine + Finance* 6 (21 July 1889): 9. B.H.V.P.

system were close enough to Western keys to sound vaguely tonal with penta-tonic tinges. This was not the case with the music from Vietnam, which, to Western ears, sounded sharply dissonant. For the most part, the reaction to this music was predictably negative. Reading the general press gives the impression of the journalists entering a competition as to who could write the most outrageous condemnation. Émile Goudeau found that the musicians accompanied the text "with frightful and continuous sounds that are able to smash the skull of a pachyderm without any visible tool."[121] After characterizing the musical ensemble as "horrible charivari of saucepan solos accompanied by drums, cymbals and tramway horns," Hippolyte Lemaire staged the interplay between actors and musicians as a competition in noise:

> Then began a deplorable emulation between [the actors] and the musicians. It is a fight: the former try hard to dominate the brouhaha in screaming, with exasperated contortions, like animals being slaughtered, while the latter furiously double their effort on their *tam-tam* and on their zebra-skins stretched to the point of ripping apart. The result is an infernal racket.

> Imaginez le plus effroyable charivari de solos de casseroles avec accompagnement de tambour, de cymbales et de cornes de tramways, voilà ce qui soutient la déclamations. . . . Alors il s'établit entre [les acteurs] et les musiciens une émulation déplorable. C'est une lutte: les premiers s'efforcent de dominer le brouhaha en poussant, avec des contorsions exaspérées, des cris de bêtes qu'on égorge, tandis que les seconds redoublent de rage sur leurs *tam-tam* et sur leurs peaux de zèbres tendues à crever. Il en résulte un tapage infernal.[122]

To add insult to injury, there are no zebras in Vietnam. However it is Jules Lemaître who deserves the prize for the most gruesome description of the music in his front-page article for *Le Figaro*:

> And what music! The most discordant charivari of lunatic amateurs would seem like a celestial harmony after this. Heavy strokes on a piece of wood or on pots; a kind of flute whose sound enters your ear like a rotary drill. It is music for torturers, made to accompany the agony of prisoners under whose fingernails one has forced sharp reeds, or whose head was put into a hermetically sealed cage that contains a rat—a pretty rat with pointed teeth to nibble on your lips, your nose, your eyes, slowly and with pauses. . . .

121. Goudeau, "Théâtres à l'Exposition," 171: "[L]es ouvriers en musique, les spécialistes de gammes annamites, soulignent ou plutôt surlignent le texte bramé par d'effroyables et continues sonorités capables de démantibuler sans ressource appréciable le crâne d'un pachyderme."
122. Lemaire, "Théâtres," 398–99.

Et quelle musique! Le charivari le plus discordant de rapins en délire sem-
blerait, après cela, une harmonie céleste. Des grands coups sur des morceaux
de bois ou sur des pots; une espèce de flûte dont le son vous entre dans l'oreille comme un vilebrequin. Musique de tortionnaires, faite pour accompagner l'agonie des prisonniers à qui l'on a enfoncé des roseaux pointus sous les
ongles, ou dont on a introduit la tête dans une cage hermétiquement close,
laquelle contient un rat,—un joli rat aux dents pointues pour vous grignoter
les lèvres, le nez, les yeux, lentement, avec des pauses. . . . [123]

All these forms of torture were, of course, viewed as particularly oriental,
and therefore Lemaître plays into the usual Western fears of Oriental
sadism. While few writers went to such extremes, descriptors such as "charivari" and "tapage infernal" were common.[124] Even some of the musicians
had difficulties with this arresting sound-world, and Gaston Paulin's wording in *Le Guide musical* echoed those of his generalist colleagues in the daily
press: "During the entire action, a bizarre orchestra would not stop making
a horrible din on the pretext of [providing] incidental music."[125] Such
attitudes did not go unopposed, however, and within a week of Paulin's ver-
dict, *The Musical World* published as its lead article the following comment,
which sharply criticized so cavalier an attitude:

Western prejudice in matters artistic has seldom been illustrated more
strongly than in an article which appears in our Belgian contemporary,
"Le Guide Musical," upon the music of the Annamite Theatre, which is so
singular a feature of the Paris Exhibition. It is not necessary to quote
from the article, but it may be said that it is written throughout in an
unsympathetic vein which is surely ill-chosen, in dealing with a subject of
such interest to all students of comparative musical science. The critic
discovers only horrible discordant noises and relics of musical barbarism,
in the art thus illustrated. We shall not go so far as to declare that to the
ears trained to appreciate the modern music of Europe, much satisfaction is to be derived from these primitive performances; but the adoption
of the tone indicated is scarcely to be commended. It displays a complete
inability to alter the critical standpoint, or to depolarise habitual convic-
tions—two things which must be accomplished by anyone who under-
takes to assess these performances at their true value. What, it may be

123. Jules Lemaitre, "Le Théâtre Annamite," *Le Figaro*, 8 July 1889, 1.
124. Charivari refers traditionally to noisy and unharmonious sound productions
that were often generated though beating on pots and pans. Given the shape of the Vietnamese instruments, the reference might be quite literal.
125. G. P. [Gaston Paulin], "A l'Exposition," *Le Guide musical* 35 (1889): 173: "Pendant toute l'action, un orchestre bizarre, sous prétexte de musique de scène, ne cesse de
faire un vacarme effroyable." The date of the issue is 23 & 30 June 1889.

wondered, would the Annamites themselves think of a Beethoven symphony?[126]

As these exchanges show, the music of the *Théâtre Annamite*—both because of its sheer volume but also because of its sonic difference—drew musicians and journalists alike into a heated debate about what kind of music it was and how it related to Western musical experience. While the popular press was mostly negative about the music, musicians' reactions were more complex, with the surprisingly forward-looking view in *The Musical World* remaining, however, the exception more than the rule.

The music that prompted such heated reactions was performed by six musicians. Five were seated on the left side of the stage, one on the right (figure 4.16). The primary instruments of the ensemble were the oboe-like wood instrument (*kèn bóp*), shown on the left of the illustration, and the battle drum (*trồng chiến*), played by the musician in the center of the group on the left. This drum "leads the ensemble with specific rhythmic patterns at the beginning and ending of pieces. It coordinates the ensemble with the actors and actresses by supporting their dance movements."[127] The other instruments in the ensemble were a two-stringed fiddle (*đàn nhị*), a "rice drum" (*trồng cơm*), and various percussion instruments (such as gong and clappers), the latter played by the musician closest to the wall. The musician on the right in the engraving used the largest drum (*trồng chầu*), which is traditionally played by an experienced musician representing the audience. His changing drumming patterns provided a running commentary on the performance from the perspective of the audience.[128]

In *hát bội*, the ensemble plays throughout the piece, "functioning both as an independent element and as an accompaniment."[129] The musicians and the actors share the same scalic material but not the same melodic material. Indeed the actors follow their own musical forms of voice production in either declamation, recitative, or song, which are related to the plot, while the musicians develop the modes into a musical realization appropriate to the represented situations.[130] This procedure results in a relatively heterophonic musical ensemble emphasizing rhythmic complexity and vertical elements in an alien tuning system, rather than the dominant melodic lines found in

126. Unsigned article [C. R. Day?], "Facts and Comments," *The Musical World* 69 (29 June 1889): 409.

127. Nguyễn, "Vietnam," 492. See also Duy, *Musics of Vietnam*, 123.

128. "Originally, this task was assumed by the chief of the village"; Nguyễn, "Vietnam," 492.

129. Ibid., 491.

130. The singers' "repertory consists of *nói loi* (declamations), *xuong, bạch*, and *thán* (recitatives), *hát khách* (songs of the 'guest' category), *hát nam* (songs of the 'native' category and in the *nam* mode), *hát bài* (songs for a particular character) and *hát noi niêu* (varied songs)." Tran Văn Khê and Nguyễn Thuyết Phong, "Vietnam," in *NGr2*.

Figure 4.16. "Le Théâtre annamite à l'Esplanade des Invalides," in *L'Exposition Universelle* 1 (1889): *Supplément no 21.*

Chinese theater music. This may explain some of the negative reaction of the Parisian audiences. Furthermore, the music sounded loud in the wooden structure of the theater, in particular with the percussion dominating the sonorities. Johannès Weber made it clear that only well-trained musicians might be able to hear something beyond a "deafening charivari" in this music.[131]

One musician tried. Benedictus's transcription again offers some fascinating insights into the musical perception of the performance (example 4.4). The fact that the collection contains a *Charivari Annamite* at all bears witness to the attention that the Vietnamese Theater received during the Exposition Universelle; it could not have been left out of such a publication as the *Musiques bizarres*. On the page preceding the score, an engraving represents a scene from *Le Roi de Duong*. But the piece itself is very short (17 mm.), limited to one page only.[132] The pianist is instructed to play as

131. Weber, "Feuilleton du *Temps*: Critique musicale": "Il est tout autrement pour le théâtre annamite; des musiciens bien exercés peuvent seuls y trouver quelque chose un peu autre qu'un assourdissant charivari."

132. Although the *Nouba des tirailleurs algériens* is equally short (17 mm.), the music spreads over two pages. All other pieces in the collection are significantly longer.

Example 4.4. Louis Benedictus, *Charivari annamite*, in *Les Musiques Bizarres à l'Exposition* (Paris: Hartmann, 1889), 57.

loudly as possible, in keeping with the noise level of the performance in the theater. The left hand seems to imitate the beats of the *trông châu*, while the melody in the right hand possibly reflects the sound of the *kèn bóp* in a vaguely Oriental-sounding idiom. However, the organisation of the short piece shows that Benedictus was at loss. The *Charivari* is, in fact, in a straight-forward ABA form. In the A section, the melody is a simple four-measure phrase (2+2). The middle section, which is condensed to three measures, offers a melodic variation in similar rhythmic patterns. The three melodic sections are introduced and separated by the beats in the left hand. Benedictus's *Charivari* and the performances at the *Théâtre Annamite* have little if anything to do with each other. While Benedictus was able to create for the piano a not unsophisticated acoustic representation of the gamelan in his *Danse javanaise*—capturing some of the ensemble's sonic qualities and musical developments for Western ears—he seemed much less at ease with the rendering of Vietnamese music, and reduced it in his piece to the low and dominating percussion sound on A with dissonant melodic fragments in E♭ without any attempt at representing the motivic variety of Vietnamese music. The tritonal relationship A–E♭ introduces the time-tested *diabolus in musica* into the harmonic equation, which might not have been entirely accidental in a charivari such as this.

Even Tiersot seemed to find it difficult to say anything substantial about the Vietnamese performances.[133] As with other non-Western musicians, he went and interviewed the Vietnamese players with the help of an interpreter. When it came to describe the music, he relied on two genres familiar to his readers: on the one hand, pantomime and melodrama to relate the relationship of music and acting, and on the other, Wagnerian music drama to describe motivic developments in the music. Indeed, Tiersot's text on the *Théâtre Annamite* resembles his later analyses of Wagner operas such as that of *Die Meistersinger*, or music critic Charles Malherbe's Wagnerian analysis of Massenet's *Esclarmonde*.[134] Tiersot thus dissects the music according to its motivic material in general and leitmotifs more specifically, for example a "motif of war" and a "motif of victory" (example 4.5).

Indeed, the Vietnamese spectacle offered no self-contained pieces, the ensemble never stopped, and the instrumentalists were perceived as contesting the priority of the voice. These were exactly the features that Parisian commentators had identified in Wagner's music drama since the 1850s.[135] It is perhaps no surprise to read in *Le Figaro* the tongue-in-check reference to the "continuous melody" as the "musical commentary on the dialogue of the comedians," or Johannès Weber's more explicit reference to the singing of the actors as "a modulated declamation that would satisfy Wagner rather than

133. Katharine Ellis, "Wagnerism and Anti-Wagnerism in the Paris Periodical Press, 1852–1870," in *Von Wagner zum Wagnérisme: Musik, Literatur, Kunst, Politik,* ed. Annegret Fauser and Manuela Schwartz, 51–83, *Transfer: Die deutsch-französische Kulturbibliothek* 12 (Leipzig: Leipziger Universitäts-Verlag, 1999). Lacombe, *The Keys to French Opera,* 78–82; Steven Huebner, *French Opera at the Fin de Siècle: Wagnerism, Nationalism, and Style* (Oxford: Oxford University Press, 1999).

134. Julien Tiersot, "Promenades musicales à l'Exposition," *Le Ménestrel* 55 (1889): 189, 195–96, at 195: "J'ai *interviewé* les Annamites." Tiersot's section on the *Théâtre Annamite* is significantly shorter than those on Javanese, Arab, or African music.

135. Charles Malherbe, *Notice sur Esclarmonde* (Paris: Fischbacher, 1890), based on his article series "Massenet and Wagner" from July 1889, given in *DE,* 196–208.

a. Motif of war (*motif de la guerre*).

Très vif

b. Motif of victory (*motif du triomphe*).

Example 4.5. Transcriptions of music at the Théâtre Annamite in 1889 in Paris, from Julien Tiersot, "Promenades musicales à l'Exposition," *Le Ménestrel* 55 (1889): 196.

the usual audience of the Paris Grand Opéra."[136] For the Anti-Wagnerian Weber, this was a back-handed compliment to the actors from Saigon. Other critics used the Vietnamese "charivari" as a weapon directed at the music from "outre-Rhin," in the context of both Wagner performance—after all, the turbulent Parisian première of *Lohengrin* had occurred only two years earlier—and French Wagnerism, of which Massenet's *Esclarmonde* was the current (and successful) example. Thus Stop's caricature for *Le Journal amusant* (figure 4.17) leaves his readers wondering whether the Vietnamese music was as bad as Wagner's, or rather whether Wagner's was as atrocious as that of the *Théâtre Annamite*. Sorel, on the other hand, compared the racket of the Vietnamese Theater with that of *Esclarmonde* (figure 4.18). The fact that the Vietnamese troupe had chosen to present four different episodes from the epic *Le Roi de Duong* only made such comparisons with Wagner's music dramas more likely.

## Once Again: Debussy and the Gamelan (with a Vietnamese Variation)

Traces of this comparison can be found even twenty-four years later in a text by Claude Debussy, in which he linked *Le Roi de Duong* with Wagner's *Ring des Nibelungen*:

> In Vietnamese Theater, one performs a kind of embryonic music drama which is influenced by the Chinese, and where one recognizes the

136. Parisis, "Le Théâtre Annamite," *Le Figaro*, 6 June 1889, 2: "Il paraît que cette mélodie continue est le commentaire musical des propos qu'échangent entre eux les comédiens." Weber: "Feuilleton du *Temps*: Critique musicale": "C'est plutôt une déclamation modulée, dont Wagner serait plus satisfait que les habitués du Grand-Opéra de Paris."

AU THÉÂTRE ANNAMITE.
Très bon petit orchestre; seulement il joue un peu
trop de Wagner.

Figure 4.17. Stop, "Promenade à l'Exposition," *Le Journal amusant*, 27 July 1889, 5.
Below the image:
At the Théâtre Annamite:
"Very good little orchestra; only it plays a bit too much Wagner."

tetralogical formula, only there are more gods and less scenery. A raging
small clarinet guides the emotion; a Tam-tam organizes the terror . . . that
is all! No more specially constructed theater, no more hidden orchestra.

Chez les Annamites on représente une sorte d'embryon de drame lyrique,
d'influence chinoise, où se reconnaît la formule tétralogique; il y a seulement plus de Dieux, et moins de décors. . . . Une petite clarinette rageuse
conduit l'émotion; un Tam-tam organise la terreur . . . et c'est tout! Plus
de théâtre spécial, plus d'orchestre caché.[137]

Like the 1889 journalists, Debussy associated—albeit ironically—the dramaturgical use of the instruments in *Le Roi de Duong* with Wagner's leitmotifs and dramaturgical use of instrumentation (*Klangfarbendramaturgie*),
while the epic subject matter and its organization in four evenings had
obvious resonances with Wagner's *Ring*. Such comparisons encourage some
different questions within the ongoing musicological debate concerning

137. Claude Debussy, *Monsieur Croche et autres écrits*, ed. François Lesure (Paris: Gallimard, 1987), 229–30.

— Comment faites-vous, malheu-
reuse ouvreuse, pour supporter tous
les soirs ce vacarme?
— Les autres deviennent folles,
monsieur; moi, je résiste parce que
j'ai subi un entraînement à l'Opéra-
Comique en entendant *Esclarmonde!*

Figure 4.18. Sorel, "A l'Exposition: Les Javanaises et Théâtre annamite,"
*La Caricature*, 1889, 237.

Below the caricature, the following dialogue explains this scene:
—You poor usherette! How can you cope with this racket every evening?
—The others become mad, Sir; I resist it because I have been trained at the
Opéra-Comique listening to *Esclarmonde*!

Debussy's encounter with exotic music at the Exposition Universelle than those that have been addressed in the past thirty years.[138]

Most writers have reduced Debussy's visits to the Exposition Coloniale to those to the *kampong javanais*, often quoting Robert Godet, who recalled in 1926 that:

> Debussy spent extremely fruitful hours in the *kampong javanais* of the Dutch section, where he went countless times, attentive to the polyrhythmic percussion of a gamelan that proved itself inexhaustible in its combination of ethereal or glittering timbres, while the famous bedajas danced, turning music into images.

> Les heures vraiment fécondes pour Debussy, c'est dans le campong javanais de la section néerlandaise qu'il les goûta sans nombre, attentif à la polyrythmie percutée d'un gamelan qui se montrait inépuisable en combinaisons de timbres éthérées ou fulgurantes, tandis qu'évoluaient, musique faite image, les prestigieuses Bedayas.[139]

Godet's memories appear as an echo of Debussy's own words addressed to Pierre Louÿs in a letter of 22 January 1895: "Do you not remember the Javanese music, which contained all the nuances, even those which one can no longer name, where tonic and dominant became naught but vain ghosts for the use of unruly children. . . ."[140] For the composer, Javanese music seemed to be the magic Other, exquisitely different from the shopworn

---

138. Some of the main texts which address this issue are: Devriès, "Les Musiques d'extrême Orient à l'Exposition Universelle de 1889"; Muller, "Javanese Influence on Debussy's *Fantaisie* and Beyond"; Arndt, *Der Einfluß der javanischen Gamelan-Musik*; Roy Howat, "Debussy and the Orient," in *Recovering the Orient: Artists, Scholars, Appropriations*, ed. Andrew Gerstle and Anthony Milner, 45–81 (Chur: Harwood Academic Publishers, 1994); Mervyn Cooke, " 'The East in the West': Evocations of the Gamelan in Western Music," in *The Exotic in Western Music*, ed. Jonathan Bellman, 258–80 (Boston: Northeastern University Press, 1998); Chazal, " 'Grand Succès pour les Exotiques.' " Arndt (19–43) offers a detailed survey of the state of research up until his own contribution (1993). In Oct. and Nov. 1998, an extensive discussion on the issue of Debussy and the gamelan gripped the "Indonesian Performing Arts List" (gamelanlistserv@dartmouth.edu).

139. Robert Godet, "En Marge de la marge," *Revue musicale* 7 (May 1926), quoted in Arndt: *Der Einfluß der javanischen Gamelan-Musik*, 14.

140. Given in Devriès, "Les Musiques d'extrême Orient à l'Exposition Universelle de 1889," 25: "Rappelle-toi la musique javanaise qui contenait toutes les nuances, même celles qu'on ne peut plus nommer, où la tonique et la dominante n'étaient plus que vains fantômes à l'usage des petits enfants pas sages. . . " This must be one of Debussy's best-known remarks, for almost every author addressing the composer's encounter with exotic music, and in particular the gamelan, has cited it. Extracts from Louÿs's original letter and Debussy's response are given in Claude Debussy, *Correspondance 1884–1918*, ed. François Lesure, 2nd ed. (Paris: Hermann, 1993), 107.

sonorities of late-nineteenth-century music. Debussy's letter to Louÿs responded to one in which the poet raved about the sounds of Seville—the music of the "real" Carmen as opposed to that of Bizet—and reminded Louÿs of the remarkable experience they had shared in Paris in the summer of 1889, just before traveling to Bayreuth in order to listen to *Parsifal.* At that time the then twenty-seven-year-old composer was on a quest not just for new music but, more fervently and all-too-often forgotten in this context of the Exposition, for a new French music drama.

Scholars have thus far focused mainly on Debussy's compositions for the piano and for the orchestra in their enterprise to show how his musical experiences at the 1889 Exposition Universelle translated into his personal style. In particular, works such as the 1890 *Fantaisie* for piano and orchestra and the 1903 *Pagodes* (from *Estampes*) became prime candidates for examining the impact of the gamelan on his music, and the chronological proximity of the *Fantaisie* could be used as additional justification. In general terms, Debussy's orchestra, especially in *Nocturnes* (1897–99) and *La Mer* (1903–5), has been described as a "stylized gamelan" because of the often layered instrumentation.[141] The superimposition of different timbral, rhythmical, and registral strata is also one of the character traits of works such as *Pagodes* and has been identified as influenced by the gamelan. If Godet's reporting is to be trusted, this multi-layered contrapuntal quality of the gamelan—which Debussy himself described as being more complex than Palestrina's—seemed to be a musical device that the composer tried to relate to the canon of Western counterpoint through heightened study of Johann Sebastian Bach.[142] In addition, the percussive quality of the piano and its tendency toward sympathetic resonance allow for cross-fertilization with the gamelan.[143] Contrary to Benedictus in his *Musiques bizarres de l'Exposition*, Debussy did not transcribe the music he heard at the Exposition Coloniale into an immediately referential piece—not even in the case of the 1890 *Fantaisie*. Rather, he appropriated structural concepts and compositional procedures from his exposure to the gamelan that became amalgamated with other influences of the 1880s, such as the music of Musorgsky and Wagner, both of which he also heard in 1889.

---

141. Constantin Brailoiu, cited in Edward Lockspeiser, *Debussy: His Life and Mind*, vol. 1: *1862–1902* (London: Cassell, 1962), 116. See also Jens Peter Reiche, "Die theoretischen Grundlagen javanischer Gamelan-Musik und ihre Bedeutung für Claude Debussy," *Zeitschrift für Musiktheorie* 3 (1972): 5–15.

142. Godet, "En Marge de la marge," 154: "les quotidiens tête-à-tête avec Jean-Sébastien Bach que s'accordait Claude Debussy, même et surtout au sortir du campong javanais."

143. See Howat, "Debussy and the Orient," 48–56. Cooke cites a 1937 assessment by E. Robert Schmitz, in which he suggests that "Debussy regarded the piano as the Balinese musicians regard their gamelan orchestras. He was interested not so much in the single tone when a note was struck, as in the patterns of resonance which that tone sets up around itself" (" 'The East in the West,' " 262).

The musical innovations of Debussy's piano music with respect to structure and harmonic language can thus be understood through his encounters with a new sound-world. His new sonorities then found their basis in complex materials appropriated from a different world, and their presence could thus be attributed to a rupture with tradition—a concept dear to the ideology of modernism—rather than to the more suspicious notion of late-nineteenth-century French eclecticism within a continuous development of the Western tradition. Such an interpretation validates Debussy as a modernist hero of innovation rather than one of the many French composers of the nineteenth century succumbing to exotic music. Moreover, most scholars have treated Debussy's experience of the Exposition selectively as an aural encounter. In addition, the vocal elements in the gamelan performances, with their male singer, or the spectacle of the Vietnamese theater, are never mentioned.[144] Yet Debussy's visits to the *Théâtre Annamite* appear to have been almost as frequent as those to the *kampong javanais*. As Robert Godet remembered: "Numerous were the hours that I spent in his company at the *Théâtre Annamite*, whose select audience he scandalized more than once with irreverent comparisons with Bayreuth."[145] Here, Debussy's view was much in accord with that of his contemporaries such as the caricaturist Stop (figure 4.17).

Can we really assume that Debussy heard a form of absolute, wordless exotic music, that he had no eyes, or that he did not care about the spectacle, which is the way in which writers such as Muller, Howat, and Cooke have presented Javanese traces in Debussy's piano music? After all, the gamelan's singer attracted comment in the contemporary press, and we know from Godet that Debussy listened closely to the performance. Yet the only references to vocal music in scholarly discussions focus on the piano parts of Debussy's songs. Thus Muller shows that Benedictus's transcription of the *Danse javanaise* (example 4.3) is echoed in the opening of Debussy's 1891 Verlaine setting, "Clair de lune."[146] Similarly, three other songs on texts by Paul Verlaine—composed in 1891 and 1892—refer to the timbre and rhythmic structure of the gamelan in their piano part: "Le son du cor," "L'Échelonnement des haies," and "En Sourdine." Debussy dedicated the first two to Robert Godet, and the last to Godet's wife.

"En Sourdine" and "Clair de lune," which now form the outer numbers in the *Fêtes galantes* (series I), followed each other directly in Debussy's

144. Devriès is the major exception in her article "Les Musiques d'extrême Orient à l'Exposition Universelle de 1889"; in his recent biography on Debussy, Roger Nichols briefly refers to the *Théâtre Annamite* as an influence on Debussy's concept of music drama. See Roger Nichols, *The Life of Debussy* (Cambridge: Cambridge University Press, 1998), 58.

145. Godet, "En Marge de la marge," 152: "Nombreuses furent les heures que l'on passa dans sa compagnie au Théâtre Annamite, dont il scandalisa plus d'une fois les rares spectateurs par des comparaisons irrévérentes avec Bayreuth."

146. Muller, "Javanese Influence on Debussy's *Fantaisie* and Beyond," 175.

first version of the song set.[147] They are in B major and G♯ minor respectively, key signatures that allow the use of all five black keys on the piano within the tonic, which is the easiest way to create a pentatonic sonority on this instrument. This is exactly how Debussy opens "En Sourdine." The right hand plays a melodic line on the five black keys before ending in a whole-tone alternation B–C♯, which recalls both melodic contour and rhythm of the *suling*, the Javanese flute (example 4.6a).[148] Save for the additional whole-tone step D♯–E♯ in measures 5 and 9, the voice remains for the entire first stanza within the pentatonic *suling* contour outlined an octave higher in measures 1–2, and explores the characteristic heterophonic relationship of a gamelan performance between melodic instrument (usually the *suling* in Sundanese gamelan) and voice in measures 8–9 (example 4.6b). Similar heterophonic counterpoint between piano and voice also exists in the second stanza (mm. 14–15), before, with the third, Debussy shifts towards a much more traditional idiom of a vocal line enveloped by arpeggios in the piano. Heterophonic elaborations of the core melody abound also in "Clair de lune." But neither "En Sourdine" nor "Clair de lune," with its echoes of the shaking sounds of the *angklung*, and the repetitive patterns of the *peking* and the *bonang panerus* in both piano and voice, could be characterized as "exotic" works in the way of, for example, Camille Saint-Saëns's *Mélodies persanes* (1875), where poetry and musical material self-consciously pose as Other. Rather, the two Verlaine poems' dream-like eroticism with their reference to masks and twilight evoke a different world that might have called for the sonic echoes of musical alterity, another musical world whose memories lingered on after the composer experienced the sounds two years earlier at the Exposition Universelle.[149] Debussy's exotic references in these songs are less obvious and often masked, but they nevertheless appropriate another culture's music to represent alterity musically.

If the gamelan performances left such obvious compositional traces in Debussy's songs, both the *kampong javanais* and *Théâtre Annamite* offered aesthetic as well as musical alternatives to the traditional French fare for the musical stage. Indeed, among the closest documents to

147. See the critical commentary in *Songs of Claude Debussy*, ed. James R. Briscoe, 2 vols. (Milwaukee, WI: Hal Leonard Publishing, 1993), 2:11. Briscoe refers to the 1891 manuscript in the collection of Robert Lehman. The songs presented in Briscoe's edition are in the original keys.

148. I am grateful to Ethan Lechner for his help with the intricate aspects of gamelan music.

149. Howat points out that soon after the 1889 Exposition Universelle, Debussy joined the circle around Edmond Bailly, the oriental scholar of the bookshop, *L'Art indépendant*, where intense discussions took place and scholarly literature was available in Bailly's personal library. See Howat, "Debussy and the Orient," 46.

Example 4.6. a. Claude Debussy, *En sourdine*, mm. 1–4, piano, right-hand part.

Example 4.6. b. Claude Debussy: *En sourdine*, mm. 8–10.

Debussy's encounter with the Exposition Universelle are Maurice Emmanuel's famous transcriptions of discussions between the composer and his teacher Guiraud.[150] And even more frequently quoted than the sentence on the gamelan in the Louÿs letter is Debussy's dream of an ideal theater where silence would have its place and where music could express the inexpressible. Caught at that time between what he perceived as stale French tradition on the one hand, and Wagnerian formulism on the other, Debussy suffered from a typical case of anxiety of influence. If we also take into account Debussy's preoccupation with opera in the late 1880s and the 1890s, his encounter with exotic musical theater at the Exposition could be seen in a different light. After all, Debussy's text on the *Théâtre Annamite* focuses on the dramaturgic use of instrumentation in music drama, his letter to Louÿs responds to one on nubile Spanish dancers, and Godet refers extensively to the Javanese "bedajas" who were turning music into images.

150. These are reproduced as an appendix to Edward Lockspeiser, *Debussy: Sa vie et sa pensée*, trans. Léo Dilé (Paris: Fayard, 1980), 751–55.

The date of Debussy's letter to Louÿs about his visit to the *kampong javanais* is 1895, and the piece with which Debussy was obsessed at that time was *Pelléas et Mélisande*. Thus Debussy's memories of the visits to the 1889 Exposition Universelle may well have played a role in the creation of this work. Our four Javanese dancers and Mélisande share a surprising number of traits: they are frail, they are young, their beauty is exotic, they come from foreign lands, they are mysterious figures. Javanese music grows in and out of silence, and we can observe this in *Pelléas*, especially in dramaturgically significant or emotionally charged moments such as the opera's beginning or the confession of love in act 4. The layering of texture and instrumentation in the opera are further, albeit rather abstract, reference to the sonority of the gamelan. Maeterlinck's text, with its dream-like atmosphere, its repetitive language, and its fragile heroine allowed Debussy to create a piece of musical theater where his experience of the different world of exotic spectacle—one termed, after all, a "symbolic ballet" creating a hypnotic, dream-like experience—could serve as a catalyst. Other elements, such as the dramaturgic use of instrumentation whose contrapuntal wizardry had impressed him so much in the Vietnamese performances, might well be echoed in his association of specific instruments with characters in the opera. While the latter is a technique of orchestration used both in French opera of the latter half of the nineteenth century and in Wagner's music dramas, Debussy associated it specifically with the dramaturgy of the *Théâtre Annamite* in both his remarks to the 1889 theater-goers and, a quarter of a century later, his 1913 essay on taste, in which he contrasts the drama of the Vietnamese, based on the "conservatory of nature," with the acquired techniques of Western composition.[151]

Some exotic traces in *Pelléas et Mélisande* might be even more specific than the more abstract structural similarities, especially with respect to the character of Mélisande. The first time we hear sound obviously relating to Mélisande in the opera is a short melodic fragment in the middle register of the oboe, soft and expressive, completely alien to the musical world of Golaud (example 4.7a). Its melodic contour and rhythm again are evocative of the *suling* and very close to Debussy's piano melody in *En Sourdine* (example 4.6a). However, this exotic melodic fragment is not the first musical reference to Mélisande in Debussy's score. Her leitmotif, again in the oboe, was already introduced earlier, though hidden within a whole-tone fabric (example 4.7b). When Mélisande's theme appears for the first time clearly linked to her character (example 4.7c), it is on the same pitch as in measures 14–15, but in the flute (or is it *suling*?), suggestive of the pentatonic pitch-material used in *En Sourdine*. While Golaud's harmonic world is colored modally (starting with the Dorian of the opening measures),

---

151. Debussy, *Monsieur Croche et autres écrits*, 229.

Example 4.7. a. Claude Debussy, *Pelléas et Mélisande*, Act 1, scene 1, mm. 46–47.

Example 4.7. b. Claude Debussy, *Pelléas et Mélisande*, Act 1, scene 1, mm. 14–15.

Example 4.7. c. Claude Debussy, *Pelléas et Mélisande*, Act 1, scene 1, mm. 102–3.

Mélisande's theme first appears in a whole-tone context and later is chromatically clouded. Furthermore, as Richard Langham Smith has observed, in Act 1, Mélisande's theme tends to be associated with either flute or oboe, and enters usually on A♭ (G♯).[152] These are abstract indicators of alterity referring to the exotic world of the bedajas rather than representing specific quotations of Javanese music, but they are distinct enough to act as semiotic markers in order to signal Mélisande's musical difference from the conspicuously Western (albeit modal) world of Golaud.

These exotic traces in *Pelléas et Mélisande* add another layer of referentiality to existing Wagnerian or symbolist interpretations and open up questions about the issues of appropriation and influence with respect to such spectacles as those of the 1889 Exposition Universelle. Edward Said's point that orientalism and exoticism always contain an element of taking possession in an unequal power relationship is still valid. We have grown accustomed to exempt Debussy from the role of the "compositeur exotique," not only because he himself denounced exoticism *à la* Delibes in his writings, but also because his piano music was far more discreet than conventional

152. Richard Langham Smith, "Motives and Symbols," in *Claude Debussy: "Pelléas et Mélisande,"* ed. Roger Nichols and Richard Langham Smith, Cambridge Opera Handbooks (Cambridge: Cambridge University Press, 1989), 84.

exoticism even in such pieces as *Pagodes*. Yet for Debussy, these exotic spectacles contained elements that clearly offered a way out of the impasse created by the Wagnerian dilemma, and he appropriated those components that might help him to write new French music, whether for the piano or for the stage. Emphasizing Debussy's debt to the colonial exhibition not only in terms of his piano music but in the wider context of his compositions can help us understand that he consumed these performances as "spectacles exotiques" in all their richness as a child of his time. In the end, those exotic articles were commodities similar to batik silk or Japanese prints. If they could be used to enrich French culture and prosperity, they fulfilled their role. In this sense, Debussy's appropriation of elements from the exotic performances to further the cause of French music is as much part of the colonial enterprise as what we habitually identify in works such as *Lakmé*. Whether Debussy's exoticism is more internalized than Delibes's is not the issue of my argument. Rather, I would suggest that we reinterpret his fascination with the spectacle of the *kampong javanais* and the *Théâtre Annamite* as an encounter with alterity not as an agent of rupture as so often posited by the modernist construction of Debussy but as a form of appropriation firmly inscribed in the tradition of French music of the 1890s.[153]

Debussy's exoticism differs from that of other composers of his generation in that his appropriation of non-Western music left traces on a structural level as well as on a surface one. In that sense, his form of musical encounter lead the way towards techniques of twentieth-century music, in which composers such as Henry Cowell, Francis Poulenc, or Colin McPhee would take such structural appropriation even further.[154] While Tiersot and Benedictus on their side offered transcriptions of their encounters with exotic music—whether scholarly or popular—most other French composers of the late nineteenth century did not musically engage with the music from the Far East, but, rather, turned to more familiar exotic sounds at the Exposition Universelle and rendered them in the well-tried mold of Orientalist compositions. Thus the Romanian folk ensemble was echoed in one of Erik Satie's *Gnossiènnes* (published as no. 5), and the rue du Caire was mirrored in such works as Ernest Alder's "mélopée orientale" for piano, *Les Almées*; Hedwige Gennaro-Chrétien's *Derbouka (Échos de la rue du*

153. Philippe Albèra comes to a similar conclusion in his "Tradizione e rottura della tradizione," in *Enciclopedia della Musica*, ed. Jean-Jacques Nattiez, vol. 1: *Il Novecento* (Turin: Giulio Einaudi Editore, 2001), 44. See also the concept of "intuitive exoticism" discussed in Christian Utz, *Neue Musik und Interkulturalität*, Beihefte zum Archiv für Musikwissenschaft 51 (Stuttgart: Franz Steiner, 2002), esp. 45–47.

154. See Ethan Lechner, "Hearing Past the Cultural Divide: Issues of Perspective and Hybridity in Colin McPhee's *Tabuh-tabuhan*" (Masters thesis, University of North Carolina at Chapel Hill, 2002).

*Caire)*; or Paul Hillemacher's *Mélodie arabe.*[155] Indeed, the rue du Caire and its Arab music was to become the most enduring sonic memory that Parisians kept of the Exposition Universelle, to the point that, five years on, the musical representation of an orgy in Jules Massenet's opera *Thaïs* was received as being modeled on that sound world.[156] While the Javanese dancers fascinated their audience with their performance, their music was quickly forgotten. The "charivari annamite" was even less of an enduring memory, save in a small circle of connoisseurs to which Debussy belonged. But their presence in Paris in 1889 laid the foundation for what was to become one of the main strains of Western music in the twentieth century: the abstract rather than picturesque engagement of alterity. Whether or not this strand is to be counted among the many manifestations of musical exoticism is still open for debate.

155. On Satie, see Steven Moore Whiting, *Satie the Bohemian: From Cabaret to Concert Hall* (Oxford: Oxford University Press, 1999), 118. See also Ernest Alder, *Les Almées* (Paris: Enoch Frères & Costallat, 1890); Hedwige Gennaro-Chrétien, *Derbouka (Échos de la rue du Caire)* (Paris: J. Naus, 1889); Paul L. Hillemacher, *Mélodie arabe*, poem by Eugène Adenis (Paris: Alphonse Leduc, 1889).

156. One of the *Thaïs* critics, Johannès Weber, describes the orgy in act 2 as molded on the sounds of the 1889 rue du Caire. The review is reproduced in Clair Rowden, ed., *Dossier de presse parisienne: Jules Massenet "Thaïs" (1894)* (Heilbronn: Musik-Edition Lucie Galland, 2000).

# Appendix

## DANSE JAVANAISE.

Example 4.3. Louis Benedictus, *Danse javanaise,* in *Les Musiques Bizarres à l'Exposition* (Paris: Hartmann, 1889), 9-17.

**Tempo 1° ma più mod<sup>to</sup>**

# Chapter 5

# Belly Dancers, Gypsies, and French Peasants

The performances from the Far East had captured the imagination of both the Parisian intelligentsia and the hundreds of thousands of visitors to the Exposition Coloniale alike. Avant-garde artistic currents such as Symbolism and Wagnerism served as a framework within which to engage with such alien music and performances, even if some of the fascination was based more on the visual splendor of these exotic representations that had come to life than on the music or dances themselves. In the *Théâtre Annamite* in particular, the glorious costumes and colorful decoration created a sense of occasion, supported by the performance character of the theatrical events. Indeed, both the Javanese and the Vietnamese stood out as offering self-contained shows from mysterious and far-away lands, with premières, processions, and program books, rather than being simply an orientalist entertainment in a *café-concert* of the kind that that had become fashionable in Paris in the 1880s, with its can-can dancers such as La Goulue and singers like Thérésa or Paulus, who performed to café patrons while they enjoyed their food and drink.[1] And although customers at the Javanese pavilion savored Javanese culinary treats such as hot chocolate or beer, the contemporary reception downplayed this facet in favor of the enthralling artistic aspects of the dance and music. What both the *kampong javanais* and *Théâtre Annamite* shared was the cachet of the exceptional if not sensational, of an art never seen or heard before.

This was not the case with other exotic and picturesque entertainments at the Exposition Universelle. They had been encountered before. Indeed, images of the Orient featured prominently in European arts and literature of the long nineteenth century, whether paintings, opera, or song. Female dancers from the Middle East had performed in the cafés of the 1867 and

---

1. By 1889, there were 203 brasseries and *cafés-concerts* in Paris. See Sylviane Leprun, *Le Théâtre des Colonies: Scénographie, acteurs et discours de l'imaginaire dans les expositions, 1855–1937* (Paris: Éditions l'Harmattan, 1986), 74. On the *café-concert*, see also the richly illustrated book by François Caradec and Alain Weill, *Le Café-concert* (Paris: Atelier Hachette & Massin, 1980).

1878 Expositions Universelles, and "oriental" dancers—both authentic and fake—appeared in select Parisian *cafés-concerts.*[2] And Africans formed part of ethnographic exhibitions at the Jardin d'Acclimatation, where they were displayed as elements of a savage landscape from afar. Furthermore, central Africa was on thousands of French minds after the exploits of France's national hero, Pierre Savorgnan de Brazza, in the early 1880s. The Middle East and Africa thus represented the more familiar face of French colonialism as it emerged and developed through the nineteenth century.

European neighbors and their folklore were likewise sufficiently different to represent a further kind of Otherness in their ways of dressing, speaking, and most importantly, performing the folk music of their people. Exotic Others thus could be encountered at the Exposition Universelle in many different ways. Visitors from countries such as Britain and Spain became subject to the observing gaze of Parisian caricaturists, while their countries exhibited that which was nationally specific in their produce or culture to gain a larger share in the economic competition of the late nineteenth century. Many exhibiting cultures played on French and (more generally) European prejudice in order to distinguish themselves and their produce as unique.[3] All the while, the national pavilions became showcases for these images in their architectural details and decorations.[4] Whether they were Romanian, Swiss, or Algerian, the presence of indigenous representatives within the exhibits added to the creation of an aura of authenticity that was reinforced through traditional cultural activities, both artisan and artistic.

Indeed, the issue of the authenticity of what was shown to the fairgoers in Paris was one of the recurring themes in the press. The topic was particularly important when it came to the French colonial exhibits. It did matter, for example, whether the goods sold in the Oriental bazaars were made in

2. The picturesque music of the 1867 Fair is described in Oscar Comettant, *La Musique, les musiciens et les instruments de musique chez les peuples du monde* (Paris: Michel Lévy Frères, 1869), 282–90.

3. This form of advertising through emphasizing picturesque details of the national origin of produce developed throughout the nineteenth century and was part of the marketing strategies in World's Fairs in general. See Peter H. Hoffenberg, *An Empire on Display: English, Indian, and Australian Exhibitions from the Crystal Palace to the Great War* (Berkeley, Los Angeles, and London: University of California Press, 2001), 146.

4. See, for example, the case built by Zeynep Çelik in the chapter "Search for Identity: Architecture of National Pavilions," in Çelik, *Displaying the Orient: Architecture of Islam at Nineteenth-Century World's Fairs* (Berkeley, Los Angeles, and Oxford: University of California Press, 1992), 95–138. For a broader discussion of the architecture on display, see Caroline Mathieu, "Invitation au Voyage," in *1889: La Tour Eiffel et l'Exposition Universelle*, ed. Caroline Mathieu, 102–29 (Paris: Éditions de la Réunion des Musées Nationaux, 1989).

Egypt or produced on the outskirts of Paris, and whether dancers and musicians really came from Algeria and Tunisia or from Montmartre, because in the concert and competition of international world's fairs—as in the 1886 Colonial and Indian Fair in London just three years earlier—the exhibition of fakes would tarnish the Exposition Universelle as being nothing but a gigantic and inconsequential amusement park. The representation of original artifacts, together with the exhibition of goods and natives from afar, provided the stamp of authenticity to the Exposition. This was not a matter to be taken lightly. Thus, when doubts arose in early July about the origin of the goods sold in the Egyptian section, inspectors of the Exposition Universelle closed the stalls until their provenance was verified. These quality controls continued throughout the Exposition, with French newspapers reporting on the efforts of the inspectors. In the same way that medieval relics and pilgrims' badges were authenticated by the church authorities, the modern relics (or tourist souvenirs) from the Exposition needed certification as authentic by the inspectors of the Exposition in order to have validity. The aura of the authentic was thus as essential to the Colonial exhibits on the Esplanade des Invalides as it was to the archaeological exhibits in the Palais des Arts Libéraux.[5] As the competitive development of museums and collections over the nineteenth century has made abundantly clear, only a truly great nation was able to show the originals.

Because "authenticity" had become such a central issue in the judgment and discussion of cultural artifacts and artistic representation at the Exposition Universelle, it pervaded the discourse in the press. In contrast to the *kampong javanais* and the *Théâtre Annamite*, where authenticity was an unproblematic though celebrated bonus, the fear of fakes brought the question of the "authentic" into the spotlight of the reception of music and dance from the Middle East, Europe and—especially—the French provinces. Like the discussions of early music and revolutionary *opéra comique* (see chapters 1 and 2), this allows for some fascinating glimpses into the debates on a category of musical aesthetics that is more usually associated with the second half of twentieth century, rather than late nineteenth, whether in the context of early music, popular music, or world music.

## Orientalism, Oriental Dancers, and Arab Music

The most visited Oriental exhibit of the Exposition Universelle was the rue du Caire, with its buildings shipped from Cairo, and its donkeys, street-vendors, and imam, plus its *cafés-concerts* at either end (figure 5.1). This

---

5. On the exhibits from the Ancient Near East in the Palais des Arts Libéraux, see Frederick N. Bohrer, *Orientalism and Visual Culture: Imagining Mesopotamia in Nineteenth-Century Europe* (Cambridge: Cambridge University Press, 2003), 244–49.

Figure 5.1. G. Traiponi, "La Rue du Caire," engraving published on the title page
of *L'Exposition de Paris*, 4 May 1889.

Traponi rendered the scene with a strong focus on the exotic architectural detail
and the picturesque Arabs in the front, while the European visitors of the
*Exposition Universelle* disappear in the background and are barely visible.

street, located at the periphery of the main exhibition of the Champ de Mars (next to the Galerie des Machines), brought a piece of apparently "authentic" Cairo to Paris. Indeed, as guidebooks and reviewers pointed out, the reproduction on the Champ de Mars was ostensibly closer to the townscapes of the time of the caliphs than to modern, late-nineteenth-century Egypt: "Neither in Cairo nor in any other Egyptian town does a street still exist so devoid of any modern construction."[6] Like the *kampong javanais*, the rue du Caire extended an invitation to "fairground visitors" to leave modern times of industrial progress behind for a lost pastoral world of fantasy situated in the era of the archetypal albeit fictional caliph, Haroun-Al-Raschid.[7] "One could believe," as Judith Gautier put it, "that one was truly transported into the Orient by the magic carpet of *The Thousand and One Nights*."[8] The sensual experience of Egypt was no longer mediated through a two-dimensional painting, a newspaper report, or an opera performance, but could be experienced in many of its tangible facets, from Arab coffee to dancing *almées*. The rue du Caire was an orientalist fantasy come true—or was it?

Scholars seem to buy into this one-dimensional orientalist fantasy promoted by the organizers of the Exposition Universelle.[9] Both modern and postcolonial discourses do not seem to question the underlying premise that the visitors of the Exposition Universelle consumed the exhibit of the rue du Caire uncritically and homogeneously as an orientalist display.[10]

6. *Exposition de 1889: Guide bleu du "Figaro" et du "Petit Journal" avec 5 plans et 31 dessins* (Paris: Le Figaro, 1889), 179: "Il n'y a plus au Caire, ni dans aucune autre ville égyptienne, de rue qui soit ainsi vierge de toute construction moderne."

7. Émile Goudeau, "La Rue du Caire," *La Revue illustrée* 4, part 2 (1889): 113–15.

8. Judith Gautier, "L'Orient: Almées, ghaziyés, derviches, rakkasas, danseuses noires," *Le Rappel*, 29 June 1889 / 11 Messidor an 97, 1–2, at 1: "On se croit transporté vraiment en Orient par le tapis magique des *Mille et une Nuits*." Just outside the main entrance of the Champ de Mars, on the avenue Rapp, was the *Pays de Fées*, an amusement park built especially for the occasion of the Exposition Universelle. One section consisted of a theme park representing some elements of the *The Thousand and One Nights*, complete with its star dancer, "the beautiful Féridjée." See Charles Rearick, *Pleasures of the Belle Époque: Entertainment & Festivity in Turn-of-the-Century France* (New Haven, CT, and London: Yale University Press, 1985), 121; and Zeynep Çelik and Leila Kinney, "Ethnography and Exhibitionism at the Expositions Universelles," *Assemblage* 13 (1990): 48–49.

9. The sources quoted tend to be limited to the official and promotional books and pamphlets such as Delort de Gléon, *L'Architecture arabe des Khalifes d'Égypte à l'Exposition Universelle de Paris en 1889: La rue du Caire* (Paris: E. Plon, 1889). Delort de Gléon was the organizer behind the construction of the rue du Caire.

10. Rearick, *Pleasures of the Belle Époque*, 139; Elaine Brody, *Paris: The Musical Kaleidoscope, 1870–1925* (New York: George Braziller, 1987), 91; Pascal Ory, *L'Expo universelle* (Paris: Éditions Complexe, 1989), 100, 125; Timothy Mitchell, "The World as Exhibition," *Comparative Studies in Society and History* 31 (1989): 217; Çelik and Kinney, "Ethnography and Exhibitionism," 43–49; Çelik, *Displaying the Orient*, 75–79.

Furthermore, these readings of the rue du Caire reveal the extent to which the binary opposition of Oriental Other and Western Self remains pervasive even in the postcolonialist critical discourse. And finally, even more than the 1889 fairgoers, modern scholars seem to dismiss the individual, non-Western performers and dancers as unworthy of their attention compared with their (mostly Western) spectators, given that all they ever receive is a brief reference, if that. Çelik and Kinney, for example, rightly criticize the essentializing Saidian discourse of orientalism in their 1990 article on belly dancing at the 1889 Exposition Universelle.[11] But while their pertinent cultural analysis of belly dancing as signifier of "the Islamic Orient" captures to some extent the complexities of Western mediation and reception, they follow the trend of all other writers who have so far engaged with the rue du Caire, in that their analysis focuses entirely on its reception as a uniform orientalist fantasy, the ubiquitous salacious quotations from Edmond de Goncourt's diaries included.[12] The two authors show in detail the effects of the Oriental dance on Parisian music halls with respect to the Parisian dancer, La Goulue, and such artists as Toulouse-Lautrec, but the Egyptian dancers at the Fair are hardly mentioned at all, save being shown in a photograph— just as they were in the nineteenth-century publication from which the image was taken. Few individuals from the Middle East who visited the 1889 Exposition Universelle have received any scholarly attention, and these were without exception male.[13] In scholarly narratives, the belly dancers of the Exposition Universelle are just "extras," representing "Oriental woman" in deconstructions of their Western reception, rather than receiving any attention as performers and individuals.[14]

Contemporary sources, however, point to a far more complex nexus of representation and reception with respect to the rue du Caire and other Middle Eastern performance venues at the Exposition Universelle. That

11. Çelik and Kinney, "Ethnography and Exhibitionism," 35–36.

12. Edmond de Goncourt's comments on his visits to the rue du Caire are among the few easily accessible contemporary sources and have become much quoted, probably starting with Rearick, *Pleasures of the Belle Époque*. Goncourt's comments on the rue du Caire and its belly dancers can be found in Edmond and Jules de Goncourt, *Journal: Mémoires de la vie littéraire*, ed. Robert Ricatte, 3 vols. (Paris: Robert Laffont, 1989), 3:290, 312–13, 320.

13. See, for example, the references to the Egyptian delegation to the orientalist conference in Timothy Mitchell, "Orientalism and the Exhibitionary Order," in *Colonialism and Culture*, ed. by Nicholas B. Dirks, 289–317 (Ann Arbor: University of Michigan Press, 1995); or Carter Vaughan Findley, "An Ottoman Occidentalist in Europe: Ahmed Midhat Meets Madame Gülnar," *American Historical Review* 103 (1998): 15–49. Madame Gülnar was the pen name for the Russian countess Olga Sergeyevna Lebedeva (p. 31).

14. On the figure of the "Oriental woman" and its continuous presence in current scholarly discourse, see Madeleine Dobie, *Foreign Bodies: Gender, Language, and Culture in French Orientalism* (Stanford: Stanford University Press, 2001), 1–5.

French orientalism of the late nineteenth century constituted a significant component of many fairgoers' horizon of expectations goes without saying, given that, by 1889, orientalist *topoi* pervaded both popular and elite culture in France, whether in novels, paintings, lithographs, operas, or interior décor.[15] But orientalism in the arts was shaded by what was represented when, by whom, and for whom. Nor should the distinction between the oriental and the exotic be neglected in this context, for not only can orientalism be defined as those artistic "dialects" of a more broadly defined Exoticism that evoke the Islamic Middle East or East and South Asia, but even within these dialects, there were some significant differences.[16] Although Japan and China were fashionable for the purpose of interior decoration—whether in the form of precious Japanese woodcuts or cheaper *chinoiserie* reproduction vases—and popular entertainments establishments such as the Ba-ta-clan *café-concert* (named after Offenbach and Halévy's 1855 operetta), references to the Far East were rather underrepresented in other art forms in France, such as painting, sculpture, and music. India, Japan, and China rarely found their way, for example, onto the opera stage before the 1890s.[17]

The Middle East, on the other hand, had become a cliché location of orientalist representation in France, paradigmatically captured in such harem scenes as Ingres's *Bain turc* (1863) or Gerôme's *L'Almée* (1864).[18]

15. For a general introduction into orientalism in nineteenth-century European arts, see John M. MacKenzie, *Orientalism: History, Theory and the Arts* (Manchester and New York: Manchester University Press, 1995). The wider political issues of imperialism in France, including its exotic component, are addressed in the review article by Edward Berenson, "Making a Colonial Culture? Empire and the French Public, 1880–1940," *French Politics, Culture, and Society* 22 (2004): 127–49.

16. I have borrowed the description of orientalism as a dialect of the broader language of Exoticism from Ralph P. Locke's article, "Orientalism," in *NGr2*. For a detailed exploration of the concept of exoticism, see Bohrer, *Orientalism and Visual Culture*, 10–41.

17. Karen Henson points to the relative absence of Chinese subjects in French opera in her "Exotisme et Nationalités: *Aida* à l'Opéra de Paris," in *L'Opéra en France et en Italie (1791–1925): Une scène privilégiée d'échanges littéraires et musicaux*, ed. Hervé Lacombe (Paris: Société Française de Musicologie, 2000), 295. Save for Saint-Saëns's 1872 *La Princesse jaune*, the fashion for Japan started with Pierre Loti's 1887 novel *Madame Chrysanthème*, which became the source for both André Messager's eponymous opera of 1893 and Giacomo Puccini's *Madama Butterfly*, premièred in 1904. Only three major operas that were located in India or Hindu culture were premièred before 1889: Georges Bizet's *Les Pêcheurs des perles* (1863), Jules Massenet's *Le Roi de Lahore* (1877), and Léo Delibes's *Lakmé* (1883), the latter also based on a novel by Pierre Loti, *Rarahu* (1880). See Jann Pasler, "India and Its Music: Imagination before 1913," *Journal of the Indian Musicological Society*, 27 (1996): 47.

18. On the representation of harem scenes in nineteenth-century painting and engraving, see Joan DelPlato, *Multiple Wives, Multiple Pleasures: Representing the Harem, 1800–1875* (Madison, NJ, and Teaneck, NJ: Fairleigh Dickinson University Press, 2002).

Turkey, Algeria, Egypt, Tunisia, and other countries of the Levant and the Maghreb provided the setting of countless operas by composers such as Rossini, Meyerbeer, Massenet, Saint-Saëns, and Thomas, and their ballets usually offered ample opportunity for the representation of lascivious oriental dance. If the stereotypical Oriental dancers and harems represented one important aspect of nineteenth-century orientalism, another field of reception is indicated by works such as Fromentin's renderings of biblical scenes in "authentic" Middle Eastern settings, familiar to French audiences not only because of his paintings but even more so because of their imitation in lithographs and engravings in illustrated bibles and religious kitsch: that of the imaginary Orient with its exotic landscapes and townscapes. As Linda Nochlin has observed, these paintings depict "a world of timeless customs and rituals, untouched by the historical processes that were drastically altering Western society."[19] The Orient thus became an alternative space, a landscape that could encapsulate nostalgia for a lost world or a golden age as much as represent the location of forbidden erotic desires. In music, works such as Félicien David's *ode-symphonie, Le Désert,* with its landscape-inspired program of desert night and sunrise, created an imaginary soundscape for the landscapes of a Fromentin or Gérôme. These orientalist landscapes, however—whether in paintings, music, or literature—carried increasingly solidified semantic layers, and because of its continuous presence in the arts, the semantic field of French orientalism was also richer than that of the less received and popularized Far East. This had a significant impact on its representation and reception at the Exposition Universelle.[20] Not for nothing was the rue du Caire a reconstruction of old Cairo and not of the modern one, and thus a timeless landscape that could well have been the backdrop of an orientalist painting.

But Oriental landscapes and townscapes found their ways into other cultural contexts in France, most notably into the set design for orientalist stage productions, whether in the opera houses or in the boulevard theaters. Stage designers for the main Parisian theaters vied with each other to produce more splendid and increasingly detailed representations of foreign locations. By the mid-nineteenth century, the centuries-old practice of recycling generic landscapes selected from a theater's stock had been replaced by production-specific sets that reflected concerns for "authenticity" similar to other visual representations. Attention to specific

19. Linda Nochlin, "The Imaginary Orient," *Art in America* 71 (1983): 122.

20. Irvin Cemil Schick, *The Erotic Margin: Sexuality and Spatiality in Alterist Discourse* (London and New York: Verso, 1999), 43–74. Simon Schama has shown how the complex, reciprocal relationship between landscape and interpretation has influenced cultural discourse as much as political decision. See Simon Schama, *Landscape & Memory* (London: HarperCollins, 1995).

details had become the marker for true locality in displays of exotic spaces, whether in the form of historic settings or of Oriental architecture. This trend was compounded in 1880 in one of the most famous cases of historical "reconstruction" in the arts, the Parisian stage designs for Giuseppe Verdi's opera *Aida*, in which the stage designer, Auguste Mariette, consulted Egyptologists and Egyptological literature for every detail.[21]

While imitations and recreations of Oriental landscapes increased on the Parisian stage, and while ballet dancers were dressed up in apparently authentic and (usually) sexually provocative orientalist costumes, the sonic and kinetic side of these performances remained firmly located within the framework of Western culture. Not until Fokine's experiments in the ballet production of Debussy's *Prélude à l'après-midi d'un faune* (1911) would a choreographer engage seriously with a style of movement markedly different from European ballet. In the same way that the music of orientalist spectacle remained thoroughly within the Western idiom, so did the movements of the ballerinas, whether they represented Egyptian dancers in Massenet's *Hérodiade* (1881) or Renaissance courtiers in Saint-Saëns's *Henry VIII* (1884). While the tableau of an opera or ballet thus emphasized difference, the dancers' movement and their music—the performance side of things—stayed securely grounded in Western sonic and kinetic experiences.[22] Indeed, the Middle East may have looked Eastern, but it sounded Western even with the added twist that composers used orientalist musical signifiers such as the augmented second and melodic arabesques to provide *couleur locale*.

This discrepancy between the xenotopic landscape of painting, photography, and stage design on the one hand, and the Western soundscape of the imaginary Orient on the other, is rarely if ever addressed in the secondary literature. But this difference defined the horizon of expectations of the fairgoers and commentators who were going to encounter "real"

---

21. See Nicole Wild, "Les Traditions scéniques à l'Opéra de Paris au temps de Verdi," in *La realizzazione scenica dello spettacolo verdiano*, ed. Pierluigi Petrobelli and Fabrizio Della Seta, 135–66 (Parma: Istituto Nazionale di Studi Verdiani, 1996).

22. One might want to make the point that orientalist painters were mediating their exotic subjects through a Western technique—Linda Nochlin shows that Gérôme in fact perfected his technique to the point of transparency—but nineteenth-century painting's realism was in collusion with "authentic" representation that could be verified through photography and visits, whereas nineteenth-century music could not employ this conceit. Nochlin, "The Imaginary Orient," 122–23. See also the discussion of Renoir's studio orientalism in Roger Benjamin, *Renoir and Algeria* (New Haven and London: Yale University Press, 2003), 17–37. On the incompatibility of Western tonality and Arab idioms in music, see Jean-Pierre Bartoli, "L'Orientalisme dans la musique française du XIXème siècle: La ponctuation, la seconde augmentée et l'apparition de la modalité dans les procédures exotiques," *Revue Belge de Musicologie* 51 (1997): 137–70.

Oriental performers in the orientalist settings of the exhibition, whose theatrical quality Edmond de Goncourt defined rather pointedly: "This Fair has no reality: it is almost as if one were walking in the set of an Oriental play. . . ."[23] Visitors thus found themselves in a field of tension between the reality of the Middle Eastern performances and the imaginary Orient of their previous cultural experiences. Instead of lushly orchestrated landscape music and members of the corps de ballet of the Opéra, they encountered women such as twenty-year-old Hanem Mohammed, a dancer from Cairo, whose performances were accompanied by fellow Egyptian musicians such as Omar-Hellal and Abou-Halaka.[24]

Oriental dancers and their performances had been among the expected attractions of the 1889 Exposition Universelle, since they had already been a successful part of the 1867 and 1878 Fairs. Arthur Pougin observed that their triumph grew over the summer of 1889, with additional performers arriving as the Exposition Universelle went on. The main attraction was the belly dance, which Pougin "found just everywhere, in the cafés of the rue du Caire, in the Tunisian market, on the Esplanade des Invalides, and which seems to have bewitched the Parisians and hypnotized the fairgoers."[25] On average, 2,000 visitors a day flocked to the various cafés to watch the spectacles from the Orient.[26] The Egyptian café alone took in more than half a million francs.[27] But while the belly-dance craze kept the cafés full and the journalists busy, it also became the focus of "orientalist dismay."[28] Its music broke the sensual orientalist dream because it intruded with sonorities that seemed loud, nasal, and "barbaric" to Western ears, while the movements were too different from Parisian ballet to be perceived as graceful. But because of the sexual attraction and physical difference of the dance, the performers received close attention from their

23. Goncourt, *Journal*, 3:271: "Cette Exposition n'a pas la réalité; il semble qu'on processionne dans les praticables d'une pièce orientale. . . ."

24. Names, origins, and age taken from the ethnographic records and photographs by Prince Roland Bonaparte, which are kept in the collection of the Société de Géographie, Bibliothèque Nationale de France, Département des Cartes et Plans, Dossier We341.

25. Arthur Pougin, *Le Théâtre à l'Exposition Universelle de 1889: Notes et descriptions, histoires et souvenirs* (Paris: Librarie Fischbacher, 1890), 102: "[La danse du ventre] que je devais retrouver partout ensuite, dans les cafés de la rue du Caire, au Souk tunisien, à l'Esplanade des Invalides, et qui pendant plusieurs mois semble avoir affolé les Parisiens et hypnotisé les visiteurs de l'Exposition."

26. Çelik, *Displaying the Orient*, 24.

27. Alfred Picard, *Rapport général sur l'Exposition universelle internationale de 1889*, 10 vols. (Paris: Imprimerie nationale, 1890–91), 3:285.

28. Timothy Mitchell defines orientalist dismay as the disappointed reaction of visitors to the Orient when they discovered that it did not correspond to their expectations as shaped by Western mediation. See Mitchell, "The World as Exhibition," 233.

audiences, as reflected in countless newspaper reports that tried to capture what made it so special. In a lead article for the mass journal *Le Petit Journal*, the anonymous author captured the tension between the visual and the sonic side of the experience of the Oriental dance:

> Gérard de Nerval declared that one dreamed of paradise when one saw the *almées* dance. Visitors to the Exposition can now offer themselves this dream a considerable number of times in a single day, if they have not had their fill after the first performance.
>
> At the Esplanade des Invalides and the rue du Caire, there are in effect seven or eight *café-concerts*, whether Egyptian, Moroccan, Algerian, or Tunisian; in each the dance of the *almées* constitutes the foundation of the show.
>
> One can recognize an African concert from afar; even before one can clearly see this Moorish house, that minaret, or this tent made out of Oriental carpets which become visible at a distance of about fifty meters, one can hear bizarre sounds escape though the openings of the *moucharabias*, the half-open windows, the gaps of the curtains; it is the *nouba*, a strange music at the same time squalling, monotonous, and melancholic, the obligatory accompaniment of the *almées*, who would not agree to dance with any other orchestra. One has to resign oneself to listen to the one if one wants to see the other, and they are worth the effort of being seen.

> Gérard de Nerval déclarait qu'on rêvait le paradis voir danser les almées. Ce rêve, les visiteurs de l'Exposition peuvent se l'offrir un nombre considérable de fois dans une même journée, à condition de n'en avoir pas été rassasiés après le premier spectacle.
>
> Tant à l'Esplanade des Invalides que dans la rue du Caire, il y a en effet sept ou huit  concerts égyptiens, marocains, algériens ou tunisiens; dans tous, ce sont les danses d'almées qui constituent le fond du spectacle.
>
> Un concert africain se reconnaît de loin; avant même d'avoir distingué nettement cette maison mauresque, ce minaret ou cette tente faite de tapis d'Orient qui se profilent à une cinquantaine de mètres, vous entendez des sons bizarres sortir par les ouvertures des moucharabies, par l'entrebâillement des fenêtres, par l'écartement des portières; musique étrange, à la fois criarde, monotone et mélancolique, c'est la *nouba*, l'accompagnement obligatoire des almées, qui ne consentiraient pas à danser avec un autre orchestre. Il faut se résigner à entendre l'une si on veut voir l'autre, et elles valent la peine d'être vues.[29]

29. "Curiosités de l'Exposition: Les Concerts Africains," *Le Petit Journal*, 10 July 1889, 1.

With rhetorical zest, the author played out the dissonance between the visual and the acoustic, for even before we see the details of the exotic locations we hear bizarre music, and in order to enjoy the sight, we are forced to tolerate the sound. The commonplace that visitors just cannot escape the phenomenological presence of the music runs through many published commentaries on the belly dances, whether in newspapers and periodicals or in reminiscences of the Exposition Universelle. In contrast to the descriptions of the Javanese gamelan—which was generally perceived as supporting the exoticist dream rather than destroying it—those of Arab music were almost uniformly negative. Writers described it as monotonous, sick, barbaric, loud, and discordant, often labeling the sounds as "noise" rather than music.[30] This contrasts with the reception only eleven years earlier, at the 1878 Exposition Universelle, when Paul Lacome reported on the strange and unknown music from the Middle East, that had musicians such as Franz Liszt and François Gevaert listening attentively to the players, in the manner of Debussy's or Chausson's encounter with the Javanese gamelan in 1889.[31]

As Çelik and Kinney have shown, the institutional model for the Arab spectacles was the Parisian *café-concert* with its musical support cast and its stars, which influenced both the performances on stage and their reception by customers and journalists.[32] One particular performer created a bridge between these worlds: "la belle Fatma," the Tunisian dancer Rachel Bent-Eny whose fame started with the 1878 Exposition Universelle and who had stayed on in Paris for the intervening eleven years as a *café-concert* performer (figure 5.2).[33] But other dancers competed for the fairgoers' attention, such as Baya, "the blond *almée* of the Moroccan café," or the Egyptian belly dancer, Aïouché. While the ethnographic photographs and notes of Prince Roland Bonaparte give a face to, and sparse information about, the sixteen-year-old dancer Bahia (Bonaparte's spelling) from Algiers (figure 5.3), Aïouché remains anonymous, although engravings published in the illustrated press show her dancing in the Café égyptien

30. See, for example, Maurice Guillenot, "La Danse du ventre," *Gil Blas*, 17 Aug. 1889, 2; Ibrahim, "La Danse du ventre," *La Vie Parisienne* 27 (1889): 333; B. Schulte-Smidt, *Bleistift-Skizzen: Erinnerungen an die Pariser Weltausstellung* (Bremen: Johann Kühtmann's Buchhandlung, 1890), 39; Th. Lindenlaub, "Le Café maure," *Revue de l'Exposition Universelle de 1889* 1 (1889): 409–15.

31. Paul Lacome, "Exposition universelle de 1878: Les Musiciens arabes," *Le Ménestrel* 44 (1878): 269: "une étrange musique" and "laissez-vous séduire par cet inconnu." On Liszt and Gevaert, further along in the same text: "J'ai vu par deux fois Listz [*sic*] et Gevaert venir prendre place auprès des virtuoses barbares et suivre le concert avec le plus grand soin." Oscar Comettant cites Paul Lacome as the reason why he went to visit the Café Tunisien at the 1867 Exposition Universelle (Comettant, *La Musique*, 284).

32. Çelik and Kinnon, "Ethnography and Exhibitionism," 43.

33. Pougin, *Le Théâtre à l'Exposition*, 120.

Figure 5.2. *La Belle Fatma*, portrait of the Tunisian dancer Rachel Bent-Eny, 1889.
B.H.V.P., Dossier photographique *Divers XXI*, 210.

Figure 5.3. Bahia, 16 years old, from Algiers, ethnographic photograph from the collection of Prince Roland Bonaparte, Bibliotheque nationale de Paris, collection of the Société de Géographie, We 342 (25). Used by permission.

Figure 5.4. Adrien Marie, "La Danse de l'almée Aïoucha au café égyptien de la rue du Caire," *Le Monde illustré*, 3 Aug. 1889, 73.

(figure 5.4). The names of dancers seem to be accessories aimed to evoke difference but not individuality. Thus when three new dancers arrived at the Tunisian café in early July, they were introduced as follows: "The three new dancers, Hadra, Sophia, and Saïda, who belong to the harem of the Mahdi, are without rivals in the Muslim world."[34] The probably fictitious attribution of the dancers to the harem of the Mahdi was all the more titillating given the political context of the famous uprising in Sudan, at which the British troops, including General George Gordon, were massacred in 1885. In another description the dancers' names themselves sound the Orient

34. "A l'Exposition," *Le Petit Parisien*, 1 July 1889, 2: "Les trois nouvelles danseuses, Hadra, Sophia et Saïda, qui faisaient partie du sérail du Madhi sont, dit-on, sans rivales dans le monde musulman."

Let us cross the seas. . . . The podium is long and covered in carpet: at the very back are the musicians and in front of them the *almées*. . . . The small stage and the hall are roofed by an awning which is held up by the trees that have been left from the Champ de Mars. . . . The *qānūn, ūd, darabukka*, resound under the fingers of the musicians. . . . The *almées* Adila, Farida, Hanem Mohamed, Kadra appear one after the other on the front of the stage in their iridescent costumes.

. . . Traversons les mers. . . . L'estrade est longue et couverte de tapis: tout au fond, les musiciens, et devant eux, les almées. . . . La petite scène et la salle sont recouvertes d'un velum que soutiennent les arbres, laissés là, du Champ de Mars. . . . Le *ganoûm*, l'*oud*, la *darbouka*, résonnent sous les doigts des musiciens. . . . Les almées Adila, Farida, Hanem Mohamed, Kadra paraissent successivement sur le devant de l'estrade, dans leurs costumes chatoyants.[35]

Other than those of Bahia and Aïouché, engravings in the illustrated press tended to represent scenes from the performances without identifying the dancers. Thus the engraving from the Moorish café of the Algerian section shows a "scarf dance;" another from the Egyptian café represents the Sudanese dancers and musicians, cobra included (figures 5.5 and 5.6).

The illustrated scenes from the Moorish and the Egyptian cafés have more to offer, however, than the simple representation of an orientalist spectacle. They contain some traces of the actual performances in their depiction of the dancers and their poses, and in the often detailed rendering of the musicians in the background. The musicians on the right in the engraving of Aïouché (figure 5.4) are, in fact, identifiable as Omar-Hellal (left, with the *ūd*) and Osman-Hassem (right, with the *qānūn*). This identification is possible because of the photographs taken at the Exposition Universelle by Prince Roland Bonaparte which show both players with their instruments (figures 5.7 and 5.8).

Even more than in the case of the Javanese and the Vietnamese, the situation of the Arab performers at the Exposition Universelle calls attention to the complexities of musico-historical phenomenology in its uncomfortable position between a lost sonic reality and documentary traces which translated the acoustic into a non-sonic medium.[36] Verbal descriptions are particularly problematic. Without exception, all the non-specialist writers that I have encountered describe a generic "Arab" sound, distinguishing between individual numbers within the performance sequence but not between different Middle Eastern cultures, even though in visual terms,

35. Adolphe Aderer, "La Musique à l'Exposition," *L'Exposition de Paris* 2 (1889): 286–87, at 287.
36. I am appropriating the concept of historical phenomenology from Bruce R. Smith's forthcoming study "Hearing Green," presented at Duke University in January 2004.

Figure 5.5. "L'Exposition Algérienne à l'Esplanade des Invalides — Le Café Maure,"
*L'Exposition de Paris* (Paris: Librairie Illustrée, 1889): 1:157.

Figure 5.6. "Les Soudanais au Café Egyptien," engraving by E. A. Jely illustrating the
article by Adolphe Aderer, "La Musique à l'Exposition," *L'Exposition* de Paris, 2:287.

Figure 5.7. Omar-Hellal, 25 years old, musician from Cairo, ethnographic photograph from the collection of Prince Roland Bonaparte, Bibliothèque nationale de France, collection of the Société de Géographie, We 341 (8). Used by permission.

Figure 5.8. Osman-Hassem, 26 years old, musician from Cairo, ethnographic photograph from the collection of Prince Roland Bonaparte, Bibliothèque nationale de
France, collection of the Société de Géographie, We 341 (9). Used by permission.

distinctions are quite clearly made between the Egyptians, Algerians, and Sudanese. But then, whose reality could they describe if not their own, in which nuances of regional difference within oral traditions might not have been evident to untrained Western ears and are thus lost entirely, in contrast to the visual specificity in the engravings.

Nevertheless, the visual representations of performances allow for the identification of instruments and possibly ensembles. Thus the performance represented in figure 5.4 shows three musicians in the background on the right, playing an *ūd* (a short-necked lute), a *qānūn* (a type of zither) and a *duff* (a frame drum with usually five sets of jingles inserted into the frame). This matches the description by the exceptionally well-informed musician Tiersot:

> Three musicians are crouched, their legs crossed, in the background, on an elevated sofa; one plays a kind of mandolin that does not seem to differ noticeably from the Algerian *qitra*, but which seems to carry another name, the *ūd*; another uses a kind of zither called, as we were told, *qānūn*; the third, who is in charge of the percussion instruments, uses in turn a *darabukka* [a goblet drum], a tambourine, and other varieties of drums.

> [A]u fond, sur un sofa élevé, trois musiciens sont accroupis, les jambes croisés; l'un joue une sorte de mandoline qui ne semble pas différer sensiblement de la *kouitre* algérienne, mais qui porte, paraît-il, un autre nom: *oud*; un autre se sert d'une espèce de cithare, dénommée, nous dit-on, *canoun*; le troisième, chargé des instruments frappés, se sert tour de rôle du *darabouka*, du tambour de basque et de différentes autres variétés du tambour.[37]

In addition, the dancer uses finger cymbals. This corresponds to what we know about *takhut*, late-nineteenth-century ensembles in urban Cairo. Indeed, the description of the music by Tiersot points to a nineteenth-century Egyptian form—again mainly practiced in urban Cairo—the *dōr*. The ensemble and thus the music are not those usually associated with popular and peasant dance, and they confirm that the Egyptian musicians represented in figure 5.4 performed probably in an urban musical style.[38]

---

37. Julien Tiersot, "Promenades musicales à l'Exposition: Les Arabes," *Le Ménestrel* 55 (1889): 292–93, at 293. For a short introduction into the instruments of pre-1918 Egypt, see Owen Wright, Christian Poché, and Amnon Shiloah, "Arab Music," in *NGr2*.

38. Magda Saleh points out that research on dance in Egypt is still in its initial stages, especially with respect to its historic side. See Magda Saleh, "Dance in Egypt," in *The Garland Encyclopedia of World Music*, vol. 6: *The Middle East*, ed. Virginia Danielson, Scott Marcus, and Dwight Reynolds (New York and London: Routledge, 2002), 623.

A distinction that none of the lay writers made but to which Tiersot at least alluded, is the difference between popular (i.e., folk) and more elaborate art music in the Arab world, which, at least in the nineteenth century, was a feature of both the Ottoman Empire and (influenced by the Ottomans) Egypt.[39] In the reception of the performances of the Exposition Universelle, however, perception again played a major role. For the visitors of the *cafés-concerts*, the music performed at the rue du Caire and other Middle Eastern cafés was popular culture. The existence of highly sophisticated traditions of Arab music such as *amal* lay beyond the horizon of most lay writers. The music on the rue du Caire was perceived either as street music or harem music, while that in the Tunisian *café-concert* was purportedly music of the desert tribes.

In this context, folk-music researcher Julien Tiersot showed himself to be well aware of the richness of Arab musical traditions, but he was even more dismissive of the Middle Eastern music in the *cafés-concerts* than his amateur counterparts because it was urban music for the *café-concert* instead of folk music performed by artisans and peasants. In his opening remarks in the section on Arab music, Tiersot reveled in the fact that "nowhere in the Exposition is music held in such honor as in the areas inhabited by the Arabs."[40] The folk-music collector in him dreamed of a rich harvest if he could only have found the time to ask the artisans brought to Paris for the Exposition about the music they performed after hours, when the visitors were gone: "It would have been a rare opportunity to study Arab music in a more thorough fashion than ever before."[41] Tiersot did not, however, introduce "true" Arab music as anything other than the living and

---

In her review article on anthropological dance scholarship, Susan Reed shows that post-colonial research on dance in the nineteenth century focuses almost exclusively on native American and Indian dance. None of the works that she cites engages with Arab dance prior to 1900. See Susan A. Reed, "The Politics and Poetics of Dance," *Annual Review of Anthropology* 27 (1998): 503–32. On developments in Arab music during the nineteenth century, see Habib Hassan Touma, "Die Musik der Araber im 19. Jahrhundert," in *Musikkulturen Asiens, Afrikas und Ozeaniens im 19. Jahrhundert*, ed. Robert Günther (Regensburg: Gustav Bosse Verlag, 1973), 53.

39. This European distinction, though problematic, is nevertheless valid and useful for some musical practices in nineteenth-century Arab cultures. See Harold S. Powers, "Classical Music, Cultural Roots, and Colonial Rule: An Indic Musicologist Looks at the Muslim World," *Asian Music* 12 (1980): esp. 5–8; Walter Feldman, "Cultural Authority and Authenticity in the Turkish Repertoire," *Asian Music* 22 (1990): 73–111; Ruth Davis, "The Art/Popular Music Paradigm and the Tunisian Ma'luf," *Popular Music* 15 (1996): 313–23.

40. Tiersot, "Promenades musicales à l'Exposition," 292: "Nulle part, à l'Exposition, la musique n'est aussi en honneur que dans les quartiers habités par les Arabes."

41. Ibid.: "Nous y aurions trouvé une rare occasion d'étudier la musique arabe d'une façon bien plus approfondie que cela a jamais été fait."

oral traditions of the various crafts people; for him, too, it was folk music, albeit one that was worth studying.

Although Tiersot described for his readers the music that he could hear in the *cafés-concerts* during the day, his approach made it clear that for him the music that accompanied the belly dance was inferior to the truly "authentic" folk music that he would have liked to hear. Whereas engaging with Javanese and Vietnamese music demanded effort and extensive interviews with musicians, the repetitiveness of the Arab melody allowed for its "exact notation" without further ado, even though percussion instruments obscured it more often than not.[42] If he granted a certain authenticity to the performances in the Egyptian café—even while he dismissed as "choreographic fantasies" the dance of the *almée* Aïouché—his report on the Moroccan and Tunisian performances was full of scathing comments: neither was authentic in his view. The music in the Moroccan café is described as "Gallicized Algerian music" with Western cadences and harmonies, even though some of the melodies were based on "ancient Arab melodies."[43] But worse was yet to come; both Tunisian venues had committed the gravest possible sin against authenticity in non-Western folk music: each ensemble included a piano. At the spectacle of the beautiful Fatma, "there is a piano on which the pianist plays Arab melodies that he accompanies with accompaniment-figures of waltzes and polkas! . . ."[44] The performances at the Souk were equally problematical in their instrumentation: "Could it be that the Tunisians have the ambition to make us believe that the piano is one of their national instruments? We found another one at the Tunisian café at the Esplanade des Invalides."[45] In an interesting twist, Tiersot then punished the upstart Tunisians who used European instruments for their Arab music: because of its tuning in equal temperament, the

42. Ibid., 293: "Toute cette percussion couvre le plus souvent les sons des instruments mélodiques; mais, comme le même dessin se reproduit fréquemment dans leur chant et que j'en ai eu plusieurs auditions, j'ai pu en prendre la notation exacte."

43. Julien Tiersot, "Promenades musicales à l'Exposition," *Le Ménestrel* 55 (1889): 299–300, at 299: "Or, ces airs, s'ils tirent leur origine d'anciennes mélodies arabes, n'en ont pas moins été retouchés et mis au point. . . . Mais, comme musique marocaine, cette musique algérienne francisée me parait faible."

44. Ibid., 299: "Enfin, au pied de la scène—ceci donne la note du sérieux de l'endroit—est un piano sur lequel un pianiste joue des airs arabes qu'il accompagne avec des formules d'accompagnement de valses et de polkas! . . ." Arthur Pougin was similarly sarcastic about the presence of the piano in his *Le Théâtre à l'Exposition*, 121: "Enfin, au bas de l'estrade, par conséquent dans la salle même, un piano tenu par une Tunisienne des Batignolles, dont le langage trahit une longue fréquentation avec la plus pure population parisienne."

45. Tiersot, "Promenades musicales à l'Exposition," 299–300: "Les Tunisiens de l'Exposition auraient-ils par hasard la prétention de nous faire prendre le piano pour un de leurs instruments nationaux? Voilà que nous en retrouvons encore un au café

piano reduced Arab music to a "melodic skeleton devoid of all charm." Consequently, the melodies that he transcribed were too commonplace to be worth publishing.[46] He was slightly more favorable in his description of the Algerian belly dances, supposedly from the desert tribes of the Ouled-Naïl. But while Tiersot dismissed orientalist mediation in art as inauthentic, he himself embodied orientalist attitudes in searching for the unspoiled, the true Orient. Just like the advertisements of the rue du Caire that presented it as an authentic Egyptian setting, without the disfigurement of modern architecture, so Tiersot's rhetoric reflected a search for the genuine article of Arab performance. He would find it not in the feminized belly dance and its urban music from the streets of Cairo but in a far more manly manifestation: the performances of the Aissaoua.

The Moroccan Sufist brotherhood of the Aissaoua fascinated the Parisians with their demonstrations of physical mortification performed to trance-inducing music. People queued to enter the spectacle whose success was such that the Moroccan *café-concert*, which housed the spectacle, changed the performance schedule from three times per week to daily shows after only four weeks.[47] Both Tiersot and his lay colleagues interpreted what they heard and saw along very similar lines. In the case of the Aissaouas, spectacle and sound were perceived as congruent in their primordial attraction, foreshadowing later primitivist discourses of the early twentieth century. For the audience, it was the display of strange religious fervor, comparable to the dark ages of European history when flagellation

Tunisien de l'Esplanade des Invalides." Again, Arthur Pougin echoed Tiersot's dismissal of the music at the Tunisian Souk in *Le Théâtre à l'Exposition*, 122–23: "Je n'en saurais dire autant du Concert installé au Souk tunisien. Celui-ci était assez vulgaire, et ne se distinguait par rien de particulier. Je me trompe: il se distinguait par ce fait que les danses des almées y étaient accompagnées—ô horreur!—par un piano européen, sur lequel les airs arabes, parfois si curieux, perdaient tout leur cachet et leur caractère. Le virtuose qui tenait ce piano était un juif arabe nommé Bennini-Semmama, à qui le séjour de Paris fut fatal: il tomba malade ici, et mourut dans les derniers jours du mois d'août. Je ne sais qui lui succéda dans son emploi."

46. Tiersot, "Promenades musicales à l'Exposition," 300: "Les notes du piano s'envolent en l'air, grêles et sèches, laissant à découvert comme un squelette mélodique dénué de tout charme. Ces airs, faits pour des instruments aux intonations indécises, aux sonorités profondes, se prêtant très bien à leurs rythmes vagues, ondulants et langoureux, perdent tout leur caractère en passant sur notre instrument moderne au tempérament égal, aux sons nets et précis, et destiné à des manifestations musicales d'une nature tout autre. J'en ai noté quelques-uns—c'était trop facile ainsi! En les relisant, ils me paraissaient d'une platitude extrême; aucun n'est digne d'être publié."

47. Henri Lavedan, "Les Aïssa-Ouas," *Revue de l'Exposition Universelle de 1889* 1 (1889): 305–10; Georges Grison, "Courrier de l'Exposition," *Le Figaro*, 3 Aug. 1889, 3. Arthur Pougin reported that the Aissaouas generated 400,000 francs of income (*Le Théâtre à l'Exposition*, 118).

and convulsion were part of organized religious practices.[48] Moreover, the repetitive sonorities of the drums and the rhythmical chant of the Aissaoua sounded as savage to the writers' ears as the spectacle they expected to witness. An "increasingly violent and pounding" music, "the only military music capable of inciting these savage creatures," made one writer refer to war in Algeria.[49] For the writer, these were not the classical and civilized heroes of the Mediterranean—such as Alexander the Great who had Timotheus play for him to raise his spirit to go to battle—but warriors so savage that their military ardor could be aroused only by this ferocious music. The hypnotic sounds, together with the gruesome spectacle of pierced arms and swallowed snakes, created the experience of a dangerous Orient, both fascinating and repulsive (figure 5.9). Not the belly dance of the *almées*, but that of a fierce-looking sword dancer—who resembles strikingly the photograph of Rachel Bent-Eny (figure 5.2)—was the only female contribution to the macabre show.

For Tiersot this music, though primitive and repetitive, had things to offer that pointed beyond itself. After the easy work with the Arab dance music, transcription had suddenly become a challenge again, and Tiersot's descriptions—rather than his earlier comparing of Arab dance-music formulas to Camille Saint-Saëns's *Rêverie arabe*—investigate matters in far greater technical detail. He could not attribute intrinsic value to the music in the ceremonies, but for the music scholar it became a fascinating case study given that music played a role in these spectacles that was "truly interesting and most conforming to its nature."[50] In a proto-primitivist conclusion to his description, Tiersot comes to the heart of his interest in this music:

> Music here plays the role in which we see it appear in the most ancient and classic legends. Its magic power exercises itself fully, and almost as much on the nerves of the spectators as on those of the main character. The power lies much more in the rhythmic accent than the form; truth be told, the violent and agitated performance is actually the essential ingredient. Is it not through analogous manifestations that music originally revealed itself in primitive times? If one considers closely the fables of Linus, Orpheus, or Amphion, does it not seem as if music as it was conceived of in legendary eras had an analogous nature to the one that was just examined?

48. "Les Aïssaoua," *Le Matin*, 1 July 1889, 1–2; Émile Michelet, "Autour de l'Exposition," *Paris illustré*, 20 July 1889, 529.

49. Lavedan, "Les Aïssa-Ouas," 307: "toujours plus violente et plus martelée, la seule musique militaire pour allumer ces sauvages créatures."

50. Tiersot, "Promenades musicales à l'Exposition," 308: "si la musique n'y jouait un rôle vraiment intéressant et des plus conforme à sa nature, malgré son peu de valeur intrinsèque dans les cérémonies en question."

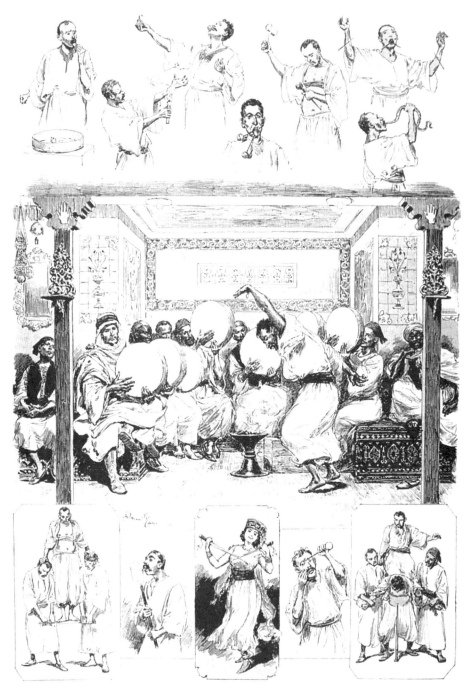

Figure 5.9. Adrien Marie, "Exposition Universelle.—Les Aïssaouas à l'Explanade des Invalides," *Le Monde illustré*, 12 Oct. 1889, 237.

Later, the pure and learned forms of the art made us forget or disdain these rudimentary formulas, this primal matter of music: but while their charm is greater, is their effect on the human spirit not less?

La musique joue ici le rôle dans lequel nous la voyons paraître dans les plus antiques et classiques légendes. Son pouvoir magique s'exerce pleine-ment, et presque autant sur les nerfs des spectateurs que sur ceux du prin-cipal personnage. Ce pouvoir réside bien plutôt dans l'accent rythmique que dans la forme; l'interprétation, violente et mouvementée, en est, en vérité, l'élément essentiel. N'est-ce pas par des manifestations analogues que, dans les temps primitifs, la musique s'est révélée tout d'abord? A bien considérer les fables de Linus, d'Orphée ou d'Amphion, n'apparaît-il pas que la musique, telle qu'on la concevait à ces époques légendaires, était d'une nature analogue à celle qui vient d'être étudiée! Plus tard, les formes pures et savantes de l'art ont fait oublier ou dédaigner ces formules rudimentaires, cette matière première de la musique: mais si leur charme est plus grand, leur action sur l'esprit de l'homme n'est-elle pas moindre?[51]

For Tiersot, the reference to origins bestowed genuineness on the Ais-saouas that no other music from North Africa could offer, and the physical effect of the sounds were his litmus test. In the eyes of their Parisian audi-ences, however, the Aissaouas paid a reassuring prize for such magic and raw masculine powers: "They usually die young."[52]

## Coloring Black Musicians at the Exposition Universelle

The Aissaouas were not the only primitivist attraction of the Middle Eastern *cafés-concerts*. Indeed, these performance venues served as a cultural axis between Europe and Africa with, on the one hand, dance numbers by the blonde Bahia and other stars in the Parisian *café-concert* style and, on the other, performances by black dancers and musicians whose representations were read in an entirely different cultural framework from those of their Arab counterparts. Africa, in the French imagination of the late nineteenth century, was not a uniformly dark continent but one with a black center and lighter fringes. The North Africa of the Maghreb and Levant could be the setting of operas such as Berlioz's *Les Troyens*, Meyerbeer's *L'Africaine*, and Verdi's *Aida*. The latter two were performed at the Opéra during the Exposition Universelle. North Africa provided Paris with dancers of a vari-ety of colors during the Fair, from light-skinned to black; they elicited such

51. Ibid., 309.
52. "Gli Aissa-Ua," *L'Esposizione di Parigi del 1889 illustra* (Milan: Edoardo Sonzogno, 1889), 487–88, at 488: "Generalmente, gli Aissa-Ua muojono giovani."

comments as "Not only the brown Ouled-Naïl with their dull skin and their tattoos on the chin nor just the ebony-colored Sudanese or the bronzed Kabyles, but even those young women who are so white and so rosy that one could confuse them with the *almées* from Montmartre or the Batignolles, they all came from the African coast to appear in the Exposition."[53] In contrast to the orientalist imaginary of the Maghreb, Africa's dark center was an exotic place of subjugation of and encounter with an Other so different that race became a much more foregrounded signifier than in discussions of the Arabs. Indeed if Arab performances were located between the West and the East, black musicians such as the Sudanese who lived just to the south of Egypt and performed in Egypt and Algeria pointed away from Europe to an alterity whose difference was constructed as an absolute in terms of race, culture, and society. The discourses about and visual representations of black performers colored them as the opposite of "white" by emphasizing difference, which included the "absence of culture."[54]

This difference was also embodied in the way African musical cultures were represented at the Exposition Universelle in the Middle Eastern *café-concert* performances on the one hand, and as part of the living ethnological exhibits in the Colonial section on the other.[55] In the context of the belly dances, black performers served as a primitivist foil for the more "decadent" Arabs, coming from a culture still unknown, not yet entirely subjugated, and thus dangerous. François de Nion describes the African performers of the *cafés-concerts* as symbols for this foreign world. When recounting the dance of the Sudanese, Nion plays on the old sexualizing metaphor that likens Africa to a female body to be conquered, and he reinscribes the power of the West's superior virility through a reassuring reference to Africa's eunuchs as mediators of sexual encounter:

53. "Curiosités de l'Exposition: Les Concerts Africains," *Le Petit Journal*, 10 July 1889, 1: "Non seulement les brunes Ouled-Naïl avec leur peau mate et leurs tatouages sur le menton, non seulement les Soudaniens couleur d'ébène ou les Kabyles bronzés, mais même ces jeunes personnes si blanches et si roses qu'on les prendrait pour les almées de Montmartre ou des Batignolles, tous sont venus de la côte africaine pour figurer à l'Exposition."

54. For an important study on French perceptions of and discourses about Africa, see Christopher L. Miller, *Blank Darkness: Africanist Discourse in French* (Chicago and London: University of Chicago Press, 1985). See in particular his introductory chapter on the deriving of the French Africanist discourses, 3–65.

55. The exhibition of humans in World's Fairs, national trade shows, and zoos has elicited a significant body of literature. For a case study related to British India that addresses several of the issues, see Saloni Mathur, "Living Ethnological Exhibits: The Case of 1886," *Cultural Anthropology* 15 (2000); 492–524; a variety of cases are examined in Nicolas Bancel et al., eds., *Zoos humains: De la Vénus hottentote aux Reality Shows* (Paris: Éditions de la Découverte, 2002).

Monstrous, lascivious, obscene Africa, a *new world*, barely known, the black world, teeming with a disquieting and robust life, the generator of a power that will one day revolutionize any exhausted societies through contact alone. This soul of Africa, that lies in the genitals, is already exposed in the spectacle of the Algerian and Tunisian concerts, however banal and amalgamated of all kinds of elements . . . this soul flourishes in these dislocations of the torso, in this extreme science—a science of eunuchs—to present and offer the pudenda of a woman. The movement of the hips which plays with the womb, promising and withdrawing, these loin pushes with their brutal jolts, this is the dance *par excellence* of all of the immense triangle whose base reaches from Suez to Tétouan and whose point is the Cape.

[L]'Afrique monstrueuse, lascive, obscène, de *nouveau monde*, à peine encore connu, le monde noir, grouillant d'une vie inquiétante et robuste, un facteur d'une puissance à bouleverser un jour par son simple contact les sociétés vidées. Cette âme de l'Afrique qui est dans le bas-ventre, elle se dénonce déjà dans le spectacle, au fond banal, de ces concerts algériens ou tunisiens si amalgamés pourtant d'éléments . . . elle s'épanouit dans ces déhanchements du torse, dans cette science extrême,—une science d'eunuques,—de présenter et d'offrir le sexe de la femme. Ce mouvement des hanches qui fait jouer le flanc, le promet, le retire, ces coups de reins aux saccades brutales, c'est la danse par excellence de tout l'immense triangle dont la base va de Suez à Tétouan et dont la pointe est au Cap.[56]

Nion described the African performers at the *cafés-concerts* as offering a glimpse of raw and primitive sexuality which offers a striking contrast to the widespread disenchantment of the broken orientalist dream when journalists and visitors encountered the Arab belly dance. Nion seems to suggest that the "black" African dance, coming from lower down the continent, focuses on a lower, more provocative part of the anatomy. Indeed, for the French, darker-skinned Africans were oversexed beings.[57]

The sexualizing of the black performers at the Exposition Universelle became a characterization that, in some instances, also related to the sonic side of the performances. In Jourdain's description, the primitive percussive music—to his ears a terrible charivari—has the ability to excite the African dancers to sexually evocative movements:

As far as the Sudanese black women are concerned, they limit themselves to the *kakeb*, a kind of big iron castanets that the virtuoso (?) agitates

56. François de Nion, "Théâtre," *Revue Indépendante*, Sept. 1889, 504.

57. William B. Cohen, *The French Encounter with Africans: White Responses to Blacks, 1530–1880* (Bloomington and London: Indiana University Press, 1980), 245.

furiously, and the tamtam that an epileptic player hits alternatively with a long stick or a wooden rounded one. This horrible charivari has the ability to excite the Negresses to shake themselves where they are standing, while turning with more enthusiasm than grace.

Quant aux noires Soudanaises, elles se contentent du Kakeb, sorte de grandes castagnettes en fer que le virtuose (?) agite avec fureur, et du Tam-Tam sur lequel un instrumentiste épileptique tape alternativement avec une longue baguette et une crosse de bois. Cet effroyable charivari a le don d'exciter les négresses, qui se trémoussent sur place, en tournant sur elles-mêmes avec plus d'entrain que de grâce.[58]

The popular link between the dominance of percussion instruments and African dance—prominently exploited by Fétis and other experienced writers on music—seemed to be the only way in which music could figure in the general-press accounts of African sound, and then only with respect to the *café-concert* performances by the Sudanese at the Middle Eastern cafés.[59] Even Tiersot, in his series on picturesque music at the Exposition Universelle, contrasted the more or less melodic music of the Arab performers with the primitive limitation of the musical means of the black performers, whose "[orchestra] has not a single melodic instrument and consists only of rhythmic instruments."[60] Yet these performances represented only a limited part of African music at the Exposition Universelle. In the colonial exhibition, Africans were part of the "villages" that were constructed to show the visitors what indigenous life was like in the countries that had made the news in the past ten years, whether Senegal or the Congo. Public interest in these African exhibits was as keen as it was for any other exotic display, and the colonialist discourses were pronounced in this context. Thus the hero of the Congo and governor-general of Gabon, Savorgnan de Brazza, took the journalist from *Le Figaro* around the Gabon village with its twenty inhabitants in order to explain their culture to the journal's readers.[61] An anecdote confirmed the apparent superiority of the white race because of their literacy

58. Frantz Jourdain, "L'Exposition algérienne," *L'Exposition de Paris* 1–2 (1889): 146–47, at 147.

59. On the close link between percussion instruments and race in French nineteenth-century imagination, see also Jann Pasler, "The Utility of Musical Instruments in the Racial and Colonial Agendas of Late Nineteenth-Century France," *Journal of the Royal Musical Association* 129 (2004): 24–76.

60. Julien Tiersot, "Promenades musicales à l'Exposition: Les arabes (*suite et fin*)," *Le Ménestrel* (1889): 307–9, at 308: "il ne possède aucun instrument mélodique, et se compose uniquement d'instruments rythmiques."

61. On the central role of Savorgnan de Brazza in the Third Republic's shifts in colonial politics, see Edward Berenson, "Unifying the French Nation: Savorgnan de Brazza

rather than their pale skin—one of the cornerstones of the *mission civil-isatrice* would be the establishment of schools—before the visit ended with the performance of a "bizarre song" that was "chanted" in antiphonal manner by the Gabonese who accompanied themselves with clapping.[62] This is one of the rare references to sub-Saharan African music in the general press, and then only because it was part of a performance for a specific audience.

To what extent such representation of Africans as "savages" was guided by a colonialist agenda as well as a primitivist desire for an authentic African landscape uncorrupted by civilization can be gathered from diverse comments, as for example the description of exotic villages in *Le Figaro* at the opening of the Exposition, which described the inhabitants of the villages as little more than members of a natural, exotic species that represents the countryside of their origin, regretting that they could not have "brought their landscape with them"—a familiar conceit of display at the Jardin d'Acclimatation:

> We arrive finally at the unknown, at the extraordinary. Behind the *Palais Central*, along the rue Constantine, are the *inhabited villages*. They are already the subject of conversation amid anthropologists. The Jardin d'Acclimatation has never offered us so many authentic and exotic curiosities at once. . . . One should not forget that, in addition to the zoological and anthropological interest offered by the importation into France of the native cultures of all the countries, the sight of the huts and unfamiliar furniture will greatly astonish the visitors.

> Nous arrivons enfin à l'inconnu et à l'extraordinaire. Derrière le Palais central, le long de la rue Constantine, sont établis les *villages habités*. Ils sont déjà le sujet des conversations entre les anthropologistes. Le Jardin d'acclimatation ne nous a jamais fourni d'un seul coup autant de curiosités exotiques et authentiques. . . . Il ne faut pas oublier qu'outre l'intérêt zoologique et anthropologique qu'offre l'importation en France de naturels de tous les pays, la vue de cases, de meubles inconnus étonnera beaucoup les visiteurs.[63]

---

and the Third Republic," in *Music, Culture, and National Identity in France, 1870–1939*, ed. Barbara Kelly (Rochester, NY: University of Rochester Press, forthcoming).

62. Charles Chincholle, "Paris jugé par les peaux jaunes et noires," *Le Figaro*, 9 May 1889, 1–2, 2: "Ici c'est M. de Brazza, gouverneur général de Gabon, qui me sert lui-même d'interprète. . . . C'est que maintenant, pour Ndjouké et pour tous ceux de sa race, les blancs sont des êtres supérieurs. 'Ce sont des écrivains.' Cela veut simplement dire que nous savons lire, correspondre, tenir des livres et compter autrement que sur nos doigts. . . . Je prie M. de Brazza de faire chanter à son intention les Gabonnais. Ils nous psalmodient, en battant des mains, une chanson bizarre."

63. "Villages Exotiques," *Le Figaro*, special issue "Exposition de 1889," 6 May 1889, 2: "apporter avec eux leur paysage."

That the exhibited subjects were very well aware of the colonialist agenda and found this deeply offensive becomes apparent in the subsequent remark by the Senegalese silversmith, Samba Lawbé Thiam, who may well be one of the three artisans represented in figure 5.10:

> Sir, we are very humiliated, he told me in very good French, to be thus exhibited like savages in huts: these hovels made of straw and mud don't give you any idea about Senegal. In Senegal, Sir, we have barracks, train stations, railways; we use electricity for lighting. The hygiene council no longer tolerates the building of such huts.

> Nous sommes très humiliés, monsieur, m'a-t-il dit en fort bon français, d'être ainsi exhibés dans des huttes comme des sauvages: ces cases en nattes et en boue ne vous donnent aucune idée du Sénégal. Au Sénégal, monsieur, nous avons des casernes, des gares, des chemins de fer; nous nous éclairons à l'électricité. Le conseil d'hygiène ne tolère plus que l'on édifie des baraques dans ce genre-là.[64]

Samba Lawbé Thiam's Senegal is that of General Faidherbe and the model colony he describes in his book, published in 1889.[65] The dissonance between the view from Senegal and the colonialist representation of Senegal is sharp. In an ironic twist, this did not stop some living exhibits, however, from playing to the perceived expectations of the organizers and visitors.

In the colonial exhibition, dark-skinned natives were shown as part of not only the African villages from Senegal and Gabon but also those from Oceania, most prominently in the "village Canaque" from New Caledonia. But whether African or Oceanian, these villages were consumed by visitors as the scenery of a "safari" trip into foreign lands, with postcards and photographs on sale as memories of this fake voyage.[66] Given that none of the villages had a performance venue comparable to that of the *kampong javanais*, African and Oceanian musics had no recognizable forum, which may account for the absence of music in reports about and visual representations of these exhibition villages. In the images from the Senegalese village, the ubiquitous prop in French representations of black visitors from abroad, the drum, is tucked away in the upper center of the silversmith's hut (figure 5.10). Music-making in the black villages—to which Tiersot

---

64. Un Badaud, "Psychologie Exotique," *Le Figaro*, 12 June 1889, 1.

65. Louis Léon César Faidherbe, *Le Sénégal: La France dans l'Afrique occidentale* (Paris: Librairie Hachette, 1889). I am grateful to my colleague at UNC, anthropologist Michael Lambert, for this reference and his helpful comments about colonial Senegal.

66. On Paul Gauguin's visits to the Exposition Universelle and his acquiring of exotic photographs at this occasion, see Elizabeth C. Childs, "The Colonial Lens: Gauguin, Primitivism, and Photography in the Fin de siècle," in *Antimodernism and Artistic*

Figure 5.10. "Le Village sénégalais," *L'Exposition de Paris 1889* 3–4 (1889): 124.

attested in his descriptions—seems to have been either ignored or perceived as environmental sound, even when it was part of festivities staged
for the fairgoers.

Save for the belly dances, only one other black performance of
the Exposition Universelle was mentioned and represented visually in the
press: the dance of the Polynesian Kanakas.[67] As in the case of the
Gabonese song, the context signaled "performance." The Kanakas had
taken part in the colonial processions of the "fête de nuit," before launch-
ing into their national dance, well choreographed under the medallion of
the "République Française." The contrast in this engraving between the
three barefoot dancers and their environment is striking (figure 5.11). The
Third-Republic trappings of the performance space, the well-heeled Western audience in the foreground, the colonial soldier guarding the performance, and the mass of barely distinguishable audience members
outside accentuate all that is associated with the "black" performers' primitivism: dark skin, primitive tools, absence of "real music" (the figure to the
right behind the dancer seems to be playing a drum), and the sheer physi-
cality of the dance. These are neither the movements of a European folk
dance nor those of the ballroom or ballet. The image shows savages in
action, but framed and contained by the empire of the French Republic,
both her symbols and her people.

While other writers and musicians shared Julien Tiersot's interest in
the music of other cultures, he was alone in his enquiries into the
sound-world of the African and Oceanian villages at the Exposition Coloniale. He gathered the results of his research in the last three installments
of his reports on the exotic musics of the Fair.[68] Tiersot starts his remarks
about this music by engaging squarely with the question as to whether it is
music at all. He is careful not to invest his black informants with too much
musicality, but stays within the confines of anthropological argument by
emphasizing the raw sensualism that writers such as Gobineau had claimed
as a main character trait of blacks.

> Studying the music of the Negroes, well, this is an idea that will seem
> bizarre and perhaps even superfluous to more than one reader. Some will
> no doubt wonder whether the essentially primitive aggregations of sound,
> which constitute the only art form of the Kanaka, Pahouins, Senegalese,

*Experience: Policing the Boundaries of Modernism*, ed. Linda Jessup (Toronto, Buffalo, and
London: University of Toronto Press, 2000), 56–57.

67. In contrast to current American usage, French nineteenth-century anthropologists and ethnographers considered Oceanian natives as "black." Julien Tierot describes
their music in his "Promenades musicales à l'Exposition: Les Nègres," *Le Ménestrel* 55
(1889): 315–16, 324–26, 331–32.

68. Ibid.

Figure 5.11. "Danse canaque," *L'Exposition de Paris 1889* 3–4 (1889): title page for 12 Oct. 1889.

etc., are in fact worthy of carrying the noble name of Music and whether, on the other hand, they deserve our full attention. It is true, of course, that those who expect us to report on Kanakian symphonies, Pahouian music dramas or even simple Senegalese *opéras comiques* will be disappointed; but in addition to the fact that, even from a technical and theoretical stand-point, the music of the Negroes is not as entirely lacking in interest as one usually assumes, it is understood that the principal aim of these articles is to explain and determine musical forms different from ours, in particular those that might give us a better idea of the primitive forms. In that respect, the Negroes of Africa and Oceania will give us elements that conform entirely to our program. . . . In truth, if one considers the sensation produced by the sound as the main component of musical pleasure, Negroes have to be recognized as passionate about music.

Etudier la musique des nègres, voilà une idée qui paraîtra bizarre, et peut-être superflue, à plus d'un lecteur. Quelques-uns se demanderont sans doute si les agrégations de sons, essentiellement primitives, qui constituent la seule forme d'art des Canaques, Pahouins, Sénégalais, etc., sont dignes, en vérité, de porter le noble nom de Musique, et si d'autre part, elles méritent de retenir sérieusement notre attention. Il est bien vrai que ceux qui s'attendraient à nous voir rendre compte de symphonies canaques, de drames musicaux pahouins, même de simples opéras-comiques sénégalais, seraient déçus; mais, outre que, même au point de vue technique et théorique, la musique des nègres n'est pas aussi complètement dépourvue d'intérêt qu'on le suppose d'ordinaire, il est entendu que ces articles ont pour objet principal d'expliquer et de fixer des formes musicales différentes de celles qui nous sont propres, et particulièrement celles qui peuvent le mieux donner l'idée des formes primitives. A ce point de vue, les nègres de l'Afrique et de l'Océanie nous apporteront des éléments absolument conformes à notre programme. . . . La vérité est que, si, dans la jouissance musicale, on considère surtout la sensation produite par le son, les nègres doivent être reconnus pour passionnés pour la musique.[69]

Thus, for Tiersot, the visit of the black musicians brings full circle the research program for the origins of music that he had outlined five months earlier in his opening text on exotic music at the Exposition Universelle (see chapter 4). Tiersot guides his readers through this music with the help of well-tried racist constructs: blacks as a childlike and womanlike race whose primitivism will not allow for sophisticated art but whose simplemindedness allows the knowledgeable scholar to trace music back to its origins.[70] What Tiersot observes and transcribes for his audience is not only sonic ethnography but also—far more importantly for his Western readers—musical archaeology. According to this argument, black music has no intrinsic value, but is ennobled through its role as a living history of universal music. This role in a universalist music history shines through several of Tiersot's accounts. His description of the Senegalese bestows them with an *Urmusik* of a Wagnerian kind, in which dance and music are inextricably linked; later, a Senegalese sings an "epic song recalling the

69. Ibid., 315.
70. Cohen, *French Encounter with Africans*, 236–45.

memory of an earlier hero (for this is among all peoples of the world the primordial form, and one necessary, so to speak, for all lyric [i.e., sung] poetry)."[71] When the French administration of the Gabon village proved difficult, Tiersot showed himself able to use the universal language of music, opening a non-mediated dialogue with the Pahouins through song: Tiersot opened the "conversation" with an unspecified melodic phrase and, bit by bit, enticed the Pahouins to respond in their own musical language and then to embark on demonstrations of their music. To describe the result, Tiesot looked at comparisons taken from the past of European music: for what Tiersot characterized first as a serenade, a European fellow listener hit upon the analogy with plainchant as the most fitting description.[72]

Tiersot's greatest "discovery," however, was that of tonal harmony in the songs from Gabon. Contrary to popular belief, Tiersot points out, his research reveals that the primitive music of both Africa and Oceania contains harmonic aggregates, and because these harmonies are entirely vocal in origin, they prove that tonal harmony is a natural and universal component of music. His transcription of "harmonic formulas" (*formules harmoniques*) brought a new and empirical argument to the ongoing debates in nineteenth-century music theory as to whether tonality was universal (and thus natural) or culture-specific. For Tiersot, the conclusion that tonality was natural may well have been the most important discovery of his musical enquiries during the Exposition Universelle.[73] If comparative musicology could prove the universality of tonal harmony (which Tiersot also attempted in his reading of the *angklung* as producing a ninth chord) then Tiersot's enterprise at the Exposition Universelle achieved the two aims of his program: it reinforced Western music as the most advanced, sophisticated, and beautiful, and it showed to his readers that ethnography could uncover traces of Western civilization in ways akin if not superior to the fashionable archaeology widely showcased at the Fair. Tiersot concluded his section on music from Africa and Oceania by declaring: "we will say again that harmony, far from being, as some believe, the exclusive product of a complex act of the brain, is, in contrast, a natural thing for man, even savage, even primitive, and that its rights in the city of Art are equal to those of melody."[74] Thus his discovery achieved a third goal, which Tiersot

---

71. Tiersot, "Promenades musicales à l'Exposition: Les Nègres," 315: "Il voulut bien me chanter une chanson: c'était un chant épique, rappelant la mémoire d'un héros d'autrefois (car c'est là, chez tous les peuples du monde, la forme primordiale et, pour ainsi dire, nécessaire de toute poésie lyrique)."

72. Ibid., 324.

73. Ibid., 325–26.

74. Ibid., 332: "Nous dirons encore que l'harmonie, loin d'être, comme d'aucuns le croient, le produit exclusif d'un travail complexe du cerveau, est, au contraire, chose

had kept quiet until that point. For him, the old French disputes over the primacy of melody or harmony had thus been solved empirically, with potentially profound consequences for the future of music. Starting with the "querelles des Piccinnistes et Ramistes," the French disputes over the primacy of harmony or melody have surfaced repeatedly, whether in the Stendhalian support of melodic Rossini against the harmonic Weber or, closer to the Exposition Universelle of 1889, the debates around the Wagnerian preference of harmony over melody.[75] Indeed, much of the debate over Massenet's *Esclarmonde* in May 1889 had focused on exactly these issues, and they remained burning questions that would surface with every major French première, whether Gustave Charpentier's *Louise* in 1900, Debussy's *Pelléas et Mélisande* two years later, or even the revival of composers such as Monteverdi in 1904.[76] If musical anthropology could show, however, that harmony was a universal human form of expression, then France could embrace it without the fear of using a musical construct developed by foreign cultures, most prominently Wagner's Germany.

## Picturesque Music of the People: Europe at the Fair

For Tiersot, the primitivist interpretation of black music was an essential building block of his universalist musical world view. For many of his contemporaries, it remained doubtful whether it was music at all. Such questions were, however, far from everybody's mind when they were listening to the folk music of many of the nineteen European nations whose products were shown at the Exposition Universelle. As was the case with the music of the Far and Middle East, European folk music served as an advertising aid for the promotion of autochthonic goods. But like the exotic performances from Java, some of the picturesque musics from Europe took on a life of their own, beyond simply furnishing the background music for the various local pavilions and restaurants. Folk music also found its way into the concert hall of the Trocadéro, both on the programs of visiting choirs

naturelle à l'homme, même sauvage, même primitif, et que ses droits dans la cité de l'Art sont égaux à ceux de la mélodie."

75. One of the key texts of that period is Camille Saint-Saëns's 1879 essay "Harmonie et mélodie," published in his essay collection *Harmonie et mélodie* (Paris: Calman-Lévy, 1885), 1–36.

76. On the discussions around *Louise* and *Pelléas et Mélisande*, see James Ross, "Crisis and Transformation: French Opera, Politics and the Press, 1897–1903" (DPhil diss., Oxford University, 1998); on the Parisian Monteverdi performances, see Annegret Fauser, "D'Indy archéologue," in *Vincent d'Indy et son temps*, ed. Myriam Chimènes and Manuela Schwartz (Sprimont: Pierre Mardaga, forthcoming).

such as those from Norway, Finland, and Spain, and in the official contest of picturesque music judged by, among others, professors of the Paris Conservatoire.

Folk music at the Exposition Universelle was "cheerful, [performed] in costumes and on instruments that were both picturesque."[77] For visitors to the Fair, it was music of the people and for the people, played on "archaic instruments that were abandoned by the kings and emperors of music." Indeed, "picturesque music here signifies naive, original, folk, rustic music, the music of those who can't read music."[78] By 1889, the rhetoric of folk music as the authentic, uncorrupted voice of the people had been firmly established in European thought, with the widespread adoption of the Herderian concept of "the people" as the cradle of a true national culture.[79] As Weckerlin put it in 1886, the people had not been corrupted by the internationalization of music which was the consequence of its written transmission from the Middle Ages onward. While art music was a universal language spoken by individuals, folk music was specific to a linguistic community and region but, at the same time, a shared, collective expression of the "génie du peuple":

> The folksongs of a country better express its type; specific physiognomy; and particular, characteristic rhythms than the music of the composers of that same country for—given that art is universal—it cannot have this or that country as its type, while the song of the people remains circumscribed by a radius usually determined by the same language if not the same dialect.

> Les chansons populaires d'un pays expriment mieux son type, sa physionomie spéciale, ses rythmes particuliers, caractéristiques, que la musique

---

77. Adolphe Aderer, "La Musique à l'Exposition," *L'Illustration*, 12 Oct. 1889, 303–5, at 303: "la musique gaie, dans des costumes et avec des instruments pittoresques."

78. Émile Goudeau, "Les Musiques pittoresques au Trocadéro," *Revue de l'Exposition Universelle de 1889* 2 (1889): 25–32, at 25: "les instruments archaïques abandonnés par les rois et empereurs de la musique"; and "Musiques pittoresques signifie ici musiques naïves, originales, populaires, rustiques, musique de ceux qui ne savent pas la musique."

79. On the issue of "the people" and folk music, see Richard Middleton, "Locating the People: Music and the Popular," in *The Cultural Study of Music: A Critical Introduction*, ed. Martin Clayton, Trevor Herbert, and Richard Middleton (New York and London: Routledge, 2003), esp. 252–53. On the role and rhetoric of folk music in France in the nineteenth century, see Jane F. Fulcher, "The Popular Chanson of the Second Empire: 'Music of the Peasants' in France," *Acta musicologica* 52 (1981): 27–37; and Annegret Fauser: "Gendering the Nations: The Ideologies of French Discourse on Music (1870–1914)," in *Musical Constructions of Nationalism: Essays on the History and Ideology of European Musical Culture, 1800–1945*, ed. Michael Murphy and Harry White, 72–103 (Cork: Cork University Press, 2001).

des compositeurs de ce même pays, parce que l'art étant universel, ne peut
avoir comme type tel ou tel pays, tandis que la chanson du peuple reste
circonscrite dans un rayon, déterminé généralement par la même langue
ou le même dialecte.[80]

The seductive conflation of national identity and popular culture had been
established in France since the late 1820s, when the French historian Jules
Michelet (among other poets and scholars concerned with post-revolutionary French identity) formulated his notion that popular traditions reflected
a distinct national character.[81] By the 1830s and 1840s, the concept of folksong as the collective musical expression of a people as a nation was firmly
in place. Consequently, in 1852, in one of his first official decrees,
Napoléon III had called for the publication of folksong collections.[82] Not
only in nineteenth-century France but throughout Europe (and—
famously—a concept also imported to the United States by Antonín
Dvořák), folksong was invested with iconic nationalism, because its collective character, perceived as that of the people, could carry nationalist ideologies.[83]

   Traditional music thus played a central role in the construction of various European national identities at the Exposition Universelle, in particular for those countries that were struggling with these issues in the late
nineteenth century: Romania, Serbia, and Hungary. Already in the
previous two Parisian Expositions Universelles, gypsy music from Hungary
was a major musical attraction that made the Austrian Empire sound
Hungarian.[84] While in 1889 the "Viennese Ladies Orchestra" played their
waltzes at the cosmopolitan Restaurant de France, it was a Hungarian gypsy
band, the "Czarda hongroise," that was installed in the Austro-Hungarian
culinary exhibition of the Galerie d'Agriculture et de Viticulture and
which also played in the Hungarian restaurant, "the simple and
unadorned hut of a straw-covered inn which brings to the border of the
Seine some of the landscape and air of the banks of the Danube."[85] In

   80. Jean-Baptiste Weckerlin, *La Chanson populaire* (Paris: Librairie de Firmin-Didot,
1886), 3.
   81. Charles Rearick, "Symbol, Legend, and History: Michelet as Folklorist-
Historian," *French Historical Studies* 7 (1971): 76. See also Stéphane Gerson, "Parisian
Littérateurs, Provincial Journeys, and the Construction of Unity in Post-Revolutionary
France," *Past and Present*, no. 151 (May 1996): 141–73.
   82. Fulcher, "The Popular Chanson of the Second Empire," 27–30.
   83. For an overview of musical nationalism with some reference to the folksong
movements, see Richard Taruskin, "Nationalism," in *NGr2*.
   84. Comettant, *La Musique*, 281.
   85. Th. Lindenlaub, "La Csarda hongroise," *Revue de l'Exposition Universelle de 1889* 1
(1889): 193–95, at 193: "la hutte simple et nue de l'auberge couverte de chaume qui
amène au bord de la Seine un peu du Paysage et de l'air des rives du Danube."

Les dames hongroises.

Figure 5.12. Illustration in Maurice Montégut, "La Musique dans les cafés," *Revue de l'Exposition Universelle de 1889* 1 (1889): 225–28, at 226.

addition, a Hungarian women's band—billed as such, even though it had some male performers, and dressed up in Magyar-style costumes—and other musicians from Hungary enchanted the fairgoers with their music *en style hongrois* (figure 5.12).

For the Parisians, the folkloric musical Hungary was the country of Liszt, of gypsy musicians (who were perceived as the true Hungarian folk musicians), and of the struggle for liberation. The Rákóczy march and its arrangement by Berlioz are mentioned repeatedly in accounts of the Hungarian folk music, and Liszt's name is present throughout most of the discussions. The improvisatory character of Hungarian music, its virtuosic embroidery of the melodic material and its rhythmic freedom became signifiers of a free-spirited people, conflating popular stereotypes about the Romani with images of Hungarian steppes and Magyar horsemen.[86]

86. On the French relationship with gypsies, see François de Vaux de Foletier, *Les Bohémiens en France au 19e siècle* (Paris: J. C. Lattès, 1981), esp. 193–231.

"Movement and life," so Tiersot wrote, were "the essential qualities of gypsy music."[87] But while these qualities make their music irresistible, they also reveal a national weakness. Tiersot uses the comparison between a French and a Hungarian rendition of their "national song," the Rákóczy march, as a case in point: the French composer Berlioz's version is heroic and long-breathed—it is truly music of the revolution; the Hungarians, however, though belligerent and vivacious, make short-breathed music that is over in a moment and whose revolutionary zeal does not last.[88] Tiersot ends his argument with these musical comparisons, but the political consequences are implied: the French achieved the political results that they sought in their revolutions, the Hungarians were still dominated by the Austrians, and their embroidered, improvised, and rhythmically unstable music offers all the clues necessary to understand why.[89]

Gypsies were perceived as a race and yet as a musically authentic part of the popular culture of their host country because of their nature-related life style.[90] As an American visitor to the Fair put it: "A good deal had been written on the subject, to which Liszt devoted an entire volume, but a Hungarian gentleman settled the question by proving authoritatively that all their melodies were popular tunes of his native country, so old that they had been generally forgotten, which the gypsies had picked up ages ago on the steppes." The author's theory could be proven, on the one hand, by "the African character of the gypsy music in Spain," while, on the other, it would account "for the absence of music among the English gypsies, England proper having no native music."[91] Ironically, the gypsies of the Exposition thus reinforced the notion of folk music as the authentic expression of a people's soul (*génie populaire*), for theirs was a music from the distant past—not their own, however, but that of their host country. It is exactly because gypsies (like Jews) were perceived as having no music of their own that they could become the true voice of a people who since had lost their heritage because of political occupation or socio-economic development.

87. Julien Tiersot, "Promenades musicales à l'Exposition: Les Tziganes de Hongrie," *Le Ménestrel* 55 (1889): 267–69, at 267: "Le mouvement, la vie: voilà donc les qualités essentielles de la musique des Tziganes."
88. Ibid., 269. He starts his comparison as follows: "La différence des deux races, française et hongroise, est marquée d'une façon singulière par la façon dont Berlioz a traité le thème de la marche Racoczy."
89. On the complex relationship of Hungarian political identity and gypsy music since the nineteenth century, see Jonathan Bellman, "The Hungarian Gypsies and the Poetics of Exclusion," in *The Exotic in Western Music*, ed. Jonathan Bellman, 74–103 (Boston: Northeastern University Press, 1998).
90. On the stereotypes about gypsy musicians, see ibid., 75–79.
91. "Loitering through the Paris Exhibition," *Atlantic Monthly*, issue 389 (Mar. 1890): 360–74, esp. 361–62. Apparently the author was more influenced by Haydn's infamous dictum than knowledge about folk music on the British Isles.

The Hungarian gypsy musicians were back in Paris because they were one of the musical magnets of the 1878 Fair, to the point of being compared to an "invasion."[92] Their success in 1889 was tempered, however, by the even more exotic and more "authentic" gypsy music from Romania and Spain.[93] The Romanian music elicited much more controversy than the established Hungarian gypsy music. For Maurice Montégut, the Romanian *lăutari* were primitives and thus true gypsies. They were so attuned to their art that they became "almost instruments themselves."[94] Indeed, the *Guide bleu* described the Romanian café as one of the "marvels" of the Exposition (figure 5.13), the "exact reproduction of a Romanian country house. . . . The interior of the chalet corresponds to the exterior; one can listen to Romanian gypsies, who should not be confused with their Hungarian colleagues, for they are still natural. . . . One is served by real Romanian women who are pretty in their picturesque costumes. . . . Those who enjoy culinary exoticism should therefore go to the Romanian chalet."[95] In such reasoning, the Romanian gypsies were perceived as more "authentic" musicians because they were unspoiled by the urban music business—a widespread approach towards Hungarian gypsies that endured well into the twentieth century with the writings of Béla Bartók, who himself favored the music of Romanian gypsies over those of Hungary.

Among the signs of artistic success for the Romanian players was the cabaret's reputation as a place where (similar to the *kampong javanais*) Parisians musicians, painters, and literati—perceived as arbiters of musical judgment—came in order to listen. That some of these artists were moving in the same circles as Prince Georges Bibesco, the patron of the Romanian exhibit, might well have helped establish the reputation of the

92. Graindorge, "Tziganes," *L'Écho de Paris*, 13 July 1889, 2: "L'invasion de la France par les Tziganes date de 1878."

93. With rhetorical flourish, the author of "La musica pittoresca" presents the gypsy musicians in sequence. The Hungarians are "zingari," then "sono zingari anche I *Lautars* della bettola Rumena," and reaches the last group: "E sono zingari anche i *Gananos* di Spagna." R. C., "La musica pittoresca," *Parigi e l'esposizione universale des 1889* (Milano: Fratelli Treves, 1889), issue of Aug. 1889, 127–28, at 127.

94. Maurice Montégut, "La Musique dans les cafés," *Revue de l'Exposition Universelle de 1889* 1 (1889): 225–28, at 226: "Eux aussi sont des primitifs, des romanichels; et, plus que les nôtres jadis, de vrais Bohémiens. Ces êtres, éminemment doués, sont presque des instruments eux-mêmes."

95. *Exposition de 1889: Guide bleu du "Figaro" et du "Petit Journal,"* 216–17: "un chalet-restaurant qui est simplement une des merveilles de l'Exposition. C'est la reproduction exacte de la maison de campagne roumaine. . . . L'intérieur du chalet répond à l'extérieur; on y entend des tziganes roumains qu'il est bon de ne pas confondre avec leurs confrères hongrois, car ils sont encore naturels. . . . On y est servi par de vraies Roumaines, fort jolies sous leurs costumes pittoresques. . . . Les amateurs d'exotisme culinaire doivent donc aller au chalet roumain."

Le cabaret roumain.

Figure 5.13. Drawing of the Romanian restaurant, in Émile Goudeau: "Une
Journée d'exposition," *La Revue illustrée* 4, part 2 (1889): 215.

Romanian gypsy performances: "Artists—those who really know their
business—come to have lunch or dinner at the Romanian cabaret with
the sole intention of hearing the gypsies. And they were often among the
most famous artists, for instance Gounod and Massenet."[96] Among the

96. Montégut, "La Musique dans les cafés," 227: "Des artistes, des gens du métier,
viennent déjeuner ou dîner au Cabaret Roumain, dans l'intention unique d'ouïr les

musicians fascinated by the music of the Romanian gypsies were not only such well-known musicians as Gounod and Massenet, but also the young Erik Satie.[97] Julien Tiersot points out that there were two *lăutari* groups, one placed inside of the establishment, the other, smaller one, outside in the courtyard, next to a picturesque fountain (figure 5.14).[98] The instrument that elicited the most comment was the pan-pipes or *nai* (seen at the center of figure 5.14). For Tiersot, the sound itself of the instrument contributed to the "effeminate" chamber-music effect of the Romanian music when compared to the more vigorous and "heroic" orchestra of the Hungarians.[99] Even a sympathetic listener such as Émile Goudeau heard the music of the Romanians as one that represented "the musical soul of a people that has been enslaved for a long time," referring to the centuries of Ottoman occupation, which had lasted until 1829, and Romania's subsequent decades as a Russian protectorate until the end of the Crimean War in 1856.[100] The French commentators' linking of popular music with the political destiny of the Romanians was echoed in the American press:

> The airs [of the Romanians] have not the originality of the Hungarian, nor a spark of their fire; they seem, like the Roumanian [*sic*] language, enfeebled, uncultivated, Italian; when they are more distinctly national they are pastoral, with a certain regretfulness which pervades even the lively tunes. It is the music of a conquered people, without the martial despair of the Polonaises or the unconquerable turbulence of the Czardas.[101]

Tziganes. Et souvent ces artistes sont les plus célèbres; je n'en veux citer pour exemple que Gounod et Massenet." Immediately after the Exposition Universelle was finished, Prince Bibesco published a book on Romania and her representation at the fair. See Prince Georges Bibesco, *1889: Exposition Universelle: La Roumanie, avant—pendant—après* (Paris: Imprimerie Typographique J. Kugelman, 1890).

97. Steven Moore Whiting, *Satie the Bohemian: From Cabaret to Concert Hall* (Oxford: Oxford University Press, 1999), 118.

98. Julien Tiersot, "Promenades musicales à l'Exposition: Les laoutars rumains— L'exotisme des Batignolles—les Espagnols," *Le Ménestrel* 55 (1889): 275–77, at 276.

99. Ibid., 275: "Outre que les bandes des musiciens roumains sont beaucoup moins nombreuses que celles des tziganes et se réduisent pour ainsi dire aux proportions des groupes destinés à l'exécution de la musique de chambre, tandis que les tziganes forment un véritable orchestre, les premiers ne possèdent aucun des instruments sonores et vibrants des seconds, clarinettes et czymbalum, et les remplacent par le *naiou* ou flûte de Pan et la *cobza*, sorte de luth. Il en résulte une sonorité plus efféminée et beaucoup moins apte à l'interprétation des sentiments héroiques."

100. Émile Goudeau, "Une journée d'exposition," *La Revue illustrée* 4, part 2 (1889): 240–244, at 241: "l'âme chantante d'un peuple qui longtemps fut esclave."

101. "Loitering through the Paris Exhibition," 363–64.

Figure 5.14. "Les Lautars roumains," *L'Illustration* 47 (1889): 304.

For Tiersot, the proof of authenticity of the *lăutari*'s music lay in their harmonic language, which was far more "primitive" than that of the Hungarians and which it shared with early French *chansons populaires* that had been transmitted in "ancient manuscripts."[102] Thus the pastoral setting on the banks of the Seine/Danube provided a perfect frame for the performances that, like their Javanese counterpart at the Exposition Coloniale, were perceived as melancholic and feminized, suffused with exotic charm but a far cry from the mythologized sounds of the Magyar steppes.[103]

While both Hungarian and Romanian gypsies were part of the national exhibits, the gypsies from Spain appeared on the stage of the Grand Théâtre de l'Exposition. The taverna that was part of the Spanish national exhibit had hired musicians from Seville—the Estudiantina sévillane—to perform for their customers. Indeed, the kingdom of Spain was a major presence at the Republican Exposition Universelle, and all things Spanish quickly became the rage in Paris during the hot summer of 1889. The Spanish pavilions took up significant space at the fair and their architecture played with the French predilection for Spanish and, in particular, Moorish culture and customs (figure 5.15).[104] Spain spilled over from the Exposition into Paris, whether via two bullfight arenas—in the rue de Pergolèse and in the Bois de Boulogne—or by way of Spanish evenings at the Vaudeville theater.[105] "Spain is in Paris," we read in the newspapers.[106] Soon, "aimez-vous l'espagnol?" became such a catchphrase in the newspapers that even Julien Tiersot employed it to open his text about Spanish music and dance, which then lists the entertainments in a style familiar to Rossini's Barber of Seville:

> Do you love things Spanish? They have put them everywhere. Bullfights to the right, bullfights to the left; Spanish choral society here, Spanish evenings there; at the Cirque d'hiver, big Spanish fiestas, orchestra, dance,

102. Tiersot, "Promenades musicales à l'Exposition: Les laoutars rumains," 276: "effet propre à toutes les musiques primitives (on le trouve dans les chansons populaires françaises et surtout dans celles qui nous sont venues par les anciens manuscrits)."

103. Ibid., 275–76 passim.

104. *Exposition de 1889: Guide bleu du "Figaro" et du "Petit Journal,"* 184. See also the report, "Il palazzo dei vini spagnuoli," *L'Esposizione di Parigi des 1889 illustrata* (Milan: Sonzogno, 1889), no. 47, 369–70, at 369: "La Spagna occupa nell'Esposizione di Parigi, del 1889, uno dei posti principali fra i paesi che vi hanno con maggior larghezza partecipato."

105. The bullfights received extensive coverage in the daily press, including the killings of bulls. See, for example, "La Mort du taureau," *Le Soir*, 7 July 1889, 2; and "Six Taureaux tués," *Le Soir*, 15 Aug. 1889, 2.

106. *Le Matin*, 6 July 1889, 2: "L'Espagne est à Paris."

Figure 5.15. "Galerie Mauresque du Pavillon Espagnol des Produits Alimentaires," *L'Exposition de Paris 1889*, vols. 3–4 (Paris: Librairie Illustrée, 1889), 256.

student groups; at the Exposition, the gypsies from Granada. Spain over-does it: in truth, it is too much for a single man to contemplate and coolly analyze so much seduction.

Aimez-vous l'espagnol? On en a mis partout. Courses de taureaux à droite, courses de taureaux à gauche; société chorale espagnole par-ci, soirées espagnoles par-là; au Cirque d'hiver, grandes fêtes espagnoles, orchestre, danse, estudiantine; à l'Exposition, les gitanas de Grenade. L'Espagne abuse: en vérité c'est trop, pour un seul homme, de contempler et froide-ment analyser tant de séduction.[107]

For the French, Spain was the most exotic of European cultures, and espe-cially Southern Spain, whether Chateaubriand's Alhambra or Carmen's Seville, had become the location for all kinds of artistic *espagnolades* on the opera stage and in the concert hall.[108] Thus Georges Bizet's *Carmen* (1875) celebrated its four hundredth performance at the Opéra Comique during the Exposition, and Emmanuel Chabrier's rhapsody for orchestra, *España* (1883), was all the rage in Parisian concerts.

While concerts and revues in Paris featured a variety of music "à l'es-pagnole" and put together shows with mass appeal—such as the evening at the Cirque d'hiver with its two hundred female dancers "selected from among the most beautiful Spanish types"[109]—the organizers at the Exposi-tion Universelle looked, again, at gypsies as the most "authentic" popular performers of a people. As with other exotic performances of the Fair, the representation at the Exposition of the "true" musical Spain—rather than the one mediated by European composers or trivialized in French popular music of the *café-concert*—had to have the stamp of authenticity. For the director of the Grand Théâtre de l'Exposition, things would not get more authentic than the gypsies, or *gitanas*, from Granada, as they became quickly known, who arrived relatively late and opened their show in mid-July. The press picked up on it quickly:

On the slope of the hill above which rises the Alhambra of Granada, the palace of the Moorish kings, there are deeply dug grottoes, in which live the gypsies, racially pure gypsies without any trace of foreign blood, and

107. Tiersot, "Promenades musicales à l'Exposition: Les laoutars roumains," 276.
108. On the musical exoticizing of Spain, see James Parakilas, "How Spain Got a Soul," in *The Exotic in Western Music*, ed. Jonathan Bellman, 137–93 (Boston: Northeast-ern University Press, 1998). See also François Lesure, "Debussy et le syndrome de Grenade," *Revue de musicologie* 68 (1982): 101–9; Robert L. A. Clark: "South of North: *Car-men* and French Nationalisms," in *East of West: Cross-Cultural Performance and the Staging of Difference*, ed. Claire Sponsler and Xioamei Chen, 187–216 (New York: Palgrave, 2000).
109. Tiersot, "Promenades musicales à l'Exposition: Les laoutars roumains," 276: "les deux cent danseuses choisies parmi les plus beaux types espagnols."

not those that one sees in Madrid or Barcelona, and which this old race treats disdainfully as Tchoulas.

Au flanc de la colline sur laquelle s'élève l'Alhambra de Grenade, le palais de rois maures, sont creusées de profondes grottes où vivent les gitanes, les gitanes de race pure sans aucun de mélange de sang étranger, et non ceux qu'on voit à Madrid ou à Barcelone et que la vieille race traite dédaigneuse-ment de Tchoulas.[110]

These dancers from Granada were represented in press accounts as com-pletely wedded to the earth of the South, entirely natural in their artistic expression, and authentic in their dance and music to the point that they reach even beyond Moorish Spain of the legendary king Boabdil to the times of the Roman Empire.[111] This last reference is rather striking in that it relates the contemporary Parisian visit of the *gitanas* to performances by Spanish dancers in ancient Rome, playing even in this context on the powerful metaphor of Republican France as the new Rome: the dances from Granada "must recall those same dances that the Romans acclaimed, when they were enthralled by the troupes of female entertainers who had come from Spain."[112] So marked had the claims to authenticity become with respect to the *gitanas* that they turned into one of the themes of Henriot's caricature of the gypsies in *Le Journal amusant* (figure 5.16). These Spanish visitors to the Exposition, the text running beneath the guitarists claims, "do not need to show their birth certificate. . . . They are authentic. . . . too authentic," with the performances becoming "more and more authentic" during the evening. In contrast to the Arab belly dancers, the Spanish performers were described as using their arms, legs and—in Henriot's caricature—their der-riere, but not their belly. As with the Eastern gypsies, the *gitanas'* gypsiness essentialized their national identity because of the prevalent view of gypsies' intimate closeness to nature, in this specific case the hills of Granada. The chronicler of *Le Soir* thus predicted after the opening of the show at the

110. "L'Exposition: Chronique du Champ de Mars," *Le Petit Journal*, 13 July 1889, 2.

111. For example: Gaston Paulin, "L'Espagne à Paris," *Le Guide musical* 35 (1889): 206; Maurice Guillemot, "Les Gitanas," *Gil Blas*, 18 Aug. 1889, 2; P. D., "Gitanos et Gitanas," *Le Soir*, 13 July 1889, 2; F. G., "Au pays des *gitanas*," *Le Gaulois*, 14 July 1889, 2; and Charles Darcours [Charles Réty], "Courrier des Théâtres," *Le Figaro*, 7 Sept 1889, 3. The reference to King Boabdil is in Eugène Clisson, "Notes Parisiennes: Gitanas de Grenade," *L'Événement*, 14 July 1889, 2.

112. Paul Margueritte, "Gitanas et Druses," *L'Exposition de Paris 1889* (Paris: Librairie Illustrée, 1889), 7: "espagnoles, [les danses] doivent rappeler ces mêmes danses qu'acclamaient les Romains, fort épris alors des troupes de saltatrices venues d'Espagne."

Figure 5.16. Henriot, "Les Gitanas de Grenade (avec leur capitan),"
*Le Journal amusant,* 17 Aug. 1889, 7.

Exposition that all those who love "authentic and characteristic exhibitions
will give the gypsies from Spain a success without precedent."[113]

Like the Javanese dancers, the *gitanas* became stars. The text for the
engraving that adorned the title page of *L'Exposition de Paris de 1889* for
9 October 1889 (figure 5.17) identifies the dancers Mlle Pepa and M.
Pigeri as dancing the *tango.* Journalists, who clearly were cued by a detailed
press release, informed their readers about the individuals of the troupe.
Like Wakiem, Seriem, Taminah, and Soekia from Java, Soledad, La Lola,
and La Maccarona became celebrities whose fame extended beyond their
immediate presence at the Exposition. Indeed, as with the Javanese and the
Vietnamese, Claude Debussy's writings provide an indicator for the impact
that the *gitanas* had on their Parisian listeners. In a review of December
1913 of a concert "of Spanish music performed by real Spaniards," Debussy

113. P. D., "Gitanos et Gitanas," 2: "Tous les amateurs d'exhibitions authentiques
et caractéristiques vont faire un succès sans précédent à ces bohèmes d'Espagne."

pointed out that real Spanish music in France was now but a "vague memory of the Exposition" with its "severe beauty of the old Moorish cantilenas." He recalled the *gitanas* by name as La Macarona and La Soledad.[114] As with the Javanese dancers, stories of the origins of the *gitanas* abounded in the press and in later reports of the Spanish performances.[115] Their origin was traceable to a specific location and to their place in the gypsy community, which ensured their authenticity in the eyes of the French press. In fact, judging from the press accounts of their première, it seems as if this was not only a concern of the journalists but also a concept played on by the organizers, who seem to have used this mounting interest in the authentic to shape their press release.

This mark of authenticity was also present in the *gitanas'* shows on the stage of the Grand Théâtre de l'Exposition, whose set reproduced the exterior of a tavern (or *pasada*) in the best Opéra-Comique tradition, palm trees included (figure 5.17). "But this is all that is theatrical in this affair; as for the rest, they behave as they do at home."[116] Theirs is not a dance accompanied by an orchestra, but by the guitar and—most importantly—the clapping of hands: "the clapping, executed in cadence by the entire performing group, constitutes in reality the true Spanish dance music."[117] Such primitive and natural instruments, for Tiersot, go with the primitive dances and songs, embodied in the performers rather than learned academically. Writers characterized the dance repeatedly as "naturally graceful," contrasting it with the artificial grace of the ballerinas at the Opéra. While the *almées* of the rue du Caire created only orientalist dismay in their spectators, the *gitanas* offered the authentic dance of Spain that, as Arthur Pougin reports, drew the entire *corps de ballet*—the Spanish-born *étoile*, Rosita Mauri, included—to watch the "lovely Soledad and the astounding Maccarona."[118] In contrast to the Arab music, the music of the *gitanas* remained reasonably consonant with expectations of musical signifiers of Spain in Western art music. Indeed, while Bizet's *Carmen* with its gypsy heroine was performed at

114. Claude Debussy, *Monsieur Croche et autres écrits*, ed. François Lesure (Paris: Gallimard, 1987), 250: "de vagues souvenirs d'exposition"; "l'âpre beauté des vieilles cantilènes mauresques restait inoubliable"; "les noms de *La Macarona, La Soledad.*"

115. See in particular the details provided painstakingly in Pougin, *Le Théâtre à l'Exposition*, 105–9.

116. Tiersot, "Promenades musicales à l'Exposition: Les laoutars Rumains," 277: "mais c'est tout ce qu'il y a de théâtral dans l'affaire; pour le reste, ils font comme chez eux."

117. Ibid.: "Les mains, tout simplement, dont les battements, exécutés en cadence par tout le personnel, constituent en réalité la véritable musique de danse espagnole."

118. Pougin, *Le Théâtre à l'Exposition*, 109: "En particulier, tout le personnel de l'Opéra y a passé, et l'on a vu plus d'une fois la gentille Rosita Mauri et la jolie Mlle Subra applaudir de toutes leurs forces l'aimable Soledad et l'étonnante Maccarona."

Figure 5.17. Mlle Pepa and M. Pigeri [Antonio de la Rosa] dance the Tango, engraving on the title page of *L'Exposition de Paris de 1889*, 9 Oct. 1889.

least once a week at the Opéra Comique, a real-life Carmen could be admired in an Andalusian setting at the Exposition Universelle.

The reception and presentation of the *gitanas*, the *Czarda*, and the *lăutari* as the authentic music of these nations' people contrast greatly with the perception of many other ensembles of folk music at the Exposition. Some were exposed as frauds. Thus the beautifully costumed "Russians" proved to have hired a second violin from the Colonne orchestra and a double-bass player from its rival orchestra, the Lamoureux.[119] Others were a motley group of non-French performers conducted by the mysterious and impoverished Russian Princess Dolgorouki, who played generic waltzes, mazurkas, and other such fare at the Volponi restaurant. Many other ensembles came and went, such as the "peculiar Austrian music" of the "Tamburaski-sbor" from Croatia.[120] *Musique pittoresque* was everywhere at the Exposition, whether authentic or fake. But as with many other issues with respect to musical culture that had been slowly developing over the course of the nineteenth century, the quest for authenticity in folk music was thrust sharply into the spotlight at the 1889 Exposition Universelle. Nowhere does this become as clear as in the treatment of the body politic of French *musique pittoresque*.

Indeed, contrary to the picturesque musics from afar, French folk music was not part of the wave of local color exhibited in tavernas, restaurants, *cafés-concerts*, or exotic theater productions at the Exposition Universelle. While some French folk-music ensembles performed in the various bandstands, the music from the French provinces was mainly located in the concert hall, in exhibitions of instruments, and in museums. Thus in the exhibition of "authentic costumes placed on mannequins modeled after nature" at the Musée d'Ethographie at the Trocadéro, visitors could admire French folk in characteristic poses that echoed the current "fashion to research the old songs and study old manners and customs."[121] One installation of this ethnographic exhibition allowed visitors to "witness the dance of the fandango by mountain-dwellers from the Pyrenees, while a Basque

119. Tiersot, "Promenades musicales à l'Exposition: Les laoutars Rumains," 276: "il reconnut un second violon du concert Colonne et une contrebasse du concert Lamoureux."

120. "Chronique de l'Exposition," *Le Soir*, 17 Aug. 1889, 2: "Une originale musique autrichienne va se faire entendre à l'Exposition. C'est la 'Tamburaski-sbor' société musicale composée de jeunes gens croates."

121. Fernand Landrin, "Anciens Costumes populaires français au Palais du Trocadéo, à Paris," *La Nature: Revue des Sciences et de leurs applications aux arts et aux industries* 17 (1889): 295–98, at 295: "les costumes authentiques, placés sur des mannequins modelés d'après nature"; "la mode de rechercher les vieilles chansons, d'étudier les anciennes mœurs ou coutumes."

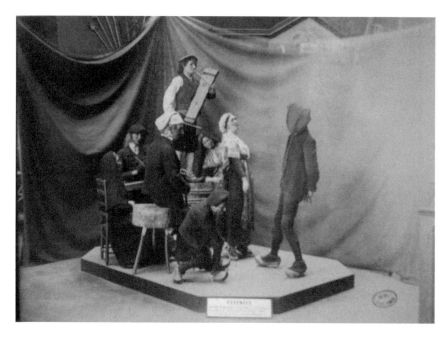

Figure 5.18. Musée de l'Ethnographie, "Anciens costumes populaires français: Les Pyrénées," B.H.V.P., Dossier photographique *Divers XXI*, 106.

plays a *tambourin à cordes* and a flute."[122] The ensemble (figure 5.18) shows a *txistulari* who traditionally plays the flute with his left hand while beating a drum with his right, using a stick.[123]

The exhibition at the Musée d'Ethnographie coincided with two music-related celebrations of folk music: the official competition at the Exposition Universelle on 4 July 1889 and the equally official Congrès International des Traditions Populaires, for which Julien Tiersot organized a concert on 1 August 1889. Neither of these events was reserved purely for French folk music, but the music of the French provinces was at the center of both. Here, where the official appreciation of a sponsored competition and scholarly work on the *chanson populaire* gave the seal of authorized recognition to the performances, French folk music could take its rightful place in the concert of picturesque authentic voices of the people.

The Concours International et Auditions de Musiques Pittoresques took place on the afternoon of 4 July 1889 at the Salle des Fêtes of the

122. Ibid., 298: "Ailleurs, on assiste à la danse du fandango par les montagnards des Pyrénées, tandis qu'un Basque joue du tambourin à cordes et de la flûte."

123. For a description of Basque dance music and instruments, see Denis Laborde, "Basque Music," in *NGr2*.

Trocadéro and lasted a good five hours, even though all its competition classes were not filled, as the missing "Class C" in the French section in the first part indicates (figure 5.19).[124] Like any other competition at the Exposition Universelle, it was decided by a jury. This one was presided over by the composer Émile Paladilhe and comprised—in addition to Julien Tiersot and Louis-Albert Bourgault-Ducoudray, who were the two best-known folk-music specialists of France at the time—Maurice Faure (founder of the meridionalist *Cigale* movement and deputy from the Drôme), Pierre Gailhard (bass and co-director of the Opéra), Léon Kerst (music critic), Théodore de Lajarte (librarian of the Bibliothèque de l'Opéra), Laurent Léon (conductor at the Théâtre-Français), Victor Leydet (deputy from Aix), Antoine Marmontel (pianist and professor at the Conservatoire), Henri Maréchal (composer), Raoul Madier de Montjau (second conductor of the Opéra), Sextius Michel (mayor of the 15th arrondissement and president of the Parisian *Félibres*; see below), and Gaston Salvayre (composer and music critic for *Gil Blas*).

The competition reflected two intertwined currents in French politics and culture of the late nineteenth century: on the one hand, the increasing interest in authenticity and folklore that had resulted, among other things, in the establishment of the Société des Traditions Populaires in 1886; on the other, the development of regionalist movements, most prominently the *Félibrige*, a meridionalist movement founded by the Provençal poet Frédéric Mistral.[125] In fact, the Concours International et Auditions de Musiques Pittoresques was a direct result of these developments, given that it was proposed by the meridionalist writer and politician Maurice Faure and presided over by the meridionalist patriot and fellow *cigalier*, Émile Paladilhe. *Félibres* such as Sextius Michel were among the jury members, while Mistral himself attended the event. The Parisian press picked up on the cultural-political context in their reporting and classed the competition as an event related to Southern French regionalism, which at that time adopted a nationalist discourse of *enracinement*: through her celebration of regional roots, especially in the Latin cultures of the Mediterranean, France was to strengthen national identity and patriotic pride.[126]

---

124. Charles Darcours [Charles Réty], "Notes de musique," *Le Figaro*, 3 July 1889, 6: "Classe C. Groupe d'instruments jouant par 2 ou 3: Biniou et Hautbois, Musette et Vielle, etc." Which instruments were missing is unclear, for the original Class C was announced as Class D in the program.

125. For a concise summary of the Félibrige and French music, see Andrea Musk, "Regionalism, *Latinité* and the French Musical Tradition: Déodat de Séverac's *Héliogabale*," in *Nineteenth-Century Music Studies*, ed. Jim Samson and Bennett Zon, 226–49 (London and Aldershot: Ashgate, 2002).

126. See, among others, Élie Fourès, "Cigalier & Félibres," *L'Événement*, 7 July 1889, 3; and Goudeau, "Les Musiques pittoresques au Trocadéro," 27. On the nationalist agenda

RÉPUBLIQUE FRANÇAISE

MINISTÈRE DU COMMERCE, DE L'INDUSTRIE ET DES COLONIES

# EXPOSITION UNIVERSELLE DE 1889

*Direction Générale de l'Exploitation*

## AUDITIONS MUSICALES – SALLE DES FÊTES DU TROCADÉRO

JEUDI 4 JUILLET à 1 heure 1/2

# CONCOURS INTERNATIONAL

ET

## AUDITIONS

DE

# MUSIQUES PITTORESQUES

### 1° PROVINCES DE LA FRANCE

**CLASSE A.** — INSTRUMENTS A VENT ET A SOUFFLET
*Biniou, Bombarde, Cornemuse, Hautbois, Musette*

**CLASSE B.** — INSTRUMENT A CORDES ET A ROUE
*Vielle*

**CLASSE D.** — INSTRUMENTS JOUANT PAR 2 OU PAR 3
*Biniou et Hautbois, Cornemuse et Vielle*

**CLASSE E.** — GROUPE D'INSTRUMENTS DIVERS JOUANT ENSEMBLE
*L'ESTUDIANTINA PROVENÇALE*

### AUDITION DE L'ACADÉMIE DU TAMBOURIN D'AIX

### 2° PAYS ÉTRANGERS

**CLASSE A.** — INSTRUMENT A CORDES PINCÉES
*Guitare, Machete de l'île de Madère, Mandoline, Théorbe*

**CLASSE B.** — INSTRUMENT A CORDES FRAPPÉES
*Cymbalum*

**CLASSE C.** — INSTRUMENT A VENT
*Flûte de Pan (Naïou)*

### CONCOURS DE GROUPES D'INSTRUMENTISTES DIVERS
Orchestre des Lautars Roumains. — Orchestres Tziganes. — Orchestre Serbe.

## GRAND CONCOURS D'HONNEUR
### INTERNATIONAL

6-89 2263 *bis* — Paris. Typ. Morris père et fils, rue Amelot, 64.        *Ce Programme ne peut être affiché.*

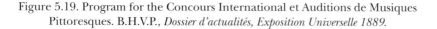

Figure 5.19. Program for the Concours International et Auditions de Musiques Pittoresques. B.H.V.P., *Dossier d'actualités, Exposition Universelle 1889.*

The structure of the competition is revealing on several levels: on the one hand, the competition for the French provinces was separated from a second one that lumped together all other, foreign countries; on the other, however, the provinces were themselves represented as the exotic within, different from the—presumably non-picturesque and definitely sophisticated—capital, Paris. The format adopted was one that reflected the Exposition's other cultural competitions—such as painting or sculpture—where French and foreign contributions were similarly divided. But in contrast to these competitions, picturesque music from France was defined as essentially non-Parisian. Indeed, the parameters of this competition were profoundly different in stressing regional authenticity in lieu of cosmopolitan achievement. The rules of the competition make this very clear in two of the nine articles:

> Art. 4: Only players of characteristic instruments such as the tambourine, the *galoubet*, the *biniou*, the bagpipes, the hurdy-gurdy, the mandolin, the guitar, etc., will be allowed to these competitions and performances.
> Art. 7: The admitted performers (soloists or ensembles) must submit to the Commission des Musiques Pittoresques a list of the pieces that they plan to perform. These programs may comprise only popular melodies from the performers' region; all arrangements, fantasies or selections from operas, or chansons from the *café-concert* will be rigorously excluded.

> Art. 4. Ne seront admis à ces concours et auditions que les joueurs d'instruments caractéristiques, tels que le tambourin, le galoubet, le biniou, la cornemuse, la vielle, la mandoline, la guitare, etc. . . .
> Art. 7. Les instrumentistes admis (solistes ou groupes d'exécutants) devront soumettre à la Commission des musiques pittoresques la liste des morceaux qu'ils se proposent d'exécuter. Ces programmes ne devront comprendre que des airs populaires des régions des exécutants; tous arrangements, fantaisies ou mosaïques d'opéras, ou chansons de cafés-concerts, en seront rigoureusement exclus.[127]

This quest for authenticity in folk music in the competition rules took the desire for the genuine (so obvious in the representation and reception of exotic and oriental musics at the Exposition) even further. It used pronounced concepts of material originality that echoed the French

---

of the meridionalists, see Musk, "Regionalism, *Latinité* and the French Musical Tradition," 229–38. On folksong in late-nineteenth-century France in more general terms, see Jann Pasler, "The *Chanson populaire* as a Malleable Symbol in Turn-of-the-Century France," in *Tradition and Its Future in Music: Report of SIMS 1990 Osaka*, ed. Yoshiko Tokumaru (Tokyo and Osaka: Mita Press, 1991), 203–9.

127. Alphonse Certeux, "Notes et Enquêtes," *Revue des traditions populaires* 4 (1889): 303–4, at 304.

nineteenth-century usage of "authentic" with respect to Natural History. According to Pierre Larousse's *Grand Dictionnaire universel du XIX^e siècle*, "authentic" was to be employed for "animals, plants, or minerals that truly belong to the country from which they are said to originate and the families in which they are classed."[128] Indeed, Article 7 of the competition rules, with its demand to exclude any music that might stem from urban contexts (whether upper-class such as opera or lower-class such as *café-concert* songs), points to the dichotomies of authenticity and corruption, region and capital, Arcadia and worldliness, peasantry and industrialization. The utopian space of an uncorrupted Arcadia was encapsulated in the sounds of its music to the point that the performance alone could evoke the landscape of rural France: "With a little bit of imagination, one saw emerge, at the threshold of dreams, the rustic landscapes of the Auvergne, Bretagne, and Provence, the village dances of our old provinces, all kinds of idyllic, fresh, and charming scenes."[129] The pastoral trope was all-pervasive in the reception of the afternoon, whether in the widespread praise for the enterprise or in those few, more critical voices such as Johannès Weber, for whom the transplantation of folk music into the ornate hall of the Trocadéro turned what was picturesque in Provence or Auvergne into something grotesque. Taken out of its rural context, the warm-up of the *biniou* (Breton bagpipes), for example, was nothing but a cacophony.[130] In a similar vein, the critic for *Le Gaulois* went so far as to call the various folk-music performances on the stage of the Trocadéro "musiques dépaysées," which could not offer the same joyous effects as they would in the pastoral idyll of their home.[131] Another commentator saw this event as a way for those Parisians who had come from the provinces

128. Article "authentique," in *Grand Dictionnaire universel du XIXe siècle*, ed. Pierre Larousse, 17 vols (Paris: Administration du Grand Dictionnaire universel, 1866–90), 1 (1866): 977–78, at 977: "Hist. Nat. Se dit des animaux, des plantes ou des minéraux qui appartiennent réellement aux pays dont on les dit originaires, et aux familles dans lesquelles on les classe."

129. Fourès, "Cigalier & Félibres," 3: "Avec un peu d'imagination, on voyait surgir, à l'horizon du rêve, les paysages rustiques de l'Auvergne, de la Bretagne et de la Provence, les danses villageoises de nos vieilles provinces, toute sorte de scènes idylliques, fraîches et douces."

130. Johannès Weber, "Critique musicale," *Le Temps*, 8 July 1889, 3: "Le galoubet peut être pittoresque en Provence, la cornemuse peut l'être dans les Abruzzes, en Auvergne, dans la Cornouailles ou chez les *Highlanders*; mais dans la salle du Trocadéro! . . . Aussi tel instrument a-t-il produit un effet grotesque. . . . Deux sonneurs [de biniou], en costume national et jouant ensemble, ont débuté par une véritable cacophonie de sons aigus et criards. Ce début a évidemment sa raison d'être dans le pays."

131. Tout-Paris, "Bloc-Notes Parisiens: Musiques pittoresques," *Le Gaulois*, 5 July 1889, 2.

to renew their ties to the land, cheering for their region as if it were a sports event.[132]

The sharpest critic, as always, was Julien Tiersot. While he celebrated the fact that, for the first time ever, all these different instruments were brought together under one roof to offer this kind of music to Parisian audiences, he was less than happy with the way authenticity was represented but not necessarily rewarded in the competition. Thus the Bourbon bagpipe player who won first prize, so Tiersot said, was less authentic (because influenced by modern music) than the second-placed one from Auvergne whose performance was much more in keeping with a folk sound.[133] But the worst was to come with the much applauded *tambourinaires* from Provence, for they played music composed in Paris in the seventeenth and eighteenth centuries, which was not of truly folk origin at all, and to add insult to injury, these musicians were able to read music. Indeed, "one player played his piece with the score before his eyes." The Estudiantina provençal that performed after the drummers appeared even less authentic in their uniforms, and recalled the *orphéon* orchestras throughout France.[134]

While Tiersot denounced these lapses to his fellow-musicians in the music journal, *Le Ménestrel*, audience and journalists reveled in another "inauthentic" moment during that afternoon. Émile Paladilhe, the president of the jury, tried to keep the public from cheering too much for the Neapolitan mandolin players, the brothers Angelizzi, who delighted the audience—among other tunes—with *Funiculi-Funicula*. When Paladilhe called the audience to order, the musicians launched—to the listeners' great enjoyment and Paladilhe's consternation—into the song *Mandolinata*, then possibly the most famous and widely known piece by

132. Goudeau, "Les Musiques pittoresques au Trocadéro," 26: "Mais tous les provinciaux parisianisés se sentaient en joie, chacun pour son clocher, chacun pour sa province."

133. Julien Tiersot, "Promenades musicales à l'Exposition: Concours de musique pittoresque," *Le Ménestrel* 55 (1889): 210–12, at 211: "Je crois voir une influence de certaine musique moderne, et non la meilleure, qui altère le caractère primitif et vraiment intéressant. L'exécutant auvergnat . . . [était] beaucoup plus dans la note populaire."

134. Ibid., 211: "Le répertoire des solistes se compose de fantaisies ou de variations sur des airs provençaux, lesquels ne sont pour la plupart que des airs de vaudevilles des XVII<sup></sup> et XVIII<sup></sup> siècles venus de Paris et acclimatés par un long séjour; ces morceaux sont assez développés, et de forme nullement populaire: ce qui l'est moins encore, c'est que la plupart de ces tambourinaires savent la musique: il y en a un qui a joué son morceau avec sa partie devant les yeux! . . . A la suite des tambourinaires est venue une Estudiantina provençale, qui, concourant seule, a eu une médaille. Ici, nous sortons de plus en plus du populaire. La société est organisée comme un orphéon, ses membres portent une uniforme."

Paladilhe.[135] The relish with which several journalists reported the breach of protocol is indicative for the multi-layered reception of this afternoon, indicating that the organizers' expectations of what folk music was did not necessarily match the notions of the musicians themselves. On one level, it was simply music performed by picturesquely dressed players; on another, it was the music that encapsulated provincial and European landscapes in a sonic time-warp; on another yet, there was a play between the familiar and the foreign, even if it was from France itself (with journalists pointing to the lack of Parisian knowledge of the French regions and their culture); finally, it was a scholarly enterprise in which a writer like Tiersot—like a botanist—tried to classify and authenticate the products brought from afar.

But the event also showed the problems inherent in the enterprise. Even though the journalists celebrated the event and the hall was filled with a distinguished audience, the programs and their reports show that the definition of folk music was still contested—for the Neapolitan brothers Angelizzi, the performance of *Funiculi-Funicula* fulfilled the notion of playing authentic folk music—and that the research enterprise was still a fledgling endeavor. After all, the event was the last official competition added to the musical offerings at the Exposition, a year and a half after the others.[136] Not all announced musicians even showed up on that afternoon in the Trocadéro; in particular the much-anticipated Russian balalaikas were missed by the audience. The program itself was rather slim in certain categories, like Class E, which had only one competitor, the *Estudiantina provençale*, as Tiersot remarked rather sarcastically.[137] Thus the reception of the competition as a major event in French cultural politics did not entirely square with the attention given to it by the folk musicians themselves.

That Tiersot was, indeed, the voice of French popular-music studies at the time becomes obvious both in the reporting of the concert on the occasion of the Congrès International des Traditions Populaires, which took place from 29 July to 1 August 1889, and in the reviews of his recently published book, *Histoire de la chanson populaire en France* (which remained a

135. Tout-Paris, "Bloc-Notes Parisiens: Musiques pittoresques," 3; Goudeau, "Les Musiques pittoresques au Trocadéro," 26. Tiersot refers, not without irony, to Paladilhe—who usually is called the "author of *Patrie*," his most famous opera—as the "author of *Mandolinata*," playing with the French custom of identifying a composer through his most famous work ("Promenades musicales à l'Exposition: Concours de musique pittoresque," 211). See Émile Paladilhe, *Mandolinata (Souvenir de Rome)*, words by A. P*** (Paris: G. Hartmann, 1869).

136. Most of the *auditions musicales* were organized in a ministerial decree of 17 October 1887, while the folk-music competition was established by a decree of 20 February 1889. Picard, *Rapport général sur l'Exposition universelle*, 3:345–46.

137. Tiersot, "Promenades musicales à l'Exposition: Concours de musique pittoresque," 211.

respected study for decades to come).[138] In contrast to other such gatherings, this Congrès had very little publicity in the regular newspaper reports that usually followed these events, given that more space than usual was taken up by the departmental elections, the trial of General Boulanger, and the visit of the Shah of Persia. Nevertheless, some coverage in newspapers reflected Tiersot's work as a musical folklorist. Indeed, the front page for the mass-circulation daily, *Le Petit Parisien*, carried a feature article by the newspaper's main Parisian columnist, Jean Frollo, on the "chansons de métiers," in which Tiersot is quoted extensively on his ideas about folksongs related to various handicrafts.[139] Frollo's opening reference to the centenary celebrations, however, sets the Congrès in the more problematic context of commemorating the French Revolution, in which popular song, in a variety of roles, had, after all, played a well-known role (witness the *Marseillaise*). While the picturesque music competition in early July became an opportunity to celebrate rural France—and, to a lesser extent, Europe—the Congrès brought to the fore more political questions about people and revolution, if not in the academic papers then in the newspapers.[140] Nevertheless, music also fulfilled an entertaining role in addition to its political potential, and Tiersot's concert of folk music from France and Europe received a good press.[141] Like the Congrès too, Tiersot's book obtained both political and musicographic commentary. It was lauded for its scholarly depth and breadth, while the subject itself gave rise to political commentary. In particular, his fellow composer Alfred Bruneau celebrated the possibilities of this new resource for the future of French music, when the closeness to nature was going to "light our art, I hope, with the beautiful ray of sun which, through its robustness, will bring it the health, the life, and the vigorous and fruitful love of the good French Earth."[142]

As with many other developments of the nineteenth century, the 1889 Exposition Universelle throws into relief what had been latent or only emerging in terms of French discourse and reception of musical alterity.

---

138. "Programme du Congrès des Traditions Populaires," *Revue des traditions populaires* 4 (1889): 364–65. Julien Tiersot, *Histoire de la chanson populaire en France* (Paris: Plon, 1889).

139. Jean Frollo, "Les Chansons de métiers," *Le Petit Parisien*, 4 Aug. 1889, 1.

140. See, in particular, Tabar, "Le Folkorisme," *L'Écho de Paris*, 31 July 1889, 2.

141. See, for example, Gaston Paulin, "Chronique parisienne," *Le Guide musical* 35 (1889): 197; "La Musique à l'Exposition," *L'Art musical* 28 (1889): 117; "Propos de Coulisses," *Gil Blas*, 1 Aug. 1889, 4; "Les Congrès: Les traditions populaires," *Le Soir*, 4 Aug. 1889, 3.

142. Alfred Bruneau, "Musique," *La Revue indépendante*, Oct. 1889, 144–51, at 151: "Il éclairera notre art, je l'espère, d'un beau rayon de soleil qui, par sa robustesse, lui apportera la santé, la vie, l'amour sain et fécond de la bonne Terre française."

In particular the romance of authenticity, though strongly rooted in French romanticism, was—perhaps for the first time—institutionalized in exhibitions of people and their arts, musical competitions, and scholarly evaluations, whether they were from Java or Provence. It was, Camille Benoît concludes, "the year of folk music."[143] The Exposition Universelle and its various musical manifestations—whether in the colonial part of the Fair or in the Trocadéro—provided Parisian ears with new sounds that could make even Wagner's music seem insipid:

> As for the Parisians, if their ears have not received their definitive educa-
> tion, one would have to despair of sound. To hear the Javanese gamelan,
> Tunisian music, Spanish castanets and tambourines, the formidable Anna-
> mite orchestra; to go from *guzla* to *biniou*, from the hurdy-gurdy to the cim-
> balom; to subject oneself to all these dissonances, all these meowings,
> screams, and howling that nature offers when ornamented by art, this is
> certainly the deed of heroic ears. . . . When we are offered Wagner this
> winter, he will appear insipid to us. This is a piece of advice to musicians
> who would truly want to invent the music of the future.

> Quant aux Parisiens, si leur Oreille n'a pas fait son éducation définitive,
> c'est à désespérer de l'acoustique. Entendre le *gamelang* javanais, la
> musique tunisienne, les castagnettes et tambours de basque espagnols, le
> redoutable orchestre annamite; aller de la guzla au biniou, de la vielle au
> czymbalum; se soumettre à toutes les dissonances, tous les miaulements,
> cris et clameurs que peut offrir la nature agrémentée par l'art, c'est cer-
> tainement le fait d'oreilles héroïques. . . . Quand, cet hiver, on nous
> offrira Wagner, il nous paraîtra fade. Avis aux musiciens qui voudront
> inventer la musique de l'avenir.[144]

The music that Parisians heard was, so Goudeau said, one based on nature, whether foreign or familiar. Its presentation in the Exposition lent it an aura of sonic authenticity that other Parisian contexts—in particular the *café-concert*—could not. Whether background music to a restaurant or music in the Théâtre Annamite, the containing of sound within the perimeters of the Exposition Universelle bestowed it with meaning beyond its sonic presence as a representation of culture, even if—as in the case of African musicians—that culture was belittled by its public. While the sonic trip around the world at the Exposition Universelle was framed by nineteenth-century prejudice and taxonomies, the actual music showed its

143. Balthasar Claes [Camille Benoît], "Chronique Parisienne: L'année de la musique populaire" *Le Guide musical* 35 (1889): 205–6. His first sentence comments on his title: "C'est bien là, en effet, la qualification caractéristique de l'année 1889."

144. Goudeau, "Les Musiques pittoresques au Trocadéro," 31.

power to transcend such boundaries by its sheer presence. Depending on the listener, this could lead to musical appropriation or rejection, but at the 1889 Exposition Universelle, exotic and picturesque music proved its capacity to penetrate even those ears that would have liked to shut it out. Few cultural manifestations during the Exposition could rival such immediate and unmitigated impact.

*Chapter 6*

# The Marvels of Technology

On 9 June yet another sonic attraction of the Exposition Universelle opened its doors to the public: the telephone display at the pavilion of the Société Générale des Téléphones, where live performances on Parisian stages could be heard through acoustic tubes connected to electronic telephone lines that transmitted the sounds. Together with the exhibition of the Edison phonograph in the Galerie des Machines, the telephone exhibition was among the best-known successes at the Exposition. The listening stations proved to be places of magic and discovery, but also of uncomfortable awe, however tamed within the secure parameters of an industrial fair. To go and listen to sounds that had no immediate source was to catch a glimpse of a future which might well bring with it some if not all of those strange and wonderful inventions so popularized in novels by Jules Verne. The prospect was at the same time enticing and frightening.

Neither the telephone nor the phonograph was entirely new in 1889. Edison's earlier, though disappointing, prototype had been shown in the 1878 Exposition Universelle, and telephonic transmissions from the opera house were already an attraction of the 1881 Exposition Internationale de l'Électricité in Paris. However, what makes their presence in the 1889 Exposition Universelle so central is the fact that here, for the first time, electroacoustic technology became an integral part of an exhibition project conceived as a gigantic taxonomy of human and industrial achievement. Electricity had become one of the main themes of the Exposition, featured not only in the various inventions of the Galerie des Machines, but also, and more visibly, in such installations as the nightly illuminated fountains and the electric lights around the Exposition, especially a spectacular electric light-sculpture by Sautter-Lemonnier and the 20,000 light bulbs that illuminated Edison's exhibit (both also in the Galerie des Machines).[1] While in 1878 electricity was in its "embryonic state," now it was a full-fledged industrial force in the competitive game of highly developed nations.[2]

---

1. *Exposition de 1889: Guide bleu du "Figaro" et du "Petit Journal" avec 5 plans et 31 dessins* (Paris: Le Figaro, 1889), 122.

2. "La Telegrafia—la Telefonia," *L'Esposizione di Parigi des 1889 illustrata* (Milan: Sonzogno, 1889), 70–71, at 70: "allo stato embrionale nel 1878."

The 1889 Exposition Universelle had turned into a celebration of the virtues of Republican France and its meritocracy, embodied in the mythologized figures of the frontier-breaking scientist and the daring explorer. Gustave Eiffel was the hero of the Champ de Mars, Louis Pasteur was regarded as a "lay saint,"[3] explorers such as Savorgnan de Brazza were fêted, and Thomas Alva Edison was received in Paris with the honors usually reserved for a head of state. This was victory in the battlefield of progress. In the end, France achieved manifold glory, not only through the accumulation of prizes but also through the overall achievement of mounting so successful a World's Fair. Republican propaganda milked every aspect of the Exposition, and even in the development and application of electro-acoustic equipment, French contributions were emphasized throughout. But while America was the place where true men of talent were able to forge personal and scientific progress, it was in France, the center of culture and science where they would come to fruition in civilized manners. That Edison, the handsome hero of the phonograph, was American proved no hindrance: he was, after all, a product of universal republicanism, the French roots of which could always be demonstrated. Indeed, the United States held endless fascination for a republican France which prided itself as a midwife in the birth of the American Republic.[4]

Accordingly, the nationalist slant came particularly to the fore with respect to the telephone, where German involvement might be claimed as rivaling the French contribution. In a popular-science publication on the telephone and its origins, conveniently published in 1889, Michelis de Rienzi laid down the gauntlet: "Do you know that the first person to have the idea was French, Monsieur Bourseul, the former director of the Telegraphs? In fact, it was in 1854 that he affirmed the possibility of using electric current to transmit the human voice."[5] De Rienzi claimed that the German professor, Philipp Reiss, appropriated the idea only in 1860, and then did it badly.[6] It took the genius of a Scottish-born inventor,

3. Pascal Ory, *L'Expo Universelle* (Paris: Éditions Complexe, 1989), 22.

4. On France's "passionate interest" in the United States in the nineteenth century, see Jean-Baptiste Duroselle, *France and the United States: From the Beginnings to the Present*, trans. Derek Coltman (Chicago and London: University of Chicago Press, 1978), 46–82. For a more critical perspective, see Philippe Roger, *L'Ennemi américain: Généalogie de l'an-tiaméricanisme français* (Paris: Édition du Seuil, 2002),

5. Michelis de Rienzi, *La Téléphonie: Ses origines et ses applications*, Bibliothèque universelle (Paris: Beaudelot, 1889), 3: "Savez-vous que le premier qui a eu l'idée est un français, M. Bourseul, ancien directeur des Télégraphes? C'est en 1854, en effet, qu'il affirma la possibilité d'utiliser le courant électrique pour transmettre la voix humaine."

6. Ibid., 4: "Un professeur allemand, le docteur Reiss, se l'appropria et, en 1860, il put faire entendre devant la société de physique de Francfort, des chants exécutés à 150 mètres de distance. Il est inutile de décrire la sensation que fit la nouvelle invention. M.

Alexander Graham Bell, and the ingenuity of the great French engineer Clément Ader, to create a technique sophisticated enough to do more than just give crude results over a short distance, and indeed to allow for such marvels as the transmission of opera by telephone. De Rienzi's popularizing account merely echoes the nationalist narrative of countless other books on the invention of the telephone that flooded the French market in the 1880s and 1890s, all of which emphasized (as one would expect) French contributions to its development.[7] But whereas such accounts stressed the nationalist aspect of French achievements in the field of technological development, descriptions of the actual experiences of these telephone and phonograph auditions at the Exposition Universelle pointed more to the visitors' fascination with the new media themselves and, in particular, with the experience of listening to music technically transmitted.

## Listening to Music without a Source: Opera through the Telephone

In the setup of its exhibit, the Société Générale des Téléphones used an already successful formula to demonstrate the telephone's sonorous power with the installation of musical listening stations, modeled on those that had made a triumph of the Exposition Internationale de l'Électricité eight years previously. Indeed, the Société Générale des Téléphones had its own pavilion, near the Eiffel Tower, the ground floor of which was dedicated to the musical listening stations with telephones (figure 6.1). But the marvels of electronic transmission of sounds were already audible before visitors entered the pavilion via the sounds of a new invention, the "Fanfare Ader," the latest electro-acoustic creation of the French telephone pioneer, Clément Ader, especially conceived for the 1889 Exposition. On the front of the tower, above the main entrance and the name plaque of the pavilion, a bank of twenty trumpet-shaped receptors alerted passers-by to the sonic possibilities of electronically transmitted and amplifed sound (figure 6.2). What they heard was a quartet of musicians who sang fanfares into the mouthpieces of the transmitters in the manner of a kazoo (figure 6.3).[8]

Reiss avait été conduit, dit-il du moins, à construire son appareil, par les recherches de Page sur l'aimantation et la désaimantation du fer doux et sur le bruit particulier qu'elles produisent."

7. On the French aspect of telephone development, see Pierre Aulas, *Les Origines du téléphone en France (1876–1914)* (Paris: Association pour le Développement de l'Histoire Économique, 1999).

8. E. H., "La Fanfare Ader à l'Exposition Universelle de 1889," *La Nature: Revue des Sciences et de leurs applications aux arts et aux industries* 17 (1889): 103–5, at 104: "En A

Figure 6.1. The Pavillon des Téléphones, in Alfred Picard, *Rapport général sur l'Exposition universelle internationale de 1889*, 10 vols. (Paris: Imprimerie nationale, 1890-91), vol. 2, plate opposite p. 201.

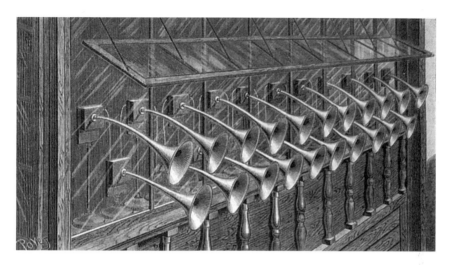

Figure 6.2. The receivers of the "Fanfare Ader," *La Nature: Revue des Sciences et de leurs applications aux arts et aux industries* 17 (1889), 105.

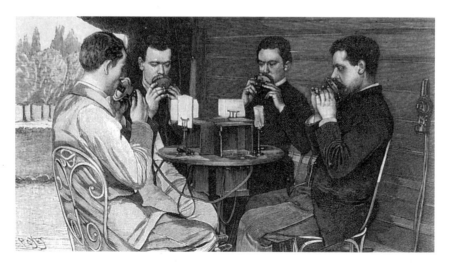

Figure 6.3. The four performers of the "Fanfare Ader," blowing into the mouthpieces, *La Nature: Revue des Sciences et de leurs applications aux arts et aux industries* 17 (1889): 104.

The small music stands in front of the performers indicate that theirs was a serious musical business, just as a traditional fanfare would be.

If the fanfare offered a taste of things to come inside the telephone exhibition, the main musical attraction of the pavilion was the transmission by telephone of operas and other musical shows from major Parisian theaters, as an advertisement placed in the daily newspaper, *Le Matin*, informed its readers:

ONE OF THE BIGGEST SUCCESSES OF THE EXPOSITION
EVERY EVENING, from 8:30 to 11 p.m.
at the Pavillon des Téléphones
TELEPHONIC AUDITIONS
from the Opéra, the Opéra-Comique, the Eden
In the afternoon: audition of the Fantaisies-Parisiennes

————

Price: evening, 1 franc per person; afternoon, 50 centimes per person
(allowing a ten-minute listening session)
The pavillon of the Société Générale des Téléphones is situated near
the Eiffel Tower, next to the Exposition du Gaz.

UN DES PLUS GRANDS SUCCÈS DE L'EXPOSITION
TOUS LES SOIRS, de 8 h ½ à 11 heures
au Pavillon des Téléphones
AUDITIONS TÉLÉPHONIQUES
de l'Opéra, de l'Opéra-Comique, de l'Eden
L'après-midi: audition des Fantaisies-Parisiennes

————

Prix: soir, 1 fr. par personne; après-midi, 50 c. par personne
(donnant droit à une audition de dix minutes)
Le pavillon de la Société Générale des Téléphones est situé près de
la tour Eiffel, à coté de l'Exposition du Gaz.[9]

The Pavilion contained two listening rooms whose floors were carpeted and whose walls and windows were heavily draped in order to smother any distracting noise. A portion of the rooms were given over to a secondary

———

[= part of transmitter] est une embouchure devant laquelle le musicien fredonne sa partie, comme sur un mirliton."

9. Advertisement placed in *Le Matin*, 4 July 1889, 3. In 1889, it cost 50 centimes to phone someone within Paris for 5 minutes and 1 franc to phone to a city outside of Paris. See *Tit-Bits Guide to Paris and the Exhibition*, 8th ed. (London: "Tit-Bits" Offices, 1889), 98.

installation of Edison phonographs, supplementary to his own display at the Galerie des Machines. Most of the space was taken up, however, with sixty listening stations in each hall (120 altogether). Half of the stations were dedicated to transmissions from the Opéra (and, on the evenings when the Opéra was closed, from the Eden-Théâtre), the other to those from the Opéra-Comique (which performed seven nights per week); the programs of Opéra and Opéra-Comique are in Appendix 2 (p. 331). All in all, close to 90,000 people visited the pavilion between 9 June and 6 November and paid their admission fee in order to listen for all of ten minutes to the telephonically transmitted music.[10]

Journal articles explained to their readers in great detail how the sound was transmitted from stage to earpiece: several microphones (or transmitters) were placed at the front edge of the stage in question, with an equal number on either side of the prompter's box.[11] These microphones were linked to telephone cables that transmitted the sound of each individual microphone to the Exposition and then served a number of receivers. Each listener had two earphones, one linked to a microphone on the left side of the stage, the other to one on the right, which created a stereophonic sound experience. One of the authors explained the need for stereophony as a result of the kinetic realities of performance:

> It has proven indispensable to furnish each listener with a double receiver: one for each ear. Here is the reason for this attentiveness to detail. A singer is not immobile on the stage. He moves frequently from one side of the scene to the other. This is, in fact, one of the rules of the art.

> On a jugé indispensable de munir chaque auditeur d'un récepteur double: un pour chaque oreille. Et voici la raison de cette particularité. Le chanteur n'est pas immobile sur la scène. Il passe fréquemment de l'un à l'autre côté de la rampe. C'est même là une des règles de l'art.[12]

The stereophonic earphones were connected to the walls along the listening halls of the Pavilion, making the visitors listen to something "behind"

---

10. The exact number of paying entries was 87,436. They divided as follows: 29,090 listened to the Opéra, 34,000 to the Opéra-Comique, 2,425 to the Eden-Théâtre, and 21,921 to the Folies-Parisiennes in the afternoon. Alfred Picard, *Rapport général sur l'Exposition universelle internationale de 1889*, 10 vols. (Paris: Imprimerie nationale, 1890–91), 2:202. In addition to the paying visitors, dignitaries such as the Shah of Persia were taken to the attraction of the musical telephones.

11. The setup is explained in detail in Louis Figuier, "Le Pavillon des Téléphones," *L'Exposition de Paris 1889* 3–4 (1889): 10–12.

12. Ibid., 11.

those walls almost like doctors listening to their patients with stethoscopes (figure 6.4). This form of acousmatic listening, where the source of the sound is invisible beyond its cause—here in the form of the acoustic tube— was one of the central issues discussed in the press with respect to the *auditions téléphoniques.*[13] Indeed, reporters investigated and observed listeners in the Pavillon des Téléphones as if it were a laboratory for acoustic experiment, as for example in the following article published in *Le Figaro* in July 1889:

> We have been told of the "auditions théâtrales" *by telephone*, organized by the Société [Générale du Téléphone], as being one of the great successes of the Exposition. Having been given the opportunity to judge *de... auditu*, we follow the crowd of visitors and enter the rooms reserved for the auditions from the Opéra-Comique. We see that Massenet's *Esclarmonde* is on the programme. We put the receivers on our ears, and we hear at once, with incredible clarity, the voices of the singers, the slightest modulations of the orchestra, in which one can distinguish, in a manner of speaking, each instrument. We recognize the voice of Miss Sanderson, who finishes a phrase with a high C, of which we lose not a single vibration and which is followed by a round of applause; if one closes one's eyes, one might believe oneself to be in the theater of the Opéra-Comique itself. One of the listeners caught by the illusion puts down his receivers in order to applaud; the laughing of his neighbors brings him back to reality. After the Opéra-Comique, it is the turn of the Opéra, which we hear with the same clarity [in the room next door]; none of the harmonic effects of *La Tempête* escapes us; at times, when the orchestra plays *piano*, we hear the steps of the ballerinas.

> On nous avait parlé des auditions théâtrales, *par téléphone*, organisées par la Société, comme un des gros succès de l'Exposition. L'occasion s'offrant à nous d'en juger *de... auditu*, nous suivons la foule des visiteurs et nous pénétrons dans une des salles réservées aux auditions de l'Opéra-Comique. Nous voyons au programme *Esclarmonde*, de Massenet. Nous portons les récepteurs à nos oreilles et nous percevons aussitôt, avec une netteté incroyable, les voix des chanteurs, les moindres modulations de l'orchestre, dont on distingue, pour ainsi dire, chaque instrument. Nous reconnaissons la voix de miss Sanderson, qui termine une phrase par un *ut*, dont nous ne perdons pas une vibration, et qui est suivi d'une salve d'applaudissement; en fermant les yeux on se croirait dans la salle même

---

13. The issues of source bonding and phenomenological disjuncture are among of the key issues in the aesthetics of electro-acoustic music. For a brief discussion of these topics, see Denis Smalley, "Spectromorphology: Explaining Sound-Shapes," *Organised Sound* 2 (1992): 111–12.

Figure 6.4. Paul Renouard, "Écoutant l'Opéra," illustration for Louis d'Hurcourt, "Téléphones et phonographes à l'Exposition Universelle," *L'Illustration* 47 (1889): 330.

de l'Opéra-Comique. Un des auditeurs, que l'illusion a gagné, dépose ses récepteurs pour applaudir;—les rires de ses voisins le ramènent à la réalité. Après l'Opéra-Comique, c'est l'Opéra que nous entendons avec la même netteté; aucun des effets harmoniques de *la Tempête* ne nous échappe;—par moments, lorsque l'orchestre joue *piano*, nous entendons le bruit des pas des danseuses.[14]

The report is rich in resonance. The first work the author hears is the great French creation of the season, Massenet's opera *Esclarmonde*, first performed on the day the Eiffel Tower was inaugurated. He then proceeds to listen to the venerable Ambroise Thomas's ballet *La Tempête*. Thus the operatic music heard could not have been more patriotic. Furthermore, in the manner of a nineteenth-century scientist, the author uses his sense perceptions to explore these new acousmatic phenomena empirically, in order to share the discovery with his readers.[15] He observes himself and the others reacting to a new medium that dislocates the experience from one of physical immediacy to one of alienation. Imagination appears to bridge the gap between invisible source and the listener caught up in his illusion of being at the performance, in ways readers had been educated to do throughout the nineteenth century in what Friedrich Kittler has termed the notation system (*Aufschreibesystem*) or discourse network of the book.[16] Thus the imagined reality of a romantic novel becomes a model of reading that could be transposed immediately to the engagement with the new medium of listening: telephonic opera. But the environment of the Exposition distorts the experience. This is no reader in an armchair following the author's flights of fantasy in private. The listener in the Pavillon des Téléphones is in public, and his fantasy-generated reaction of applause—as if he were there in the theater—in the inappropriate environment of the listening hall can only bring ridicule from those who observe. After all, part of the game is not to get caught up in the fantasy and take the imagined for the real. Thus the setup in the Pavillion des Téléphones problematizes the listener's reaction to music in new ways: because the internalized listening on the ear-tubes causes social alienation, the act of applause—albeit shared with the theatergoers on the other side of the telephone lines—is no longer an appropriate reaction, for there is no one present to whom it can be reasonably addressed. The inappropriate clapping thus becomes a symbol for the dislocation between activity and space.

The gap between acousmatic source and listener was already an issue in the 1881 experiments, when Parisians could hear opera by telephone for the very first time. The illustrator in *Le Monde illustré* tried to capture the process

14. Nemo, "Le Théâtre par Téléphone à l'Exposition," *Le Figaro*, 2 July 1889, 2.

15. On nineteenth-century techniques of observation and the separation of senses, see Jonathan Crary, *Techniques of the Observer: On Vision and Modernity in the Nineteenth Century* (Cambridge, MA, and London: MIT Press, 1990), esp. 67–96.

16. Friedrich Kittler, *Aufschreibesysteme 1800/1900* (Munich: Fink, 1985), trans. Michael Matteer and Chris Cullens as *Discourse Networks 1800/1900* (Stanford, CA: Stanford University Press, 1990).

DU THÉÂTRE DE L'OPÉRA                    TRANSMISSION DU SON. — AUDITIONS THÉÂTRALES A DISTANCE.                    AU PALAIS DES CHAMPS-ÉLYSÉES.

Figure 6.5. Morin, "Transmission du son.—Auditions théâtrales à distance," *Le Monde illustré*, numéro spécial exclusivement consacré à l'Exposition de l'Electricité, 22 Oct. 1881, 12.

in an engraving with the title "Transmission of sound; the theatrical auditions at a distance" (figure 6.5).[17] In the top-left corner, the source of sound, two small figures on the stage of the Opéra, produce the stream of notes—I assume one system per singer rather than a piano reduction. This stream penetrates the walls of the Palais des Champs-Élysées to be channeled down the acoustic tube that leads to the ear of an excited female listener. As one commentator wrote: "It is certain that every person who hears for the first time a telephone is struck by surprise; this mysterious voice, which comes from so far, has something strange about it."[18]

"To watch people listening"—in other words, the investigation of the listener and her or his reaction to the new medium—became one of the favorite approaches to the telephone and phonograph exhibitions of 1889.

17. Morin, "Transmission du son.—Auditions théâtrales à distance," *Le Monde illustré*, numéro spécial exclusivement consacré à l'Exposition de l'Électricité, 22 Oct. 1881, 12.

18. Frank Géraldy, "Téléphonie," *Le Monde illustré*, numéro spécial exclusivement consacré à l'Exposition de l'Électricité, 22 Oct. 1881, 14–15, at 14: "Il est certain que toute personne qui entend pour la première fois un téléphone est frappée d'étonnement; cette voix mystérieuse venant de si loin a quelque chose d'étrange."

Both the widely read weekly *L'Illustration* and Sonzogno's *L'Esposizione di Parigi del 1889 illustrata* ran an illustrated article showing enraptured listeners (figure 6.4).[19] As in the previous report published in *Le Figaro*, the figure of the enchanted opera lover is one whose spontaneous reaction of applauding the singers of the opera performance causes most amusement to the writer. This time, it is a young woman who is bewitched by the "warm voice of the baritone" at the end of a love duet. "She closed her eyes, and the illusion was so strong that, once the piece was finished, she put down the receivers and applauded noisily, forgetting that the sound of her small clapping hands would never reach the object of her enthusiasm"[20] (figure 6.6). Here the notion of the alienated listener receives an additional twist in that not only is the listener cut off from the source of sound, but also the performer is separated from his customary audience. Thus the feedback loop of live performance is cut irrevocably by the interpolation of the new medium, even though performers perform and listeners listen simultaneously. McLuhan's concept that "the medium is the message" may rarely have been so visible as in the process of listening to these telephone transmissions in 1889, especially when the medium disappears for those observed listeners who react as if they were in the imagined space and applaud, and then realize their mistake.[21]

The two opera lovers who were surprised applauding the singers, immersing themselves fully in their experience of listening, represented a new type of listener who, over the nineteenth century, had been educated to rely on one of her or his individual senses, whether sight or sound, to read the world through observation. The stethoscope, for example, allowed doctors to use their ears to detect health or illness beneath the barrier of a patient's skin and to construct a full diagnosis on the basis of the heard.[22] Similarly, the setup in the Pavillon des Téléphones was one that

19. Louis d'Hurcourt, "Téléphones et phonographes à l'Exposition Universelle," *L'Illustration* 47 (1889): 328–30; translated as "Telefoni e fonografi," *L'Esposizione di Parigi del 1889* (Milan: Edoardo Sonzogno, 1889), 387–89. Quotation at p. 330 ("regarder écouter") or at p. 387 ("guardare chi ascolta").

20. D'Hurcourt, "Téléphones et phonographes à l'Exposition Universelle," 330: "La dernière, dilettante sans doute, a choisi l'appareil en communication avec l'Opéra-Comique; le hasard l'a servie, on achève un duo d'amour. Bercée par la voix chaude du baryton, elle a fermé les yeux, et l'illusion a été si forte que, le morceau terminé, elle pose les récepteurs et applaudit bruyamment, oubliant que le bruit de ses petites mains entrechoquées ne saurait arriver jusqu'à l'objet de son enthousiasme."

21. On the mediality of the gramophone, see Friedrich Kittler, *Grammophon, Film, Typewriter* (Berlin: Brinkmann & Bose, 1986), trans. Geoffrey Winthrop-Young and Michael Wutz as *Gramophone, Film, Typewriter* (Stanford, CA: Stanford University Press, 1999).

22. On the invention of the stethoscope in the nineteenth century and the resulting changes in listening technique, see Jonathan Sterne, *The Audible Past: Cultural Origins of Sound Production* (Durham, NC, and London: Duke University Press, 2003), 99–127.

Une distraction.

Figure 6.6. Paul Renouard, "Une distraction," illustration for Louis d'Hurcourt, "Téléphones et phonographes à l'Exposition Universelle," *L'Illustration* 47 (1889): 330.

deprived the listeners of visual input for reconstructing the reality of the sound. What they saw—tubes coming out the wall, and other visitors—had no relation to what they heard. With the rooms "set up to extinguish all exterior noise" and nothing to look at (unless the profession of journalist turned someone into a self-conscious observer), the listener needed to construct a parallel reality based on the sign-character of the sounds they heard:

> Thanks to these ingenious dispositions, one literally attends a perform-ance at the Opéra. One recognizes the voice of the singers. This is not the effect of a far-away dream, but that of an auditory reality. The choruses and the sung words reach the ear, fully and harmoniously, and one does not miss a single chord from the orchestra. In the breaks, one hears even the noises of the hall, right down to the voices of the newspaper boys and pro-gram vendors!

> Grâce à ces ingénieuses dispositions, on assiste littéralement à une représentation de l'Opéra. On reconnaît la voix des chanteurs. Ce n'est pas l'effet d'un rêve lointain, mais celui d'une réalité auditive. Les chœurs et les paroles chantées arrivent à l'oreille, pleins et harmonieux, et l'on ne perd pas un accord de l'orchestre. Pendant les entr'actes, on entend même les bruits de la salle, et jusqu'à la voix des crieurs de journaux et des marchands de programmes![23]

In order to convey to his readers the novelty of listening to a musical per-formance through the telephone, Louis Figuier introduced here the key distinction between the experience of a "faraway dream" and of an "audi-tory reality." Indeed, both the opera lovers earlier and Figuier were listen-ing for something new through their earpieces when compared to the traditional listening experience in music during the nineteenth century.[24]

Neither acousmatic nor associative listening was anything novel in terms of musical consumption. Sounds whose source remains invisible were particularly prevalent within the Catholic domain, whether the disem-bodied voices of nuns emerging from behind convent walls or the sound of an organ whose performer is invisible on the balcony.[25] In these cases, music was usually received as either an ethereal experience of pure sound, listened to in contemplation, or a titillating trace of musical practice taking place just behind the separating walls or emanating from afar. In the latter case, the sound acted as both a sonic and a geographical marker, pointing

23. Figuier, "Le Pavillon des Téléphones," 11.

24. James H. Johnson traces the changes in the collective listening attitudes in Paris from the late eighteenth to the mid-nineteenth centuries in his *Listening in Paris: A Cul-tural History* (Berkeley, Los Angeles, and London: University of California Press, 1995). See also the review article by Rémy Campos, "Traces d'écoute: Sur quelques tentatives historiennes de saisie du corps de la musique," *Circuit: Musiques contemporaines* 14 (2003): 7–17.

25. Ingrid Sykes has traced these issues throughout the nineteenth century in France in her dissertation, "Female Piety and the Organ: Nineteenth-Century French Women Organists" (PhD diss., City University, London, 2001).

to the source in physical proximity. This was not the case with the listening experience at the Pavillon des Téléphones, where the "traditional link between physical and social space" was broken and therefore created a "place-less" encounter with a musical event.[26] The telephone thus significantly transformed the listeners' auditory relationship to space by relying on their imagination to evoke the source of a sound no longer in physical proximity, but somewhere distant, albeit at a specific location. To push things even further, when listening to a theatrical performance, the imaginary relocation of the Exposition Universelle listeners was that of a spectator in the audience, rather than a performer onstage, where the microphones were placed. Thus the traditional experience of listening to acousmatic sound was transposed into the hearing of the telephone performances. Instead of imagining their position within the performance (where the receivers amazingly put them), the listeners distanced themselves from the much closer source of sound (i.e., the opera singers) by locating themselves in the audience.

The response of the fairgoers to these telephonic transmissions relied on listening strategies that were fairly new. Indeed if the acousmatic experience of sound has a long history, contemplative listening to music was a more recent phenomenon, emerging in Europe in the late eighteenth century, especially in the context of Romanticism and the notion of *Kunstreligion* (art-religion).[27] Contemplative listening as cultural practice had been formed in France by the 1830s, and had found its way into literature, such as Honoré de Balzac's 1834 novel, *La Duchesse de Langeais*, in which the hero, general Montriveau, listens to a convent organ in Spain during a military campaign. Balzac translates his hero's listening experience over several pages, summing up the quality of the hidden source of sound:

> The organ is in truth the grandest, the most daring, the most magnificent of all instruments invented by human genius. It is a whole orchestra in itself. It can express anything in response to a skilled touch. Surely it is in some way a pedestal on which the soul poises for a flight forth into space, essaying on her course to draw picture after picture in an endless series, to paint human life, to cross the Infinite that separates heaven from earth?

> L'orgue est certes le plus grand, le plus audacieux, le plus magnifique de tous les instruments créés par le génie humain. Il est un orchestre entier,

26. Kurt Blaukopf, "Mediamorphosis and Secondary Orality: A Challenge to Cultural Policy," in *World Music, Music of the Worlds: Aspects of Documentation, Mass Media and Acculturation*, ed. Max Peter Baumann (Wilhelmshaven: Florian Noetzel Verlag, 1992), 20.

27. Elizabeth Kramer, "The Idea of *Kunstreligion* in German Musical Aesthetics of the Early Nineteenth Century" (PhD diss., University of North Carolina at Chapel Hill, 2005). See also Wilhelm Seidel, "Absolute Musik und Kunstreligion um 1800," in *Musik und Religion*, ed. Helga de la Motte-Haber, 89–114 (Laaber: Laaber Verlag, 1995).

auquel une main habile peut tout demander, il peut tout exprimer. N'est-ce pas, en quelque sorte, un piédestal sur lequel l'âme se pose pour s'élancer dans les espaces lorsque, dans son vol, elle essaie de tracer mille tableaux, de peindre la vie, de parcourir l'infini qui sépare le ciel de la terre?[28]

Balzac's rhetoric here echoes countless texts by (among others) E. T. A. Hoffmann, Hector Berlioz, or Franz Liszt relating music's power to express beyond words, or—again in Balzac's term—to express "what is forbidden to language and renders speech powerless."[29] Such Romantic topoi of music's ability to express the inexpressible remained an aesthetic mainstay throughout the nineteenth century.[30]

This kind of music demanded new forms of listening in concert and opera, in which the sense of hearing became a conduit for experiencing the world more completely than other senses would allow, slowly shifting listening techniques from communal contemplation in a concert as a shared experience to one of individualized meditation, excluding all other senses, especially vision. In the course of the nineteenth century, the ideal listener became blind, either temporarily or permanently. Thus the symbolist poet Stéphane Mallarmé needed to close his eyes during a concert in order to listen completely, when he "intoxicated himself with the opium of the symphony."[31] This temporary blindness related to the notion of a superior musical sense of the blind that compensated for the loss of vision and which, as Ingrid Sykes has shown, had become a wide-spread concept in France by the end of the nineteenth century.[32] Such separation of senses is, according to Maurice de la Sizeranne, what the

28. Honoré de Balzac, *Histoire des Treize: La Duchesse de Langeais* (Paris: Flammarion, 1988), 49.

29. Ibid., 46: "dont l'expression est interdite à la parole, et la rend impuissante." On changes in musical aesthetics in the early nineteenth century, see Carl Dahlhaus, *Klassische und romantische Musikästhetik* (Laaber: Laaber Verlag, 1988), esp. 86–166.

30. Brian Hart has examined these issues with respect to the symphony in his "The Symphony in Theory and Practice in France, 1900–1914" (PhD diss., Indiana University, 1994). See also Brian Hart, "Wagner and the Franckiste 'Message-Symphony' in Early Twentieth-Century France," in *Von Wagner zum Wagnérisme: Musik, Literatur, Kunst, Politik*, ed. Annegret Fauser and Manuela Schwartz, 315–37, Transfer: Die deutsch-französische Kulturbibliothek 12 (Leipzig: Leipziger Universitäts-Verlag, 1999).

31. Camille Mauclair, *Servitude et grandeur littéraire* (1922), quoted in Annegret Fauser, *Der Orchestergesang in Frankreich zwischen 1870 und 1920*, Freiburger Beiträge zur Musikwissenschaft 2 (Laaber: Laaber Verlag, 1994), 142: "Au promenoir du concert Lamoureux—son seul luxe dominical—[Mallarmé] allait chaque semaine s'enivrer de l'opium de la symphonie; je m'y suis souvent assis auprès de lui, il ne parlait pas, mais, replié, les yeux clos, il semblait en prière."

32. Sykes, "Female Piety," 362–421.

blind can offer to the sighted: "The sighted person who wants to reflect, to meditate profoundly, closes his eyes and finds himself through this act almost entirely separated from the exterior world, and it is this separation, this isolation, that he borrows from the blind."[33] The voluntary disassociation from the source of sound in a concert through the closing of eyes thus allows the listener to focus on music's sonic quality rather than the visual presence of the music-making

As Jonathan Sterne has shown convincingly, sound-technological inventions correspond to changes in listening technique rather than simply generating new ways of listening after they are released to the public. Indeed, "sound-reproduction technologies are shot through with the tensions, tendencies, and currents of the culture from which they emerged, right down to their most basic mechanical functions. . . . For many of their inventors and early users, sound-reproduction technologies encapsulated a whole set of beliefs about the age and place in which they lived."[34] But if sound-reproduction technologies reflect changing practices of listening, they also allow assumptions about auditory (rather than simply audible) pasts through the ways in which the sonorous, inside world of listening had emerged and became perceptible through its exterior manifestations.[35]

Indeed, the sound-reproduction technologies of the Pavillon des Téléphones and their use in the Exposition Universelle permit some unique insights into the auditory past of the late nineteenth century. The two forms of live transmission that were part of the telephone exhibit reflected two very different forms of musical reception with respect to two very different repertoires: fanfares on the one hand, and opera on the other. The fanfares were broadcast on a series of proto-loudspeakers mounted on the outside of the pavilion (figures 6.1 and 6.2), providing public background music in a similar way to the competing fanfares on the bandstands scattered throughout the Exposition. One might, in fact, characterize the "fanfare Ader" as an electronic bandstand.

The operatic telephone transmissions relied on a different type of equipment. Each listener had her or his own set of individual earphones, even though the technology for loudspeakers would have been available, given Edison's invention of the megaphone in 1878 and Ader's electronic

---

33. Maurice de la Sizeranne, *Les Femmes aveugles* (Paris: Lecoffre, 1901), 28, quoted in Sykes, "Female Piety," 365: "Le clairvoyant qui veut réfléchir, méditer profondément, ferme les yeux et se trouve, par ce fait, presque entièrement séparé du monde extérieur, et c'est cette séparation, cet isolement qu'il prête à l'aveugle."

34. Sterne, *The Audible Past*, 8–9.

35. I am turning Sterne's argument on its head. He argued (*The Audible Past*, 13) that rather than describing "people's interior experience of listening—an auditory past," a history of sound needs to focus on the exterior manifestations of sound for a more documented and less subjective account.

fanfare.[36] Thus the technology of telephonic transmission through head-sets built on listening techniques that aimed to separate the specific physi-cal experience—sitting in the third row of a theater—from the auditory appreciation of the music, focusing entirely on the listening imagination.[37] Unless telephone listeners engaged specifically in the act of spectatorship—watching other people listen—the setup of the rooms encouraged listeners to close their eyes and focus on listening, just like the two opera-lovers described in the press. Such listening could create the illu-sion of geographical relocation within the performance, in other words: an "auditory reality."[38] The concept of experiencing such a parallel reality is not far from notions of hysteria in contemporary psychology. The famous Jean Martin Charcot's patients at the psychiatric hospital of the Salpêtrière heard voices that—for them—were an auditory reality, and the image of the female opera lover (figure 6.6) who claps her hands at something she alone heard was not unfamiliar to readers of Charcot's publications.[39] In this sense, the listening experience of the telephone auditions was almost diametrically opposed to that of the dream-like evocation through music of a visual correlate in the way that the sound of picturesque folk music could evoke the Auvergne and its dances.[40] Listening to a stage production through the telephone headset offered the possibility of an out-of-body experience triggered by the technological setup, but like the hysterics at the Salpêtrière, the listener could fall prey to her or his illusion when the

36. "Paris et Départements," *Le Ménestrel* 44 (1878), 279: "Une nouvelle invention touchant à l'acoustique vient compléter les deux merveilleux instruments tout récem-ment découverts. C'est le mégaphone qui rend tout simplement l'ouïe aux sourds en grossissant les sons comme les lentilles grossissent les objets visibles. Le mégaphone est la dernière création du professeur Edison, l'inventeur du phonographe."

37. The modes of listening to music described by Pierre Schaeffer developed fur-ther by Denis Smalley could provide a useful framework for this discussion. The tele-phone transmissions focus the attention of the listeners on the musical object in an allocentric way, appreciating and responding to the meaning of the sounds. See Denis Smalley, "The Listening Imagination: Listening in the Electroacoustic Era," in *Compan-ion to Contemporary Musical Thought*, ed. John Paynter et al., 2 vols. (London and New York: Routledge, 1992), 1:515–20.

38. Both the authors in *Le Figaro* and *L'Illustration* (see notes 14 and 19, pp. 288 and 290) use the word "illusion" to explain the behavior of the two opera lovers.

39. I am grateful to Debora Silverman for drawing this parallel to my attention. Charcot's writings and illustrations were published widely by the 1880s. He was closely linked with writers and other artists since the 1860s, and his theories influenced in par-ticular writers of the *decadence* movement. See Jean-François Six, *1886: Naissance du XX<sup>e</sup> siècle en France* (Paris: Seuil, 1986), 120–31; Clair Rowden, *Republican Morality and Catholic Tradition in the Opera: Massenet's "Hérodiade" and "Thaïs"* (Weinsberg: Musik-Edition Lucie Galland, 2004), 157–65.

40. See chapter 5, pp. 273.

listening imagination conjured an auditory reality. A ten-minute slot in public, at a World's Fair exhibition, may have been just safe enough.

With the telephonic transmission of opera, the Société Générale des Téléphones clearly had tapped into a form of musical consumption that had a commercial future. Already during the Exposition Universelle, a competing company had installed across Paris a "rather curious reduction" of telephone transmission which became known as *théâtrophones*, fitted with a money slot for a 50-centime coin.[41] Placed in public spaces, from hotel lobbies to bars, they quickly became all the rage in Paris and led, in 1890, to the establishment of the Compagnie du Théâtrophone.[42] *Théâtrophones* were widely distributed in public, and soon, Parisians could subscribe to them at their home for 180 francs per year, making a reality of the "theater in an armchair." One of the first beneficiaries of these telephonic transmissions of operas was the French president whose apartments remained telephonically linked to the Opéra until 1932.[43] Within two years, the *théâtrophone* had become, in the words of an American correspondent from Paris, "a machine they use here very much."[44]

## *Le Roi Edison*, or the Triumph of the Phonograph

If the telephone auditions conjured an "auditory reality" of a simultaneous but geographically distant musical event, the phonograph lured fairgoers with another dream: that of preserving humanly generated sound for—so the hyperbole went—eternity.[45] Edison's phonographs drew a record number of visitors who wanted to hear with their own ears what these "canned voices" would sound like in their improved format.[46] While the early version of the phonograph had shown, in 1878, the possibility of sound storage, it was not until the 1889 Exposition that Edison's phonograph was an industrial reality. The prototype of the new machine had been built only in June 1888, but by the time of the opening of the Exposition in May 1889, Edison's production lines were turning out close

41. Figuier, "Le Pavillon des Téléphones," 11: "une assez curieuse réduction des *auditions théâtrales* imaginée par MM. Marinovitch et Szanady [*sic*]."

42. Aulas, *Les Origines du téléphone en France (1876–1914)*, 88.

43. The setup of the *théâtrophone* is described in great detail in L. Montillot, *Téléphone pratique*, 2 vols. (Paris: A. Grelot, 1893), 2:460–69. The cost of 180 francs per year is mentioned on p. 461.

44. "The Theatrophone in Paris," *Electrical Review*, 29 Aug. 1891, 4, reproduced at http://earlyradiohistory.us/1891thea.htm (accessed 5 May 2004).

45. Edison's comment that "speech has become, as it were, immortal" is quoted in Kittler, *Gramophone, Film, Typewriter*, 21.

46. Victor Meunier, "*Le Rappel* à l'Exposition: Conserves de voix," *Le Rappel*, 8 June 1889, 3.

to fifty machines a day.[47] Edison's phonograph was not the only sound-reproduction device presented at the Exposition, but it was the only one to receive significant attention by the press and the fairgoers.[48]

The Edison exhibition was touted as "one of the great attractions of the Galerie des Machines" and occupied a space of $675 \text{ m}^2$ (ca. 7,266 square feet).[49] It consisted of two pavilions within the Galerie, one dedicated to electric light, the other to the phonograph. The exhibition was carefully staged so as to represent Edison the inventor rather than Edison the businessman. In contrast to the telephone auditions on the other side of the Champ de Mars, Edison's phonograph auditions were free; indeed, any attempt to charge for them was forbidden expressly by the inventor himself in a letter to the organizer in charge of the Parisian exhibit, William Joseph Hammer:

> It is my intention that the phonograph, as well as all my other inventions, shall be exhibited in Paris upon a purely scientific basis, excluding all commercial or speculative elements. . . . I will not countenance any exhibition of the phonograph for mony [*sic*] anywhere within the City of Paris during the time the Exposition is in progress.[50]

The phonograph's introduction to the European market via the Exposition Universelle was painstakingly orchestrated. Still several weeks before the Exposition opened, on 15 April, George E. Gouraud—Edison's French-born representative in Great Britain—had presented the phonograph to the Institut de France, where the *doyen* of French composers, Charles Gounod, was among the musical guinea pigs: "They say that Charles Gounod sang and then had reproduced several times the song 'Il pleut, bergère,' and that this roll, a new sort of musical autograph, will be preserved as carefully as an ancient document."[51] The French press was

47. Alexander Boyden Magoun, *Shaping the Sound of Music: The Evolution of the Phonograph Record, 1877–1950* (PhD diss., University of Maryland, 2000), 78.

48. Only one competing device, the graphophone of Charles Summer Tainter, received some mention in the French press. On the development of the gramophone and sound reproduction, see Roland Gelatt, *The Fabulous Phonograph, 1877–1977*, 2nd edition (London: Cassell, 1977).

49. V.-F. M., "Les Auditions du phonographe dans la Galerie des Machines," *L'Exposition de Paris 1889* 3–4 (1889): 307–10, at 307: "Une des grandes attractions de la Galerie des Machines est l'exposition de M. Edison, qui occupe deux pavillons entiers, l'un consacré à l'éclairage électrique, l'autre au phonographe, devenu un instrument pratique." For the footprint of $675 \text{ m}^2$, see *Exposition de 1889: Guide bleu du "Figaro" et du "Petit Journal,"* 125.

50. Letter by Thomas Alva Edison to William Joseph Hammer, 20 April 1889, in *Thomas A. Edison Papers*, ed. by Paul B. Israel, Rutgers University, Letterbook, LB-029 (April–May 1889), 177; http://edison.rutgers.edu (accessed 6 Jan. 2004).

51. Julien Tiersot, "Promenades musicales à l'Exposition," *Le Ménestrel* 55 (1889): 188–89, at 188: "[L]'on a raconté que M. Gounod y avait chanté, puis fait reproduire à

introduced to the new machine as soon as it arrived in Paris. Indeed, as the author of the *Guide bleu* put it, the new phonographs "had spoken to the entire press," and now, "from the moment that the Exposition opened, the entire press has spoken about them."[52] In August, the excitement about the Edison exhibition reached new heights, after the inventor himself embarked on his first trip ever to Europe to spend a month in Paris on the occasion of the Exposition Universelle.[53]

While the operatic transmissions of the French Société Générale des Téléphones channeled the press reception into questions of audience response, the Edison exhibition generated a wider field of debate which bifurcated into two distinct topics. Edison himself served as a symbolic figure—especially to the Republican press, led by *Le Figaro*—to draw attention to the contentious issue of meritocracy versus aristocracy in Third-Republic France. The phonograph auditions, on the other hand, led to observations and speculations about sound-reproduction, its sonic qualities, and its uses in replicating speech and music.

Edison's visit to Paris in the middle of August 1889 occurred at a politically charged moment in an already turbulent year of centenary celebrations of the French Revolution, the Exposition Universelle itself, and political upheaval caused by the former war minister, General Boulanger. In the four weeks leading up to his visit, republican and monarchist politics had dominated the public sphere with the national commemoration of 14 July; the departmental elections at the end of July; the glamorous state visit of a reigning monarch, the Shah of Persia, to the French Republic in early August; the republican celebration of 4 August; and finally, the trial and condemnation in absentia, on 14 August, of General Boulanger. The arrival of Edison—an ostentatiously non-political, self-made celebrity from America, an engineer, and a "benefactor to humanity"—brought some distraction from the political tensions in France, while it also served to exhort the French government to rethink some of its fundamental values with respect to merit and nobility.[54] Who else should be honored, the question

---

plusieurs reprises la chanson: *Il pleut, bergère,* et que le rouleau, autographe musical d'un genre nouveau, serait conservé précieusement, comme un document faisant date." Unfortunately, the recording has not been preserved.

52. *Exposition de 1889: Guide bleu du "Figaro" et du "Petit Journal,"* 125: "On y voit les nouveaux phonographes qui ont parlé à toute la Presse et dont toute la Presse a parlé au moment même de l'ouverture de l'Exposition universelle."

53. Edison's visit coincided with the publication of the first French biography by Émile Durer, *Edison: Sa vie—ses œuvres: Esquisses américaines* (Paris: Victor Marchesson, 1889).

54. Gaston Tissandier, "Th. A. Edison," *La Nature: Revue des Sciences et de leurs applications aux arts et aux industries* 17 (1889): 215–18, at 215: "Edison . . . appartient par ses découvertes à la classe privilégiée des bienfaiteurs de l'humanité."

ran, if not the true royalty of the future: a "modern majesty," that "king of science."[55]

In the French reception of Edison, concepts of modernity and aristocracy were conflated into a powerful campaign to honor this exceptional meritocrat of the present as a member of the true aristocracy of the future.[56] This proved a very timely discussion, as the political events in 1889 were leading already toward the *Ralliement*, the informal alliance in 1890 between the old conservative elites with "middle-class republicans increasingly fearful of a resurgent left."[57] The press campaign for Edison was started on 8 August by the preeminent Republican broadsheet, *Le Figaro*, with a long article splashed over half of the front page that was provocatively entitled "Sa Majesté Edison."[58] Within the first few paragraphs, the author progressively increased his use of superlatives, turning Edison from the "king of the elements" and "sage of Llewellyn" into the conqueror and transformer of the "old world"; the article reached its climax with the author transforming him into a modern god, more powerful that the Zeus of antiquity: "Thus the modern god, who throws out lightning bolts and even more dangerous sparks than those of that old beast Zeus who has now been set aside, honored France by leaving his Olympus."[59] For Edison's arrival in Le Havre on 11 August, *Le Figaro* had sent its young star reporter, Gaston Calmette, to recount the event in detail for its readers and to extend an invitation for a *soirée* to be given by the journal in Edison's honor.[60] By that time, most other Parisian newspapers had picked up on the story, following *Le Figaro*'s lead in turning the visit of Edison to France into a "continuous apotheosis" of republican meritocracy.[61]

55. Georges Robert, "Sa Majesté Edison," *Le Figaro*, 8 Aug. 1889, 1: "cette majesté moderne"; Scaramouche, "Edison," *Le Gaulois*, 14 Aug. 1889, 1: "le roi de la science."

56. Concepts of aristocracy and meritocracy overlapped in the nineteenth century, especially with respect to the medicine and science. See Robert A. Nye, "Medecine and Science as Masculine 'Fields of Honor,'" *Osiris* 12 (1997): 60–79.

57. Edward Berenson, *The Trial of Madame Caillaux* (Berkeley, Los Angeles, and London: University of California Press, 1992), 183.

58. Robert, "Sa Majesté Edison."

59. Ibid., 1: "le roi des éléments"; "le *sage* de Leweln [*sic*]"; "ce vieux monde, qu'il a superbement conquis"; "Donc, le Dieu moderne, qui lance des éclairs et des étincelles plus dangereuses que celles de cette vieille bête de Zeus, désormais remisé, fait à la France l'honneur de quitter son Olympe."

60. Gaston Calmette, "Edison en France," *Le Figaro*, 12 Aug. 1889, 1–2. In 1889, Gaston Calmette was the editor of the "Échos" column and rapidly rising through the ranks. He was appointed as the journal's editor-in-chief in 1896. He died in 1914 when he was shot by Henriette Caillaux over his threat to publish her adulterous love letters in the journal as part of an attack on her husband, cabinet minister Joseph Caillaux. For a biographical sketch, see Berenson, *The Trial of Madame Caillaux*, 220–23.

61. Ory, *L'Expo universelle*, 23.

Many a newspaper reporter contrasted the state visit of the Shah of Persia, with its troop inspections, presidential welcome, and other honors, with the entirely private arrival of Edison, and used this comparison to question the role of aristocracy and royalty in the context of a republic. As one might expect, the radical newspaper *Le Rappel* pushed things furthest with a polemical article that compared the French fascination with royalty, especially after 1789 and 1793, to African (thus savage) ritual in which a crowned head serves as fetish. While monarchs such as François I or Frederick the Great of Prussia had wielded genuine power in the past, "crown-bearers" such as Queen Victoria or Czar Alexander were nothing in this progressive modern world when compared to "the real contemporary sovereigns that are the Edisons, Pasteurs, Listers, Kochs, if one remains only in the world of science."[62] Newspapers and journals played on the contrast between rites of the "old world" and what should be appropriate ceremony in the modern one. Even a more moderate journal such as *Le Monde illustré* repeated the trope when it contrasted—with a colonialist jibe—the way in which "our old world . . . full of prejudices . . . welcomes with fanfares and feasts even the most African of monarchs," and the fact that "it receives the king of thought with neither drums nor trumpets, without troop inspections and without hurrahs."[63] Indeed, we read in the daily *Gil Blas* that no other monarch has so powerful a kingdom as Edison, "for he embraces the universality of modern ideas."[64]

This modern, meritocratic realm in which science reigns supreme has all the traces of revolutionary ideology—with the "fée Électricité" as the "être suprême" of the future—transported into the bourgeois context of the Third Republic.[65] Edison was celebrated as an almost priest-like figure, a genius who shared deafness with Beethoven yet invented progressive sonic devices, whose looks resembled men of science and letters such as Jean Martin Charcot or François Coppée, and who would bring enlightened

---

62. "Chronique du jour: Le roi Edison," *Le Rappel,* 17 Aug. 1889/30 Thermidor an 97, 1–2, at 1: "En dépit des 89 et des 93, une tête couronnée, par la filiation, par le hasard ou par le crime, apparaît toujours comme une tête à part dans le troupeau humain. . . . Nos fétiches couronnés paraîtront aussi grossiers que ceux des naturels du Congo apparaissent à l'heure actuelle. . . . Les vrais souverains contemporains, ces sont les Edison, les Pasteur, les Lister, les Koch, pour ne rester que dans l'ordre scientifique."

63. G. Lenôtre, "Edison et le phonographe," *Le Monde illustré,* 17 Aug. 1889, 99: "notre vieux monde . . . plein de préjugés . . . il accueille par des fanfares et des fêtes les monarques les plus africains; et il reçoit ce roi de la pensée sans tambours ni trompettes, sans haies de troupes et sans *hourras.*"

64. Jean Parvais, "Edison à Paris," *Gil Blas,* 14 Aug. 1889, 2: "son domaine est plus vaste que celui de n'importe quelle puissance, car il embrasse l'universalité des idées modernes."

65. On the "Fairy Electricity," see Ory, *L'Expo Universelle,* 24–26.

peace in the face of France's atavistic opponent, Bismarck.[66] Edison's visit allowed the future to be painted as a utopian world of science, in which "men of genius, representing what is highest in humanity, the victory over nature" will create a world "overflowing with work and prosperity."[67]

The campaign of the ever-powerful French press to acknowledge Edison as modern royalty resulted not only in medals and honors from the Republic—including his being made a commander of the Légion d'honneur—and from the City of Paris, but also in a flood of private receptions and dinners.[68] Edison and his wife were offered the presidential box for their visit to the Opéra on 21 August, which for this occasion was decorated with both the American and the French flags. During the intermission, the orchestra performed the American national anthem, just as it would for an official delegation.[69] Even today, a plaque on the top floor of the Eiffel Tower commemorates the dinner that Gustave Eiffel gave in Edison's honor.[70] So many dinners were offered that a report in the *New York World* claimed in early September that Edison was "made ill by too many banquets."[71]

While the press celebrated the king of science, the banquets honored Edison, the inventor of the phonograph. One major event was the soirée organized by *Le Figaro* on 26 August, consisting of a dinner and entertainment. The program needed to be a "summary of what there is in Paris that is typical and indicative of national art, and also, thanks to the Exposition, of exotic art."[72] The performance started with the Romanian *lăutari*, followed by performances by Parisian artists from the Comédie-Française, the Opéra, and some variété stages. Then came the "highlight of the

---

66. Max de Nansouty, "Edison," *L'Événement*, 17 Aug. 1889, 1; Scaramouche, "Edison"; Paul Degouy, "Edison," *La Justice*, 14 Aug. 1889, 1; "Edison en France," *Le Petit Journal*, 13 Aug. 1889, 2; Robert, "Sa Majesté Edison."

67. Scaramouche, "Edison": "hommes qui ont du génie, représentant ce qu'il y a de plus haut dans l'humanité, la victoire sur la nature"; "qui découle tout travail et toute prospérité."

68. The foreign minister's letter to Edison about the decoration is reproduced in Gaston Calmette, "Edison à Paris," *Le Figaro*, 27 Sept. 1889, 1–2.

69. "Courrier des Théâtres," *Le Figaro*, 22 Aug. 1889, 3: "M. et Mme Edison assistaient, hier, à la représentation de l'Opéra, dans la loge du Président de la République, qui avait été pour la circonstance décorée de drapeaux français et américains. . . . Le spectacle se composait de *Rigoletto* et du ballet *la Tempête*. Dans un entracte, on a exécuté l'hymne national américain, qui a été salué de chaleureuses acclamations."

70. I am grateful to Peter Lamothe for this information.

71. "Edison Talks about Paris," *New York World*, 8 Sept., 1889; newspaper clipping, Archives of the Edison National Historic Site, Series D-89-46: "Paris Exposition."

72. Parisis, "Edison au *Figaro*," *Le Figaro*, 21 Aug. 1889, 1: "Mais il s'agissait, cette fois, de composer un programme qui fût comme une sélection, un résumé de ce qu'il y a de typique, de suggestif à Paris au point de vue de l'art national et aussi, grâce à l'Exposition, de l'art exotique."

program," "furnished by Edison himself," of a phonograph performance for the guests.[73] After that, the actor Coquelin improvised a comic scene about Edison, and Jeanne Granier some "couplets de circonstance" about the phonograph, set to music by Gaston Serpette. The evening ended with performances by the Javanese dancers and the *gitana*, La Maccarona. The composition of the program was itself a reflection not only of Edison's place in the "brotherhood of letters and science," but even more of the ideology of progress as encapsulated in the structure of the evening.[74] At the fringes were the most celebrated exotic musicians and dancers from Europe and the Far East, while the middleground was occupied by performances from the Parisian theater world. The center, however, was dedicated to the future, with speech and music rendered by the phonograph.

Several days earlier, the Société Générale des Téléphones had invited the Edisons to a dinner followed by "experiments" with Edison's phonograph, before the guests "went to the Pavillon des Téléphones to attend the hearing of a performance at the Opéra Comique."[75] There might have been ulterior motives for this program by offering comparative listening between telephone and phonograph, since—compared to the telephone—the phonograph's quality of sound reproduction was still in its infancy so far as music was concerned. Another dinner, offered by the British Committee, also combined phonograph and telephone as futuristic entertainment:

> They had phonographs in which tunes and famous voices, and dialogues spoken by famous actors and actresses, were stored up. Any number of apparatus for conducting sound to pairs of ears were in communication. Then there was the magnifying phonograph, which enabled you to hear in the ordinary manner [i.e., without the help of acoustic tubes]. Besides these wonders of science, which have, from use, ceased to be marvelous, there were telephonic means of enabling a score of us to hear the opera of the evening.[76]

It seems as if the phonograph and its sonic possibilities had become the main theme of Edison's visit to Paris given that, in its redesigned version, it

---

73. Ibid., 1: "Mais voici le clou du programme. C'est Edison lui-même qui l'a fourni."

74. Ibid., 1: "fraternité des lettres et de la science."

75. *Champ de Mars*, 24 Aug. 1889, newspaper clipping, Archives of the Edison National Historic Site, Series D-89-46: "Paris Exposition": "Après quelques expériences faites dans la salle même du banquet, avec le phonographe de M. Edison, tous les invités se sont rendus au Pavillon des Téléphones, pour assister à l'audition d'une représentation de l'Opéra-Comique."

76. "Notes from Paris: A Scientific Soirée," *Truth*, 5 Sept. 1889; newspaper clipping, Archives of the Edison National Historic Site, Series D-89-46: "Paris Exposition."

was his latest invention and the one most conducive to publicity. Also, Edison and his company had created an interactive display that allowed for both listening and recording. The exhibition space itself had being arranged so that six people could listen to each phonograph simultaneously (figure 6.7). The engraving shows Edison's engineers and other employees matching the poses of listeners at the Exposition. The structure behind them seems to be the recording and private listening studio to which only selected guests were admitted. "The walls of this bureau are about a foot in thickness and filled with sawdust in the center in order to deaden the sound of the machinery outside."[77]

The phonographs in the Edison exhibition played mostly music. The repertoire consisted of the French and American national anthems, songs, short solo and ensemble pieces, and band music. For the most part, they were recorded in Edison's studios in New Jersey and shipped over to Paris.[78] The "Musical Cylinder Accounts" preserved at the Archives of the Edison National Historic Site allow for some reconstruction of the kinds of music offered to the visitors to the Galerie des Machines. These early wax cylinders were all originals, recorded onto several machines simultaneously: in order to produce multiple copies of popular pieces, the performers had to record the same piece over and over again.[79] Judging from the recording logs, the wax cylinders sent to Paris offered a broad selection of light music with popular waltzes, polkas and marches, including works by Johann Strauss, Emil Waldteufel, and Franz Lehar. But they also contained some opera extracts and other classical repertoire that would have been played in any bourgeois salon of the time, whether in New York or Paris (see table 6.1).

Save for references to the two national anthems, and to piano or band music in generic terms, the reports in the French press remained rather vague, however, on the specific repertoire that was being played on the phonographs of the Galerie des Machines. Rather, the discussion in the press seemed to focus more on issues of sound reproduction as such, and on its uses in the near and more distant future. One of the main issues in

---

77. "The Wizard in Paris," *Gazette*, 13 July 1889; newspaper clipping, Archives of the Edison National Historic Site, Series D-89-46: "Paris Exposition." Lenôtre reports on his attempts to be admitted to the studio during Edison's visit to Paris, but to no avail. See Lenôtre, "Edison et le phonographe," 99.

78. The entry for 13 June 1889 details that 654 cylinder records were sent to Paris. See Allen Koenigsberg, *Edison Cylinder Records, 1889–1912, with an Illustrated History of the Phonograph* (New York: Stellar Productions, 1969), 112.

79. Koenigsberg, *Edison Cylinder Records, 1889–1912*, xvii. While a process for duplicating cylinders was developed in 1890, its cost was prohibitive at first, which meant that cylinders were still produced by creating sets of originals. See Marsha Siefert, "Aesthetics, Technology, and the Capitalization of Culture: How the Talking Machine Became a Musical Instrument," *Science in Context* 8 (1995): 429.

Figure 6.7. "Auditions des phonographes d'Edison dans la Galerie des Machines à l'Exposition Universelle de 1889," *La Nature: Revue des Sciences et de leurs applications aux arts et aux industries* 17 (1889): 217.

these texts was the question of the reproduction's "fidelity" to the original and its meaning.[80] Metaphors such as the description of recordings as a "photography of the voice" tried to capture the essence of phonograph recordings through the comparison with earlier experiences with reproduction technology.[81]

The 1889 phonograph was both a recording and a reproduction device, a machine to replicate speech and a musical instrument. Recent scholarship on the development of the phonograph has focused on Edison's apparent resistance to marketing the phonograph as a musical instrument instead of as an office machine, locating the beginning of that development in the 1890s as driven by the musical market rather than the machine's producer.[82] This seems to be contradicted, however, by the high

80. (Hi-)Fidelity was a major point in the promotion, reception, and technical developments of the phonograph in its first fifty years. See Emily Thompson, "Machines, Music, and the Quest for Fidelity: Marketing the Edison Phonograph in America, 1877–1925," *Musical Quarterly* 79 (1995): 131–71.

81. George E. Gouraud, "Le Nouveau Phonographe d'Edison," *L'Exposition de Paris* 3–4 (1889), 111–12, at 111: "la photographie de la voix."

82. Siefert, "Aesthetics, Technology, and the Capitalization of Culture"; Thompson, "Machines, Music, and the Quest for Fidelity."

Table 6.1. Recordings of classical repertoire by the Edison Laboratory assumed to have been included in the Paris shipment of 15 June 1889.

| Date | Artist | Instrument | Composer | Title | No of cylind. |
|------|--------|------------|----------|-------|---------------|
| 25 May | Alfred Arnheim | violin | Auber | *Fra Diavolo* (overture) | 3 |
| 28 May | John Mittauer | cornet | Wagner | *Lohengrin* ("King's Air") | 14 |
| | | | Verdi | *Rigoletto* | 5 |
| 29 May | C. Aug. Joepel Henry Giese | flute clarinet | Gounod | *Faust* (selection) | 18 |
| 31 May | Henry Giese | clarinet | Bizet | *Carmen* (selection) | 15 |
| | | | Rossini | *Barbiere di Siviglia* (air) | 8 |
| | | | Schumann | *Spring Song* ("Frühlingslied") | 8 |
| 1 June | Miss Lankow Max Franklin | voice piano | Schumann | *Spring Song* ("Frühlingslied") | 15 |
| 6 June | Mr. Wehnert | flute | Schubert | "Song" | 8 |
| | Messrs. Wehnert, Rose, & Gast | flute trio | Kuhlau | Scherzo | 8 |
| | | | Beethoven | Op. 67, Adagio | 6 |
| | | | | Op. 67, Scherzo | 8 |
| 13 June | Theodore Hoch | cornet | Donizetti | *Anna Bolena* (theme and variations) | 3 |

**Note:** The table is based on Allen Koenigsberg: *Edison Cylinder Records, 1889–1912, with an Illustrated History of the Phonograph* (New York: Stellar Productions, 1969), 111–12. The recordings were almost certainly included in the shipment sent to Paris on 13 June.

volume of musical recordings shipped from the Edison Laboratories to Paris on the one hand, and by the exhibition setup with its focus on mainly musical recordings on the other. As Julien Tiersot recalls, music played a major role right from the beginning, to the point that he characterized the phonograph as an "essentially musical instrument".[83]

---

83. Tiersot, "Promenades musicales à l'Exposition," 188: "un instrument essentiellement musical."

I myself had previously, on the first day when the instrument was shown to a French public, the opportunity to see and hear repeated before me a flute solo performed by M. de Vroye, the *Concert à la cour* aria by Auber, and even a French folksong, quite apart from the sounds of trumpets and piece of military music performed in America, which seemed to come directly from the room in which they were created. If only the phonograph did not seem to take a roguish pleasure in reproducing, with a scrupulous fidelity bordering on exaggeration, the slightest imperfections of the song, whether in its intonation or its pronunciation, it would be a perfect instrument.

J'avais eu moi-même antérieurement, le premier jour où l'instrument fut montré à un public français, l'occasion de voir et d'entendre répéter devant moi un solo de flûte, joué par M. de Vroye, l'air du *Concert à la Cour*, d'Auber, et même une chanson populaire française, sans compter des sonneries de trompettes et des morceaux de musique militaire exécutés en Amérique et qui paraissent sortir de la salle même où avait lieu l'expérience. N'était que le phonographe semble se faire un malin plaisir à reproduire avec un scrupule de fidélité qui frise l'exagération les moindres imperfections du chant, soit dans l'intonation, soit dans la prononciation, ce serait un instrument parfait.[84]

Thus right from the beginning, musical performances were an important part of the display, demonstrating the "faithful" rendering of both speech and music. Because "fidelity" became such a catchword as a sound-quality indicator at the turn of the century, its use in the earlier reception as indicator of reliability is often overlooked.[85] When Gounod exclaimed: "How glad I am that I did not make any mistakes! How faithful this is! But this is faithfulness without rancor!" he made a judgment not on the quality of sound reproduction but on a significant attribute of the medium itself: its lack of neurological differentiation.[86] The human ear is trained "to filter voices, words, and sounds out of noise;" the machine records it all indiscriminately.[87] While such fidelity of the medium might offer all kinds of interesting applications in terms of record-keeping—the Italian parliament had just started a trial of phonographs to document its sessions[88]—it

84. Ibid.
85. Sterne refers to this earlier use in passing before focusing on issues of authenticity and fidelity a decade later. Sterne, *The Audible Past*, 222.
86. Gouraud, "Le Nouveau Phonographe d'Edison," 111: "Un de vos célèbres compositeurs, M. Gounod, s'écria, après avoir entendu le phonographe répéter son *Ave Maria* qu'il avait chanté en s'accompagnant lui-même: 'Que je suis heureux de n'avoir pas fait de fautes! Comme c'est fidèle! mais c'est la fidélité sans rancune.'"
87. Kittler, *Gramophone, Film, Typewriter*, 22.
88. Léon Millet, "Chroniques: Phonographies," *La Justice*, 17 July 1889, 1.

proved a double-edged sword when it came to the recording of music. Because the primitive loudspeakers of the 1877 model were replaced with acoustic tubes inserted into the listeners' ears, the "sensory data stream" from the wax cylinder now was received in a reduced-listening context of acoustic privacy, literally putting sound in one's ear.[89] Tiersot praised these tubes as one of two improvements that had turned the original speech-recording device into a musical instrument, because it allowed the listener to "perceive with absolute fidelity the slightest nuances of timbre and intensity of the recorded sounds."[90] Here Tiersot revealed himself as a modern listener, someone who focuses not on the message (i.e., the music) but on the sonic medium (i.e., the reproduction of sound) in ways that bring to mind modernist musical concerns about musical materiality worked out much later in compositions such as Olivier Messiaen's piano etude, *Modes de valeurs et d'intensités* (1949), in which the sonic spectrum of musical sound is divided up into its components and recomposed.

Tiersot seemed to use his earphones as if they were a stethoscope to diagnose the abilities and problems of the new musical instrument. His sound analysis focused on the tonal spectrum of the instrument, which was still very limited, albeit more developed than in 1877.[91] On the plus side, the wax-cylinder phonograph could record "simultaneous sounds," which, for Tiersot, was key to his being able to declare the apparatus a musical instrument.[92] But this apparatus still had musical limitations:

Even after these precious results, it is certain that not all has been said. The reason is that the harmonies that were reproduced so clearly in the cases above [performed by two cornets and piano] came from instruments of the same nature or of homogeneous timbres, but it remains to be seen whether the complex sonorities of the modern orchestra can be preserved with the same perfection.

Il est certain que, même après ces précieux résultats, tout n'est pas encore dit. Car les harmonies si clairement reproduites provenaient, dans les cas ci-dessus, d'instruments de même nature ou de timbres homogènes, mais

89. Kittler, *Gramophone, Film, Typewriter*, 22, 37.

90. Tiersot, "Promenades musicales à l'Exposition," 188: "percevoir avec une fidé-lité absolue les moindres nuances de timbre et d'intensité des sons enregistrés."

91. From a mid-twentieth-century perspective, Robert Gelatt judged the sound quality very severely: "[T]he quality of reproduction was extremely poor. Only a fraction of the tonal spectrum could be caught in wax, and even that fraction issued from the ear tubes in so blurred and indistinct a manner as to make any resemblance to real music almost coincidental" (*The Fabulous Phonograph*, 46).

92. Tiersot, "Promenades musicales à l'Exposition," 188: "Mais le résultat le plus considérable qu'aient produit les derniers perfectionnements, du moins au point de vue musical, c'est la possibilité d'enregistrer les sons simultanés."

il reste à savoir si les sonorités complexes de l'orchestre moderne pourront être conservées avec la même perfection.[93]

Thus the Edison exhibit of the phonograph was, in the end, presenting a music of the future rather than of the present, a promise of things to come. After all, "one can no longer say that something might be impossible."[94]

Many of those who described the imagined sound of faithful rendition or reacted to it as listeners seemed to respond to the sheer fact of sound reproduction itself. As in 1878, they appeared to have been more impressed by the possibility than the actuality of the recorded sound. In a "comparative study of dismay" (figure 6.8), the caricaturist, Paul Léonnec, may have captured the moment of discovering the existence of recorded sound by a sample of French society—from officer to peasant—but his drawing also illustrates a degree of surprise at the recorded sound's sonic limitations:

> Whether one hears them through the acoustic tube or on open machines, the sounds of the orchestra, the choruses, and the words retain that timbre of a buffoon's voice and that extraneous noise that remove all illusion and all charm. The listeners look at each other without daring to express their disappointment, but finding that the result did not live up to their expectation.

> Qu'on les écoute par le tube acoustique, ou par l'appareil libre, les sons d'orchestre, les chœurs ou les paroles, conservent ce timbre de voix de polichinelle et ce bruit de friture, qui ôtent toute illusion et tout charme. Les auditeurs se regardent entre eux, n'osant trop exprimer leur désappointement, mais trouvant que le résultat n'a pas répondu à leur attente.[95]

Indeed, Figuier's disappointment with the realities of recorded sound closely echoes similar dismay with the tangible Orient expressed by those visiting the rue du Caire just outside the Galerie des Machines. But this lone voice who described the actual sound of the phonograph as an obstacle to the listening imagination stood out in a chorus of admirers, who celebrated the faithful rendering of sound as a signpost towards the future: thanks to the phonograph, the dream of a "spectacle in an armchair" would come true.[96] In the future, journalists predicted, music would be available at the drop of a hat to serve as sleeping aid or to change someone's mood; to entertain the disabled at home, and to preserve the

---

93. Ibid.
94. Ibid.: "L'on ne peut plus dire désormais qu'il y ait rien d'impossible."
95. Figuier, "Le Pavillon des Téléphones," 11.
96. Millet, "Chroniques: Phonographies," 1: "spectacle dans un fauteuil."

AUTOUR DU PHONOGRAPHE D'EDISON.
Étude d'abrutissement comparé.

Figure 6.8. Paul Léonnec, "L'Exposition comique," *Le Journal amusant*,
24 Aug. 1889, 2.

voices of great singers for all eternity; to allow for repeated enjoyment of
the most beautiful in music and rhetoric.[97] Then the phonograph would
be, so Tiersot said, "a proud instrument."[98] Then, instead of listening to
Gossec's version of the *Marseillaise* (recorded by two cornets) as played at
the Edison exhibition, one might revel in Richard Wagner's *Tristan* or *Parsifal*, recorded in Bayreuth, so that one "might attend [their] performances
in the Galerie des Machines."[99]

Total media control over both the ecstatic and the sonic in music became
a vision in 1889, one which has lasted into our age of digital remastering

97. Durer, *Edison: Sa vie—ses œuvres*, 57; Millet, "Chroniques: Phonographies"; V.-F.
M., "Les Auditions du phonographe dans la Galerie des Machines."

98. Tiersot, "Promenades musicales à l'Exposition," 188: "un fier instrument."

99. Lenôtre, "Edison et le phonographe," 99: "[P]ourquoi ne pas réjouir, à l'aide de
ces appareils, toute une classe de dilettantes, en leur faisant ouïr des mélodies nouvelles
et dignes d'être écoutées; rien ne serait plus simple que d'enregistrer à Bayreuth par
exemple les opéras de Wagner et de nous faire assister, de la Galerie de Machines, aux
représentations de *Tristan* ou de *Parcifal* [*sic*]."

and electronic music.[100] Such preservation of music for the twin objectives of continuous *jouissance,* to be repeated at will, and archival preservation of what is deemed worthy, might be achieved even against the will of the recorded object, as when Adelina Patti's voice was recorded without her knowledge by means of a cleverly disguised phonograph.[101] Secret recordings of that kind might include not only the "stolen voice" of a diva such as Patti or Jules Verne's fictitious soprano, "La Stilla," in his 1892 novel *Le Château des Carpathes,* but even "the voice of the dead" themselves.[102] After all, "as Klaus Theweleit noted, media are always flight apparatuses into the great beyond."[103]

By recording and transmitting music, sound-reproduction devices not only "immortalize" the performers themselves, but become the technical mirror of musical aesthetics of the late nineteenth century. The phonograph is the opposite side of the coin of Diémer's archaeological enterprise of reconstructing lost sounds of the musical past. The operatic telephone transmissions represent an "auditory reality" of a technological kind, while the exotic musics transport the visitors into the unknown realm of Java or Romania. Sounds that have no visible source are sounds that retain an aura of mystery, that express what may be inexpressible, that become sonic symbols of music. Like the Exposition itself, with its twin perspectives of progress and retrospection, the sound-reproduction technologies presented at the Fair offered both: the present as the future past (through the reality and potential of musical recordings), and the future as present through its display of auditory technologies. While this generated excitement about coming riches—both cultural and economic—it also created anxieties for a generation "which has seen these surprising leaps of progress one after another" but which claims the right "to remain sometimes fearful and frightened," even though subsequent generations might share none of those fears.[104]

At the 1889 Exposition Universelle, music was indeed an overwhelmingly present phenomenon that was perceived as one of the defining character traits of this event. Memoirs, newspapers, and images bear witness to the extent of this event's sonic nature and the acoustic awareness of the fairgoers. For scholars today, these sounds are no more than faint traces

100. See Friedrich Kittler, "Wagners wildes Heer," in *Die Symbolisten und Richard Wagner,* ed. Wolfgang Storch with Josef Mackert, 37–43 (Berlin: Edition Hentrich, 1991).

101. A.-Mathieu Villon, *Le Phonographe et ses applications* (Paris: Bernard Tignol, [1894]), 18.

102. Ibid.: "la voix d'un mort." On Jules Verne, see Franc Schuerewegen, *A distance de voix: Essai sur les "machines à parler"* (Lille: Presses Universitaires de Lille, 1994), 38–40.

103. Kittler, *Gramophone, Film, Typewriter,* 13.

104. De Nansouty, "Edison," 1: "qui a vu ces étonnants progrès se presser coup sur coup"; "rester apeurée et craintive parfois."

contained in two-dimensional documents, engendering the dream of time-machine travel that would allow once more for those sounds to come alive, although they would be distorted even then, because our own ears have already heard the music of the future that the listeners to the Edison phonograph only imagined. But for its limitations, my study has shown the intensity with which both professional musicians and lay visitors to the Exposition Universelle experienced the sound world of the fair; it has offered insight into the richness and diversity of musics that were performed by musicians from Java, Paris, Russia, or the United States; and it has engaged with the listeners at the end of telephone transmitters, and those of the Trocadéro concerts, the opera, and the belly dancers. From this thick description of music-making and listening at the Exposition Universelle have emerged broader issues such as authenticity, gender, identity, history, and alterity, which not only characterized the presentation and reception of music in 1889 but which also had their impact on much of musical life during the twentieth century. Thus the 1889 Exposition Universelle in Paris represents a pivotal moment in the history of music in Europe that contained its past, present, and even future.

*Appendix 1*

# Programs of Concerts at the Exposition Universelle

## A. French Concerts at the Trocadéro[1]

### 1. Concerts Lamoureux (conducted by Charles Lamoureux), 23 May 1889

Soloists: Numa Auguez, Marie-Hélène Brunet-Lafleur, Camilla Landi, Jean-Louis Lassalle, Marguerite Martini, Paul Mounet, M. Narçon, Edmond Vergnet.

| | |
|---|---|
| *Patrie!* Ouverture (1873) | Georges Bizet |
| *Le Désert* (1844), part 1 | Félicien David |
| *Loreley* (1882), extracts | Paul and Lucien Hillemacher |
| Symphonie en *ré* mineur (1884) | Gabriel Fauré |
| Andante | |
| *Béatrice et Bénédict* (1862) | Hector Berlioz |
| Duo | |
| *Velleda* (1882) | Charles Lenepveu |
| Scène de la Conjuration | |

\* \* \*

| | |
|---|---|
| *Le Camp de Wallenstein* (1873) | Vincent d'Indy |
| *Eve* (1875), part 1: | Jules Massenet |
| Prologue – La naissance de la femme – | |
| Prélude, scène et duo | |
| *Matinée de Printemps* (1885) | Georges Marty |
| *Geneviève*, légende française (1888) | William Chaumet |

1. The listings are based on the printed programs for all five concerts kept in the "Dossier d'actualités" for 1889, Bibliothèque Historique de la Ville de Paris (B.H.V.P.).

| | |
|---|---|
| *La Mer* (1881) | Victorin Joncières |
| *España* (1883) | Emmanuel Chabrier |

### 2. Association Artistique (conducted by Édouard Colonne), 6 June 1889

Soloists:   Numa Auguez, Jacques Joseph André Bouhy, Émilie Durand-Ulbach, Mme Franck-Duvernoy, André-Joseph Quirot, Edmond Vergnet, Mlle X...

Organ:   Alexandre Guilmant

| | |
|---|---|
| *Béatrice* (1880) | Émile Bernard |
| Overture | |
| *Les Béatitudes* (1880), no. 8 | César Franck |
| *La Korrigane,* ballet (1880) | Charles Marie Widor |
| Adagio – Scherzettino – Valse lente | |
| *Aben-Hamet* (1884) | Théodore Dubois |
| Grand duo of Act 3 | |
| *Rapsodie norvégienne* (1879) | Edouard Lalo |
| Andantino – Presto | |
| *Ludus pro patria* (1888), extract: *La Nuit d'amour* | Augusta Holmès |
| Prélude instrumental – Chœur | |
| *L'Arlésienne* (1872) | Georges Bizet |
| Prélude – Minuetto – Entr'acte du 3e acte | |

* * *

| | |
|---|---|
| *Requiem* (1837), no. 2 | Hector Berlioz |
| *Dies irae* – *Tuba mirum* | |
| *Air de danse varié* (1878), for strings | Gaston Salvayre |
| *La Tempête* (1880), extracts from Part 2 | Alphonse Duvernoy |
| *Première Suite d'orchestre* (1883) | Gabriel Pierné |
| Entrée en forme et Menuet – Intermezzo | |
| *Symphonie Légendaire* (1886) | Benjamin Godard |
| Dans la Cathédrale | |
| *Judith,* drame lyrique (1879), extracts from Part 1 | Charles Lefebvre |
| Air de Judith – Chœur | |
| *Danse persane* (1880) | Ernest Guiraud |

### 3. Société des Concerts du Conservatoire (conducted by Jules Garcin), 20 June 1889

Soloists:   Numa Auguez, Rose Caron, Camilla Landi, Mme Franck-Duvernoy, Edmond Vergnet

Symphonie en *ut* mineur (1886)     Camille Saint-Saëns
  I. Introduction, allegro, poco adagio – II. Scherzo,
  Finale
*Les Abencérages* (1813)     Luigi Cherubini
Symphonie no. 3 en *mi bémol*     Henri Reber
  Andantino
*Psyché* (1857), extracts     Ambroise Thomas
  Introduction – Chœur des Nymphes – Récit et
  Romance du Sommeil – Invocation de la nuit –
  Scène de l'Extase – Bacchanale

\* \* \*

*Sigurd* (1884), extracts     Ernest Reyer
  Ouverture – final du 2e acte
*La Muette de Portici* (1828)     Daniel-François-Esprit
  Prière     Auber
*Le Roi d'amuse*, Airs de danse dans le style ancien     Léo Delibes
  (1882)
  I. Gaillarde – II. Scène du Bouquet – II. Madrigal –
  IV. Passepied – V. Reprise de la Gaillarde
*Mors et Vita*, oratorio (1885), extracts     Charles Gounod
  Lacrymosa – Quid Sum Miser – Felix Culpa –
  Judex – Agnus Dei, Communion, Épilogue
  instrumental

**4. Opéra-Comique (conducted by Jules Danbé), 5 September 1889**

Soloists:   Mathilde Auguez, Esther Chevalier, Henry Cobalet, Blanche
Deschamps, Sylvain Dupuis, Mlle Mary, Cécile Simonnet,
Gabriel Soulacroix, Émile-Alexandre Taskin

Organ:   Auguste-Ernest Bazille

*Zampa* (1831)     Ferdinand Hérold
  Overture
*Joseph* (1807), extracts     Étienne-Nicolas Méhul
  A. Duo – B. Cantique
*Joli Gille* (1884)     Ferdinand Poise
  Entracte
*Jean de Nivelle* (1880), extracts     Léo Delibes
  A. *Chœur des Vendageuses* – B. *Ballade de la
  Mandragore*
*Capitaine Fracasse* (1878)     Émile Pessard
  Menuet des petits violons

*Proserpine* (1887)                                          Camille Saint-Saëns
    Finale du 2e acte


\* \* \*


*Le Domino noir* (1837)                              Daniel-François-Esprit Auber
    Overture
*La Déesse et le Berger* (1863)                         Jules-Laurent Duprato
    Romance
*La Statue* (1861), extracts                                       Ernest Reyer
    A. *Introduction* du 2e acte – B. Récit et
    Air de Margyane à la Fontaine – C. Grand
    récit de Sélim – D. *Marche de la caravane* et
    Air de Margyane
*Giralda* (1850)                                                  Adolphe Adam
    Overture
*Les Saisons* (1855), sélection                                   Victor Massé
    A. Entr'acte du troisième acte –
    B. *Andante* (orgue) – C. Air: "Ah!
    Pourquoi suis-je revenue" – D. *Chanson du
    Blé*
*La Jolie Fille de Perth* (1866), extracts                       Georges Bizet
    A. *Danse Bohémienne* – B. *Trio* du 1$^{er}$ acte –
    C. *Quatuor* – D. Chœur de la *Saint-Valentin*
*Les Amoureux de Catherine* (1876)                            Henri Maréchal
    Finale

### 5. Opéra (conducted by Auguste Vianesi), 19 September 1889

Soloists:   Ada Adiny, Mme Agussol, Rosa Bosman, M. Dubullé, Valentin
          Duc, M. Muratet, M. Plançon

*La Muette de Portici* (1828)                        Daniel-François-Esprit Auber
    A. Ouverture – B. Duo "Amour sacré
    de la patrie"
*Herculanum* (1859)                                              Félicien David
    A. Chœur des Chrétiens – B. Prière
*Patrie!* (1886)                                              Émile Paladilhe
    Ballet: A. Passe-Pied – B. Pavane – C. Valse –
    D. Andante et Finale
*Le Roi de Lahore* (1877)                                       Jules Massenet
    Final du 1er acte


\* \* \*

*Françoise de Rimini* (1882)     Ambroise Thomas
    Prologue
*Sapho* (1851)     Charles Gounod
    A. Final du 1er acte – B. Stances
*Guido et Ginevra* (1838)     Fromental Halévy
    Scène et air du Tombeau
*La Vestale* (1807)     Gaspare Spontini
    Final du 2e acte

## B. Organ Concerts at the Trocadéro[2]

| | |
|---|---|
| 20 May | Henri Dallier (organist of Saint Eustache, Paris) |
| 27 May | Jules Stoltz (organist of Saint-Ambroise, Paris) |
| 3 June | Edmond Lemaigre (organist of the Cathedral of Clermont-Ferrand) |
| 13 June | Alexandre Guilmant (organist at La Trinité and resident organist at the Trocadéro; *concert with orchestra*) |
| 17 June | Ernest Gigout (organist of Saint Augustin, Paris) |
| 27 June | Alexandre Guilmant (*concert with orchestra*) |
| 3 July | Charles-Marie Widor (organist of Saint Sulpice, Paris) |
| 25 July | Adhémar Decq (organist of Saint Honoré, Paris) |
| 2 August | Clarence Eddy (organist of the First Presbyterian Church, Chicago) |
| 31 August | Walter Handel Thorley (organist from the Blackburn Cathedral) |
| 9 September | Alexandre Guilmant ("*historic*" organ concert) |
| 15 September | Filipo Capocci (organist of San Giovanni in Laterano, Rome) |
| 23 September | Émile Bouchère (*maître de chapelle* of La Trinité, Paris) |

## C. Transcription of Programs for the Two Concerts of *Musique française ancienne et moderne*, 25 and 31 May 1889[3]

N.B.: Both programs contain the following note: "La Partie ancienne sera jouée sur les instruments du temps."

---

2. I am grateful to Arthur Lawrence for his help with the names and positions of the organists.

3. Source: Concert programs in the collection of the B.H.V.P.

### 1. Palais du Trocadéro, 25 May 1889

1. *Trio* pour Piano, Violon et Violoncelle      C. Saint-Saëns
   MM. Diémer, Rémy et Delsart
2. *Les Berceaux*      G. Fauré
   *Le Doux Appel*      Ch. M. Widor
   Mlle Lépine
3. *Suite* pour Violon et Piano      E. Bernard
   MM. Rémy et Diémer
4. *Suite* pour Hautbois et Piano      L. Diémer
   MM. Gillet et Diémer
5. *Canzonetta* du 3e quatuor à cordes      G. Alary
   *Sérénade* pour instruments à cordes      E. Lalo
   MM. Rémy, Parent, Van Waefelghem
   et Delsart

* * *

6. *Sonate* pour violoncelle      Berteau (1700)
   M. J. Delsart      (Fondateur de l'École de Violoncelle)
7. *Le Carillon de Cythère*      F. Couperin (1720)
   *Le Coucou*      Claude Daquin (1735)
   *Gavotte*      Rameau (1741)
   Clavecin: M. L. Diémer
8. a. *Sarabande grave* pour la Viole de gambe      Marais (1692)
   M. J. Delsart
   b. *Menuet* pour la Viole d'amour      Milandre (1770)
   Van Waefelghem
9. Ariette de la Belle Arsène      Monsigny (1775)
   Mlle Lépine
10. *Pièces en concert* (Clavecin, Flûte et Basse)      Rameau (1741)
    *Menuets, Tambourin, L'Indiscrète*
    MM. Diémer, Taffanel et Delsart

Clavecin de P. Taskin (1769)

### 2. Palais du Trocadéro, 31 May 1889

1. *Trio* pour Piano, Violon et Violoncelle      E. Lalo
   MM. Diémer, Rémy et Delsart
2. *La Jeune Captive*      Ch. Lenepveu
   Mlle Lépine
3. *Adagio* et *Vivace* de Pièces pour Violoncelle      Ch. M. Widor
   et Piano (Transcrits par J. Delsart)
   MM. J. Delsart et Widor

4. *Barcarolle mélancolique* et *Scherzo*                     Ch. Lenepveu
   M. Taffanel
5. *Duos* pour deux Violons                                   B. Godard
   (*Berceuse, Minuet, Sérénade*)
   MM. Rémy et Parent

* * *

6. *Sarabande* et *Menuet* pour Quinton                       Marais (1692)
   Viole d'amour et Viole da gambe
   MM. Balbreck, Van Waefelghem et Delsart
7. *Musette en rondeau*                                       Rameau (1741)
   *Le Rappel des Oiseaux*                                    Rameau
   *Le Réveil-Matin*                                     F. Couperin (1720)
   Clavecin: M. L. Diémer
8. *Andante* pour Viole d'amour                               Milandre (1770)
   Van Waefelghem
   *Sarabande* et *Musette* pour Viole de gambe               Marais (1692)
   M. J. Delsart
9. *Romance*                                                  Garat
   *Vieille Chanson normande*                            (Auteur inconnu)
   Mlle Lépine
10. *Le Tambourin*, pièce pour Violon                         Leclair (1738)
    M. Rémy
11. *Pièces en concert* (Clavecin, Flûte et Basse)            Rameau (1741)
    *La Forqueray, la Timide, la Pantomime*
    MM. Diémer, Taffanel et Delsart

Clavecin de Pascal Taskin (1769)

## D. Reconstructed Programs for the Two Concerts of *Musique italienne ancienne et moderne*, 5 and 12 June 1889[4]

### 1. Théâtre de la Gaîté, 5 June 1889

Ouverture d'*Il matrimonio segreto*        Domenico Nicola Cimarosa
                                                    (1749–1801)
*Scherzo* à trois voix                     Giovanni Battista Martini
   chanté par les chœurs                            (1706–1794)

---

4. Source: Concert announcements and reviews in *Le Figaro, Gil Blas, Le Temps*, and *Le Soir.*

| | |
|---|---|
| *Air d'église* | Alessandro Stradella |
| exécuté par l'orchestre | (1639–1682) |
| Cantate *Povera pellegrina* | Domenico Scarlatti |
| par Mlle Bevilacqua | (1685–1757) |
| *Gavotte*, pour instruments à vents | Jean-Baptiste Lulli |
| | (1632–1687) |
| | |
| Air *Pur dicesti* | Antonio Lotti |
| chanté par Mlle Calvé | (1666–1740) |
| *Ronda* | Luigi Cherubini |
| chantée par les chœurs | (1760–1842) |
| *Pastorale* | Giuseppe Sammartini |
| orchestrée par Giuseppe Martucci | (1695–1750) |

* * *

| | |
|---|---|
| Scène et air du troisième acte de l'opéra *Stella* | Salvatore Auteri |
| par Mlle Jodici et les chœurs | (1845–1924) |
| *Romance* sans paroles, pour instruments à cordes | Giovanni Bolzoni |
| | (1841–1919) |
| | |
| Cavatine de *Ernani* | Giuseppe Verdi |
| chantée par Mlle Calvé | (1813–1901) |
| *Gavotte* pour instruments à cordes | Giovanni Sgambati |
| orchestrée par Luigi Mancinelli | (1841–1914) |
| *Confutatis maledictis* de la Messe de *Requiem* | Giuseppe Verdi |
| chanté par M. Navarrini | (1831–1901) |
| *Symphonie* en *mi* mineur | Alberto Franchetti |
| A. Allegro – B. Larghetto – | (1860–1942) |
| C. Vivace | |

## 2. Théâtre de la Gaîté, 12 June 1889

| | |
|---|---|
| Ouverture de *Le due giornate* | Luigi Cherubini |
| | (1760–1842) |
| *Madrigal Sulle rive del Tebro* | Giov. Pierluigi da Palestrina |
| chanté par les chœurs | (1525/26–1594) |
| Air de la *Biondina in gondoletta* | Ferdinando Paër |
| chanté par Mme Muller de la Source | (1771–1839) |
| *Gavotte* | Giovanni Battista Martini |
| | (1706–1784) |
| | |
| Ballata: *La Zingara* | Gaëtano Donizetti |
| chanté par Mlle Calvé | (1797–1848) |
| Madrigal *Il giocatore sfortunato* | Giovanni Clari |
| chanté par les chœurs | (1677–1754) |

* * *

| | |
|---|---|
| *Danse des fleurs* et *Sarabande* | Spiro Samara |
| de l'opéra *Flora mirabilis* | (1861–1917) |
| exécuté par l'orchestre | |
| Air du 3e acte de *Flora mirabilis* | Spiro Samara |
| chanté par Mlle Calvé | (1861–1917) |
| Trio de *L'Italiana in Algeri* | Gioacchino Rossini |
| chanté par MM. Fagotti, Navarrini et | (1792–1868) |
| Frigiotti | |
| *Symphonie* en *mi* mineur | Alberto Franchetti |
| A. Allegro – B. Larghetto – C. Vivace | (1860–1942) |
| *La Forza del destino* | Giuseppe Verdi |
| Air, chœur et final du 3e acte | (1813–1901) |
| chanté par Mme Jodici, M. Navarrini | |
| et les chœurs | |
| *Symphonie* en *do* | Luigi Forino |
| | (1868–1936) |

# E. Programs of Major Foreign Concerts at the Trocadéro[5]

## 1. First Russian Concert, 22 June 1889

Piano solo: Lavrov
        The piano was by the manufacturer J. Becker (Saint Petersburg)
Musicians from the Orchestre Colonne, conducted by Nikolay Rimsky-Korsakov

| | |
|---|---|
| *Ruslan and Ludmilla* (1842) | Mikhail Ivanovich Glinka |
| Overture | |
| *In Central Asia* (1880) | Aleksandr Borodin |
| Concerto no. 1 in B-flat Major for piano | Pyotr Il'ych Tchaikovsky |
| and orchestra, Op. 23 (1875) | |
| Allegro | |
| *Antar*, symphony no. 2, Op. 9 (1875) | Nikolay Rimsky-Korsakov |

* * *

| | |
|---|---|
| *Second Overture on Russian Themes* (1884) | Mily Alekseyevich Balakirev |
| *Marche solennelle* in E-flat Major, Op. 18 (1881) | Cesar Cui |
| Works for Piano Solo | |
| A. *Impromptu* from Op. 35 (1881) | Cesar Cui |
| B. *Intermezzo* in B-flat Major, Op. 8, no. 1 (1883) | Anatoly Lyadov |
| C. *Prelude* in B-flat Major, Op. 13, no. 2 (1887) | Anatoly Lyadov |
| D. *Novelette* in C Minor, Op. 20 (1889) | Anatoly Lyadov |

    5. Unless otherwise stated, the listings in 1E are based on the printed programs for
the concerts kept in the "Dossier d'actualités" for 1889, B.H.V.P.

*Fantasy over Finnish Airs* (1867)          Aleksandr Dargomïzhsky
*Stenka Razine*, symphonic poem, Op. 13 (1885)    Aleksandr Glazunov
    conducted by the composer

## 2. Second Russian Concert, 29 June 1889

Piano solo:   Lavrov
             The piano was by the manufacturer J. Becker (Saint
             Petersburg)
Musicians from the Orchestre Colonne, conducted by Nikolay
Rimsky-Korsakov

Symphony no. 2, in F-sharp Minor, Op. 16 (1886)    Aleksandr Glazunov
    conducted by the composer
    I. Andante maestoso, Allegro –
    II. Andante – III. Allegro vivace –
    IV. Intrada, Allegro sostenuto,
    Finale-Allegro
Concerto in C-sharp Major for piano    Nikolay Rimsky-Korsakov
    and orchestra, Op. 30 (1883)
*Kamarinskaya*, fantasy on Russian themes (1848)    Mikhail Ivanovich
                                     Glinka

                        * * *

*Prince Igor*    Aleksandr Borodin
    I. Polovtsian March – II. Polovtsian Dances (1875)
*A Night on the Bald Mountain* (1867)    Modest Musorgsky
Works for Piano Solo
    A. *Mazurka* no 4 in G-flat Major (1886)    Mily Alekseyevich
                                        Balakirev
    B. *Barcarolle* in G Minor, from    Pyotr Il'ych Tchaikovsky
       *Les Saisons* (1873)
    C. *Étude* in A Major    Felix Blumenfeld
*Scherzo for Orchestra* in D Major, Op. 16 (1886)    Anatoly Lyadov
*Capriccio Espagnol*, Op. 34 (1887)    Nikolay Rimsky-Korsakov

## 3. First Finnish Concert, 6 July 1889[6]

Muntra Musikanter (Helsinki University Student Choir), conducted by
Gösta Sohlström

*March of the "MM"* ("Muntra Musikanter")    Karl August Riccius

---

6. Based on the documents at the B.H.V.P., and Helena Tyrväinen, "Suomalaiset Pariisin maailmannäyttelyiden 1889 ja 1900 musiikkiohjelmissa," *Musiikkitiede* 1–2 (1994): 30–31.

| | |
|---|---|
| *Song of Suomi* ("Suomis Sång") | Fredrik Pacius |
| *Dans la forêt* ("Metsässä") | Carl Amand Mangold |
| *Les Adieux* ("Virran reunalla") | |
| Solo by Filep Forsten (baritone), | |
| accompanied by the choir | |
| *Olav Trygvason* | Friedrich August Reissiger |

* * *

| | |
|---|---|
| *Cortège nuptial de Hardanger* | Halfdan Kjerulf |
| ("Brudefærden i Hardanger") | |
| *Ma Bien-Aimée est loin* | |
| *La Sérénade au bord de l'eau* | Halfdan Kjerulf |
| ("Serenade ved Strandbredden") | |
| Solo by Filep Forsten (baritone), | |
| accompanied by the choir | |
| *Chant Suédois* | |
| *March of Björneborg* ("Björneborgarnes Marsch") | Fredrik Pacius |
| *Les Noces villageoises à la ferme* | August Söderman |
| ("Ett bondbröllop") | |
| *Le Départ pour l'église – A l'église –* | |
| *Chanson des souhaits – A la ferme* | |

## 4. Second Finish Concert, 8 July 1889

Soloist: Filep Forsten (baritone)
Muntra Musikanter (Helsinki University Student Choir), conducted by
Gösta Sohlström

| | |
|---|---|
| *March of the "MM"* ("Muntra Musikanter") | Karl August Riccius |
| *Le Départ du Paquebot* ("Sångfåglarna") | Otto Jonas Lindblad |
| *Les Sons des Cloches* | Karl Flodin |
| *Chant populaire finlandais* | |
| *Chant Suédois* (*Fredmans epistlar*, no 38) | Carl-Michael Bellman |

* * *

| | |
|---|---|
| *Les Sons* ("Tonerna") | Gustaf Lagercrantz |
| *Le Repos à la Source* | Carl-Michael Bellman |
| *La Sérénade au bord de l'eau* | Halfdan Kjerulf |
| ("Serenade ved Strandbredden") | |
| *Olav Trygvason* | Friedrich August Reissiger |

* * *

*Chant populaire Suédois*
*Chant populaire Finlandais*

*Les Noces villageoises à la ferme*                                            August Söderman
    ("Ett bondbröllop")
    *Le Départ pour l'église – A l'église – Chanson*
    *des souhaits – A la ferme*
*Les Étoiles*
*March of Björneborg* ("Björneborgarnes Marsch")              Fredrik Pacius

### 5. American Concert, 12 July 1889[7]

Soloists:   Edward MacDowell (piano), Willis Nowell (violin), Maude
            Starvetta (mezzo-soprano), Emma Sylvania (soprano)
Orchestre de l'Opéra-Comique, conducted by Frank van der Stucken

*In the Mountains*, overture, Op. 14 (1886)                     Arthur Foote
Concerto no. 2 in D Minor for piano                     Edward MacDowell
    and orchestra, Op. 23 (1886)
    Larghetto calmato; Piu mosso,
    con passione – Presto giocoso –
    Largo; Molto allegro
Three Songs
    *In Bygone Days*                            George Whitefield Chadwick
    *Milkmaid's Song*                                          Arthur Foote
    *Where the Lindens Bloom*                                   Dudley Buck
*La Tempête*, orchestral suite, op. 8 (1882)        Frank van der Stucken
    Invocation of Prospero; Dance of the
    Gnomes – Mélodrama – Dance of the
    Harvesters – Dance of the
    Nymphs – Infernal Hunt

* * *

*Melpomene*, dramatic overture (1887)          George Whitefield Chadwick
*Romance et Polonaise* for violin and                 Henry Holden Huss
    orchestra
*Oedipus Tyrannus*, incidental music,                 John Knowles Paine
    Op. 35 (1881)
    Prelude
*Carneval Scene*, Op. 5 (1887)                           Arthur Bird
Three Songs
    *Moonlight*                                 Frank van der Stucken

---

7. For additional information for the American program, see Douglas Bomberger: *"A Tidal Wave of Encouragement": American Composers' Concerts in the Gilded Age* (Westport, CT, and London: Praeger, 2002), 190.

| | |
|---|---|
| *Ojala*, text by George Eliot (1889) | Margaret Ruthven Lang |
| *Early Love* | Frank van der Stucken |
| Festival overture on *The Star-Spangled Banner* | Dudley Buck |

## 6. First Norwegian Concert, 27 July 1889[8]

Soloist:   Thorvald Lammers (voice)
Sociétés chorales norvégiennes (Christiana), conducted by Olams-
Andreas Grøndahl
Orchestre de l'Opéra-Comique, conducted by Gabriel Marie

| | |
|---|---|
| *Le Carnaval à Paris*, fantaisie pour orchestre, Op. 9 (1872) | Johan Svendsen |
| *Salut!* ("Sangerhilsen"), words by S. Skavlan (1883) | Edvard Grieg |
| *Charivari* | Johan Peter Selmer |
| *Dans la Forêt*, words by Johan Behrens | Olams-Andreas Grøndahl |
| *Magnus aveugle*, words by Bjørnstjerne Bjørnson | Olams-Andreas Grøndahl |
| *Olaf Trygvason*, words by Bjørnstjerne Bjørnson | Friedrich August Reissiger |
| *Two Elegiac Melodies* for String Orchestra, Op. 34 (1880) | Edvard Grieg |
| *Røtnamsknut*, Album for Male Voices, no. 12 (1878) | Edvard Grieg |
| *Jour d'été* ("Sommervise") | Halfdan Kjerulf |
| *La Sérénade au bord de l'eau* ("Serenade ved Strandbredden") | Halfdan Kjerulf |
| *Cortège nuptial de Hardanger* ("Brudefærden i Hardanger") | Halfdan Kjerulf |
| *Terre!* ("Landkjenning"), op. 31, words by Bjørnstjerne Bjørnson (1881) | Edvard Grieg |
| Symphony no. 2 in B-flat Major, Op. 15 (1874) | Johan Svendsen |

## 7. Second Norwegian Concert, 29 July 1889

Soloist:   Agathe Ursula Backer-Grøndahl (piano)
Sociétés chorales norvégiennes (Christiana), conducted by Olams-
Andreas Grøndahl
Orchestre de l'Opéra-Comique, conducted by Gabriel Marie

8. Program of first Norwegian concert reconstructed after the detailed review by Balthasar Claes [Camille Benoît], "Chronique parisienne," *Le Guide musical* 35 (1889), 196–97.

| | |
|---|---|
| *L'Automne* ("I høst"), grande ouverture de concert, Op. 11 (1887) | Edvard Grieg |
| *Les Montagnes de la Norvège*, words by Henrik Wergeland | Halfdan Kjerulf |
| *Røtnamsknut*, Album for Male Voices, no. 12 (1878) | Edvard Grieg |
| *Dans la Forêt*, words by Johan Behrens | Olams-Andreas Grøndahl |
| *Magnus aveugle*, words by Bjørnstjerne Bjørnson | O.-A. Grøndahl |
| *La Tempête*, words by J.-G. Welkeren | Johan Selmer |
| *Jotunheimen*, words by O.-P. Monrad | Ole Olsen |
| Concert for piano and orchestra in A Minor, Op. 16 (1868) | Edvard Grieg |
| *Chant à la Norvège* ("Norsk faedrelandssang"), words by Bjørnstjerne Bjørnson (1864) | Rikard Nordraak |
| *Hymne*, words by Henrik Wergeland | Catharinus Elling |
| *Olaf Trygvason*, words by Bjørnstjerne Bjørnson | Friedrich August Reissiger |
| *Two Elegiac Melodies* for string orchestra, Op. 34 (1880) | Edvard Grieg |
| *Terre!* ("Landkjenning"), Op. 31, words by Bjørnstjerne Bjørnson (1881) | Edvard Grieg |

## 8. First Concert of the Spanish Choral Society, 20 August 1889

Orphéon Coruñès, no. 4, conducted by Pascual Veiga

"Audition d'œuvres des Compositeurs Espagnols, Chants Populaires de l'ancienne Ibérie Européenne"

## 9. Second Concert of the Spanish Choral Society, 24 August 1889

Orphéon Coruñès, no. 4, conducted by Pascual Veiga

| | |
|---|---|
| *Maladie d'amour*, polka | Pascual Veiga |
| *Les Astrabos* | Pascual Veiga |
| *Souvenir à M. Péreire* | Pascual Veiga |
| *O Esprito Gallego* (Muiñeira) | Pascual Veiga |

* * *

| | |
|---|---|
| *La Escala* (Muiñeira) | Gonzalo Vidal |
| *Une Soirée à Naples* | Pascual Veiga |
| *Sérénade* | Pedro Tintorer |
| *L'Aubade* | Pascual Veiga |

## 10. "Grandes Fêtes Espagnoles," 29 August 1889

Part 1

Union Artistico Musical de Madrid, conducted by M. Perez

*El primer dia Feliz*, symphony (1872)                    Manuel Fernandez Caballero
*La Corte de Granada*, fantaisie                                    Ruperto Chapì
   mauresque (1873)
   A. Grenada (Marche au tournoi) –
   B. Méditation – C. Sérénade – D. Final
*Bolero de Concert*                                    Adolfo Llanos y Alcaraz

Part 2

Estudiantina "El Figaro" (40 mandolin players), conducted by M. Mora

*Turkish March*                                    Wolfgang Amadeus Mozart
*Luisito*, waltz                                    Antonio L. Mora
Défilé and dances by the corps de ballet,
   representing the nine regions of Spain

La Infantil Rondella Aragonese, conducted by M. Pera y Nebot

*El Certamen* (Jota)                                    Ruperto Chapì
*Valse Espagnole*                                    M. Pera y Nebot

Part 3
Grandes Danses by the Corps de Ballet,
accompanied by the Union Artistico Musical de Madrid

## 11. First Concert of the Russian National Choir, 12 September 1889

Chapelle nationale russe (*Slavyanskaya Kappella*), conducted by Dmitri
Slavyansky d'Agrenev

*Sviatogor*, poème épique ("Bylona o Sviatgore")
*La Neige blanche dans les champs*, chanson champêtre ("Ne belli snegui")
*Ma Fille aux joues roses*, ronde villageoise ("Belolitza, krouglolotza")
*Le Coucher du soleil (Le Crépuscule)*, chanson champêtre ("Zaria vetcherniaia")
*Le Bouleau dans les champs*, chanson joyeuse ("Vo pole beresa stoiala")
*Kamarinskaia*, célèbre chanson à danser ("Ah, tchoudak je ti,
   kamarisnki mougik")

\* \* \*

*Le Sarafane rouge*, complainte d'une jeune fille ("Krasni sarafane")
*Dans le Bosquet du petit père*, chant de jeune fille ("Kak ou batiouchki")
*Devant notre Portail*, chanson à danser ("Kak ou nachikh ou vorote")

Polish Folk Songs
  *Attends, ma blanche colombe!* ("Podogedi moia krassolka!")
  *L'Arrivée des faucons* ("Priletali sokoli")
*Les Beaux Yeux bleus,* mazurka polonaise ("Otchi, otchi goloubiia")
*Oh! Gémis, mon pieu!,* chanson des charpentiers ("Aie, doubinouchka, okhni!")

### 12. Second Concert of the Russian National Choir, 15 September 1889

Chapelle nationale russe (*Slavyanskaya Kappella*), conducted by Dmitri Slavyansky d'Agrenev

*Poème épique, chantant le célèbre héros du onzième siècle, Dobrynia Nikititeb*
*Cherchez mon Anneau que je cache,* chant de bonne aventure
*A toi mon cœur, jeune homme aux yeux noirs!* chant dialogué
*Le Sommeil m'accable,* chanson des mœurs
*Le Petit Obier et le petit framboisier* ("Kalinka, Malinka, Moia")
*Gloire à l'astre du jour, Gloire!* Hymne ancien

* * *

*En Descendant le Wolga,* célèbre chanson ancienne ("Vnis po matuchke po Wolgue")
*Ivoutchka,* chanson lyrique
*Oh! Pourquoi me marie-t-on si tôt,* chanson petit-russienne
*L'Obier de la montagne,* ballade sibérienne
*El Oukhnem*
*Il Passe un Jeune Homme le long du village,* chanson à danser

### 13. Third Concert of the Russian National Choir, 18 September 1889

Chapelle nationale russe (*Slavyanskaya Kappella*), conducted by Dmitri Slavyansky d'Agrenev

### 14. Concert of the Choir from Saint-Sébastien, 20 September 1889

Société Chorale de Saint-Sébastien and its Estudiantina, conducted by Mariano Arnao

| | |
|---|---|
| *Viva la Francia* (Pas redoublé) | Manuel Garcia |
| *Charmangarria* (Zortzico) | José Juan Santezteban |
| *Danse américaine* | J. Perez |
| *Orannena* (Zortzico) | Felipe Gorriti |
| *Le Secret de ma Dame,* seguidillas | Barvieri |
| *Soirée d'automne* | Laurent de Rillé |
| *Mémoire d'un étudiant* (Jota) | Audrid |
| *Ume eder bar* (Zortzico) | José Juan Santezteban |

\* \* \*

| | |
|---|---|
| *Chanson de la brise* | J. Carlez |
| *El Centenario de Calderon* (Pas redoublé) | Erviti |
| *Madrid* | François-Auguste Gevaert |
| *La Cubana*, dance | H. Rodriguez |
| *Oh Euskal erri maitea* (Zortzico) | Sarriegui |
| *El Barberillo de Lavapies*, seguillas | Barvieri |
| *Sérénade d'hiver* | Camille Saint-Saëns |
| *Les Déesses de l'Olympe* | Audrid |

### 15. Fourth Concert of the Russian National Choir, 21 September 1889

Chapelle nationale russe (*Slavyanskaya Kappella*), conducted by Dmitri Slavyansky d'Agrenev

### 16. Belgian Concert, 28 September 1889

Soloists: Rosa Bosman, Blanche Deschamps, Eva Dufranne, M. Fournets, Gabriel Soulacroix, Alexandre Talazac
Piano: Gabrielle Ferrari
Violin: Martin Marsick
Orchestre de l'Opéra-Comique, conducted by Léon Jehin

| | |
|---|---|
| *Yolande* | Emiel Wambach |
|    Marche des Corporations | |
| *Richard, Cœur de Lion* | André Ernest Modeste Grétry |
|    Air | |
| *Scènes de ballet* | Léon Jehin |
|    Jeux et Danses – Intermezzo – Pàs | |
|    guerrier – Apparition et Bacchanale | |
| Two Songs | |
|    *Sonnet* | Gustave Huberti |
|    *Les Porcherons*, romance | Albert Grisar |
| *Daphnis et Chloé* | Fernand Le Borne |
|    Prélude, scène et duo | |
| Piano Pieces | Edgard Tinel |
| *Kermesse flamande*, extract from the ballet *Milenka* | Jan Blockx |
|    Kermesse – Danse des sabots – Entrée des | |
|    rhétoriciens (thème ancien) – Scène d'amour – | |
|    Entrée des zingari – Finale | |

\* \* \*

| | |
|---|---|
| *Charlotte Corday* | Peter Benoit |
|    Overture | |

*Anacréon*                                         André Ernest Modeste Grétry
    Air
Concerto no. 1 in E Major for                              Henri Vieuxtemps
    violin and orchestra
    First movement
*Patria*                                               Théodore Radoux
    Prelude to the third part, *La Paix*
*L'Apollonide,* Élégie funèbre                             Franz Servais
    Introduction to Act 3
*J'avais rêvé*                                          Edouard Lassen
*Le Capitaine Henriot*                           François-Auguste Gevaert
    Duo
*Quentin Durward*                                François-Auguste Gevaert
    Romance – Air – Trio
*Polonaise* in D Major                                  Auguste Dupont

# *Appendix 2*

# Performances at the Opéra and the Opéra-Comique during the Exposition Universelle

## Works Performed[1]

Opéra:

Delibes, Léo. *Coppélia, ou La Fille aux yeux d'émail* (1870), 2 acts, libr. by Charles Nuitter.

Gounod, Charles. *Faust* (1859), 5 acts, libr. by Jules Barbier and Michel Carré.

Gounod, Charles. *Roméo et Juliette* (1867), 5 acts, libr. by Jules Barbier and Michel Carré.

Halévy, Fromental. *La Juive* (1835), 5 acts, libr. by Eugène Scribe.

Massenet, Jules. *Le Cid* (1885), 4 acts, libr. by Adolphe d'Ennery, Edouard Blau, and Louis Gallet.

Meyerbeer, Giacomo. *Les Huguenots* (1836), 5 acts, libr. by Eugène Scribe and Émile Deschamps.

Meyerbeer, Giacomo. *Le Prophète* (1849), 5 acts, libr. by Eugène Scribe.

Meyerbeer, Giacomo. *L'Africaine* (1865), 5 acts, libr. by Eugène Scribe, François Joseph Fétis, et al.

Paladilhe, Émile. *Patrie!* (1886), 5 acts, libr. by Victorien Sardou and Louis Gallet.

Rossini, Gioacchino. *Guillaume Tell* (1829), 5 acts, libr. by Étienne de Jouy and Hippolyte-Louis-Florent Bis.

Saint-Saëns, Camille. *Henry VIII* (1883), 4 acts, libr. by Léonce Détroyat and Armand Silvestre.

1. This list is based on the daily listings of *Le Figaro*, on the *Journal de bord* of the Opéra and on the *Journal de bord* of the Opéra-Comique (both archived in the Bibliothèque de l'Opéra, Paris).

Thomas, Ambroise. *Hamlet* (1868), 5 acts, libr. by Jules Barbier and Michel Carré.

Thomas, Ambroise. *La Tempête* (1889), 3 acts, libr. by Jules Barbier.

Verdi, Giuseppe. *Rigoletto* (1851), 3 acts, libr. by Francesco Maria Piave.

Verdi, Giuseppe. *Aida* (1871), 4 acts, libr. by Antonio Ghislanzoni, after a scenario by Auguste Mariette.

Opéra-Comique:

Adam, Adolphe. *Le Chalet* (1834), 1 act, libr. by Eugène Scribe and Mélesville [Anne-Honoré-Joseph Duveyrier].

Auber, Daniel-François-Esprit. *Fra Diavolo* (1830), 3 acts, libr. by Eugène Scribe.

Auber, Daniel-François-Esprit. *Le Domino noir* (1837), 3 acts, libr. by Eugène Scribe.

Bemberg, Hermann. *Le Baiser de Suzon* (1888), 1 act, libr. by Pierre Barbier.

Bizet, Georges. *Carmen* (1875), 4 acts, libr. by Henri Meilhac and Ludovic Halévy.

Boieldieu, François-Adrien. *La Dame blanche* (1825), 3 acts, libr. by Eugène Scribe.

Dalayrac, Nicholas-Marie. *Raoul, Sire de Créqui* (1789), 3 acts, libr. by Bernard Boutet de Monvel.

Dalayrac, Nicholas-Marie. *La Soirée orageuse* (1790), 1 act, libr. by Jean Baptiste Radet.

Deffès, Louis. *Le Café du roi* (1861), 1 act, libr. by Henri Meilhac.

Donizetti, Gaetano. *La Fille du régiment* (1840), 2 acts, libr. by Jules Henri Vernoy de Saint-Georges and Jean-François Alfred Bayard.

Gounod, Charles. *Philémon et Baucis* (1860), 2 acts, libr. by Jules Barbier and Michel Carré.

Grétry, André Ernest Modeste. *Richard, Cœur de Lion* (1784), 3 acts, libr. by Michel Jean Sedaine.

Hérold, Ferdinand. *Zampa* (1831), 3 acts, libr. by Mélesville [Anne-Honoré-Joseph Duveyrier].

Hérold, Ferdinand. *Le Pré aux clercs* (1832), 3 acts, libr. by François Antoine Eugène de Planard.

Isouard, Niccolò. *Les Rendez-vous bourgeois* (1807), 1 act, libr. by François Benoît Hoffmann.

Lacome, Paul. *La Nuit de Saint Jean* (1882), 1 act, libr. by M. M. A. Delacour and J. de Lau Lusignan.

Lalo, Edouard. *Le Roi d'Ys* (1888), 3 acts, libr. by Edouard Blau.

Maillart, Louis Aimé. *Les Dragons de Villars* (1859), 3 acts, libr. by Lockroy [Joseph Philippe Simon] and Cormon [Pierre Étienne Piestre]

Maréchal, Henri. *Les Amoureux de Catherine* (1876), 1 act, libr. by Jules Barbier.

Massé, Victor. *Galathée* (1852), 2 acts, libr. by Jules Barbier and Michel Carré

Massé, Victor. *Les Noces de Jeannette* (1853), 1 act, libr. by Jules Barbier and Michel Carré.

Massenet, Jules. *Esclarmonde* (1889), 4 acts, libr. by Louis de Gramont and Alfred Blau.

Paër, Ferdinand. *Le Maître de chapelle* (1821), 2 acts, libr. by Sophie Gay.

Paisiello, Giovanni. *Le Barbier de Séville* (1782), 4 acts, libr. by Giuseppe Petrosellini.

Pérronnet, Joanni. *La Cigale madrilène* (1889), 2 acts, libr. by Léon Vernoux [Amélie Pérronnet].

Rossini, Gioacchino. *Il Barbiere di Siviglia* (1816), 2 acts, libr. by Cesare Sterbini.

Thomas, Ambroise. *Mignon* (1866), 3 acts, libr. by Jules Barbier and Michel Carré.

Verdi, Giuseppe. *La traviata* (1853), 3 acts, libr. by Francesco Maria Piave.

| Date | Opéra | Opéra Comique |
| --- | --- | --- |
| May | | |
| 1 | 8:00 *Roméo et Juliette* | 8:00 *Carmen* |
| 2 | | 8:15 *Le Roi d'Ys* |
| 3 | 8:00 *Aida* | 8:00 *Mignon* |
| 4 | 8:00 *Roméo et Juliette* | 8:00 *Richard, Cœur de Lion* / *Philémon et Baucis* |
| 5 repr. grat. | 7:30 **Guillaume Tell** / **La Marseillaise** / **Free Performance, Centenary** | 1:15 **Matinee: Carmen** / 7:45 **Les Noces de Jeannette,** / **La Marseillaise** / **Le Barbier de Séville** / **(Rossini)** |
| 6 | Closed (Centenary 1789–1889) | 7:45 *Le Domino noir* / *Les Rendez-vous bourgeois* |
| 7 | 8:00 *Faust* | 8:15 *Le Roi d'Ys* |
| 8 | 8:00 *Hamlet* (début of Nelly Melba) | 8:00 *Carmen* |

| Date | Opéra | Opéra Comique |
| --- | --- | --- |
| 9 | | 8:00 *Mignon* |
| 10 | 8:00 *Roméo et Juliette* | 8:15 *Le Roi d'Ys* |
| 11 | Bal annuel de l' Association des artistes dramatiques | 7:45 *Le Maître de chapelle* *Galathée* *Les Rendez-vous bourgeois* |
| **12** | | **1:00 Matinee:** *Les Noces de Jeannette* *Le Pré aux clercs* |
| | | **7:45** *Les Dragons de Villars* *Les Rendez-vous bourgeois* |
| 13 | 8:00 *Hamlet* | 7:30 *Esclarmonde* Dress rehearsal |
| 14 | | 8:00 *Mignon* |
| 15 | 8:00 *Les Huguenots* | 8:00 *Esclarmonde* Première |
| 16 | | 8:00 *Le Roi d'Ys* |
| 17 | 8:00 *Hamlet* | 8:00 *Carmen* |
| 18 | 8:00 *Roméo et Juliette* | 8:00 *Esclarmonde* |
| **19** | | **7:15** *Galathée* *Le Pré aux clercs* |
| 20 | 8:00 *Roméo et Juliette* | 8:00 *Esclarmonde* |
| 21 | | 8:00 *Carmen* |
| 22 | 8:00 *Hamlet* | 7:30 *Le Chalet* *Zampa* |
| 23 | | 8:00 *Esclarmonde* |
| 24 | 8:00 *Roméo et Juliette* | 8:15 *Le Roi d'Ys* 100th performance |
| 25 | 8:00 *Hamlet* | 8:00 *Esclarmonde* |
| **26** | **"Représentation offerte à MM. les membres étrangers du jury intern**[al] **des récompenses de l'Expos. 1889"** | **8:00** *Mignon* |

| Date | Opéra | Opéra Comique |
|------|-------|---------------|
| 27 | 8:00 *Roméo et Juliette* | 8:00 *Esclarmonde* |
| 28 | | 7:30 *La Cigale madrilène* <br> *La traviata* |
| 29 | 8:00 *Patrie!* <br> Revival | 8:00 *Esclarmonde* |
| • 30 | | 7:30 *Le Chalet* <br> *La Dame blanche* |
| 31 | 8:00 *Roméo et Juliette* | 8:00 *Esclarmonde* |
| June | | |
| 1 | | 8:00 *Carmen* |
| **2** | | **7:30 Les Noces de Jeannette** <br> **Les Dragons de Villars** |
| 3 | 8:00 *Patrie!* | 7:30 *Le Chalet* <br> *Zampa* <br> Représentation <br> populaire[2] |
| 4 | | 8:00 *Esclarmonde* |
| 5 | 8:00 *Roméo et Juliette* | 8:00 *Le Baiser de Suzon* <br> *Le Roi d'Ys* |
| 6 | | 8:00 *Esclarmonde* |
| 7 | 8:00 *L'Africaine* | 8:00 *Mignon* |
| 8 | 8:00 *Les Huguenots* | 8:00 *Esclarmonde* |
| **9** | | **7:30 Le Chalet** <br> **Zampa** |
| 10 | 8:00 *Roméo et Juliette* | 8:00 *Carmen* |
| 11 | | 8:00 *Esclarmonde* |
| 12 | 8:00 *L'Africaine* | 8:15 *Le Roi d'Ys* |
| 13 | | 8:00 *Esclarmonde* |
| 14 | 8:00 *Patrie!* | 8:00 *Mignon* |
| 15 | 8:00 *Faust* | 8:00 *Esclarmonde* |

2. A *représentation populaire* was for inhabitants of Paris at discounted prices.

| Date | Opéra | Opéra Comique |
|------|-------|---------------|
| **16** | | **8:00 *La Nuit de Saint Jean*** <br> ***La Dame blanche*** |
| 17 | 8:00 *Guillaume Tell* | 8:15 *Carmen* |
| 18 | | 8:00 *Esclarmonde* |
| 19 | 8:00 *Roméo et Juliette* | 8:30 *Le Roi d'Ys* |
| 20 | | 8:00 *Esclarmonde* |
| 21 | 8:00 *Le Prophète* | 8:15 *Mignon* |
| 22 | 8:00 *L'Africaine* | 8:00 *Esclarmonde* |
| **23** | **8:00 *La Tempête*** <br> **Dress rehearsal** | **8:00 *Les Dragons de Villars*** <br> ***Les Rendez-vous*** <br> ***bourgeois*** |
| 24 | 8:00 *Le Prophète* | 8:00 *Esclarmonde* |
| 25 | | 8:30 *Le Roi d'Ys* |
| 26 | 8:30 *La Tempête* <br> First performance | 8:00 *Esclarmonde* |
| 27 | | 8:30 *Le Barbier de Séville* <br> (Paisiello) |
| 28 | 8:30 *La Tempête* | 8:00 *Esclarmonde* |
| 29 | 8:00 *Le Prophète* | 8:15 *Mignon* |
| **30** | | **7:30 *La Cigale Madrilène*** <br> ***Zampa*** |
| July | | |
| 1 | 8:00 *Roméo et Juliette* | 8:15 *Carmen* |
| 2 | 8:00 *La Tempête* <br> Gala performance <br> for the "Membres <br> du Jury de l'Exposition" | 8:00 *Esclarmonde* |
| 3 | 8:00 *Le Prophète* | 8:15 *Le Roi d'Ys* |
| 4 | | 8:00 *Esclarmonde* |
| 5 | 7:30 *Rigoletto* <br> *La Tempête* | 8:30 *Raoul, Sire de Créqui* <br> *La Soirée orageuse* |

| Date | Opéra | Opéra Comique |
|---|---|---|
| 6 | 8:00 *Faust*<br>Gala performance for<br>the Shah of Persia | 8:00 *Esclarmonde* |
| 7 | | 7:30 **Les Noces de Jeannette**<br>**La Dame blanche** |
| 8 | 7:30 *Rigoletto*<br>*La Tempête* | 8:15 *Mignon* |
| 9 | | 8:00 *Esclarmonde* |
| 10 | 8:00 *Le Prophète* | 8:15 *Le Roi d'Ys* |
| 11 | | 8:00 *Esclarmonde*<br>Extraordinary Performance<br>offered by the city of Paris to<br>the Hungarian Delegation<br>After Act 3: *The Rákóczi*<br>*March*<br>After Act 4: *La Marseillaise* |
| 12 | 8:00 *Roméo et Juliette* | 8:15 *Carmen* |
| 13 | 7:30 *Rigoletto*<br>*La Tempête* | 8:00 *Esclarmonde* |
| **14**<br>**Free Perf.** | **1:00 *L'Africaine***<br>**La Marseillaise** | **1:00 Les Amoureux de**<br>**Catherine**<br>**La Fille du régiment**<br>**La Marseillaise**<br>**Les Rendez-vous Bourgeois** |
| 15 | 8:00 *Les Huguenots* | 7:45 *Les Noces de Jeannette*<br>*Le Pré aux clercs* |
| 16 | | 8:00 *Esclarmonde* |
| 17 | 8:00 *Roméo et Juliette* | 8:15 *Le Roi d'Ys* |
| 18 | | 8:00 *Esclarmonde* |
| 19 | 7:30 *Henry VIII*<br>*La Tempête* | 8:15 *Mignon* |
| 20 | 8:00 *La Juive* | 8:00 *Esclarmonde* |
| **21** | | 7:45 **Les Noces de Jeannette**<br>**Le Pré aux clercs** |

| Date | Opéra | Opéra Comique |
|------|-------|---------------|
| 22 | 8:00 *Patrie!* | 7:45 *Le Chalet*<br>    *La Dame blanche* |
| 23 | 8:00 *Roméo et Juliette*<br>    "exceptional<br>    performance" | 8:00 *Esclarmonde* |
| 24 | 7:30 *Henry VIII*<br>    *La Tempête* | 8:15 *Le Roi d'Ys* |
| 25 | | 8:00 *Esclarmonde* |
| 26 | 8:00 *La Juive* | 8:15 *Carmen* |
| 27 | 8:00 *Henry VIII*<br>    *La Tempête* | 8:00 *Esclarmonde* |
| **28** | | **8:15 *Mignon*** |
| 29 | 8:00 *Aida* | 8:00 *Esclarmonde* |
| 30 | 8:00 *Les Huguenots* | 8:15 *Le Roi d'Ys* |
| 31 | 8:00 *Patrie!* | 8:00 *Esclarmonde* |
| August | | |
| 1 | | 8:15 *Mignon* |
| 2 | 7:30 *Henry VIII*<br>    *La Tempête* | 8:00 *Esclarmonde* |
| 3 | | 8:15 *Carmen* |
| **4** | **8:00 *Guillaume Tell*** | **8:00 *La Nuit de Saint Jean*<br>    *Les Dragons de Villars*** |
| 5 | 8:00 *Faust* | 8:15 *Mignon* |
| 6 | 8:30 *Le Cid* (Act 2)<br>    *La Marseillaise*<br>    *La Tempête*<br>    Gala evening for the<br>    Shah of Persia | 8:00 *Esclarmonde* |
| 7 | 8:00 *Le Cid* | 8:15 *Le Roi d'Ys* |
| 8 | | 8:00 *Esclarmonde* |
| 9 | 8:00 *Roméo et Juliette* | 8:15 *Carmen* |
| 10 | 8:00 *Aida* | 8:00 *Esclarmonde* |
| **11** | | **7:45 *Les Noces de Jeannette*<br>    *Les Dragons de Villars*<br>    Représentation Populaire** |

| Date | Opéra | Opéra Comique |
|------|-------|---------------|
| 12 | 7:30 *Roméo et Juliette* <br> *La Tempête* | 8:15 *Mignon* |
| 13 | 8:00 *La Juive* | 8:00 *Esclarmonde* |
| 14 | 8:00 *Faust* | 8:15 *Le Roi d'Ys* |
| 15 | | 7:30 *Les Noces de Jeannette* <br> *La Dame blanche* |
| 16 | 7:30 *Henry VIII* <br> *La Tempête* | 8:15 *Carmen* |
| 17 | 8:00 *Les Huguenots* | 8:00 *Esclarmonde* |
| **18** | | **8:15 *Carmen*** |
| 19 | 8:00 *Guillaume Tell* <br> *La Marseillaise* <br> Gala evening for the <br> mayors of France | 7:30 *Les Noces de Jeannette* <br> *La Dame blanche* <br> *La Marseillaise* <br> Gala evening for the mayors <br> of France |
| 20 | 8:00 *Faust* | 8:00 *Esclarmonde* |
| 21 | 7:30 *Rigoletto* <br> *La Tempête* | 8:15 *Mignon* |
| 22 | | 8:00 *Esclarmonde* |
| 23 | 8:00 *Le Cid* | 8:15 *Carmen* |
| 24 | 8:00 *Roméo et Juliette* | 8:00 *Esclarmonde* |
| **25** | | **7:45 *Les Noces de Jeannette*** <br> ***Le Pré aux clercs*** |
| 26 | 7:30 *Henry VIII* <br> *La Tempête* | 8:15 *Mignon* |
| 27 | 8:00 *L'Africaine* | 8:00 *Esclarmonde* |
| 28 | 8:00 *Aida* | 8:15 *Carmen* |
| 29 | 8:00 *Faust* | 8:00 *Esclarmonde* |
| 30 | 7:30 *Henry VIII* <br> *La Tempête* | 8:15 *Le Roi d'Ys* |
| 31 | 8:00 *Roméo et Juliette* | 8:00 *Esclarmonde* |

September

| | | |
|------|-------|---------------|
| **1** | | **1:00 Matinee: *Fra Diavolo*** <br> ***Le Chalet*** <br> **8:15 *Carmen*** |
| 2 | 8:00 *Guillaume Tell* | 8:15 *Mignon* |
| 3 | 8:00 *Les Huguenots* | 8:00 *Esclarmonde* |
| 4 | 8:00 *Le Cid* | 7:45 *Les Noces de Jeannette* <br> *Zampa* |

| Date | Opéra | Opéra Comique |
|------|-------|---------------|
| 5 | 8:00 *La Juive* | 8:00 *Esclarmonde* |
| 6 | 8:00 *Roméo et Juliette* | 8:15 *Le Roi d'Ys* |
| 7 | 8:00 *L'Africaine* | 8:00 *Esclarmonde* |
| **8** | | **1:00 Matinee: *Les Dragons de Villars* *Les Rendez-vous bourgeois* 7:45 *Les Noces de Jeannette* *Zampa*** |
| 9 | 8:00 *Rigoletto* *Coppélia* | 8:15 *Mignon* |
| 10 | 8:00 *Aida* | 8:00 *Esclarmonde* 50th performance |
| 11 | 8:00 *Faust* | 8:15 *Le Roi d'Ys* |
| 12 | 8:00 *Roméo et Juliette* | 8:00 *Esclarmonde* |
| 13 | 8:00 *Henry VIII* *Coppélia* | 8:15 *Carmen* 400th performance |
| 14 | 8:00  *Les Huguenots* | 8:00 *Esclarmonde* |
| **15** | | **1:00 *Zampa* *Les Rendez-vous bourgeois* 7:45 *Les Noces de Jeannette* *Les Dragons de Villars*** |
| 16 | 8:00 *La Juive* | 7:45 *Les Noces de Jeannette* *Le Pré aux clercs* |
| 17 | 8:00 *Guillaume Tell* | 8:00 *Esclarmonde* |
| 18 | 8:00 *Rigoletto* *Coppélia* | 8:15 *Mignon* |
| 19 | 8:00 *L'Africaine* (Act 1) *Aida* (Act 2) *Coppélia* Gala Performance for Railroad Engineers | 8:00 *Esclarmonde* |
| 20 | 8:00 *Roméo et Juliette* | 8:15 *Le Roi d'Ys* |
| 21 | 8:00 *L'Africaine* | 8:00 *Esclarmonde* |
| **22** | | **1:00 Matinee: *Richard, Cœur de Lion* *Le Pré aux clercs* 7:45 *Les Noces de Jeanette* *Fra Diavolo*** |

| Date | Opéra | Opéra Comique |
|---|---|---|
| 23 | 8:00 *Faust* | 8:30 *Carmen* |
| 24 | 8:00 *Les Huguenots* | 8:00 *Esclarmonde* |
| 25 | 8:00 *La Juive* | 8:15 *Le Roi d'Ys* |
| 26 | 8:00 *Roméo et Juliette* | 8:00 *Esclarmonde* |
| 27 | 8:00 *Rigoletto* *Coppélia* | 8:15 *Mignon* |
| 28 | 8:00 *Faust* | 8:00 *Esclarmonde* |
| **29** | | **1:00 Matinee:** *Philémon et Baucis* *Les Noces de Jeannette* *Les Rendez-vous bourgeois* **7:45** *Le Café du roi* **First performance** *Zampa* |
| 30 | 8:00 *Roméo et Juliette* | 8:15 *Carmen* |
| October | | |
| 1 | 8:00 *L'Africaine* | 8:00 *Esclarmonde* |
| 2 | 8:00 *Aida* | 8:15 *Mignon* |
| 3 | 8:00 *Guillaume Tell* | 8:00 *Esclarmonde* |
| 4 | 8:00 *La Juive* | 8:15 *Le Roi d'Ys* |
| 5 | 8:00 *Aida* | 8:00 *Esclarmonde* |
| **6** | | **1:00 Matinee:** *Les Noces de Jeannette* *La Dame blanche* **8:15** *Carmen* |
| 7 | 8:00 *Roméo et Juliette* | 8:15 *Mignon* |
| 8 | 8:00 *Faust* | 8:00 *Esclarmonde* |
| 9 | 8:00 *Hamlet* | 8:15 *Le Roi d'Ys* |
| 10 | 8:00 *Rigoletto* *Coppélia* | 8:00 *Esclarmonde* |
| 11 | 8:00 *Aida* | 8:15 *Carmen* |
| 12 | 8:00 *Hamlet* | 8:00 *Esclarmonde* |
| **13** | | **1:00 Matinee:** *Richard, Cœur de Lion* *Les Dragons de Villars* **8:15** *Mignon* |

| Date | Opéra | Opéra Comique |
|---|---|---|
| 14 | 8:00 *Les Huguenots* | 8:00 *Le Café du roi*<br>*Le Pré aux clercs* |
| 15 | 8:00 *Hamlet* | 8:00 *Esclarmonde* |
| 16 | 8:00 *Roméo et Juliette* | 8:15 *Carmen* |
| 17 | 8:00 *L'Africaine* | 8:00 *Esclarmonde* |
| 18 | 8:00 *Hamlet* | 8:15 *Le Roi d'Ys* |
| 19 | 8:00 *La Juive* | 8:00 *Esclarmonde* |
| **20** | | **1:00 Matinee:**<br>***La Fille du régiment***<br>***Le Pré aux clercs***<br>**8:15 *Carmen*** |
| 21 | 8:00 *Faust* | 8:15 *Mignon* |
| 22 | 8:00 *Roméo et Juliette* | 8:00 *Esclarmonde* |
| 23 | 8:00 *La Juive* | 8:15 *Carmen* |
| 24 | 8:00 *Les Huguenots* | 1:00 *Les Noces de Jeannette*<br>*Fra Diavolo*<br>Représentation populaire<br>8:00 *Esclarmonde* |
| 25 | 8:00 *Roméo et Juliette* | 8:15 *Le Roi d'Ys* |
| 26 | 8:00 *L'Africaine* | 8:00 *Esclarmonde* |
| **27** | | **1:00 Matinee:**<br>***La Cigale madrilène***<br>***La Dame blanche***<br>**8:15 *Mignon*** |
| 28 | 8:00 *Hamlet* | 8:15 *Carmen* |
| 29 | 8:00 *Aida* | 8:00 *Esclarmonde* |
| 30 | 8:00 *Roméo et Juliette* | 8:15 *Mignon* |
| 31 | 8:00 *Faust* | 8:00 *Esclarmonde* |
| November | | |
| 1 | 8:00 *Rigoletto*<br>*Coppélia* | 1:00 Matinee: *La Cigale*<br>*madrilène*<br>*Le Pré aux clercs*<br>8:15 *Le Roi d'Ys* |
| 2 | 8:00 *Roméo et Juliette* | 8:00 *Esclarmonde* |

| Date | Opéra | Opéra Comique |
|------|-------|---------------|
| **3** | | **1:00 Matinee:** *Les Amoureux de Catherine Les Dragons de Villars;* **8:15** *Carmen* |
| 4 | 8:00 *Roméo et Juliette* | 8:15 *Mignon* |
| 5 | 8:00 *Les Huguenots* ("last additional performance") | 8:00 *Esclarmonde* |
| 6 | 8:00 *Hamlet* | 8:15 *Carmen* |
| 7 | | 8:00 *Esclarmonde* |
| 8 | 8:00 *Roméo et Juliette* | 8:15 *Le Roi d'Ys* |
| 9 | | 8:00 *Esclarmonde* |
| **10** | | **1:00 Matinee:** *Carmen* **8:15** *Mignon* |

# Dramatis Personae

ALPHAND, JEAN CHARLES ADOLPHE (1817–91). French engineer. He was charged by Haussmann with the creation and maintenance of Parisian parks in 1854. From 1878 to 1891, he presided over all Parisian commissions overseeing the organization of festivities. In 1889, he was the Directeur Général des Traveaux de l'Exposition Universelle.

ANEH (ca. 1854–89). Javanese musician from Parakan Salak, a Sundanese tea plantation near Sukabumi. He died in Paris on 4 July 1889 from a ruptured aneurism. His death and funeral were much discussed in the Parisian press.

BAHIA (b. ca. 1873): Algerian dancer who performed in the Café Égyptien of the Exposition Universelle.

BARBIER, JULES (1825–1901). French playwright and librettist, often in collaboration with Michel Carré. Among their most famous works are *Faust*, set by Charles Gounod (1859), and *Hamlet*, set by Ambroise Thomas (1868). He wrote the libretto for Ambroise Thomas's ballet *La Tempête*, premiered at the Théâtre de l'Opéra in 1889.

BENEDICTUS, LOUIS. Dutch composer, naturalized French. Active in the circle around Judith Gautier, for whose plays he wrote incidental music. In 1889, he published *Les Musiques Bizarres de l'Exposition*.

BENT-ENY, RACHEL (b. ca. 1871). Dancer of Algerian Jewish origin known under the stage name of "La belle Fatma." She performed as a seven-year-old during the 1878 Exposition Universelle. She stayed in Paris and performed in various *cafés-concerts*. In 1889, she first appeared at the Grand Théâtre before moving into her own space, the Concert Tunisien. She married in 1889 in Paris.

BERGER, GEORGES (1834–1910). French engineer. Already in 1867, he was responsible for the foreign section of that world's fair. In 1876, he was appointed professor at the École Supérieure des Beaux-Arts. In both 1878 and 1889, he was the Directeur Général de l'Exploitation de l'Exposition Universelle. He was elected to the Chambre des Députés in 1889 as a Paris deputy, a position he held until his death in 1910.

BLAU, ALFRED (d. 1896). French librettist born in Blois. He wrote the libretto for Ernest Reyer's opera *Sigurd*, and co-signed, with Louis de Gramont, the text for Massenet's *Esclarmonde*.

BOULANGER, GENERAL GEORGES (1837–91). French general and politician. After a successful career in the Infantry, Boulanger became Minister of War in 1886. After being dismissed as minister, he ran an election campaign in 1888–89 which came close to leading to a coup d'état in January 1889. He fled France in April 1889 and committed suicide in exile, in 1891.

CALLIAS, HORACE DE (d. 1921). French painter educated at the École des Beaux-Arts. Exhibited in the Parisian *salons*. In 1889, he showed his painting, *La Soirée de clavecin*, which depicted Louis Diémer at the harpsichord.

CARNOT, SADI (1837–94). French engineer and politician. Grandson of the hero of the French Revolution, Lazare Carnot. Elected president in 1887, he pushed the Franco-Russian alliance, which was formalized in 1893. He was assassinated in 1894.

CLÉMENT, FELIX (1822–85). French composer and anti-Wagnerian music historian. One of the founders of the École Niedermeyer. Wrote numerous instruction manuals and historic texts, including his *Dictionnaire lyrique, ou Histoire des opéras*, published in 1867–81 with Pierre Larousse. In 1885, he published his *Histoire de la musique depuis les temps anciens jusqu' à nos jours*.

COLONNE, ÉDOUARD (1838–1910). French violinist and conductor. In 1873, he founded the Concerts Colonne, one of the major concert societies in Paris. His programs championed French music, especially Berlioz. Already in 1878, Colonne conducted concerts at the Trocadéro during the Exposition Universelle. In 1889, he lead one of the official concerts and conducted the première of Augusta Holmès's *Ode triomphale en l'honneur du Centenaire de 1789*.

DIÉMER, LOUIS (1843–1919). French composer, pianist, and harpsichordist. Professor of piano at the Conservatoire from 1887. With Jules Delsart, he organized historic concerts in Paris on authentic instruments, including two concerts at the 1889 Exposition Universelle. Their success led to the founding of the Société des Instruments Anciens, which promoted the historically informed performance of early music. Diémer was named a Chevalier de la Légion d'Honneur in 1889.

EDISON, THOMAS ALVA (1847–1931). American inventor. His inventions covered a wide field, including the lightbulb, the telephone, the phonograph, and motion picture film. In 1889, Edison presented a major exhibition at the Exposition Universelle, concentrating on electric light and the phonograph. His visit to Paris in August was broadly covered in the media and brought him the honor of being named Commandant de la Légion d'Honneur.

ELLES (b. ca. 1874). Javanese dancer from Parakan Salak, a Sundanese tea plantation near Sukabumi, who performed more popular dances from Sunda during the Exposition Universelle. Her brother was one of the musicians.

FÉTIS, FRANÇOIS-JOSEPH (1784–1871). Belgian musicologist, critic, and composer. The first part of his career was in Paris, where, in 1827, he founded the music journal *La Revue musicale* (later: *La Revue et Gazette musicale de Paris*). From 1832, he organized a series of *Concerts historiques*. He was appointed director of the Conservatoire of Brussels in 1833. Fétis was one of the most influential critics and music historians in nineteenth-century France and Belgium.

GAILHARD, PIERRE [PIETRO] (1848–1918). French bass and opera director. Engaged at the Opéra from 1870 to 1879. In 1884, he became director of the Opéra jointly with Eugène Ritt until 1891. From 1893 to 1899, he was co-director of the Opéra with Eugène Bertrand, and after Bertrand's death he directed the house on his own until 1906.

GARCIN, JULES (1830–96). French violinist and conductor. After several decades as first violinist of the Orchestre de la Société des Concerts du Conservatoire, he was appointed the orchestra's director in 1885. In 1871, he was one of the founding members of the Société Nationale de Musique.

GAUTIER, JUDITH (1850–1917). French novelist and ardent Wagnerian. Wrote numerous orientalist novels and propagated the work and ideas of Richard Wagner in published reminiscences. Published articles on music and dance at the 1889 Exposition Universelle in the radical newspaper, *Le Rappel*, and collaborated eleven years later with Louis Benedictus on *Les Musiques bizarres à l'Exposition de 1900*.

GOBINEAU, JOSEPH ARTHUR COMTE DE (1816–82). French diplomat and anthropologist. His *Essai sur l'inégalité des races humaines* (1853–55) is one of the key texts of French polygenic anthropology, propagating hierarchical racial theories that placed white, Aryan races at the top of the pyramid.

GRAMONT, LOUIS DE (1854–1912). French playwright, novelist and librettist. Contributed to journals such as *Le Mot d'ordre* and *L'Intransigeant*, and published realist novels such as *Loulou* (1888). Wrote, with Alfred Blau, the libretto for Massenet's *Esclarmonde*.

GUILMANT, ALEXANDRE (1837–1911). French organist and composer. In 1871, he became the organist of La Trinité, one of the major Parisian churches. The year 1878 brought his additional appointment as resident organist of the Palais du Trocadéro. In 1889, he organized the organ-concert series for the Exposition Universelle.

HEUGEL, HENRI (1844–1916). French music publisher. Heugel was one of the main publishing houses of France. In addition to music by Félicien David, Ambroise Thomas, Camille Saint-Saëns and many other leading French composers, Heugel published the weekly music journal, *Le Ménestrel*, to which he contributed as a critic under the pseudonym H. Moreno.

HOLMÈS, AUGUSTA (1847–1903). French composer of Irish descent. Composed for all genres and became one of the composers whose works were championed by Édouard Colonne in his concert series. In 1895, the Théâtre de l'Opéra premièred her *La Montagne noire*. To commemorate the Centenary of the French Revolution, Holmès wrote, in 1889, the *Ode triomphale en l'honneur du Centenaire de 1789*.

LACOME D'ESTALENX, PAUL (1838–1920). French composer and music critic. He was a successful operetta composer with works such as *Jeanne, Jeannette et Jeanneton* (1876). He published extracts from historic operas and *opéras comiques*, and organized, for the 1889 Exposition Universelle, a retrospective of *opéras comiques* dating form the years of the French Revolution (1788–94).

LAMOUREUX, CHARLES (1834–99). French conductor and ardent supporter of Wagner. He founded several short-lived concert societies before he established, in 1881, the Société des Nouveaux-Concerts (or Concerts Lamoureux). In 1873, he conducted the Parisian performance of Handel's *Messiah*, followed by other Baroque repertoire such a Bach's *Saint Matthew Passion*. His performance of Wagner's *Lohengrin* in Paris in 1887 was a major and scandalous event.

MASSENET, JULES (1842–1912). French composer. In the 1880s and 1890s, Massenet was the leading French opera composer with such works as *Hérodiade* (1881), *Manon* (1884), *Le Cid* (1885), and *Thaïs* (1894). His opera *Esclarmonde* was premièred on 15 May 1889 at the Théâtre de l'Opéra-Comique.

MAURI, ROSITA (1856–1923). Spanish-born ballet dancer, who became the *étoile* dancer at the Théâtre de l'Opéra. In 1889, she created the role of Miranda in Ambroise Thomas's new ballet, *La Tempête*. From 1902 to 1920, she was *sous-directeur* of the Opéra's École de Danse and professor of the "classe de perfectionnement."

MOHAMMED, HANEM (b. ca. 1869). Dancer born in Cairo, who performed at the Egyptian Café during the Exposition Universelle.

OMAR-HELLAL (b. ca. 1864). Musician from Cairo who played the *ūd* at the Egyptian Café during the Exposition Universelle.

OSMAN-HASSEM (b. ca. 1863). Musician from Cairo who played the *qānūn* at the Egyptian Café during the Exposition Universelle.

PALADILHE, ÉMILE (1844–1926). French composer. He won the Prix de Rome in 1860. In Italy, he composed one of his greatest successes, the song *Mandolinata*. His opera *Patrie!* (1886), on a libretto by Sardou and Gallet, became a staple in the repertoire of the Opéra. He was elected to the Institut de France in 1892, and became an Officier of the Légion d'Honneur in 1897.

POUGIN, ARTHUR (1834–1921). French critic. After starting as a violinist, he became one of the leading French music historians and critics, contributing to *Le Ménestrel, La France musicale,* and *L'Art musical,* among others. He edited the music articles in the Larousse *Dictionnaire universel.* In 1885 he became chief editor of *Le Ménestrel.* In 1889–90, he published a series of articles in *Le Ménestrel* which appeared in book form as *Le Théâtre à l'Exposition Universelle de 1889* (1890).

RENAN, ERNEST (1823–92). French historian, philosopher and writer. Best known for this *Vie de Jesus* (1863) and his 1872 lecture, *Qu'est qu'une nation.* 1883 he was appointed the director of the Collège de France. Like Gobineau, he supported polygenic racial theories.

RIMSKY-KORSAKOV, NIKOLAY (1844–1908). Russian composer and conductor. One of the leading Russian composers of the late nineteenth century, with works such as *Mlada* (1892), *Stazka o Care Saltane* (1900), and *Zolotoj petušok* (1909). In 1889, he conducted the two Russian concerts at the Exposition Universelle, which promoted the composers of the "Mighty Handful" (*Moguchaya kuchka*).

SAINT-SAËNS, CHARLES-CAMILLE (1835–1912). French composer, pianist, and critic. He was one of the major nineteenth-century French composers, with works such as *Samson et Dalila* (1877) and *Henry VIII* (1884). His opera *Ascanio* was supposed to be premiered at the Théâtre de l'Opéra in 1889, but delayed until the following year. He published several articles on music at the Exposition Universelle in 1889 in the radical newspaper *Le Rappel.*

SANDERSON, SIBYL (1865–1903). American soprano. Pupil of Mathilde Marchesi in Paris and protégé of Jules Massenet, who wrote several parts for her, including the title roles in *Esclarmonde* (1889) and *Thaïs* (1894). She moved from the Théâtre de l'Opéra-Comique to the Opéra in 1894. In 1895, she made her debut at the Metropolitan Opera in New York.

SERIEM (b. ca. 1874). Dancer from the princely court of Surakarta, Java, and daughter of Djayamoerdassing, a soldier in the service of the prince. She was one of the four *tandak* who performed the Javanese epic *Damarwulan* at the 1889 Exposition Universelle.

SOEKIA (b. ca. 1875). Dancer from the princely court of Surakarta, Java. Her sister Kariosmito was a batik artist. Soekia was one of the four *tandak* who performed the Javanese epic *Damarwulan* at the 1889 Exposition Universelle.

SONZOGNO, EDOARDO (1836–1920). Italian music publisher of composers such as Mascagni and Leoncavallo. He published a review of the 1889 Exposition Universelle and organized between April and June a season of Italian opera at the Théâtre de la Gaîté.

STUCKEN, FRANK VAN DER (1858–1929). American conductor and composer of Dutch descent. After several years in Germany, he returned to the United States, where, in 1884, he was hired as the conductor of the Arion Society, a male chorus in New York. In 1889, he organized the "American Concert" at the Exposition Universelle. In 1895, he became the first conductor of the Cincinnati Symphony Orchestra.

TAMINAH (b. ca. 1873). Dancer from the princely court of Surakarta, Java. Her mother was a batik artist. Taminah was one of the four *tandak* who performed the Javanese epic *Damarwulan* at the 1889 Exposition Universelle.

THOMAS, AMBROISE (1811–96). French composer. He wrote numerous operas for the Parisian stage, including *Mignon* (1866) and *Hamlet* (1868). In 1871, Thomas became the director of the Conservatoire. His ballet, *La Tempête*, was premiered in 1889. He was the president of the Commission des Auditions Musicales of the Exposition Universelle, which was concerned with the attribution of prizes in class 13 and the organization of musical events during the Exposition Universelle.

TIERSOT, JULIEN (1857–1936). French musicologist and one of the founders of ethnomusicology in France. From 1883, assistant librarian at the Bibliothèque du Conservatoire, and from 1909 its director. In 1885, he won the Bodin Prize of the Académie des Beaux-Arts with his *Histoire de la chanson populaire en France* (published in 1889). His interest in folk music lead to a series of articles on music at the Exposition Universelle, which were published as *Promenades musicales à l'Exposition*.

VIANESI, AUGUSTE CHARLES (1837–1908). Italian conductor, naturalized French in the 1880s. In 1887, he was appointed musical director of the

Opéra. In 1889, he conducted the première of *La Tempête*, the official concert of the Opéra at the Trocadéro, and the performance of Handel's *Messiah*.

VICAIRE, GABRIEL (1848–1900). French poet. Wrote poetry and novels focusing on local color and the French countryside. In 1885, *Les Déliquescences d'Adoré Floupette*, a parody of Verlaine, Mallarmé, and Moréas written in collaboration with Henri Beauclair, caused a minor scandal. Vicaire won the 1889 competition for a cantata text celebrating the centenary of the French Revolution.

WAKIEM (b. ca. 1876): Dancer from the princely court of Surakarta, Java. She was one of the four *tandak* who performed the Javanese epic *Damarwulan* at the 1889 Exposition Universelle.

WEBER, JOHANNÈS (1818–1902): French music critic of Alsatian descent, who wrote for *Le Temps* from the newspaper's beginnings in 1861 to 1895. A prominent anti-Wagnerian critic, he supported French music.

WILDER, VICTOR (1835–92). Belgian music critic, translator, and writer. From 1883 to 1892, he was the music critic for *Gil Blas*. Ardent Wagnerian and translator of Wagner's operas, from *Lohengrin* onwards. He was also involved with various other translations, including Handel's *Messiah*, which was performed at the 1889 Exposition Universelle.

# Bibliography

The bibliography consists of the following sections:
  Newspapers and Periodicals
  Primary and Contemporary Sources, Scores and Editions
    Archival Collections
    Guides to the Exposition Universelle
    Other Materials
  Secondary Sources

Note: Publication information for the many contemporary reports in newspapers and journals is given in the footnotes; for reasons of brevity, the individual articles are not listed here.

## Newspapers and Periodicals

*L'Art musical*
*Atlantic Monthly*
*L'Autorité*
*La Bataille*
*La Caricature*
*The Century*
*Le Charivari*
*Le Courrier français*
*Le XIXe siècle: Journal républicain*
*L'Écho de Paris*
*L'Éclair*
*L'Esposizione di Parigi del 1889 illustra*
*L'Estafette*
*L'Événement*
*L'Exposition de Paris 1889*
*Le Figaro*
*Le Gaulois*
*Gil Blas*
*Le Guide musical*
*L'Illustration*
*L'Intransigeant*
*Le Journal amusant*
*Le Journal de Paris*
*Le Journal des débats*
*Le Journal illustré*
*La Justice*

*Le Matin*
*Le Ménestrel*
*Le Monde artiste*
*Le Monde illustré*
*Le Moniteur universel*
*The Musical Times*
*The Musical World*
*La Musique des familles (Musique populaire)*
*Le National*
*La Nature: Revue des sciences et de leurs applications aux arts et*
   *aux industries*
*L'Observateur français*
*Parigi e l'Esposizione Universale del 1889*
*Paris illustré*
*Le Petit Journal*
*Le Petit Parisien*
*Le Rappel*
*La République française*
*La Revue bleue*
*La Revue de l'Exposition Universelle de 1889*
*La Revue des deux mondes*
*La Revue illustrée*
*La Revue indépendante*
*La Revue musicale*
*Revue des traditions populaires*
*Le Soir*
*Il teatro illustrato e la musica popolare*
*Le Temps*
*L'Univers*
*L'Univers illustré*
*La Vie parisienne*
*Le Voltaire*

## Primary and Contemporary Sources

Archival Collections

"Actualités." Collection of documents relating to the 1889 Exposition
   Universelle. Bibliothèque Historique de la Ville de Paris.
*Journal de bord* of the Opéra and the *Journal de bord* of the Opéra-Comique,
   1889. Both archived in the Bibliothèque de l'Opéra, Paris.
Archives of the Edison National Historic Site, Series D-89-46: "Paris
   Exposition."

Thomas A. Edison Papers. Edited by Paul B. Israel, Rutgers University. http://edison.rutgers.edu (accessed 6 Jan. 2004).

Russell Collection of Early Keyboard Instruments, Edinburgh. On-line catalogue of the collection: http://www.music.ed.ac.uk/russell/instruments/hd5jg176329/table.html (accessed 28 May 2004).

Guides to the Exposition Universelle

*1889/Exposition Universelle/Java/Programme Explicatif Illustré.* Paris: n.p., 1889.

"*Concerts russes de la célèbre chapelle nationale Dmitri Slaviansky d'Agréneff.*" Program Booklet. Paris: Maison Rapide, 1889.

*Cook's Guide to Paris and the Universal Exhibition. Special Edition . . . Compiled under the Personal Superintendence of Thomas Cook & Son.* London: Thomas Cook & Son, 1889.

*Exposition de 1889: Guide bleu du "Figaro" et du "Petit Journal" avec 5 plans et 31 dessins.* Paris: Le Figaro, 1889.

*Fêtes du Centenaire / Commission de Contrôle / Séance du 8 Juin 1889 / Procès-verbal.* Paris: Imprimerie Chaix, 1889.

*Tit-Bits Guide to Paris and the Exhibition.* 8th edition. London: "Tit-Bits" Offices, 1889.

Other Materials

Alder, Ernest. *Les Almées.* Paris: Enoch Frères & Costallat, 1890.

Amiot, Joseph-Marie. *Mémoire sur la musique des Chinois, tant anciens que modernes.* Paris, 1779; reprint: Geneva: Minkoff, 1973.

Balzac, Honoré de. *Histoire des Treize: La Duchesse de Langeais.* Paris: Flammarion, 1988.

Bellaigue, Camille. *Un Siècle de musique française.* Paris: Librairie Ch. Delagrave, 1887.

Benedictus, Louis. *Les Musiques bizarres de l'Exposition.* Paris: Hartmann & Cie, 1889.

Bibesco, Prince Georges. *1889: Exposition Universelle: La Roumanie, avant—pendant—après.* Paris: Imprimerie Typographique J. Kugelman, 1890.

Bourgault-Ducoudray, Louis-Albert. "L'Enseignement du chant dans les lycées." *La Revue musicale* 3 (1903): 725–28.

———. *Études sur la musique ecclésiastique grecque: Mission musicale en Grèce et en Orient, janvier—mai 1875.* Paris: Librairie Hachette, 1877.

———. *Rapsodie cambodgienne.* Paris: Au Ménestrel, n.d.

Chabrier, Emmanuel. *Correspondance.* Edited by Roger Delage and Frans Durif with the contribution of Thierry Bodin. Paris: Klincksieck, 1994.

Chausson, Ernest. *Ernest Chausson: Écrits inédits.* Edited by Jean Gallois. Paris: Éditions du Rocher, 1999.

Chausson, Ernest. "Lettres inédites à Vincent d'Indy." *Revue musicale (numéro spéciale Ernest Chausson)* 6 (December 1925): 128–36.

Clément, Félix. *Histoire de la musique depuis les temps anciens jusqu'à nos jours.* Paris: Librairies Hachette et Cie, 1885.

Cohen, Robert H., et al. *Les Gravures musicales dans L'Illustration, 1843–1899.* Quebec: Les Presses de l'Université Laval, 1982–83.

Combarieu, Jules. "L'Étude du chant à l'école primaire." *La Revue musicale* 10 (1910): 314–17, 339–43.

Comettant, Oscar. *La Musique, les musiciens et les instruments de musique chez les peuples du monde.* Paris: Michel Lévy Frères, 1869.

Debussy, Claude. "Conversations avec Ernest Guiraud." In Edward Lockspeiser, *Debussy: Sa vie et sa pensée.* Translated by Léo Dilé, 751–55. Paris: Fayard, 1980.

———. *Correspondance 1884–1918.* Edited by François Lesure. 2nd edition. Paris: Hermann, 1993.

———. *Monsieur Croche et autres écrits.* Edited by François Lesure. Paris: Gallimard, 1987.

———. *Songs of Claude Debussy.* A Critical Edition by James R. Briscoe. 2 vols. Milwaukee, Hal Leonard Publishing, 1993.

Durer, Émile. *Edison: Sa vie—ses œuvres: Esquisses américaines.* Paris: Victor Marchesson, 1889.

Faidherbe, Louis Léon César. *Le Sénégal: La France dans l'Afrique occidentale.* Paris: Librairie Hachette, 1889.

Fauser, Annegret, ed. *Dossier de presse parisienne: Jules Massenet "Esclarmonde" (1889).* Heilbronn: Musik-Edition Lucie Galland, 2001.

Fétis, François-Joseph. *Biographie universelle des musiciens et Bibliographie générale de la musique.* 2nd ed. 8 vols. Paris: Didot, 1860–65.

———. *Histoire générale de la musique depuis les temps les plus anciens jusqu'à nos jours.* 6 vols. Paris: Firmin-Didot, 1869–76.

Gautier, Judith. *Les Musiques bizarres à l'Exposition de 1900.* Paris: Société d'Éditions Littéraires et Artistiques, 1900.

Gennaro-Chrétien, Hedwige. *Derbouka (Échos de la rue du Caire).* Paris: J. Naus, 1889.

Gléon, Delort de. *L'Architecture arabe des Khalifes d'Égypte à l'Exposition Universelle de Paris en 1889: La rue du Caire.* Paris: E. Plon, 1889.

Godet, Robert. "En Marge de la marge." *Revue musicale* 7 (May 1926): 147–82.

Goncourt, Edmond, and Jules de Goncourt. *Journal: Mémoires de la vie littéraire.* Edited by Robert Ricatte. 3 vols. Paris: Robert Laffont, 1989.

Gossec, François-Joseph. *Offrande à la Liberté. Scène composée de l'Air Veillons au Salut de l'Empire et de la Marche de Marseillois.* Paris: chez Imbault, 1792.

Gossec, François-Joseph. *Le Triomphe de la République, ou le camp de Grand-Pré, divertissement lyrique, en un acte; représenté par l'Académie de Musique, le 27 janvier, l'an deuxième de la République Française. La Musique est du Citoyen Gossec, Le Ballets, du Citoyen Cardel* [*sic*]. Paris: chez Baudoin, Desenne & Bailly, [1793].

Gréville, Henry. *Angèle*. Paris: Plon, 1883.

Hillemacher, Paul L. *Mélodie arabe*. Poem by Eugène Adenis. Paris: Alphonse Leduc, 1889.

Holmès, Augusta. *L'Ode triomphale en l'honneur du Centenaire de 1789*. Libretto and drafts. *F-Pn*, Département de la Musique, shelf mark: Réserve ThB 56 (2).

———. *L'Ode triomphale en l'honneur du Centenaire de 1789*. Autograph score, dated "15 août 1889." *F-Pn*, Département de la Musique. Shelf mark: Ms. 6693.

———. *L'Ode triomphale en l'honneur du Centenaire de la République*. Piano-vocal score. Paris: C.-Durdilly et Cie, 1889.

———. *L'Ode triomphale en l'honneur du Centenaire de 1789*. Printed libretto. Paris: Imprimerie Chaix, 1889.

Koenigsberg, Allen. *Edison Cylinder Records, 1889–1912, with an Illustrated History of the Phonograph*. New York: Stellar Productions, 1969.

Lacome, Paul. *Les Fondateurs de l'opéra-comique: Transcriptions pour piano et chant*. Paris: Enoch Père et Fils, 1878.

———. *Les Fondateurs de l'opéra français: Transcriptions pour piano et chant*. Paris: Enoch Père et Fils, 1878.

La Fage, Juste Adrien de. *Histoire générale de la musique et de la danse*. Paris: Au Comptoir des Imprimeurs Unis, 1844.

Larousse, Pierre, ed. *Grand Dictionnaire universel du XIXe siècle*. 17 vols. Paris: Administration du Grand Dictionnaire universel, 1866–90.

Lenôtre, G. *Voyage merveilleux à l'Exposition Universelle de 1889*. Paris: Duquesne et fils, n.d.

Malherbe, Charles. *Notice sur Esclarmonde*. Paris: Fischbacher, 1890.

Massenet, Jules. *Esclarmonde*. Piano-vocal score. Paris: Hartmann & Cie, 1889. Proofs with autograph annotations (private collection).

Monod, Émile, ed. *L'Exposition Universelle de 1889: Grand ouvrage illustré historique, encyclopédique, descriptif publié sous le patronage de M. le Ministre du Commerce, de l'Industrie et des Colonies*. 3 vols. Paris: E. Dentu, 1890.

Montillot, L. *Téléphone pratique*. 2 vols. Paris: A. Grelot, 1893.

Noël, Edouard, and Edmond Stoullig. *Les Annales du théâtre et de la musique (1889)*. Paris: Bibliothèque Charpentier, 1890.

Paisiello, Giovanni. *Le Barbier de Séville, opéra en quatre actes, musique de Paisiello, traduit et arrangé d'après le texte de Beaumarchais et l'ancienne version française par Victor Wilder, instrumentation nouvelle et accompagnement de piano par Charles Constantin*. Paris: Léon Escudier, 1868.

Paladilhe, Émile. *Mandolinata (Souvenir de Rome)*. Poem by A. P***. Paris: G. Hartmann, 1869.

Paris, Gaston. *Littérature française au moyen-âge.* Paris: Hachette, 1888.

Paris, Paulin, ed. and trans. *Les Romans de la Table Ronde.* 5 vols. Paris: Léon Techener, 1868–77.

Picard, Alfred. *Rapport général sur l'Exposition universelle internationale de 1889.* 10 vols. Paris: Imprimerie nationale, 1890–91.

Pierre, Constant. *La Facture instrumentale à l'Exposition Universelle de 1889: Notes d'un musicien sur les instruments à souffle humain nouveaux et perfectionnés.* Paris: Librairie de l'Art Indépendant, 1890.

———. *Musique des fêtes et cérémonies de la Révolution française.* Paris: Imprimerie nationale, 1899.

Puget, Loïsa. *La Bayadère.* Paris: J. Meissonnier, 1839.

Pougin, Arthur. *Le Théâtre à l'Exposition Universelle de 1889: Notes et descriptions, histoires et souvenirs.* Paris: Librarie Fischbacher, 1890.

Renan, Ernest. *Qu'est-ce qu'une nation? et autres textes choisis.* Edited by Joël Roman. Paris: Presses Pocket, 1992.

Rienzi, Michelis de. *La Téléphonie: Ses origines et ses applications.* Bibliothèque universelle. Paris: Beaudelot, 1889.

Rowden, Clair, ed. *Dossier de presse parisienne: Jules Massenet "Thaïs" (1894).* Heilbronn: Musik-Edition Lucie Galland, 2000.

Saint-Saëns, Camille. "A Augusta Holmès." Manuscript poem. *F-Pn*, Département de le Musique. Shelf mark: *l.a. Saint-Saëns 75.*

———. *Harmonie et mélodie.* Paris: Calman-Lévy, 1885

Schulte-Smidt, B. *Bleistift-Skizzen: Erinnerungen an die Pariser Weltausstellung.* Bremen: Johann Kühtmann's Buchhandlung, 1890.

Tiersot, Julien. *Histoire de la chanson populaire en France.* Paris: Plon, 1889.

———. *Promenades musicales à l'Exposition.* Paris: Fischbacher, 1889.

Villon, A.-Mathieu. *Le Phonographe et ses applications.* Paris: Bernard Tignol, [1894].

Wagner, Richard. *Richard et Cosima Wagner—Arthur Gobineau: Correspondance (1880–1882).* Edited by Eric Eugène. Saint-Genouph: Librairie Nizet, 2000.

Weckerlin, Jean-Baptiste. *La Chanson populaire.* Paris: Librairie de Firmin-Didot, 1886.

———, ed. *Ci commence le jeu de Robin et de Marion qu'Adam fit.* Paris: Durand & Schoenewerk, 1875.

## Secondary Sources

Ackerman, Gerald M. *Jean-Léon Gérôme: Monographie révisée, catalogue raisonné mis à jour.* Courbevoie: ACR, 2000.

Adcock, Michael. "The 1889 Paris *Exposition*: Mapping the Colonial Mind." *Context: A Journal of Music Research*, no. 21 (Spring 2001): 31–40.

Agulhon, Maurice. *Marianne au pouvoir: L'imagerie et la symbolique républicaines de 1880 à 1914*. Paris: Flammarion, 1989.

———. "Paris: La traversée d'est en ouest." In *Les France III: De l'archive à l'emblème*. Vol. 6 of *Les Lieux de mémoire*, edited by Pierre Nora, 868–909. Paris: Gallimard, 1984.

———. *La République: L'élan fondateur et la grande blessure (1880–1932)*. Paris: Hachette, 1990.

———. *La République de Jules Ferry à François Mitterand, 1880 à nos jours*. Paris: Hachette, 1990.

Aimone, Linda, and Carlo Olmo. *Les Expositions Universelles, 1851–1900*. Translated by Philippe Olivier. Paris: Belin, 1993.

Albèra, Philippe. "Tradizione e rottura della tradizione." In *Enciclopedia della Musica*, edited by Jean-Jacques Nattiez. Vol. 1: *Il Novecento*, 27–47. Turin: Giulio Einaudi Editore, 2001.

Alpers, Paul. *What is Pastoral?* Chicago and London: University of Chicago Press, 1996.

Angenot, Marc. *1889: Un état du discours social*. Longeuil, Quebec: Éditions du Préambule, 1989.

Arndt, Jürgen. *Der Einfluß der javanischen Gamelan-Musik auf Kompositionen von Claude Debussy*. Frankfurt/Main: Peter Lang, 1993.

Aubain, Laurence. "La Russie à l'Exposition Universelle de 1889." *Cahiers du Monde Russe* 37 (1996): 349–68.

Aulas, Pierre. *Les Origines du téléphone en France (1876–1914)*. Paris: Association pour le Développement de l'Histoire Économique, 1999.

Bancel, Nicholas, Pascal Blanchard, Gilles Bietsch, Éric Deroo, and Sandrine Lemaire. *Zoos humains: De la Vénus hottentote aux Reality Shows*. Paris: La Découverte, 2002.

Barthes, Roland. "The Eiffel Tower." In *Rethinking Architecture: A Reader in Cultural Theory*, edited by Neil Leach, 171–80. London and New York: Routledge, 1997.

Bartlet, M. Elizabeth C. "Gossec, l'*Offrande à la Liberté* et l'histoire de la *Marseillaise*." In *Le Tambour et la Harpe: Œuvres, pratiques et manifestations musicales sous la Révolution, 1788–1800*, edited by Jean-Rémy Julien and Jean Mongrédien, 123–46. Paris: Éditions du May, 1991.

Bartoli, Jean-Pierre. "L'Orientalisme dans la musique française du XIXème siècle: La ponctuation, la seconde augmentée et l'apparition de la modalité dans les procédures exotiques." *Revue Belge de Musicologie* 51 (1997): 137–70.

Bellman, Jonathan. "The Hungarian Gypsies and the Poetics of Exclusion." In *The Exotic in Western Music*, edited by Jonathan Bellman, 74–103. Boston: Northeastern University Press, 1998.

Ben-Amos, Avner. *Funerals, Politics, and Memory in Modern France, 1789–1996*. Oxford and New York: Oxford University Press, 2000.

Ben-Amos, Avner. "The Uses of the Past: Patriotism between History and Memory." In *Patriotism in the Lives of Individuals and Nations*, edited by Daniel Bar-Tal and Ervin Straub, 129–47. Chicago: Nelson-Hall Publishers, 1997.

Benjamin, Roger. *Renoir and Algeria*. New Haven and London: Yale University Press, 2003.

Berenson, Edward. "Making a Colonial Culture? Empire and the French Public, 1880–1940." *French Politics, Culture, and Society* 22 (2004): 127–49.

———. *The Trial of Madame Caillaux*. Berkeley, Los Angeles, and London: University of California Press, 1992.

———. "Unifying the French Nation: Savorgnan de Brazza and the Third Republic." In *Music, Culture, and National Identity in France, 1870–1939*, edited by Barbara Kelly. Rochester, NY: University of Rochester Press, forthcoming.

Berger, Karol. *A Theory of Art*. New York and Oxford: Oxford University Press, 2000.

Birnbaum, Pierre. "Nationalisme à la française." In *Théories du nationalisme: Nation, nationalité, ethnicité*, edited by Gil Delannoi and Pierre-André Taguieff, 125–38. Paris: Éditions Kimé, 1991.

Blacking, John. *How Musical is Man?* London: Faber & Faber, 1976.

Blanckaert, Claude. "On the Origins of French Ethnology: William Edwards and the Doctrine of Race." In *Bones, Bodies, Behavior: Essays on Biological Anthropology*, edited by George W. Stocking, 18–55. History of Anthropology, 5. Madison: University of Wisconsin Press, 1988.

Blaukopf, Kurt. "Mediamorphosis and Secondary Orality: A Challenge to Cultural Policy." In *World Music, Music of the Worlds: Aspects of Documentation, Mass Media and Acculturation*, edited by Max Peter Baumann, 19–36. Wilhelmshaven: Florian Noetzel Verlag, 1992.

Bohlman, Philip V. "The European Discovery of Music in the Islamic World and the 'Non-Western' in 19th-Century Music History." *Journal of Musicology* 5 (1987): 147–63.

———. "Representation and Cultural Critique in the History of Ethnomusicology." In *Comparative Musicology and Anthropology of Music: Essays on the History of Ethnomusicology*, edited by Bruno Nettl and Philip V. Bohlman, 131–51. Chicago and London: University of Chicago Press, 1991.

Bohrer, Frederick N. *Orientalism and Visual Culture: Imagining Mesopotamia in Nineteenth-Century Europe*. Cambridge: Cambridge University Press, 2003.

Bomberger, Douglas. *"A Tidal Wave of Encouragement": American Composers' Concerts in the Gilded Age*. Westport, CT: Praeger, 2002.

Bor, Joep. "The Rise of Ethnomusicology: Sources on Indian Music c. 1780–c. 1890." *Yearbook for Traditional Music* 20 (1988): 51–73.

Brisson, Dominique. *La Tour Eiffel: Tours et détours.* CD-Rom. Paris: arte Editions, 1997.

Brody, Elaine. *Paris: The Musical Kaleidoscope, 1870–1925.* New York: George Braziller, 1987.

———. "The Russians in Paris (1889–1914)." In *Russian and Soviet Music: Essays for Boris Schwarz,* edited by Malcolm Hamrick Brown, 157–83. Ann Arbor, MI: UMI Research Press, 1984.

Brooks, Jeanice. "Italy, the Ancient World and the French Musical Inheritance in the Sixteenth Century: Arcadelt and Clereau in the Service of the Guises." *Journal of the Royal Musical Association* 121 (1996): 147–90.

Burns, Michael. *Dreyfus: A Family Affair, 1789–1945.* London: Chatto & Windus, 1992.

Bußmann, Klaus. *Paris und die Ile de France.* Cologne: DuMont, 1980.

Campos, Rémy. "Traces d'écoute: Sur quelques tentatives historiennes de saisie du corps de la musique." *Circuit: Musiques contemporaines* 14 (2003): 7–17.

Caradec, François, and Alain Weill. *Le Café-concert.* Paris: Atelier Hachette & Massin, 1980.

Carter, Tim. "The Sound of Silence: Models for an Urban Musicology." *Urban History* 29 (2002): 8–18.

Çelik, Zeynep. *Displaying the Orient: Architecture of Islam at Nineteenth-Century World's Fairs.* Berkeley, Los Angeles, and Oxford: University of California Press, 1992.

Çelik, Zeynep, and Leila Kinney. "Ethnography and Exhibitionism at the Expositions Universelles." *Assemblage* 13 (1990): 34–59.

Chazal, Jean-Pierre. "'Grand succès pour les Exotiques': Retour sur les spectacles javanais de l'Exposition Universelle de Paris en 1889." *Archipel* 63 (2002): 109–52.

Childs, Elizabeth C. "The Colonial Lens: Gauguin, Primitivism, and Photography in the Fin de siècle." In *Antimodernism and Artistic Experience: Policing the Boundaries of Modernism,* edited by Linda Jessup, 50–70. Toronto, Buffalo, and London: University of Toronto Press, 2000.

Christensen, Thomas. "Fétis and Emerging Tonal Consciousness." In *Music Theory in the Age of Romanticism,* edited by Ian Bent, 27–56. Cambridge: Cambridge University Press, 1996.

———. *Rameau and Musical Thought in the Enlightenment.* Cambridge, MA: Harvard University Press, 1993.

Citron, Marcia J. *Gender and the Musical Canon.* Cambridge: Cambridge University Press, 1993.

Clark, Robert L. A. "South of North: *Carmen* and French Nationalisms." In *East of West: Cross-Cultural Performance and the Staging of Difference*, edited by Claire Sponsler and Xioamei Chen, 187–216. New York: Palgrave, 2000.

Cohen, William B. *The French Encounter with Africans: White Responses to Blacks, 1530–1880.* Bloomington and London: Indiana University Press, 1980.

Conklin, Alice L. *A Mission to Civilize: The Republican Idea of Empire in France and West Africa, 1895–1930.* Stanford, CA: Stanford University Press, 1997.

Cook, Nicholas. *Music, Imagination & Culture.* Oxford: Clarendon Press, 1992.

Cooke, Mervyn. "'The East in the West': Evocations of the Gamelan in Western Music." In *The Exotic in Western Music*, edited by Jonathan Bellman, 258–80. Boston: Northeastern University Press, 1998.

Cooper, Tom. "French Empire and Musical Exoticism to the End of the Nineteenth Century." PhD diss., Liverpool University, 1998.

Corbin, Alain. *Les Cloches de la terre: Paysage sonore et culture sensible dans les campagnes au XIXe siècle.* Paris: Éditions Albin Michel, 1994.

Crary, Jonathan. *Suspensions of Perception: Attention, Spectacle, and Modern Culture.* Cambridge, MA, and London: MIT Press, 1999.

———. *Techniques of the Observer: On Vision and Modernity in the Nineteenth Century.* Cambridge, MA, and London: MIT Press, 1990.

Dahlhaus, Carl. *The Idea of Absolute Music.* Translated by Roger Lustig. Chicago: University of Chicago Press, 1989.

———. *Klassische und romantische Musikästhetik.* Laaber: Laaber Verlag, 1988.

———. *Die Musik des 19. Jahrhunderts.* Laaber: Laaber Verlag, 1980.

Davis, Ruth. "The Art/Popular Music Paradigm and the Tunisian Ma'luf." *Popular Music* 15 (1996): 313–23.

Dean, Winton. *Bizet.* London: J. M. Dent & Sons, 1948.

DelPlato, Joan. *Multiple Wives, Multiple Pleasures: Representing the Harem, 1800–1875.* Madison, NJ, and Teaneck, NJ: Fairleigh Dickinson University Press, 2002.

Denham, A. E. "The Moving Mirrors of Music: Roger Scruton Resonates with Tradition." *Music & Letters* 80 (1999): 411–32.

Devriès, Anik. "Les Musiques d'extrême Orient à l' Exposition Universelle de 1889." *Cahiers Debussy* 1 (1977): 24–37.

Dobie, Madeleine. *Foreign Bodies: Gender, Language, and Culture in French Orientalism.* Stanford, CA: Stanford University Press, 2001.

Duroselle, Jean-Baptiste. *France and the United States: From the Beginnings to the Present.* Translated by Derek Coltman. Chicago and London: University of Chicago Press, 1978.

Duy, Pham. *Musics of Vietnam.* Carbondale and London: Southern Illinois University Press and Feffer & Simons, 1973.

Ellis, Katharine. "The Fair Sax: Women, Brass-Playing and the Instrument Trade in 1860s Paris." *Journal of the Royal Musical Association* 124 (1999): 221–54.

———. "Female Pianists and Their Male Critics in Nineteenth-Century Paris." *Journal of the American Musicological Society* 50 (1997): 353–85.

———. "François-Joseph Fétis." In *NGr2*.

———. *Interpreting the Musical Past: Early Music in Nineteenth-Century France*. New York and Oxford: Oxford University Press, 2005.

———. *Music Criticism in Nineteenth-Century France: "La Revue et Gazette Musicale de Paris" (1838–1880)*. Cambridge: Cambridge University Press, 1995.

———. "Palestrina et la musique dite 'palestrinienne' en France au XIXe siècle." In *La Renaissance et sa musique au XIXe siècle*, edited by Philippe Vendrix, 155–90. Paris: Klincksieck, 2000.

———. "Wagnerism and Anti-Wagnerism in the Paris Periodical Press." In *Von Wagner zum Wagnérisme: Musik, Literatur, Kunst, Politik*, edited by Annegret Fauser and Manuela Schwartz, 51–83. Transfer: Die deutsch-französische Kulturbibliothek 12. Leipzig: Leipziger Universitäts-Verlag, 1999.

Elste, Martin. "Nostalgische Musikmaschinen: Cembali im 20. Jahrhundert." In *Kielklaviere: Cembali, Spinette, Virginale*, edited by John Henry van der Meer, Martin Elste, and Günther Wagner, 239–77. Berlin: Staatliches Institut für Musikforschung Preußischer Kulturbesitz, 1991.

Espagne, Michel, and Michael Werner. "Deutsch-französischer Kulturtransfer als Forschungsgegenstand: Eine Problemskizze." In *Transferts: Les Relations interculturelles dans l'espace franco-allemand (XVIIIe et XIXe siècle)*, edited by Michael Werner and Michel Espagne, 11–34. Paris: Éditions Recherche sur les Civilisations, 1988.

Eugène, Eric. *Wagner et Gobineau: Existe-t-il un racisme wagnérien?* Paris: Le Cherche Midi, 1998.

Farrell, Gerry. *Indian Music and the West*. Oxford: Clarendon Press, 1997.

Fauser, Annegret. "Alterity, Nation and Identity: Some Musicological Paradoxes." *Context: A Journal of Music Research*, no. 21 (Spring 2001): 1–18.

———. "De arqueología musical: La música barroca y la Exposición Universal de 1889." In *Concierto barroco: Estudios sobre música, dramaturgia e historia cultural*, edited by Juan José Carreras and Miguel Ángel Marín, 289–307. Logroño: Universidad de La Rioja, 2004.

———. "D'Indy archéologue." In *Vincent d'Indy et son temps*, edited by Myriam Chimènes and Manuela Schwartz. Sprimont: Pierre Mardaga, forthcoming.

———. "Gendering the Nations: The Ideologies of French Discourse on Music (1870–1914)." In *Musical Constructions of Nationalism: Essays* on the History and Ideology of European Musical Culture, 1800–1945, edited by Michael Murphy and Harry White, 72–103. Cork: Cork University Press, 2001.

———. "*La Guerre en dentelles*: Women and the *Prix de Rome* in French Cultural Politics." *Journal of the American Musicological Society* 51 (1998): 83–129.

———. *Der Orchestergesang in Frankreich zwischen 1870 und 1920.* Freiburger Beiträge zur Musikwissenschaft, 2. Laaber: Laaber Verlag, 1994.

———. "'L'Orchestre dans les sons brave l'honnêteté. . .': Le rôle de l'élément érotique dans l'œuvre de Massenet." In *Massenet en son temps: Actes du colloque organisé en 1992 à l'occasion du deuxième Festival Massenet,* edited by Gérard Condé and Patrick Gillis, 156–79. St. Étienne: Association du Festival Massenet, 1999.

———. "Die Sehnsucht nach dem Mittelalter: Ernest Chausson und Richard Wagner." In *Les Symbolistes et Richard Wagner—Die Symbolisten und Richard Wagner,* edited by Wolfgang Storch with Josef Mackert, 115–20. Berlin: Edition Hentrich, 1991.

———. "Visual Pleasures—Musical Signs: Dance at the Paris Opéra." *South Atlantic Quarterly* 104, no. 1 (2005): 99–121.

———. "Die Welt als Stadt: Weltausstellungen in Paris als Spiegel urbanen Musiklebens." In *Musik und Urbanität,* edited by Christian Kaden and Volker Kalisch, 139–48. Essen: Blaue Eule, 2002.

———. "World Fair—World Music: Musical Politics in 1889 Paris." In *Nineteenth-Century Music Studies,* edited by Jim Samson and Bennett Zon, 179–223. London and Aldershot: Ashgate, 2003.

———. "Zwischen Professionalismus und Salon: Französische Musikerinnen des *Fin de siècle.*" In *Professionalismus in der Musik,* edited by Christian Kaden and Volker Kalisch, 261–74. Essen: Blaue Eule, 1998.

Fauser, Annegret, and Manuela Schwartz, eds. *Von Wagner zum Wagnérisme: Musik, Literatur, Kunst, Politik.* Transfer: Die deutsch-französische Kulturbibliothek 12. Leipzig: Leipziger Universitäts-Verlag, 1999.

Feilhauer, Ingeborg. "Augusta Holmès (1847–1903): Biographie—Werkverzeichnis—Analysen." Master's thesis, University of Heidelberg, 1987.

Feldman, Walter. "Cultural Authority and Authenticity in the Turkish Repertoire." *Asian Music* 22 (1990): 73–111.

Findley, Carter Vaughan. "An Ottoman Occidentalist in Europe: Ahmed Midhat Meets Madame Gülnar." *The American Historical Review* 103 (1998): 15–49.

Fischer, Jens Malte. "Singende Recken und blitzende Schwerter: Die Mittelalteroper neben und nach Wagner—Ein Überblick." In *Mittelalterrezeption: Ein Symposium,* edited by Peter Wapnewski, 511–30. Stuttgart: Metzler, 1986.

Frolova-Walker, Marina. "Against Germanic Reasoning: The Search for a Russian Style of Musical Argumentation." In *Musical Constructions of Nationalism: Essays on the History and Ideology of European Musical Culture, 1800–1945*, edited by Michael Murphy and Harry White, 104–22. Cork: Cork University Press, 2001.

Fulcher, Jane F. *French Cultural Politics & Music: From the Dreyfus Affair to the First World War*. New York: Oxford University Press, 1999.

———. *The Nation's Image: French Grand Opéra as Politics and Politicized Art*. Cambridge: Cambridge University Press, 1987.

———. "The Popular Chanson of the Second Empire: 'Music of the Peasants' in France." *Acta musicologica* 52 (1981): 27–37.

Gefen, Gérard. *Augusta Holmès, l'outrancière*. Paris: Belfond, 1987.

Gelatt, Roland. *The Fabulous Phonograph, 1877–1977*. 2nd edition. London: Cassell, 1977.

Gerson, Stéphane. "Parisian Littérateurs, Provincial Journeys, and the Construction of Unity in Post-Revolutionary France." *Past and Present*, no. 151 (May 1996): 141–73.

Gifford, Terry. *Pastoral*. London and New York: Routledge, 1999.

Gildea, Robert. *The Past in French History*. New Haven and London: Yale University Press, 1994.

———. *The Third Republic from 1870 to 1914*. London and New York: Longman, 1988.

Gillis, Patrick. "Genèse d'*Esclarmonde*." *L'Avant-Scène Opéra: Esclarmonde*, no. 148 (September–October 1992): 22–33.

———. "*Thaïs* dans tous ses états: Genèse et remaniements." *Avant-Scène Opéra: Thaïs*, no. 109 (May 1988): 66–74.

Goehr, Lydia. *The Imaginary Museum of Musical Works*. Oxford: Clarendon Press, 1992.

Gossman, Lionel. "History as Decipherment: Romantic Historiography and the Discovery of the Other." *New Literary History* 18 (1986): 23–57.

Groth, Renate. *Die französische Kompositionslehre des 19. Jahrhunderts*. Beihefte zum Archiv für Musikwissenschaft 22. Wiesbaden: Franz Steiner, 1983.

Haine, Malou. "Concerts historiques dans la seconde moitié du 19e siècle." In *Musique et société: Hommages à Robert Wangermée*, edited by Henri Vanhulst and Malou Haine, 121–42. Brussels: Éditions de l'Université de Bruxelles, 1988.

Haines, John. "Généalogies musicologiques aux origines d'une science de la musique vers 1900." *Acta musicologica* 73 (2001): 45–76.

Haraszati, Émile. "Fétis fondateur de la musique comparée: Son étude sur un nouveau mode de classification des races humaines d'après leurs systèmes musicaux." *Acta musicologica* 4 (1932): 97–103.

Hart, Brian. "The Symphony in Theory and Practice in France, 1900–1914." PhD diss., Indiana University, 1994.

———. "Wagner and the Franckiste 'Message-Symphony' in Early Twentieth-Century France." In *Von Wagner zum Wagnérisme: Musik, Literatur,*

*Kunst, Politik,* edited by Annegret Fauser and Manuela Schwartz, 315–37. Transfer: Die deutsch-französische Kulturbibliothek 12. Leipzig: Leipziger Universitäts-Verlag, 1999.

Henson, Karen. "Exotisme et Nationalités: *Aida* à l'Opéra de Paris," In *L'Opéra en France et en Italie (1791–1925): Une scène privilégiée d'échanges littéraires et musicaux,* edited by Hervé Lacombe, 263–97. Paris: Société Française de Musicologie, 2000.

———. "In the House of Disillusion: Augusta Holmès and *La Montagne noire.*" *Cambridge Opera Journal* 9 (1997): 233–62.

Herresthal, Harald, and Danièle Pistone, eds. *Grieg et Paris: Romantisme, symbolisme et modernisme franco-norvégiens.* Caen: Presses Universitaires de Caen, 1996.

Herresthal, Harald, and Ladislav Reznicek. *Rhapsodie norvégienne: Les musiciens norvégiens en France au temps de Grieg.* Translated by Chantal de Batz. Caen: Presses Universitaires de Caen, 1994.

Hobsbawm, Eric J. *Echoes of the Marseillaise: Two Centuries Look Back on the French Revolution.* New Brunswick, NJ: Rutgers University Press, 1990.

Hoffenberg, Peter H. *An Empire on Display: English, Indian, and Australian Exhibitions from the Crystal Palace to the Great War.* Berkeley, Los Angeles, and London: University of California Press, 2001.

Howat, Roy. "Debussy and the Orient." In *Recovering the Orient: Artists, Scholars, Appropriations,* edited by Andrew Gerstle and Anthony Milner, 45–81. Chur: Harwood Academic Publishers, 1994.

Huebner, Steven. "*Carmen* as *corrida de toros.*" *Journal of Musicological Research* 13 (1993): 3–29.

———. *French Opera at the Fin de Siècle: Wagnerism, Nationalism, and Style.* Oxford: Oxford University Press, 1999.

Ihl, Olivier. *La Fête républicaine.* Paris: Gallimard, 1996.

Jam, Jean-Louis. "Marie-Joseph Chénier and François-Joseph Gossec: Two Artists in the Services of Revolutionary Propaganda." In *Music and the French Revolution,* edited by Malcolm Boyd, 221–35. Cambridge: Cambridge University Press, 1992.

Johnson, James H. *Listening in Paris: A Cultural History.* Berkeley, Los Angeles, and London: University of California Press, 1995.

Kaden, Christian. *Des Lebens wilder Kreis: Musik im Zivilisationsprozeß.* Kassel: Bärenreiter-Verlag, 1993.

Kasson, Joy S. *Buffalo Bill's Wild West: Celebrity, Memory, and Popular History.* New York: Hill and Wang, 2000.

Kenyon, Nicholas, ed. *Authenticity and Early Music.* Oxford: Oxford University Press, 1988.

Kisby, Fiona, ed. *Music and Musicians in Renaissance Cities and Towns.* Cambridge: Cambridge University Press, 2001.

Kittler, Friedrich. *Discourse Networks 1800/1900.* Translated by Michael Matteer and Chris Cullens. Stanford, CA: Stanford University Press, 1990.

Kittler, Friedrich. *Grammophon, Film, Typewriter*. Berlin: Brinkmann & Bose, 1986. Translated by Geoffrey Winthrop-Young and Michael Wutz as *Gramophone, Film, Typewriter*. Stanford, CA: Stanford University Press, 1999.

———. "Wagners wildes Heer." In *Die Symbolisten und Richard Wagner*, edited by Wolfgang Storch with Josef Mackert, 37–43. Berlin: Edition Hentrich, 1991.

Klein, Kerwin Lee. "In Search of Narrative Mastery: Postmodernism and the People without History." *History and Theory* 34 (1995): 275–98.

Kottrick, Edward L. *A History of the Harpsichord*. Bloomington and Indianapolis: Indiana University Press, 2003.

Kramer, Elizabeth. "The Idea of *Kunstreligion* in German Musical Aesthetics of the Early Nineteenth Century." PhD diss., University of North Carolina at Chapel Hill, 2005.

Kretschmer, Winfried. *Geschichte der Weltausstellungen*. Frankfurt and New York: Campus Verlag, 1999.

Laborde, Denis. "Basque Music." In *NGr2*.

Lacombe, Hervé. *The Keys to French Opera in the Nineteenth Century*. Translated by Edward Schneider. Berkeley, Los Angeles, and London: University of California Press, 2001.

Launay, Florence. "Les Compositrices françaises de 1789 à 1914." PhD diss., Université de Rennes 2, 2004.

Lauvergnier, Dominique. "François-Joseph Gossec: Compositeur dramatique." In *Fêtes et musiques révolutionnaires: Grétry et Gossec*, edited by Roland Mortier and Hervé Hasquin, 61–89. Études sur le XVIIIe Siècle, 8. Brussels: Éditions de l'Université de Bruxelles, 1990.

Lechner, Ethan. "Hearing Past the Cultural Divide: Issues of Perspective and Hybridity in Colin McPhee's *Tabuh-tabuhan*." Masters thesis, University of North Carolina at Chapel Hill, 2002.

Legrand, Raphaëlle, and Nicole Wild. *Regards sur l'Opéra-Comique: Trois siècles de vie théâtrale*. Paris: CNRS Éditions, 2002.

Leprun, Sylviane. *Le Théâtre des Colonies: Scénographie, acteurs et discours de l'imaginaire dans les expositions, 1855–1937*. Paris: Éditions l'Harmattan, 1986.

Lester, Joel. "Rameau and Eighteenth-Century Harmonic Theory." In *The Cambridge History of Western Music Theory*, edited by Thomas Christensen, 753–77. Cambridge: Cambridge University Press, 2002.

Lesure, François. *Claude Debussy: Biographie critique*. Paris: Klincksieck, 1994.

———. "Debussy et le syndrome de Grenade." *Revue de musicologie* 68 (1982): 101–9.

Lewis, Reina. *Race, Femininity and Representation*. London and New York: Routledge, 1996.

Locke, Ralph P. "Constructing the Oriental 'Other': Saint-Saëns's *Samson et Dalila*." *Cambridge Opera Journal* 3 (1991): 261–302.

————. "Cutthroats and Casbah Dancers, Muezzins and Timeless Sands: Musical Images of the Middle East." In *The Exotic in Western Music*, edited by Jonathan Bellman, 104–36. Boston: Northeastern University Press, 1998.

————. "Exoticism." In *NGr2*.

————. "The French Symphony: David, Gounod, and Bizet to Saint-Saëns, Franck, and Their Followers." In *The Nineteenth-Century Symphony*, edited by D. Kern Holoman, 163–94. New York: Schirmer Books, 1997.

————. "Orientalism." In *NGr2*.

Lockspeiser, Edward: *Debussy: His Life and Mind*. Vol. 1: *1862–1902*. London: Cassell, 1962. In French as *Debussy: Sa vie et sa pensée*. Translated by Léo Dilé. Paris: Fayard, 1980.

Lowenthal, David. "Authenticity? The Dogma of Self-Delusion." In *Why Fakes Matter: Essays on Problems of Authenticity*, edited by Mark Jones, 184–92. London: British Museum Press, 1992.

Loyrette, Henri. "La Tour Eiffel." *Les France III: De l'archive à l'emblême*. Vol. 6 of *Les Lieux de mémoire*, edited by Pierre Nora, 474–503. Paris: Gallimard, 1984.

MacKenzie, John M. *Orientalism: History, Theory and the Arts*. Manchester and New York: Manchester University Press, 1995.

Magoun, Alexander Boyden. "Shaping the Sound of Music: The Evolution of the Phonograph Record, 1877–1950." PhD diss., University of Maryland, 2000.

Martin-Fugier, Anne. *La Bourgeoise: Femme au temps de Paul Bourget*. Paris: Grasset, 1983.

Mathieu, Caroline. "Invitation au Voyage," In *1889: La Tour Eiffel et l'Exposition Universelle*, edited by Caroline Mathieu, 102–29. Paris: Éditions de la Réunion des Musées Nationaux, 1989.

Mathur, Saloni. "Living Ethnological Exhibits: The Case of 1886." *Cultural Anthropology* 15 (2000): 492–524.

McClary, Susan. "The Blasphemy of Talking Politics during Bach Year." In *Music and Society: The Politics of Composition, Performance and Reception*, edited by Richard Leppert and Susan McClary, 13–62. Cambridge: Cambridge University Press, 1987.

————. *Feminine Endings: Music, Gender, and Sexuality*. Minneapolis and Oxford: University of Minnesota Press, 1991.

Middleton, Richard. "Locating the People: Music and the Popular." In *The Cultural Study of Music: A Critical Introduction*, edited by Martin Clayton, Trevor Herbert, and Richard Middleton, 251–62. New York and London: Routledge, 2003.

Miller, Christopher L. *Blank Darkness: Africanist Discourse in French.* Chicago and London: University of Chicago Press, 1985.

Mitchell, Timothy. "Orientalism and the Exhibitionary Order." In *Colonialism and Culture,* edited by Nicholas B. Dirks, 289–317. Ann Arbor: University of Michigan Press, 1995.

———. "The World as Exhibition." *Comparative Studies in Society and History* 31 (1989): 217–36.

Mongrédien, Jean. *La Musique en France des Lumières au Romantisme (1789–1830).* Paris: Flammarion, 1986.

Montagnier, Jean-Paul. "Julien Tiersot: Ethnomusicologue à l'Exposition Universelle de 1889. Contribution à une histoire française de l'ethnomusicologie." *International Review of the Aesthetics and Sociology of Music* 21 (1990): 91–100.

Muller, Richard. "Javanese Influence on Debussy's *Fantaisie* and Beyond." *19th-Century Music* 10 (1986): 157–86.

Murphy, Kerry. "Race and Identity: Appraisals in France of Meyerbeer on his 1891 Centenary." *Nineteenth-Century Music Review* 1, no. 2 (2004): 27–42.

Murphy, Michael, and Harry White, eds. *Musical Constructions of Nationalism: Essays on the History and Ideology of European Musical Culture, 1800–1945.* Cork: Cork University Press, 2001.

Musk, Andrea. "Regionalism, *Latinité* and the French Musical Tradition: Déodat de Sévérac's *Héliogabale.*" In *Nineteenth-Century Music Studies,* edited by Jim Samson and Bennett Zon, 226–49. London and Aldershot: Ashgate, 2002.

Nattiez, Jean-Jacques. *Music and Discourse: Toward a Semiology of Music.* Translated by Carolyn Abbate. Princeton, NJ: Princeton University Press, 1990.

Nguyễn, Phong T. "Vietnam." In *The Garland Encyclopedia of World Music.* Vol. 4: *Southeast Asia,* edited by Terry E. Miller and Sean Williams, 444–517. New York and London: Garland Publishing, 1998.

Nguyễn, Phong T., and Tran Van Khê. "Vietnam." In *NGr2.*

Nichols, Roger. *The Life of Debussy.* Cambridge: Cambridge University Press, 1998.

Nichols, Roger, and Richard Langham Smith. *Claude Debussy: "Pelléas et Mélisande."* Cambridge Opera Handbooks. Cambridge: Cambridge University Press, 1989.

Nochlin, Linda. "The Imaginary Orient." *Art in America* 71 (1983): 119–29, 186–91.

Nye, Robert A. "Medicine and Science as Masculine 'Fields of Honor.'" *Osiris* 12 (1997): 60–79.

Oechslin, Werner. "Le Goût et les nations: Débats, polémiques et jalousies au moment de la création des musées au XVIIIe siècle." In *Les Musées en Europe à la veille de l'ouverture du Louvre*, edited by Edouard Pommier, 367–414. Paris: Service Culturel du Louvre and Klincksieck, 1995.

Ory, Pascal. "Le Centenaire de la révolution française: La preuve par 89." In *Les Lieux de mémoire*, edited by Pierre Nora. Vol. 1: *La République*, 523–60. Paris: Gallimard, 1984.

———. *L'Expo Universelle*. Paris: Éditions Complexe, 1989.

Parakilas, James. "How Spain Got a Soul." In *The Exotic in Western Music*, edited by Jonathan Bellman, 137–93. Boston: Northeastern University Press, 1998.

Pasler, Jann. "Building a Public for Orchestral Music: Les Concerts Colonne." In *Le Concert et son public: Mutations de la vie musicale en Europe de 1780 à 1914 (France, Allemagne, Angleterre)*, edited by Hans Erich Bödecker, Patrice Veit, and Michael Werner, 209–38. Paris: Éditions de la Maison de l'Homme, 2002.

———. "The *Chanson populaire* as a Malleable Symbol in Turn-of-the-Century France." In *Tradition and Its Future in Music: Report of SIMS 1990 Osaka*, edited by Yoshiko Tokumaru, 203–9. Tokyo and Osaka: Mita Press, 1991.

———. "Countess Greffulhe as Entrepreneur: Negotiating Class, Gender, and Nation." In *The Musician as Entrepreneur, 1700–1914: Managers, Charlatans, and Idealists*, edited by William Weber, 221–55. Bloomington and Indianapolis: Indiana University Press, 2004.

———. "India and Its Music: Imagination before 1913." *Journal of the Indian Musicological Society* 27 (1996): 27–51.

———. "The Ironies of Gender, or Virility and Politics in the Music of Augusta Holmès." *Women & Music: A Journal of Gender and Culture* 2 (1998): 1–25.

———. "Paris: Conflicting Notions of Progress." In *Man and Music: The Late Romantic Era from the Mid-19th Century to World War I*, edited by Jim Samson, 389–416. London: Macmillan, 1991.

———. "Reinterpreting Indian Music: Albert Roussel and Maurice Delage." In *Music-Cultures in Contact: Convergences and Collisions*, edited by Margaret J. Kartomi and Stephen Blum, 122–57. Basel: Gordon and Breach, 1994.

———. "The Utility of Musical Instruments in the Racial and Colonial Agendas of Late Nineteenth-Century France." *Journal of the Royal Musical Association* 129 (2004): 24–76.

Powers, Harold S. "Classical Music, Cultural Roots, and Colonial Rule: An Indic Musicologist Looks at the Muslim World." *Asian Music* 12 (1980): 5–39.

Rearick, Charles. *Pleasures of the Belle Époque: Entertainment & Festivity in Turn-of-the-Century France.* New Haven, CT, and London: Yale University Press, 1985.

————. "Symbol, Legend, and History: Michelet as Folklorist-Historian." *French Historical Studies* 7 (1971): 72–92.

Reed, Susan A. "The Politics and Poetics of Dance." *Annual Review of Anthropology* 27 (1998): 503–32.

Reiche, Jens Peter. "Die theoretischen Grundlagen javanischer Gamelan-Musik und ihre Bedeutung für Claude Debussy." *Zeitschrift für Musiktheorie* 3 (1972): 5–15.

Reiff, Daniel D. "Viollet le Duc and Historic Restoration: The West Portals of Notre Dame." *Journal of the Society of Architectural Historians* 30 (1971): 17–30.

Roger, Philippe. *L'Ennemi américain: Généalogie de l'antiaméricanisme français.* Paris: Édition du Seuil, 2002.

Ross, James. "Crisis and Transformation: French Opera, Politics and the Press, 1897–1903." DPhil diss., Oxford University, 1998.

Rowden, Clair. *Republican Morality and Catholic Tradition in the Opera: Massenet's "Hérodiade" and "Thaïs."* Weinsberg: Musik-Edition Lucie Galland, 2004.

Ruscio, Alain. *Le Credo de l'homme blanc.* Paris: Éditions Complexe, 2002.

Sachs, Klaus-Jürgen. "Musiktheorie." In *Die Musik in Geschichte und Gegenwart.* 2nd edition, edited by Ludwig Finscher. 25 vols. Kassel and Stuttgart: Bärenreiter and Metzler, 1994– Sachteil, vol. 6: cols. 1714–35.

Said, Edward W. *Culture and Imperialism.* London: Vintage, 1994.

————. *Orientalism: Western Conceptions of the Orient.* London: Penguin Books, 1991.

Saleh, Magda. "Dance in Egypt." In *The Garland Encyclopedia of World Music.* Vol. 6: *The Middle East,* edited by Virginia Danielson, Scott Marcus, and Dwight Reynolds, 623–33. New York and London: Routledge, 2002.

Schaeffer, Pierre. *Traité des objets musicaux: Essai interdisciplines.* Paris: Éditions du Seuil, 1966.

Schama, Simon. *Landscape & Memory.* London: HarperCollins, 1995.

Schellhous, Rosalie. "Fétis's 'Tonality' as a Metaphysical Principle: Hypothesis for a New Science." *Music Theory Spectrum* 13 (1991): 219–40.

Schick, Irvin Cemil. *The Erotic Margin: Sexuality and Spatiality in Alterist Discourse.* London and New York: Verso, 1999.

Schmidt, Alexander. "Deutschland als Modell? Bürgerlichkeit und gesellschaftliche Modernisierung im deutschen Kaiserreich (1871–1914) aus der Sicht der französischen Zeitgenossen." In *Jahrbuch für Wirtschaftsgeschichte,* 221–42. Berlin: Akademie-Verlag, 1992.

Schuerewegen, Franc. *A Distance de voix: Essai sur les "machines à parler."* Lille: Presses Universitaires de Lille, 1994.

Schwartz, Vanessa R. *Spectacular Realities: Early Mass Culture in Fin-de-Siècle Paris.* Berkeley, Los Angeles, and London: University of California Press, 1998.

Scruton, Roger. *The Aesthetics of Music.* Oxford: Clarendon Press, 1997.

Seidel, Wilhelm. "Absolute Musik und Kunstreligion um 1800." In *Musik und Religion,* edited by Helga de la Motte-Haber, 89–114. Laaber: Laaber Verlag, 1995.

Seipt, Angelus. *César Francks symphonische Dichtungen.* Kölner Beiträge zur Musikforschung, 116. Regensburg: Bosse Verlag, 1981.

Shelemay, Kay Kaufman. "Toward an Ethnomusicology of the Early-Music Movement." *Ethnomusicology* 45 (2001): 1–29.

Siefert, Marsha. "Aesthetics, Technology, and the Capitalization of Culture: How the Talking Machine Became a Musical Instrument." *Science in Context* 8 (1995): 417–49.

Silverman, Debora L. "The 1889 Exhibition: The Crisis of Bourgeois Individualism." *Oppositions: A Journal for Ideas and Criticism in Architecture.* Special Issue: "City and Ideology: Paris under the Academy" (Spring 1977): 71–91.

Six, Jean-François. *1886: Naissance du XXe siècle en France.* Paris: Seuil, 1986.

Smalley, Denis. "The Listening Imagination: Listening in the Electroacoustic Era." In *Companion to Contemporary Musical Thought,* edited by John Paynter, Tim Howell, Richard Orton, and Peter Seymour. 2 vols. 1:514–54. London and New York: Routledge, 1992.

———. "Spectromorphology: Explaining Sound-Shapes." *Organised Sound* 2 (1992): 107–26.

Smith, Bruce R. "Hearing Green." Paper presented at Duke University, January 2004.

Smith, Marian. *Ballet and Opera in the Age of Giselle.* Princeton, NJ: Princeton University Press, 2000.

Smith, Richard Langham. "Motives and Symbols." In *Claude Debussy: "Pelléas et Mélisande,"* edited by Roger Nichols and Richard Langham Smith, 78–106. Cambridge Opera Handbooks. Cambridge: Cambridge University Press, 1989.

Stanley, Glenn. "Historiography." In *NGr2.*

Sterne, Jonathan. *The Audible Past: Cultural Origins of Sound Production.* Durham, NC, and London: Duke University Press, 2003.

Sternhell, Zeev. *La Droite révolutionnaire, 1885–1914.* Paris: Gallimard, 1997.

Strohm, Reinhard. *Music in Late Medieval Bruges.* Rev. ed. Oxford: Clarendon Press, 1990.

Sutton, R. Anderson, Endo Suanda, and Sean Williams. "Java." In *The Garland Encyclopedia of World Music.* Vol. 4: *Southeast Asia,* edited by Terry E.

Miller and Sean Williams, 630–728. New York and London: Garland Publishing, 1998.

Sykes, Ingrid. "Female Piety and the Organ: Nineteenth-Century French Women Organists." PhD diss., City University, London, 2001.

Taruskin, Richard. "Nationalism." In *NGr2*.

Theeman, Nancy Sarah. "The Life and Songs of Augusta Holmès." PhD diss., University of Maryland, 1983.

Thiesse, Anne-Marie. *Le Roman du quotidien: Lecteurs et lectures populaires à la Belle Époque.* Paris: Le Chemin Vert, 1984.

Thompson, Emily. "Machines, Music, and the Quest for Fidelity: Marketing the Edison Phonograph in America, 1877–1925." *Musical Quarterly* 79 (1995): 131–71.

Todorov, Tzvetan. *On Human Diversity: Nationalism, Racism, and Exoticism in French Thought.* Translated by Catherine Porter. Cambridge, MA, and London: Harvard University Press, 1993.

Touma, Habib Hassan. "Die Musik der Araber im 19. Jahrhundert." In *Musikkulturen Asiens, Afrikas und Ozeaniens im 19. Jahrhundert,* edited by Robert Günther, 49–71. Regensburg: Gustav Bosse Verlag, 1973.

Treitler, Leo. "The Politics of Reception: Tailoring the Present as Fulfilment of a Desired Past." *Journal of the Royal Musical Association* 117 (1992): 280–98.

Tyrväinen, Helena. "Sibelius at the Paris Universal Exhibition of 1900," In *Sibelius Forum: Proceedings from The Second International Jean Sibelius Conference, Helsinki, 25–29 November, 1995,* edited by Veijo Murtomäki, Kari Kilpeläinen, and Risto Väisänen, 114–28. Helsinki: Sibelius Academy, 1998.

———. "Suomalaiset Pariisin maailmannäyttelyiden 1889 ja 1900 musiikkiohjelmissa." *Musiikkitiede* 1–2 (1994): 22–74.

Utz, Christian. *Neue Musik und Interkulturalität.* Beihefte zum Archiv für Musikwissenschaft 51. Stuttgart: Franz Steiner, 2002.

Van, Gilles de. "Fin de Siècle Exoticism and the Meaning of the Far Away." *Opera Quarterly* 11, no. 3 (1995): 77–94.

Vaux de Foletier, François de. *Les Bohémiens en France au 19e siècle.* Paris: J. C. Lattès, 1981.

Vendrix, Philippe. *Aux Origines d'une discipline historique: La musique et son histoire en France aux XVIIe et XVIIIe siècles.* Liège: Bibliothèque de la Faculté de Philosophie et Lettres de l'Université de Liège, 1993.

———. "L'Opéra comique sans rire." In *Die Opéra Comique und ihr Einfluß auf das europäische Musiktheater im 19. Jahrhundert,* edited by Herbert Schneider and Nicole Wild, 31–41. Hildesheim, Zurich, and New York: Georg Olms Verlag, 1997.

Wagstaff, John. "Messager, André (Charles Prosper)." In *NGr2*.

Weber, Eugen. *France: Fin de siècle.* Cambridge, MA, and London: Belknap Press of Harvard University Press, 1986.

Whiting, Steven Moore. *Satie the Bohemian: From Cabaret to Concert Hall.* Oxford: Oxford University Press, 1999.

Wild, Nicole. "Eugène Lacoste et la création de *Henry VIII* à l'Opéra de Paris en 1883." In *Échos de France et d'Italie: Liber amicorum Yves Gérard,* edited by Marie-Claire Mussat, Jean Mongrédien, and Jean-Michel Nectoux, 213–32. Paris: Buchet/Chastel, 1997.

———. "Les Traditions scéniques à l'Opéra de Paris au temps de Verdi." In *La realizzazione scenica dello spettacolo verdiano,* edited by Pierluigi Petrobelli and Fabrizio Della Seta, 135–66. Parma: Istituto Nazionale di Studi Verdiani, 1996.

Williams, Rosalind H. *Dream Worlds: Mass Consumption in Late Nineteenth-Century France.* Berkeley, Los Angeles, and Oxford: University of California Press, 1982.

Wright, Lesley. "Leoncavallo, *La Bohème* and the Parisian Press." In *Nazionalismo e Cosmopolitanismo nell' opera fra '800 e '900: Atti del 3° Convegno Internazionale "Ruggero Leoncavallo nel Suo Tempo,"* edited by Lorenza Guiot and Jürgen Maehder, 165–80. Milan: Sonzogno, 1998.

———. "Music Criticism and the *Exposition Internationale Universelle* of 1900." *Context: A Journal of Music Research,* no. 21 (Spring 2001): 19–30.

Wright, Owen, Christian Poché, and Amnon Shiloah. "Arab Music." In *NGr2.*

Yeğenoğlu, Meyda. *Colonial Fantasies: Towards a Feminist Reading of Orientalism.* Cambridge: Cambridge University Press, 1998.

# Index

# Eastman Studies in Music

# Musical Encounters at the 1889 Paris World's Fair

Annegret Fauser

The 1889 Exposition Universelle in Paris has become famous as a turning point in the history of French music, and modern music generally. For the first time, Debussy and his fellow composers could be inspired by Javanese gamelan music, while the Russian concerts conducted by Rimsky-Korsakov brought recent music by the Mighty Five to Parisian ears.

But the 1889 World's Fair had much wider musical and cultural ramifications; one contemporary described it as a "gigantic encyclopedia, in which nothing was forgotten." Music was so pervasive at the 1889 Exposition Universelle that newspaper journalists compared the sonic side of the affair to a "musical orgy." Musical encounters at the fair ranged from bandstand marches to folk and non-Western ensembles to symphonic and operatic premieres by Massenet to the mass-marketed Edison phonograph.

A rich and vivid literature (from newspaper columns to memoirs that are plumbed here for the first time) comments about this sonic landscape, reflecting the reactions and responses of composers (Saint-Saëns), writers (Judith Gautier), and journalists (Gaston Calmette).

*Musical Encounters at the 1889 Paris World's Fair* explores the ways in which music was used, appropriated, exhibited, listened to, and written about during the six months of the Exposition Universelle. It thereby also reveals the role and the sociopolitical uses of music in France and, more generally, Europe during the late nineteenth century.

Annegret Fauser is Associate Professor of Music at the University of North Carolina at Chapel Hill. Her many publications include books on French Wagnerism, Massenet's opera Esclarmonde, and French orchestral songs from Berlioz to Ravel.

"As *Musical Encounters at the 1889 Paris World's Fair* makes vividly clear, all of Paris, and much of the rest of the world, was 'on display' at the Exposition Universelle. Annegret Fauser provides a long-needed window on late nineteenth-century French musical culture—Massenet, the young Debussy—and the ways in which other musics—from the French provinces, from the Congo and Vietnam—and new devices such as Edison's phonograph were presented and experienced in the metropolis."

—Steven Huebner, author of *French Opera at the fin de siècle*

"A work of striking originality. Fauser's 'thick description' of the 1889 World's Fair introduces us to a vibrant sonic world usually left silent in the mute halls of cultural history. Brilliantly researched and written, this book doesn't just tell us about empire, nationalism, and the 'exotic'; it allows us to heed their often dissonant sounds."

—Edward Berenson, Director, Institute of French Studies, New York University